CENTERS OF POWER IN THE ARAB GULF STATES

KRISTIAN COATES ULRICHSEN

Centers of Power in the Arab Gulf States

OXFORD
UNIVERSITY PRESS

OXFORD
UNIVERSITY PRESS

Oxford University Press is a department of the
University of Oxford. It furthers the University's objective
of excellence in research, scholarship, and education
by publishing worldwide.

Oxford New York

Auckland   Cape Town   Dar es Salaam   Hong Kong   Karachi
Kuala Lumpur   Madrid   Melbourne   Mexico City   Nairobi
New Delhi   Shanghai   Taipei   Toronto

With offices in

Argentina   Austria   Brazil   Chile   Czech Republic   France   Greece
Guatemala   Hungary   Italy   Japan   Poland   Portugal   Singapore
South Korea   Switzerland   Thailand   Turkey   Ukraine   Vietnam

Oxford is a registered trade mark of Oxford University Press
in the UK and certain other countries.

Published in the United States of America by
Oxford University Press
198 Madison Avenue, New York, NY 10016

Library of Congress Cataloging-in-Publication Data is available

ISBN: 9780197776452

Printed in the United Kingdom by Bell & Bain Ltd, Glasgow

CONTENTS

ACKNOWLEDGMENTS

The seeds of *Centers of Power in the Arab Gulf States* were planted during a liquid lunch in London with Michael Dwyer in October 2019. The pandemic intervened and with it came a change in circumstances which slowed my research for many months. Writing finally began in the summer of 2021 but I was struck by a car while walking home from work the week before Christmas and this caused additional delay. A prolonged period of writer's block which lasted for much of 2022 meant further progress came in fits and starts. For all these reasons, this book has been a long time in the making. My thanks and gratitude are due to my family, especially my parents and my brother, sister-in-law, nephew, and niece, for their support, as well as to my colleagues at the Baker Institute who provide such a wonderful working environment. This book is dedicated to Edward and Françoise Djerejian for their extraordinary help at the time of my accident and for creating the scholarly space that has given me an institutional home for the past decade.

LIST OF ABBREVIATIONS

ACPRA	Saudi Civil and Political Rights Association
ARAMCO	Arabian American Oil Company
AWACS	Airborne Warning and Control System
BAPCO	Bahrain Petroleum Company
CDLR	Committee for the Defense of Legitimate Rights
DLF	Dhofar Liberation Front
EDB	Economic Development Board
FNC	Federal National Council
GCC	Gulf Cooperation Council
ISIS	Islamic State of Iraq and Syria
LNG	Liquefied Natural Gas
MAN	Movement of Arab Nationalists
PDRY	People's Democratic Republic of Yemen
PFLOAG	Popular Front for the Liberation of the Occupied Arabian Gulf
PIF	Public Investment Fund
RAK	Ras al-Khaimah
SAS	Special Air Service
UAE	United Arab Emirates
UAQ	Umm al-Quwain
VAT	Value Added Tax

INTRODUCTION

This book explores how different types of power and authority are accumulated and wielded across the six Gulf States and examines the relational dynamics that exist within the states, societies, and political economies that have become such assertive and visible global actors in the twenty-first century. The chapters herein draw upon theoretical and empirical insight and utilize historical and contemporary examples to analyze the centers of power, the nature of its projection, and the constraints on its exercise. The material is organized around eight themes which are designed to illustrate underlying and comparative trajectories which consider both the regionwide similarities and the country specificities that make each of the states distinct even as they are often referred to collectively as 'the Gulf States.' In so doing, it is the aim of this book to build upon and complement the many excellent studies which examine aspects of each of the states individually or in groups of two or three.

Much scholarly and practitioner analysis of the hereditary monarchies on the Arabian Peninsula—Bahrain, Kuwait, Oman, Qatar, Saudi Arabia, and the United Arab Emirates (UAE) has taken place under the shadow of rentier state theory, as developed in the 1970s and further refined over the following two decades. Recent years have seen a number of studies that have drawn attention to the shortcomings of rentier state theory and the practical difficulties of shoehorning complex empirical nuance into a rigid theoretical straitjacket in which the region and its states and societies are reduced to oil-dominated stereotypes.[1] Writing in 2005, the social anthropologist Paul Dresch observed that 'The Gulf is not just oil, and the polities of the Gulf are not simply counters on a strategic game-board,' and, as such, 'In writing about the Gulf, we need to analyze the forms of government as they are seen to connect with society at large.'[2] This is the spirit which animates this book which seeks also to extend its analysis beyond what one writer labeled 'the three pillars of the old order—clans, tribes and clerics.'[3]

In addition to providing a counterpoint to rentier state theory, this book demonstrates that there was no binary division between the 'pre-oil' and 'oil era' but instead a process of change that unfolded over four decades, between the 1930s and the 1970s, at different speeds and scales of intensity and without a master plan or defined end-goal. There are as many continuities as there are ruptures in the relationships among political, economic, and societal constituencies within and between Gulf States. Writing about this 'in between' period in Kuwait, Farah Al-Nakib observes that the labels 'tradition' and 'modern' often have become synonymous with the pre-oil and the current oil era but adds that 'this narrative leaves something crucial out: at least the three or four decades of what happened in between the pre-oil past and the "globalized" present.'[4]

The emergence of a contemporary political order which replicates and largely reinforces aspects of 'traditional' dynamics of power does not mean that its structures are somehow static, impervious to change, or wholly resistant to contestation. The fall of other regional monarchies, including in nearby Iraq and Iran, and the predictions of their own imminent demise by some social scientists in the early oil era, raises the questions of why and how the Gulf States evolved as they did. As such, their undeniably distinct characteristics repay study on their own terms, just as Fred Halliday (himself the author of a seminal study which predicted an *Arabia without Sultans*), reminded his audience, in a valedictory lecture shortly before his retirement in 2009, that 'The starting point for understanding the Middle East of today is not the remote past, nor ancient texts, nor any assumption of timeless cultural forces, behavior patterns and fault-lines.'[5]

Another trope in much of the discourse about the contemporary Gulf States that this book seeks to push back against is the notion that the rulers can be reduced to the last remaining 'absolute' monarchs in the world.[6] It is certainly the case that the six dynasties have maintained control over the levers of political and economic power and that the nature of authority has arguably become more, rather than less, authoritarian and based on intrusive structures of state security. However, this does not mean that the architecture of ruling (and political) institutions is monolithic or precludes any space for the assertion of interests and the projection of influence through formal mechanisms or informal channels. The modern history of the Gulf States is replete with examples that illustrate the importance of contingency in which a range of outcomes was possible. Analyzing the factors that went into decision-making can assist in determining how the states got to where they are today and in assessing how the next phase of development and change, against the global backdrop of climate action and the various energy transitions, may evolve.

Power is relational and is distributed among multiple nodes within a political community which itself is embedded within the state as the ultimate source of authority. Ruling families' control of state institutions, and the sometimes-blurred distinction (and overlap) between the two, can disguise but does not alter the fact that multiple centers and different types of power do exist alongside one another, and that the overall dynamic reflects 'the intersecting and often overlapping interests' of 'social constituencies, their development and relation with the center of power.'[7] Within this rubric, tribes (and tribalism) represent sub-national nodes of authority while Islam constitutes a supra-national marker that transcends national boundaries and runs through each of the eight chapters in this book. A rich literature has emerged on the intersection of tribal and state interests, on how tribalism has become fused into forms of political, economic, and social power; on conceptions of personal and collective identity; and on patterns in access to and distribution of patronage, resources, and employment in state agencies.[8]

The historical sociologist W. G. Runciman argued that any study of social interaction must be rooted in the analysis of relations of power, that is, how forms of power relate to each other, whether they be institutional, or related to the roles and practices of component actors or competing groups in society.[9] Runciman listed three types of power, economic, ideological, and coercive, and further distinguished between 'forms of power,' which he defined as 'the different kinds of inducements and sanctions which people can bring to bear on one another,' and the 'means' of exercising power, 'the different institutions through which those inducements and sanctions are applied.'[10] In his own multi-volume study, *The Sources of Social Power*, Michael Mann identified four sources of social power, namely control over political, ideological, economic, and military resources, and examined the 'logistics of power' through the study of overlapping and intersecting networks and flows among them.[11] A common thread is that whichever type or manifestation power takes it is inseparable from the study of the historical setting within which it occurs.

Turning back to the region, Saudi political analyst Turki Al-Hamad suggested that the imposition and growth of institutional structures superseded but did not entirely replace older and more fluid relationships of power and that 'the mix of this historical background with the modern state gives the Arabian Peninsula much of its singularity.'[12] Sulayman Khalaf observed that when looking at the rapid transition of the dynastic sheikhdoms into modern states in the twentieth century, 'the important question is how groups that control the state are able to widen its legitimacy base and subsequently increase its strength.'[13] For Madawi Al-Rasheed, a pre-eminent historian of Saudi Arabia, the Al Saud dynasty 'began to show state-like features' when Ibn Saud's 'authority and power took precedence over other groups and institutions.' Al-Rasheed contends that the polity ruled by Ibn Saud during the early years of his reign (which began in 1902) resembled 'a tribal dynasty with a web of tribal alliances' with (in the Saudi case) a 'strong religious dimension that proved to be essential for its expansion.'[14] Elsewhere, after Sultan Qaboos assumed power, he formed what Khalid Al-Azri labels 'political alliances' with religious and tribal groups which became key features of the social and political structure in post-1970 Oman, albeit under the firm political control of the government, and this was true of Bahrain and other states as well.[15]

Perhaps the best summation of power in the context of the regional states in the Gulf (including Iran as well as Iraq) is given by Mehran Kamrava, a longtime Qatar-based political scientist, who noted that 'politics is the art and science of the exercise of power' and added that

> power relationships are by nature bound to go beyond the composition and functions of institutions through which they are exercised. They are just as consequentially influenced by precedents and pre-existing traditions (history), by the actual and symbolic forces that shape relationships among individuals and their communities (society and culture), by the sources of wealth and patterns and consequences of its accumulation and expenditure (economy), and by matters of defense and interactions with other countries (security and international relations).[16]

Decision-making choices represented the political outcomes of the competition by different groups of actors for influence and resources. Rulers (and ruling families) stood at the apex of the structure of power, but while the state institutions and government agencies they led were elevated above other economic and social interests, they were neither autonomous from nor immune to societal pressures and demands. There were multiple pathways and spaces by which influence could be channeled and power wielded, in informal as well as formal settings and within as well as beyond institutional or bureaucratic frameworks. The focus of the chapters in this book is on the ways in which groups interacted and shaped policies and decision-making, based around eight key themes to facilitate a comparative approach that illustrates patterns of continuity as well as change and areas of convergence or divergence among the six states. While states remain the dominant unit of analysis in much of the academic literature, the strong transnational linkages that historically have connected the peoples and the societies of the Arabian Peninsula to each other, and within broader zones of exchange, is another core element of this book.

1

RULERS

Any book about power and authority in the Gulf, whether contemporary or historical, must begin with an examination of the dynastic families that continue to rule, rather than merely reign as has become the practice in constitutional monarchies in other parts of the world. In 2006, the Saudi academic Khalid Al-Dakhil observed that 'the ruling family is a political institution' and while he made this point about the royal family in Saudi Arabia it applies to ruling families in the other five Gulf States as well.[1] A similar point was made by Michael Herb in his pathbreaking study, *All in the Family*, published in 1999, which placed monarchies (as political institutions) at the heart of the study of Gulf politics.[2] Importantly, Herb focused on the need to examine the families as dynastic entities rather than individual rulers, as family members formed the ruling elite at the apex of the bureaucratic states that emerged in the twentieth century. Examining ruling families as political institutions also enables the study of factionalism that has been such a feature of rulership and guards against any notion of monolithic entities when talking about 'the' Al Saud, 'the' Al Sabah, 'the' Al Thani, 'the' Al Khalifa, 'the' Al Nahyan, 'the' Al Maktoum, or 'the' Al Said.

Individual rulers in the Gulf States have frequently faced more of a threat to their position from members of their own family than from societal pressures which, while often genuine, lacked the mobilizing capacity to pose a systemic risk to the leadership of the day. By contrast, sitting rulers were toppled, whether by forced abdication, palace coups, or even assassination, in Kuwait (1896), Abu Dhabi (1922, 1926, 1928, 1966), Bahrain (1923), Sharjah (1924, 1965, 1972), Ras al-Khaimah (1948), Qatar (1960, 1972, 1995), Saudi Arabia (1964, 1975), and Oman (1970). When the United Arab Emirates (UAE) was formed in 1971–2, five of the seven leaders of the constituent emirates had come to power after ousting an incumbent.[3] While intra-family disputes accounted for many of the enforced changes in leaderships, external pressure, primarily from British officials during the era of British protection, was significant in Bahrain in 1923, Sharjah in 1965, Abu Dhabi a year later, and Oman in 1970.[4]

There are three major sections to this chapter, which begins with a set of four opening observations about the nature of the ruling dynasties in the six Gulf States which establish the variations among them and provide context to their emergence as contemporary political entities, or polities. This leads into a second section which examines the nature of political authority in the Arabian Peninsula, especially in the period prior to the discovery and extraction of oil and the settling of national boundaries. The chapter ends with a third section that assesses some of the tools of control that ruling families deployed as they consolidated power domestically and transitioned into modern states in the middle decades of the twentieth century.

Opening observations

Before examining the nature of the political authority wielded by rulers—and ruling families—in contemporary Gulf States, four observations are in order. The first is that no two families are the same, whether in size, structure, historical origin, or indeed in the ways they maintain themselves in power.[5] The ruling families of Kuwait, Abu Dhabi, Dubai, Qatar, and Oman emerged in a far more organic manner than did the ruling family of Bahrain, which was part of a tribal migration from Najd, in central Arabia, to the

Arabian Gulf coastline in the early eighteenth century and which then split from the Al Sabah in Kuwait and moved down the coast to conquer the archipelago of Bahrain, along with its indigenous inhabitants, in 1783. The Al Saud are a mixture of the two, as a 'first' and then a 'second' iteration of an organic 'Saudi' state existed between 1744 and 1818 and from 1824 to 1892 before Abdulaziz bin Abdulrahman Al Saud, known internationally as Ibn Saud, embarked on a process of conquest of the Eastern Province, the Hijaz, and regions of southern Saudi Arabia along the border with Yemen between 1902 and 1932.[6]

A similar variation among ruling families is evident in patterns of succession. In Bahrain and Oman, the practice of son succeeding father was the major characteristic of successions in the twentieth century just as it was in Qatar, albeit alongside the aforementioned palace coups that altered lines of succession. In Abu Dhabi, power passed from one brother to another in the 1920s, again in 1966 when Sheikh Zayed ousted Sheikh Shakhbut, and did the same when Mohammed bin Zayed succeeded Khalifa bin Zayed in 2022. Succession in Saudi Arabia after the death of the founder King, Abdulaziz bin Abdulrahman Al Saud, in 1953 passed among the sons of Ibn Saud until King Salman came to power in 2015 and decisively changed the line of Saudi succession by appointing first his nephew, Mohammed bin Nayef, and then his son, Mohammed bin Salman, as Crown Prince, signifying a generational transfer of power. Such a transition from one generation to another only happened twice in Kuwait in the century that followed the initial shift in 1915 to the sons of Sheikh Mubarak the Great, the 'father of modern Kuwait,' in 1921 and 1977. This variation may nevertheless be coming to an end as a growing trend of rulers naming one of their sons as Crown Prince has been observable across the region, with the three most recent examples being the naming as heir of Mohammed bin Salman in Saudi Arabia (2017), Theyazin bin Haitham in Oman (2021), and Khalid bin Mohammed in Abu Dhabi (2023), even if the process remains opaque to family outsiders.[7]

Patterns and 'rules' of succession thus evolved, with one especially significant change taking place in Saudi Arabia with the introduction of the Basic Law by King Fahd in 1992. While much of the focus, at the time, was on the provision in the Basic Law (the closest approximation Saudi Arabia has to a written constitutional document) for the creation of a Shura Council to widen forms of political representation, one of the decrees issued at the time of the Basic Law empowered the sitting monarch to appoint and dismiss the Crown Prince and annulled the automatic right of the Crown Prince to become King.[8] The full implications of this decree only became clear a quarter-century later as Fahd's successor-but-one, King Salman, removed two Crown Princes (Muqrin bin Abdulaziz and Mohammed bin Nayef) in April 2015 and June 2017 as he paved the way for his younger son and preferred successor, Mohammed bin Salman. Ruling family councils also played an often informal and uncodified role in regulating issues of succession, with King Abdullah creating a formal, yet ultimately toothless, Allegiance Council in Saudi Arabia in 2006.[9]

Historical contingency and external recognition are a second and third factor that should be examined when considering the emergence of the dynasties that rule in the six Gulf States. Much was made, for example, of the 'alliance' between Mohammed bin Saud and Mohammed bin Abdul-Wahhab in 1744 that created the 'first Saudi state.'[10] This eighteenth-century alignment is said to have demarcated an (imprecise) division of temporal power (*imarah*) and religious authority (*mashyakhah*), although, on occasions when the former was challenged by the latter, as in 1929 and again in 1979, Al Saud leaders moved to crush the religious opposition to their political rule.[11] The (self-perceived) legacy of the collapse of the first and second Saudi states, in 1818 and 1892, under the weight of foreign intervention and factional intra-familial fighting respectively, have also resonated with contemporary family members, and were raised in two letters written by an anonymous prince in 2015 expressing alarm at the rise of Mohammed bin Salman.[12] A decree issued by King Salman in 2022 designating a national 'Founding Day' commemorating the start of Mohammed bin Saud's rule in 1727, was seen by Sultan Alamer as 'a radical break with the Wahhabi political influence that had legitimized the Saudi political projects since 1744.'[13]

Other examples of historical contingency that continued to resonate into the contemporary era include the tensions between Qatar and Bahrain, as well as boundary issues among the seven emirates that came together to form the UAE in 1971–2. Despite both becoming independent sovereign states in 1971, Bahrain and Qatar did not establish full diplomatic relations until 1997, over a quarter of a century later and sixteen years after they became fellow founder members of the Gulf Cooperation Council in 1981.[14] A large part of the animosity that persisted for so long was the legacy of a Bahraini claim to Zubarah, on the western coast of the Qatari peninsula, where the Al Khalifa had settled in the mid-eighteenth century in between their migration from Kuwait in 1766 and their conquest of Bahrain seventeen years later. The Al Khalifa continued to claim Zubarah even after the British Political Resident in the Gulf warned them in 1875 to cease interfering in the affairs of the town, and in 1920 British officials again reaffirmed that Zubarah was part of Qatar when they 'firmly refused' a Bahraini request to set up port facilities there.[15]

Tensions flared again in the mid-1930s after a representative of the newly formed Petroleum Development (Qatar) Ltd visited Zubarah in 1937, prompting the Ruler of Bahrain, Sheikh Hamad bin Isa Al Khalifa, to resurrect his claim on the town. This was in spite of an offer of mediation from the Ruler of Kuwait, Sheikh Ahmad al-Jabir Al Sabah, and renewed warnings from British officials that 'Zubarah belonged to Qatar and that this was the final verdict of the British government.'[16] In response, the Bahraini Ruler declared an embargo on travel and trade with Qatar that caused significant disruption in Doha as Bahrain had been an important regional market for a Qatari economy that was itself suffering considerable hardship after the collapse of the pearl-diving economy in the early 1930s. Bahraini rulers continued to harbor a grievance over Zubarah into the 1980s, when the Emir, Sheikh Isa bin Salman Al Khalifa, kept a map in his office that displayed Zubarah as part of Bahrain, albeit with a line crossed very lightly through it, while a naval standoff between Bahraini and Qatari forces took place in April 1986.[17] It was thus of little surprise that Bahrain joined the Saudi- and Emirati-led moves to isolate Qatar in 2013–14 and again in 2017, and that Bahrain took longer to reconcile with Qatar after the blockade ended in 2021.[18]

Intra-emirate relations and legacies of conflict and boundary disputes from the era of the Trucial States also persisted long after the seven emirates formed the UAE between December 1971 (when six emirates, led by Abu Dhabi and Dubai came together) and March 1972 (when Ras al-Khaimah belatedly joined). The ruling families of Abu Dhabi and Dubai both belong to the Bani Yas tribal confederation which originated in the Najd region (in contemporary Saudi Arabia) and established a power base in the Liwa oasis region, south-west of the modern city of Abu Dhabi, in the sixteenth century. The Bani Yas are thus distinct from the ruling families of Bahrain, Kuwait, and Saudi Arabia, which trace their lineage to the 'Anaza tribal confederation.[19] During the eighteenth century, power within the Bani Yas coalesced around a respected elder, Falah, and his son, Nahyan, who became the founder of the Al Nahyan line that rules Abu Dhabi. A separate sub-section of the Bani Yas, the Al Bu Falasah, split from the Al Bu Falah in 1833 and established themselves further north up the coastline at Dubai, where they constituted the ruling Al Maktoum line.[20]

As the ruling lineages in Abu Dhabi and Dubai consolidated power in the nineteenth century they each faced local and regional challenges to their authority. In Abu Dhabi, the threat came from Wahhabi forces from central Arabia who repeatedly threatened the oasis villages around Al-Ain—the same region which became the focus of the Buraimi crisis between Saudi Arabia, Abu Dhabi, and Oman in the 1950s.[21] It was only after the Wahhabis were ejected from Al-Ain in 1869 that Abu Dhabi was able to enjoy a period of political and economic consolidation under the leadership of Sheikh Zayed bin Khalifa Al Nahyan, known also as 'Zayed the Great,' who ruled from 1855 until 1909.[22] Dubai meanwhile was located along a tribal front-line between the confederacies of the Bani Yas, from whom the Al Maktoum had effectively seceded, and the Qawasim branch of the regional maritime power in Sharjah, just across the creek from Dubai.[23] On several occasions in the 1830s, tensions between the Bani Yas and the Qawasim threatened to draw Dubai into a regional conflict. However, by 1845, hitherto strained relations between Dubai and Abu Dhabi had improved while the threat to Dubai from the Qawasim also receded. The greater political and economic stability afforded Dubai the space to develop commercially and benefit from its advantageous location astride a wide creek and natural harbor.[24]

Dubai and Abu Dhabi went to war with each other over a boundary dispute in 1947 in a conflict that killed dozens of people, and while they agreed to join forces within the UAE in 1971, the first decade of the federation was marked by disagreement over the degree of centralized control over individual emirates. In 1976, Sheikh Zayed, the Ruler of Abu Dhabi, threatened to step down as President of the UAE, unless a deadlock over aspects of the provisional constitution (which was not made permanent until 1996) was broken.[25] One of the casualties of the rulers' inability to agree on key issues in the provisional constitution was that a new capital, earmarked for Al Karama on the Abu Dhabi-Dubai boundary, was never built. (A reminder of Al Karama is in the UAE's telephone code, which begins at '02' for Abu Dhabi as '01' was earmarked for the capital that never was.[26]) It also took nearly two decades before the Dubai Defense Force and the Ras al-Khaimah National Guard were fully integrated into the Union Defense Force in 1996. The difficulties of amalgamating previously independent emirate-level forces into UAE-wide structures had been illustrated during the coup in Sharjah in 1972 when three separate forces intervened in the affair, and in an incident the following year, when soldiers of the Sharjah National Guard reportedly fired on a helicopter carrying the UAE Defense Minister (and, since 2006, the Ruler of Dubai), Sheikh Mohammed bin Rashid Al Maktoum.[27]

External recognition—by British authorities in a series of treaty agreements signed between 1820 and 1916—was also an important factor in elevating and formalizing the role of the ruling families as the paramount political authorities in each of the proto-states in the Gulf. Britain (and British-ruled India) had by the early nineteenth century become the dominant regional and maritime power, and British officials signed a General Treaty in 1820 and a Maritime Truce in 1835 with the leaders of the coastal sheikhdoms of the southern Gulf (which henceforward became known as the

Trucial States and in 1971 as the UAE). The General Treaty and Maritime Truce outlawed 'piracy' and maritime warfare in the Gulf and British officials later signed agreements with the ruling families of Bahrain (1861), Kuwait (1899 and again in 1914), and Qatar (1916). From a ruler's perspective there was substance to the agreements. James Onley has calculated that, between 1805 and 1861, the British Residency in the Persian Gulf (based in Bushehr on the Persian coast) received ninety-eight requests for protection from the rulers of the Trucial States, in addition to twenty-one requests from Bahrain, twelve from Oman, and one from Kuwait.[28] Paul Rich observed that, in practice, 'a rule of thumb is that when something interested the British, they found a reason for interfering.'[29]

As British policy was focused primarily on the maintenance of maritime security and less on the internal affairs within the sheikhdoms, the agreements consolidated and enhanced the internal legitimacy and power of the local ruler co-signatories and introduced a measure of external protection of their survival.[30] Separately, Frederick Anscombe has suggested that the more visible Ottoman presence in parts of the Arabian Peninsula in the nineteenth century 'started a process of territorial definition, in the course of which Arab sheikhly families used great power sponsorship to define themselves against rivals.'[31] Although Saudi Arabia never became a 'British protected state' as did the other (smaller) sheikhdoms, the Treaty of Darin signed in 1915 performed a broadly similar function as, in the words of David Rundell, 'the British government first recognized Abdulaziz and his sons as rulers' of the Najd.[32]

Bahrain was the exception to the convention that British officials focused more on matters of external policy than on domestic political developments within the treaty-protected sheikhdoms. This in part was due to concerns by British officials for the potentially destabilizing impact of the mistreatment of Bahrain's (majority) Shia communities by members of the ruling family and allied (Sunni) tribal groups. Major C.K. Daly, the British Political Agent in Bahrain between 1921 and 1926, acknowledged that allegations of misrule by the Al Khalifa had implications for British interests, 'as the Sheikh is under our protection and they [Daly's Bahraini petitioners] urge, with some reason, that we ought, in consequence, to take steps to prevent the Sheikh from abusing his authority.'[33] British intervention took the form of a series of Orders in Council (approved by the Privy Council in London) between 1919 and 1927 which 'gave full administrative oversight to the British political agent' in matters of criminal justice, education, land use, and taxation, as well as British involvement in a change of ruler in Bahrain in 1923.[34]

The fourth and final opening observation is that the ruler is not always the most powerful member of the family and that familial power bases through blocs of full brothers and marriage ties, as well as force of personality, are significant contingent factors. This dynamic became visible in Abu Dhabi and Saudi Arabia in the 2010s as Mohammed bin Zayed Al Nahyan and Mohammed bin Salman Al Saud became indisputably the most powerful members of their families as the Crown Prince rather than the Ruler.[35] Another example was in Bahrain, where the long-serving Prime Minister of forty-nine years (1971–2020), Sheikh Khalifa bin Salman Al Khalifa, was the effective power base during the reign of his brother, Emir Isa bin Salman Al Khalifa, and overshadowed the first decade of the reign of his nephew, King Hamad bin Isa Al Khalifa, after his succession in 1999. Along with Emir Tamim bin Hamad Al Thani in Qatar, both Mohammed bin Salman and Mohammed bin Zayed are sons of their father's favored wife, also illustrating the significance of maternal status in determining which of a ruler's often many sons may rise to prominence.

Restraints on sitting rulers from members of their own family as well as, on occasion, from social pressures and domestic opposition forces, provided sufficient constraints on the unchecked exercise of personal power to draw a distinction between the Gulf monarchies and the notion of a 'sultanistic regime' as described by H.E. Chehabi and Juan Linz in their eponymous 1998 book. In their reading, sultanism represented an extreme form of personal rule in which one person could shape, make, and undo the institutions that supported their rule.[36] Only Oman, where successive sultans, including Qaboos bin Said after 1970, monopolized power and policymaking in their own person and largely kept family members at bay, approached the basis of a sultanistic regime, although Mohammed bin Salman has started to replicate the characteristics of such a regime in his concentration of power in Saudi Arabia since 2015.[37]

Nature of authority

C.A. Bayly has observed how, in the nineteenth century in many parts of the world, 'The state became located in a particular place, rather than moving around wherever the king went' and noted that, in areas where the modern 'state' was not (yet) present, there nevertheless existed 'a set of diverse and competing interests' whose 'stability waxed and waned over time.'[38] In the context of the pre-oil Arabian Peninsula, and specifically of the Trucial States, J.P. Bannerman observed that political units were 'people-centered' and based on personal agreements and relationships rather than defined by fixed territorial markers.[39] This persisted well into the twentieth century until bureaucracies began to formally institutionalize some of the mechanisms of rulership just as the drawing up of political borders imposed a structure on state-society relations in identifiable national units. For Saudi academic Haifa Alangari, there were three key attributes to political authority that sustained leaders in power in the Arabian Peninsula in the pre-oil era: social consent, coercive force, and (traditional) religious authority, as well as the interplay among them.[40] In tribal societies, the characterization of the Sheikh as the 'father figure' was also a marker of authority.[41]

Writing about Bahrain but in terms applicable to much of the Arabian Peninsula, especially the coastal settlements on the Gulf and Red Sea shorelines, Staci Strobl described Gulf society in the pre-modern period as one of:

> ... a history of loose political networks which allowed the Indian Ocean culture to flourish as a maritime system of small businesses, trade by dhow, pearling and fishing endeavors, and agriculture (...) Despite social cohesion around trade, the political

structure was devoid of a center and could be characterized as a system of negotiated economic relationships between sea-faring commercial families or clans.[42]

In the harsh conditions of the pre-oil political economy on the Arabian Peninsula, a relationship of mutual dependence grew up around the provision of stable and secure market conditions from which both ruling and merchant families derived material benefit. One recent study introduced the concept of 'negotiated governance' among local tribal leaders and occasional centralizing authorities.[43] This produced a set of political and social arrangements that emphasized the principles of consultative rule and the linkage of governing 'stakeholders' through social institutions such as marriage and the *majlis* (council). (The significance of consultation will be examined more fully in Chapter 2.)

The social anthropologist Peter Lienhardt conducted some of the earliest anthropological fieldwork in Kuwait and other Gulf sheikhdoms in the 1950s and 1960s and coined the expression 'political family business' to describe the nature of rulership. Lienhardt observed that 'Kuwait could not simply be "ruled" by the Ruler in absolutist terms, because the ruling family also conspicuously participated in the government of the country.'[44] Such visibility and direct involvement was especially the case during the formative years of state-building when institutions and bureaucracies were still in the process of creation. As such, Lienhardt noted that:

> How far the scope of individual shaikhs in reaching final decisions extended, or whether they considered their authority to be delegated, and, if so, delegated by what superior authority— these were questions which could not be answered without an intimate knowledge of the ruling family.[45]

During this period, ruling families needed to coexist alongside prominent families and merchants, and not infrequently relied on them for economic and financial assistance.[46] The exercise of political authority at this time was, in the words of Sulayman Khalaf and James Onley, 'frail, vulnerable, and precarious' as the ruler's family was:

... both the source of the ruler's hereditary legitimacy and strength, and a constant constraint on his rulership; it supported him against the merchants and tribes, but it produced his strongest rivals (...) To maintain their rulerships and the wellbeing of their shaikhdoms, the rulers had to engage in a never-ending juggling act (...) constantly observing, balancing and rebalancing situations; forever negotiating and renegotiating the various options available to them at any one moment.[47]

A biography of Sheikh Jassim bin Mohammed Al Thani, the 'founder' of modern Qatar, published by a member of the ruling family in 2012, described a set of qualities that Sheikh Jassim had wished in the late 1880s to see in his successor, namely that

The ruler of Doha should at once be both a soldier and a statesman, able to beat out the tribes and to march long distances whenever necessary, and while in Doha to keep order in the town, to remain conciliatory with the different tribes and to keep himself out of playing into the hands of the Turks.[48]

There was also a distinction between rulers (*umara*) and religious scholars (*ulama*) which denoted a conceptual division of political and religious authority formulated most explicitly in the relationship between the Al Saud and the Wahhabi establishment in Saudi Arabia and in the Ottoman-era distinction between the Governor of the Hijaz and the *Sharif* of Mecca.[49] Across the Arabian Peninsula, the relationship between the political and religious aspects of authority was rooted in the expectation that governance (*siyasa*) must accommodate Islamic law (*sharia*).[50] George Joffe observed that 'sovereignty' as a concept was 'legitimized as being a divine attribute and not linked to temporal power' as 'it was concerned with creating the appropriate environment for the legally sanctioned practices and authority of an Islamic society.'[51] However, it should be noted that whereas Ibn Saud mobilized religious fervor in his campaign of territorial expansion in the 1910s and 1920s through the *Ikhwan*, he acted decisively against the religious forces when he perceived the *Ikhwan* to be a political threat to him in the late 1920s.[52]

Conceptually, the German sociologist Max Weber identified and defined three ideal types of political authority in terms of the legitimate power exercised by one group over another in society—traditional authority, charismatic authority, and legal-rational authority. At the time of Weber's death in 1920, all the rulers in the Gulf would have been classified as exercising traditional authority and, in some respects, they still do, albeit that institutionalization has added a legal authority onto traditional sources of power.[53] Traditional authority in the pre-oil era was vested in power itself rooted in the local economic resources that were under the control of each group, and which could fluctuate significantly over time.[54] That said, decision-making continues to be driven by a top-down process in which policies (if not outcomes) are still largely set by senior members of ruling families, including the ruler, and where institutions exist primarily to implement, rather than determine, decisions taken by small groups of policymaking elites.[55]

In his famous 'Politics as a Vocation' (*Politik als Beruf*) lecture in Munich in January 1919, Weber outlined his definition of a state as 'a human community that (successfully) claims the monopoly of the legitimate use of physical force within a given territory.' Later in his lecture, Weber added that

> … the development of the modern state is initiated through the action of the prince. He paves the way for the expropriation of the autonomous and 'private' bearers of executive power who stand beside him, of those who in their own right possess the means of administration, warfare, and financial organization, as well as politically usable goods of all sorts.[56]

While Weber was lecturing in revolutionary Bavaria in the aftermath of Germany's defeat in the First World War, in conditions about as far removed from the Arabian Peninsula as can be imagined, the 'Weberian' notion of the state has become deeply embedded in scholarly and practical analysis. Several of the Weberian characteristics of statehood—territorial integrity and monopoly over the use of legitimate force—strengthened the position and the power of the ruling families over Gulf societies. The Gulf monarchies are virtually the only 'traditional' leaderships that survived the processes of socio-economic change without losing power to what Weber termed the class of 'professional politicians.'

Rulers in the Gulf, moreover, managed to channel, largely though not exclusively on their own terms, the transformative impact on their societies brought about by the entry into the 'oil era' after 1945. There is thus comparative utility in studying how and why 'the princes' were able to retain control of a set of processes that some at the time believed might overcome them and lead to an 'Arabia without Sultans.'[57]

Patrimonial forms of rule, buttressed enormously by the receipt and spread of oil revenues, underpinned a process of state formation in which power was centralized in a 'state' which essentially was a set of institutions whose core ministries functioned as a bureaucratic outgrowth of ruling family control.[58] Oil wealth consolidated both the distributive and the coercive power of the state in monarchies and non-monarchies, such as Saddam Hussein's Iraq and Muammar Qaddafi's Libya, alike.[59] The distribution of resources created interlocking networks of patrons and clients that flowed downward from the ruler at the apex of the pyramid and evolved into 'neopatrimonialism' as they permeated state institutions.[60] The political culture that came to define the oil era in the Gulf States was also rooted in traditional notions of leadership in tribal societies in the Arabian Peninsula in which 'pockets of fiefdom-like collective identities (…) combined both paternalistic and patriarchal characteristics vital for survival in that environment.'[61]

In this patrimonial system, proximity to the ruler was vital, and royal advisors became significant 'gatekeepers' especially in the early years of the transition into the oil era. Many of these gatekeepers were of foreign origin and wielded significant access as they controlled access to the ruling sheikhs. In Kuwait, the Ruler's secretary, Mulla Saleh, a Persian, was in post for four decades between the 1890s and the 1930s, by which latter point his son was also the Ruler's representative to the Kuwait Oil Company.[62] Examples in other Gulf States included Fuad Hamza, Hafiz Wahba, and Yusuf Yassin in Saudi Arabia, Charles Belgrave in Bahrain, and a coterie of British and Arab advisors, labeled in one history 'the Muscat mafia,' who coexisted, sometimes uneasily, around Sultan Qaboos in Oman; as well as powerful local advisors such as Abdullah al-Sulayman al-Hamdan in Riyadh and Abdullah Darwish in Doha.[63] In Saudi Arabia, Hamza, a Lebanese national, Hafiz, an Egyptian, and Yassin, a Syrian, were among six non-Saudi members of an eight-strong political committee within the royal court set up by Ibn Saud to assist in the governance of the fledging Kingdom.[64] John Thomson, a young British diplomat stationed in Jeddah in the 1950s near the end of Ibn Saud's life, recalled later how Ibn Saud's court:

> ... really consisted of non-Saudi Arabs who were thrown out of other places. This was quite sensible because it meant that none of them had any constituency in the country (...) They were a very clever, highly competitive group of people, and not altogether co-operative with each other. The important thing, the crucial thing, was to have the King's ear, to be able to go in and see the King at more or less any time and for it to be seen by everybody that the King trusted you.[65]

In his historiography of Saudi Arabia, Jörg Matthias Determann observed that Ibn Saud preferred to employ foreign advisors in part because they did not have a local power base, and also 'to keep the old Hijazi elite away from real power.' Their influence at court remained a focus of resentment for many of the Hijazi notables who continued to refer to them dismissively as 'the Syrians' long after they had been granted Saudi citizenship.[66] In the UAE, Egyptian, Iraqi, and Palestinian advisors played key roles in growing the fledgling government ministries after the creation of the federal state in 1971 and during the formative years of state-building and development that followed. Their influence was a source of some concern to British officials who had been accustomed to wielding advisory authority but reflected the fact that the Foreign Office in London paid little, if any, attention to developing local institutional capabilities prior to Britain's withdrawal from its protected state relationships with the Gulf in 1971.[67]

Tools of control

Rulers (and members of their families) had numerous tools at their disposal as they sought to acquire, consolidate, and wield power. The nature of these tools evolved over time and proved sufficiently adaptive and responsive to changing conditions so as to position the Gulf monarchies as the great survivors of regional politics, even as monarchical figures elsewhere were swept away in Egypt (1953), Iraq (1958), Yemen (1962), Libya (1969), and Iran (1979). By contrast, the six Gulf monarchies not only defied the predictions of modernization theorists that 'traditional' forms of leadership would struggle to survive the processes of socio-economic development but also consolidated political authority through their control of oil revenues and the enabling mechanisms of distributive (and coercive) power. As such, works such as Samuel Huntingdon's *Political Order in Changing Societies* (published in 1968) and Fred Halliday's *Arabia without Sultans* (published in 1974) have only limited use in explaining rulers' political durability.[68]

Marriage has long served as a 'political strategy,' as Saudi historian Madawi Al-Rasheed puts it, to establish ties of kinship within branches of ruling families and between ruling families and prominent members of local tribes (and other ruling dynasties) and to integrate social groups into an extended power structure.[69] In addition, marriages could send visible signals that branches (and members) of ruling families who had, for whatever reason, been marginalized, were being rehabilitated; an example, from Qatar, was the reintegration of the family of Sheikh Hamad bin Jassim bin Hamad Al Thani after he was implicated in the February 1996 attempt to topple Emir Hamad bin Khalifa Al Thani; Sheikh Hamad was later pardoned, members of his family were folded back into the core of the ruling family through marriages in 2006, and one of his sons, Sheikh Abdulrahman bin Hamad Al Thani, was, much later, appointed Minister of Culture by Emir Tamim bin Hamad Al Thani in an October 2021 government reshuffle.[70]

The creation of kinship alliances was especially significant in the early periods of consolidation of ruling families' authority in binding together coalitions of tribes. This practice was particularly evident as King Abdulaziz (Ibn Saud)—who had twenty-two wives throughout his life, although no more than four at any one time—expanded his control of territory in Saudi Arabia. For example, in the early 1920s, after the Al Saud conquest of the rival emirate of Ha'il in 1921, Ibn Saud married a daughter of the defeated Ruler, while a decade later he married a daughter-in-law of Faisal al-Duwaish, the leader of the *Ikhwan* movement that had initially been co-opted by Ibn Saud but later vanquished after military defeat by Al Saud forces in 1929. Ibn Saud's sons, and especially his two successors, Saud and Faisal, who, in turn, both became King of Saudi Arabia, also married strategically into prominent tribal families.[71] Longtime U.S. diplomat David Rundell has observed that 'Over time these marriages transformed the Al Saud family into a unifying super-tribe, and the only institution that encompasses most of Central Arabia's traditional elites.'[72]

Interpersonal ties have been examined in depth by Andrea Rugh in her study of the political culture of leadership in the UAE and in a context where governance is based both on personal relations and formal institutions as well as proximity to centers of power.[73] Dynastic marriages among the members of the seven ruling families and with influential (non-ruling) merchant families illustrate the enduring importance of personalized connections that persist alongside (and sometimes complicate) the formal mechanisms of bureaucratic institutionalization. As one example of many, Rugh described the dense network of familial ties of Sheikh Humaid bin Rashid Al Nuaimi, who became Ruler of Ajman in September 1981:

> … Counting his wives, mother, and grandmother, Sheikh Humaid is linked to wealthy merchant families [such as the al-Ghurair], the critical Bani Qitab, the Nahyans (albeit from a section that is not in favor), and the Rulers of RAK [Ras al-Khaimah], UAQ [Umm al-Quwain], and the Bu Falasa of Dubai. In addition, his sister married the Ruler of Fujairah, and her son is now ruler there. One could not be better positioned from the point of view of marriage relations to form political alliances with all parties in the area.[74]

More contemporary examples of politically significant marriages include the 2005 union between Sheikh Mansour bin Zayed Al Nahyan, one of the sons of Sheikh Zayed, and Sheikha Manal bint Mohammed Al Maktoum, a daughter of the Ruler of Dubai.

Their marriage served as a contemporary drawing together of the most senior lineages of the Al Nahyan and the Al Maktoum and has helped position Sheikh Mansour—at the time of writing, the owner of Manchester City Football Club as well as the UAE Vice President and Minister of Presidential Affairs—as a key powerbroker in the federation. In Kuwait, much was made of the 'wedding of the century' in April 2015 between Sheikh Fahd bin Nasser Al Sabah, a grandson of Emir Sabah, and Fay bint Luay Al Kharafi, a granddaughter of Jassim Al Kharafi, a former speaker of the National Assembly and scion of one of the oldest and most connected merchant families in the country.[75]

Marriages between members of different ruling families also created dynastic alliances akin to those within the UAE but on a regional level. In the 1950s, for example, Sheikh Ahmed bin Ali Al Thani, then the heir apparent and subsequently the Ruler of Qatar (from 1960 to 1972) married Maryam bint Rashid Al Maktoum, a daughter of the Ruler of Dubai (and a sibling of the current Ruler, Sheikh Mohammed bin Rashid). Their marriage was just one of several anchors of a close relationship between Qatar and Dubai in a period which also saw Dubai become a major regional market for Qatari goods; a common currency, the Qatar and Dubai riyal, replace the Gulf rupee as the unit of circulation from 1966 to 1973; and the two emirates take similar positions against Bahrain and Abu Dhabi in the (ultimately unsuccessful) negotiations to create a nine-member Union of Arab Emirates prior to the termination of British protection agreements in 1971.[76]

A more recent example of a dynastic marriage occurred in June 2011 when Princess Sahab bint Abdullah Al Saud, a daughter of King Abdullah of Saudi Arabia wedded Prince Khalid bin Hamad Al Isa, a son of the King of Bahrain, just weeks after units of the Saudi Arabian National Guard were deployed to Bahrain to assist in the restoration of political order in the country after the Pearl Roundabout uprising in February to March of that year. While there is no evidence to suggest any political or geopolitical element to the marriage, *Gulf States Newsletter* observed that 'it was possibly the first time that the daughter of a Saudi king had married into another royal family since an episode in the late 19th century.'[77]

Such a match between the (then) reigning branches of the Al Saud and the Al Khalifa gave, at the least, a highly visible demonstration of the dynastic links between the families at a time when the Al Khalifa was facing significant domestic pressure. The sons of King Hamad are the most dynastically interlinked in the region as Prince Nasser bin Hamad Al Khalifa married Sheikha bint Mohammed Al Maktoum, a daughter of the Ruler of Dubai, in 2009, thereby establishing a dynastic link with the other state—the UAE—that also deployed forces to Bahrain in 2011.[78]

The suppression of alternative power bases was another tool of control that enabled ruling families and individual rulers to consolidate political authority and eliminate potential and actual rivals. The *Ikhwan* rebellion against Al Saud rule between 1927 and 1929 was the first major challenge to Al Saud authority after Ibn Saud recaptured Riyadh in 1902.[79] The destruction of the *Ikhwan* in battle by 1929 had the practical effect of eliminating the Bedouin tribes as alternative centers of political, economic, or military power in the Saudi Arabia that was taking shape with the creation of the modern Kingdom in 1932. Their military defeat meant that the *Ikhwan* no longer posed a challenge to the monopoly of force enjoyed by Ibn Saud in the emerging Saudi state while the abolition of grazing rights and the resettlement of Bedouin tribes had the effect of marginalizing tribal groups and reordering them into controllable economic units.[80]

Oman was the only Gulf State, other than Saudi Arabia, that required the ruler (albeit with far greater and more direct international assistance) to militarily defeat a threat to political control during the formative years of creating modern state institutions, which in Oman's case was several decades later, in the 1970s. The Dhofar War began in 1965 as an armed struggle launched by disaffected tribes angered at the lack of economic development in Dhofar.[81] It quickly assumed political overtones and became radicalized by 1968 when the Dhofar Liberation Front (DLF) morphed into the Popular Front for the Liberation of Oman and the Arab Gulf and received logistical and ideological support from the (Marxist) People's Democratic Republic of Yemen.[82] Omani forces gradually gained the upper hand in the war with covert support from British units of the Special Air Service (SAS) and a large deployment of Iranian troops on the ground, and by 1975 most fighting ceased (with Sultan Qaboos officially declaring an end to the war in a broadcast to the nation on 11 December[83]), although sporadic incidents continued until 1980.[84]

The end of the Dhofar War was followed by a 'hearts and minds' campaign carefully designed to associate the benefits (and opportunities) of development with Sultan Qaboos, whose own mother was from a prominent Dhofari tribe,[85] and to remove all claims to autonomous political authority. The objective was to create a sense of belonging to a 'new' Oman that came into being with the 'renaissance' of Qaboos's takeover of power in 1970, and erode alternative forms of tribal or political loyalty.[86] Civil centers, which included schools and mosques as well as medical clinics and shops, were constructed throughout Dhofar and in most cases constituted the first signs of the Omani state for local communities, while new wells were dug to provide a water supply for livestock and agriculturalists. J.E. Peterson has noted that the wells were sited carefully 'at the junctions of tribal boundaries in order to prevent any single tribe from claiming ownership,'[87] while Dawn Chatty has observed that Qaboos linked his name 'with all that was new, modern, and progressive' as schools, mosques, hospitals, roads, and countless other visible manifestations of the Omani state infrastructure were named after him.[88]

Both in Oman (in the 1970s) and in Saudi Arabia (in the 1920s and 1930s) an (unstated) aim of the civil development programs was to resettle nomadic and pastoralist groups around administrative centers that not only provided visible manifestations of state authority but also were easier to control.[89] The twentieth century also saw the fixing of national boundaries which defined the sheikhdoms as formal political units. This process of identifying and demarcating borders that overlay the traditionally fluid political geography of the Arabian Peninsula was necessitated by, among other factors, the awarding of oil concessions in the 1920s and 1930s that needed to cover geographically definable territorial areas rather than the more mobile conception of tribal grazing grounds (*dirah*):[90] 'an orbit or a softly defined zone by which points of contact with other tribes, often at oases, were negotiated and renegotiated.'[91] As J.E. Peterson has noted, traditionally 'territoriality was not an important element of sovereignty (...) Instead, sovereignty depended principally on control of or influence over people.'[92] The ability of sheikhs to extract *zakat* (a form of alms) and provide protection to local tribes were additional measures of jurisdictions which altered as circumstances changed.[93]

The creation of boundaries and the later formulation of citizenship regulations that defined the categories of 'belonging' in the new political entities cut across the intensely transnational connections of tribal, agricultural, nomadic, and business relationships in the Arabian Peninsula. As a multi-volume history of boundary-making in south-eastern Arabia published between 2018 and 2020 noted, 'defined frontiers' and the 'concept of territorial sovereignty in the Western sense' did not exist in the region prior to the twentieth century.[94] New nationality laws in the 1950s and 1960s which defined citizenship and its criteria for eligibility were a top-down process that excluded as well as included communities on terms established firmly by the ruling elites whose own power became more deeply cemented.[95] Moreover, the emergence of welfare states based on the distribution of oil revenues also meant that, over time, citizenship became imbued with economic and social privileges that could be granted, but also taken away, by rulers.[96] Rulers in Kuwait and Bahrain naturalized thousands of people in the 1970s and 2000s, respectively, with the aim of creating a bedrock of pro-government political support (in Kuwait) and altering the sectarian balance of the citizen population (in Bahrain).[97]

Abdulhadi Khalaf, a Bahraini sociologist who was himself stripped of his citizenship in the 2000s, has noted that examples of collective naturalization of large groups of people for political or demographic purposes, as in Kuwait and Bahrain, as well as the withdrawal of citizenship from critics and dissidents, as in Qatar, Kuwait, Bahrain, and the UAE, illustrate how 'a passport is not a right of citizenship, but rather an honour bestowed by the ruling family, given to whom it wants and taken from whom it wants.'[98] Kuwaiti sociologist Khaldoun Al-Naqeeb made a similar point that 'loyalty is to the person of the ruler and his family.'[99] The withdrawal of Qatari citizenship from several thousand members of the Al-Ghafran clan of the Al-Murra tribe in 2005 (and, for most of those affected, its subsequent reinstatement), reinforced the point that citizenship could be granted, and taken away, at a moment's notice and with little apparent redress.[100] As the Bahraini scholar of citizenship and migration, Noora Lori, observed in 2020, rulers' ability, often seemingly arbitrarily, to determine who does or does not belong 'affects every aspect of their lives, including education, health care, social benefits, employment opportunities, and marriage prospects.'[101]

The fact that the delineation of political boundaries was followed relatively quickly by the first inflows of significant oil revenues strengthened the hold of the dynastic families over the societies they ruled. The first concessions to oil companies in the 1920s and 1930s typically were granted in the name of the ruler who retained control over the subsequent distribution of revenues and the choice of recipient.[102] In Saudi Arabia, Ibn Saud's long-serving Minister of Finance, Abdullah al-Sulayman al-Hamdan, negotiated the 1933 concession with the forerunner of Aramco and himself counted the 35,000 gold sovereigns that constituted the initial payment.[103] A decade later in Qatar, the Ruler 'personally granted oil concessions, personally received the oil income, and personally decided the distribution of wealth.'[104] As institutions were developed to handle the growing complexity of governing, they functioned essentially as the bureaucratization of ruling family control and were dominated initially by members of the ruler's family.[105]

Oil revenues fundamentally changed the relationship between the ruler (and his family) and other economic actors, such as the merchant classes in Gulf societies, as control of the receipts (which accrued to the state) elevated ruling families above their societal peers and reduced their reliance on them for resources. In the pre-oil era, a significant proportion of 'state' revenues came from taxes and duties on economic activities, and members of ruling families frequently were in partnership with, or indebted to, prominent local merchants.[106] Ibn Saud also used merchants to represent him and act as purchasing agents in neighboring and regional states, including Egypt and India, in the 1930s.[107] In this environment, where the leading merchants in pre-oil Gulf societies were at least the economic equal of the ruling families who relied on them for taxes and duties, they represented a practical constraint on the exercise of untrammeled power by the ruling elite, and an interest group with very real influence.

In this context, and in the period when boundaries were still fluid, merchants had the option of moving from one sheikhdom to another, taking with them their economic resources and commercial connections, if they felt aggrieved at any ruler's policies or decisions. A famous example of this occurred in 1910 when several leading Kuwaiti merchants withdrew to Bahrain and al-Hasa after Sheikh Mubarak doubled taxes to fund a military campaign in the desert against Sa'dun Pasha of the powerful Muntafiq tribal confederation (in modern-day southern Iraq). The merchants, led by Hilal bin Fajhan Al-Mutairi, took seventeen ships and *zakat* payments of more than 50,000 rupees with them, prompting Sheikh Mubarak to make concessions in a (successful) attempt to entice them back to Kuwait.[108] Seventy years earlier, a merchant exodus had occurred in the opposite direction as Bahraini merchants 'fled en masse' to Kuwait and also to Lingah on the Persian coastline of the Gulf as they sought refuge from a period of civil conflict, and in doing so reduced the size of the commercial fleet in Bahrain by three-quarters.[109] As the ability to leave became harder once boundaries and citizenship became fixed, this form of merchants' leverage over rulers waned.

The ways in which the subsequent allocation and distribution of oil revenues altered the balance of economic and political power within Gulf societies will be examined in Chapter 7. It was not the passive receipt of 'oil rents' but rather the active decisions on how and for what ends to use them that created the pathways of co-optation that structured and came to dominate the distinctive political economy in the 'oil monarchies' that emerged in the second half of the twentieth century. Political choices mattered in the distribution of economic resources, and those making the political decisions remained the key figures in ruling families in all six of the Gulf States. The growth of welfare structures underpinned by the (selective) distribution of oil wealth at a time of small citizen populations and seemingly limitless resources did, however, create path dependencies that have proven stubbornly hard to reform.[110]

The advent of the oil era and the fact that oil revenues were declared the property of the ruler (and later the state) elevated the position of ruling families over and above other economic actors with whom they had hitherto coexisted *primus inter pares*. Mahdi Al Tajir, a Bahraini merchant who later became Head of Customs in Dubai and a senior Emirati diplomat, observed that, 'In reality their share of the oil wealth went far beyond what was originally intended (...) the industry provided them with financial power which had previously been the domain of the pearlers and merchants and this further strengthened the political dominance of the Ruling Family.'[111] Ruling family (and state) power was further reinforced by control over land (and, later, land reclamation), which provided additional sources of wealth and became a point of tension with opposition groups, especially in already contested political communities such as Bahrain.[112]

The states that emerged in the 1960s and 1970s thus had considerable (though not complete) autonomy from social classes and, to a lesser extent, societal pressures through ruling elites' control over the processes of wealth distribution. Aspects of personalism and family rulership described in this opening chapter have endured and have enabled the ruling families to adapt to the significant changes to the political economy of all six Gulf States since the advent of the oil era. Their survival into the twenty-first century has marked the ruling families of the Arabian Peninsula as the great survivors of Middle Eastern politics, in ways that were not necessarily foreseen by academics or much of the scholarly literature at the time. And yet, any eventual 'post-oil' shift, which may be accelerated by global climate action policies, will likely pose a harder set of challenges to the monarchies, not least by calling into question the viability of some of the networks and tools of control examined in this and subsequent chapters.

2

CONSULTATION

For all the power of the ruler and his family described in Chapter 1, neither the ruler nor the state is fully autonomous from vested political and economic interests. While the 'state' is by far the most powerful actor in Gulf societies, it coexists alongside social groups that retain the capacity to mobilize support in formal and informal ways and exert varying degrees of influence and checks and balances over decision-making, especially in contested issues of policy such as the distribution of resources. *Shura* (consultation) was, historically, a link that connected the ruling elite to those over whom they ruled and a key element of the conduct of 'politics' in informal settings with weak institutional structures, as was the importance of establishing *ijma'* (consensus). More recently, the legacy of *shura* (both real and reimagined) has been raised by advocates of political reform who have cast their calls for greater representation in decision-making processes as an evolution of the traditional principle of consultation.

This chapter examines the evolution of the principle of consultation from a 'traditional' practice rooted in Islamic and tribal governance into a basis for some of the representative structures as they emerged in the second half of the twentieth century. Networks of relationships within and among social groups have long coexisted alongside tribal and kinship ties and mediated interactions between 'state' and 'society' before and after the development of formal institutions and structures.[1] At various times the consultative process has been used by rulers to rally and solidify domestic constituencies during periods of external danger and by others to justify calls for greater participation in decision-making. Examples of both sides of the coin form case studies, including the famous meeting between the exiled Kuwaiti leadership and prominent Kuwaitis that took place in Jeddah in Saudi Arabia two months after the Iraqi invasion in 1990.

In addition, the chapter explores how politics is conducted in informal settings, such as the *diwaniya* or the *majlis* as well as through mechanisms such as petitions to express and communicate citizens' views on contentious issues to their leaders, as well as quiet outreach by leaders to disaffected groups. Ellen Lust-Okar has observed of the Middle East as a whole that 'Political participation is best understood through the interface of informal and formal politics.'[2] Observing (Shah-era) Iran, James Bill drew attention to the 'politics of informality' where most channels to power were informal and access was mediated through personal ties and proximity. Power relationships were defined in this context by fluidity, flexibility, and elasticity, and the exercise of power in practice was 'played out primarily within networks of informal groups.'[3] While the many differences between Pahlavi Iran and Arab Gulf monarchies render any comparison inexact, the role of intermediaries and petitions is relevant to the Gulf States as well.

Consultation and consensus

Consultation—*shura*—and the search for consensus—*ijma'*—are two concepts rooted in the Quran that were also features of the tribally-based forms of governance in the Arabian Peninsula. *Shura* is mentioned in the Quran in the context of Allah encouraging the Prophet Mohammed to seek the advice of his companions.[4] Over time, *shura* and *ijma'* began to approximate 'local norms that derived from both tribal and religious foundations' and, in practical terms, widened the range of expertise available to decision-makers and underpinned any decision with a sense of collective responsibility.[5] These two concepts were significant aspects of the informal exercise of political power in pre-oil societies where (certain privileged) social groups often had direct access to ruling elites unmediated by state institutions.[6] They also formed parts of the 'glue' that could hold together the coalitions of familial and interest groups at the centers of power and tie them more closely to the societies over which they ruled. This was the case for influential members of the merchant community who were frequently connected to ruling families through marriage, shared business interests, and informal proximity to the court and regular access to the ruler.[7]

In her seminal work, *The Making of the Modern Gulf States*, Rosemarie Said Zahlan noted that, while in principle the rulers had absolute power, in practice:

> ... they generally consulted a small, informal council (*majlis*) according to the Islamic principle of *shura* (consultation). The concept of *shura* was essential to the administration of authority (...) The administrative infrastructure was very limited, and the functions of government varied from place to place. But the rulers remained accessible to their people: they gave daily audiences of several hours; they heard petitions and acted on them; they also gave judgements on personal and commercial disputes.[8]

A *majlis* was created in Dubai in the early 1900s to provide the ruler 'advice and political assistance.' It consisted of between fifteen and forty members both from the merchant class and from tribal elites in the emirate. In her analysis of the historical emergence of Dubai, Fatma Al-Sayegh documented how the merchants were 'the spokesmen for popular grievances and demands' and, through their direct access to the ruler, 'wielded a great deal of influence over the economic and political decision-making process.'[9] Meanwhile, writing for the (then) Dubai-based Gulf Research Centre, Giacomo Luciani described how:

> Very few decisions are made without extensive consultation (...) If the required degree of consensus is not present, matters are left pending, so that the issue can ripen. This normally happens either because key people become convinced and change their

minds, or, more frequently, because tradeoffs are arranged and compromises shaped (…) The essential task of the ruler is to set up the system of consultation, i.e. define the circle of people whose opinion matters.[10]

Across the Gulf, the *majlis* (or, in Kuwait, the *diwaniya*) has become an organic feature of social and political culture as it remains a space for gatherings in which information and opinions are shared on a regular and semi-structured basis.[11] Members of ruling families, including the ruler himself, will frequently visit the weekly *majlis* or *diwaniya* of prominent members of society, and the walls of many meeting spaces are adorned with photographs of such occasions, alongside photographs of visits by other local and international dignitaries. The *majlis* and *diwaniya* also became the focal point for meetings of networks of like-minded individuals, including scholars, often involving visitors from across the Gulf who came together to discuss the issues of the day. In Qatar, a rare, more recent example of political dissidence came when a local academic, Ali Khalifa Al-Kuwari, published a 2012 manifesto entitled *The People Want Reform…in Qatar, Too*. The manifesto arose out of monthly meetings of intellectuals at Al-Kuwari's *majlis* and contained contributions from eleven Qatari contributors who wanted to raise 'a collective voice for reform in Qatar' after they felt that official channels of making their views heard were inadequate.[12]

In Kuwait, Mary Ann Tétreault observed that the *diwaniya* was:

> the product of a merger between two traditional patterns of social life. One is the old practice of seafaring businessmen gathering in the evenings to trade information about weather, markets, and where the fish were running. The other is the primary role of the family in social, economic, and political interactions.[13]

The *majlis* and the *diwaniya* operated largely along social class lines and extended downward from the ruler and his family to other prominent members of society such as merchants, intellectuals, and religious scholars. The *diwaniya* in Kuwait was particularly embedded in local political culture and underpinned the 'personalized networks of family, neighborhood, and trust' that came to play a pivotal role in the often-informal discussion and practice of politics, and could also be a site for local conflict resolution as well.[14] *Diwaniyas* functioned also as alternative 'avenues for the conduct of politics' especially during the periods in modern Kuwaiti history when the National Assembly was suspended, most recently between 1986 and 1992.[15]

Rulers perceived a special need to consult more widely in times of danger. In 1923, after Ibn Saud blocked trade between Kuwait and the Al Saud territory of Najd and demanded that Najdi customs duties be collected in Kuwait as a condition for reallowing trade, the Ruler of Kuwait, Sheikh Ahmad al-Jaber Al Sabah, invited five prominent notables in Kuwait City to discuss the issue before he made his decision on how to respond. Kuwaiti historian Farah Al-Nakib has described how, at the meeting with the Ruler:

> The notables believed that the question of reopening trade with Najd warranted an even wider consultation with all the town's big merchants. The following day a larger meeting of twenty-one notables was held in the *diwaniya* of a leading merchant, Hamad al-Khalid, without any members of the Al Sabah present in order to debate the issue before taking the group's collective opinion to the ruler.[16]

A similar example occurred in Riyadh in November 1928 when Ibn Saud convened a meeting of 800 tribal sheikhs, religious scholars, *Ikhwan* leaders, urban notables, and other prominent figures. Ibn Saud called the meeting in the face of mounting attacks by *Ikhwan* forces that drew reprisals from British forces stationed in Iraq, which in themselves highlighted Ibn Saud's apparent inability to maintain control within his claimed territorial land. Ibn Saud offered to release the assembly from the oath of loyalty they had sworn to him but instead received a reassertion of their allegiance as well as an affirmation from the religious scholars present of their obligation to obey his political authority.[17] Several years later, in Dubai, after a period of political turbulence in 1934, the Ruler, Sheikh Saeed bin Maktoum Al Maktoum, called a *majlis* at which he demanded the loyalty of Dubai's citizens, the same day as he publicly received the support of British authorities and a cache of British weapons, illustrating how the internal and external dimensions of security were inextricably linked.[18]

Elements of this personalized rule continued into the transition away from the pre-oil era, even as bureaucracies created new formal layers of control and degrees of 'official' separation between ruler and ruled. King Faisal, for example, met each week to consult with the religious authorities and tribal clerics and held a daily *majlis* at which (fatally, as it turned out, for him) members of his family and other prominent Saudis could attend.[19] Faisal's half-brother, Salman, who himself became King of Saudi Arabia in 2015, held a *majlis* twice a day for much of his decades-long tenure as Governor of Riyadh, which began in 1963, at which he would receive petitions and direct those not under his purview to relevant state entities.[20] Access to policymakers and the political 'system' in other Gulf States, including Kuwait with its National Assembly, was still at this time mediated primarily through personal and consultative channels, even after the creation of notionally representative institutions, which created parallel tracks of access to decision-makers that complicated and undermined their functioning.[21]

One of the innovations that Sultan Qaboos introduced in Oman after the Dhofar War ended in 1975 was to initiate weeks-long 'Meet the People' tours each spring. First held in 1977, the tours initially 'had an open and spontaneous quality to them' as Qaboos 'camped out in the desert and at each site received foreign and national guests as well as local petitioners in an elaborate circular tent.'[22] The social anthropologist Dawn Chatty observed how Qaboos's 'convoys through the country became instruments for keeping in touch with local people and for measuring the public mood and sentiment,' but that, over time, the Meet the People tours became more elaborate, formal, and ritualized as the 'tradition and ceremony started to become overgrown, intricate, and incapable of inflexibility.'[23] This evolution was captured by Calvin Allen and W. Lynn Rigsbee in their modern history of Oman published in 2000, as:

> The tour, usually held in late winter or early spring when the weather is cool, began as an informal sallying forth from the

palace, but by the 1990s had become a major two-week formal event in which the sultan is joined by a full retinue of ministers and other officials complete with a cavalcade of automobiles and helicopters (...) The issues [raised] tend to be trivial by national standards (...) but the effort is most important for the symbolism of the sultan physically addressing the needs of the people.[24]

A more contemporary instance of the central (and unpredictable) role that consultation could play in a time of crisis came in October 1990, two months into the Iraqi occupation of Kuwait, when the ruling family-in-exile in Saudi Arabia organized a meeting with prominent Kuwaitis in Jeddah. Senior members of the Al Sabah intended that the gathering between 13–15 October 1990 would signify a show of unity in the face of Saddam Hussein's aggression and support the buildup of international efforts to force an Iraqi withdrawal from Kuwait either through diplomacy or by force. The meeting was therefore conceived initially as a 'traditional' ceremony of allegiance at which prominent citizens would pledge their loyalty to the ruling family and, by extension, to a liberated Kuwait. Indeed, the Kuwaiti authorities-in-exile sought to limit the resolutions that could be raised at the conference to those that related directly to the Iraqi aggression rather than any broader issues, such as the suspension of parliament, to minimize division and any appearance of a lack of consensus.[25] At the meeting, the Emir, Sheikh Jabir al-Ahmad Al Sabah, emphasized the importance of national unity while Crown Prince Sheikh Sa'ad Abdullah Al Sabah urged attendees to 'show the world you are united in a single front.'[26]

Ahmad Muhammad Al-Khatib, whose involvement in the campaign for political reform in Kuwait began in the 1950s and continued for more than half a century, later claimed that the ruling family had acted as if it wanted the Jeddah conference 'to be a festival to support the Sabahs' and called for a national unity government to represent all Kuwaitis; while another critic, the businessman Abdullah Yusuf Al-Ghanem, stated trenchantly that 'In any normal situation, a government that loses a country is not simply returned to power with no questions asked.'[27] Al-Khatib attended the meeting in Jeddah and, in an interview with the Irish academic Fred Halliday, asserted that 'Kuwaitis are having second thoughts about what Kuwait should be after liberation (...) It is only natural that the whole government has to be questioned after this affair. It was not a small mistake, it was a catastrophe. The Al Sabah have to be accountable.'[28]

The delegates, who included representatives of business, academic, and diplomatic circles as well as former members of the National Assembly (which had been suspended since 1986), intended that the Jeddah meeting be far more interactive than the display of loyalty envisaged by the ruling family. In labeling the event the 'Kuwait People's Conference' it became clear that many attendees anticipated a negotiation with the ruling family to secure a commitment to restore the parliament.[29] A behind-the-scenes meeting between the Crown Prince, the head of the Kuwait Chamber of Commerce and Industry, Abdul Aziz Al-Saqr, and the Speaker of the last National Assembly prior to its dissolution, Ahmed Sadoun, agreed a compromise whereby the Crown Prince committed to restoring the National Assembly and the opposition dropped their call for a national government. Al-Saqr, a scion of one of the oldest merchant families in Kuwait, declared at the end of the conference that the meeting had opened the way for 'a new and serious dialogue aimed at establishing the fundamental principles which will serve as the basis for the construction of tomorrow's liberated Kuwait.'[30]

One must not, however, overplay the concepts of consultation and consensus or imply that the holding of a regular *majlis* was an indication of 'desert democracy' at work, as periodically claimed by its advocates, as there were clear if unwritten limits regarding the scope of debate.[31] In the 1990s, for example, an article in *Foreign Affairs* magazine described the *majlis* of Prince Salman bin Abdulaziz Al Saud, then the Governor of Riyadh, as 'a touching scene of desert governance transposed to modern times.'[32] The ability to attend a *majlis*, especially one that provided regular access to senior ruling family members, was limited for most people, and the meetings themselves were heavily hierarchical.[33] Moreover, as Tim Niblock has noted, the 'ability to express views to the decision-maker is not equivalent to having a share in determining what decisions are made.'[34]

Just as rulers consulted more often during times of external danger, so they did also at times of economic difficulty, such as the period of low oil prices in the 1980s and 1990s, when there was more active dialogue with members of the business community and chambers of commerce.[35] After the collapse of the unofficial *Suq al-Manakh* stock market in Kuwait in 1982, for example, which resulted in investor losses that were seventeen times the value of Kuwait's foreign reserves at the time, Sheikh Saad Abdullah, the Prime Minister (as well as Crown Prince), visited *diwaniyas* to speak with Kuwaitis of many backgrounds.[36] The need to be seen to be consulting with other domestic actors did not always change the policymaking response but it did provide a safety valve at times of economic, if not always political, stress. Consultative processes were able to channel aspects of public or popular opinion upward and provide an informal basis by which figures in political power and decision-making authority could better keep in touch with the mood 'on the ground.' A search for consensus was thus an operative consideration both within ruling families and between rulers and domestic constituencies in evaluating potential decisions.[37]

Contested legacies

Memories of the 'traditional' role of consultation have continued into the oil era and survived the rapid socio-economic transformation of Gulf societies between the 1950s and the 1980s. This was reflected in the fact that societal advocates of political evolution cast their demands for reform in terms consistent with consultation as a customary practice of governance. For their part, regimes sought to formalize the practice of *shura* in the new Consultative Councils that came into being and which they cast as an organic fusion of indigenous and Western forms of political organization.[38] This is evident in the inclusion of *shura* and *majlis* into the names of the institutions that were formed largely by top-down processes with ringfenced limitations on their ability to alter the structure or balance of political power away from governments and the ruling families that continued to dominate them.[39]

An illustrative example of the legacy of *shura* in structuring contemporary political expectations came on the eve of Qatar's first elections to its Shura Council in October 2021, following two decades of delay, as a Qatari academic (and a former appointed member of the council), Hend Al Muftah, argued that the elections were consistent with the principle of consultation rather than 'western democracy':

> Historically, the Qatari government has always governed through consultation and cooperation between the ruling family, business families, and tribes—a system that could be described by some as a unique form of consensus between different state stakeholders.

For Al Muftah, the electoral process:

> ... is more of a '*Shura*,' consultative concept and practice that emphasizes participation in making decisions and policies based on trust and accountability, rather than the western model of democracy which is based on a political concept and practices that, in contrast, include parties, organizations and groups.[40]

Whereas the various forms of political representation in each of the Gulf States is examined in detail in Chapter 4, this section focuses on some of the ways in which the legacy of consultative practice has been co-opted by political actors from across the regime-opposition spectrum. Advocates of political reform drew upon memories of consultative processes and access to the ruler in their claims for greater participation in contemporary decision-making processes. In 1995, for example, Mohammed Al-Massari, a physics professor who went into exile in London after participating in the formation of the Committee for the Defense of Legitimate Rights (CDLR) in Saudi Arabia, asserted that:

> In the 1960s, professors were regularly consulted by the government. Nearly every week we would receive legislative bills and they would solicit our opinion. We would respond or we wouldn't, depending on our qualifications and our interest. This practice has disappeared with King Fahd.[41]

Another dissident, Khalid Al-Fawwaz, raised a similar point as he also hearkened back to a past period of supposedly greater consultation, remembering that 'The officials, even the king, held weekly public meetings where they received individual grievances. They made promises.'[42] One of the petitions, entitled 'A Vision for the Present and Future of the Nation,' put forward to then Crown Prince Abdullah during the period of (comparative) opening of dialogue in Saudi Arabia, after the shock to the Kingdom of their citizens' involvement in the terrorist attacks of 11 September 2001, argued that consultation was a necessary basis for the next step of creating 'a nation of institutions and of constitutionality.'[43]

In 2005, Sheikh 'Awad Al-Qarni, a prominent member of the Islamic Awakening movement in Saudi Arabia in the 1990s, urged people to vote in the municipal elections that year on the grounds that 'elections were a way to implement the religious imperative of consultation.' Al-Qarni stated that

> In public affairs consultation is compulsory; nobody can claim they can do without it. And through elections, we consult each other. This is what is also called opinion, and it is a fundamental principle of Islamic legality (…) One can also implement the principle of consultation through elections, to give all force to Islamic legality.[44]

Without waiting for government authorization, local community leaders in the Saudi Eastern Province city of Qatif had held weekly meetings for at least three years at which they gathered 'to discuss local politics, social issues, and their vision of how best to become more, not less, integrated into Saudi society.'[45]

In response to a combination of international pressure after 9/11 and the domestic shock of terrorist attacks within Saudi Arabia in 2003, the Saudi leadership began a series of national dialogues in and after 2003 that started with a National Forum for Dialogue which convened religious scholars and clerics that included Salafi, Shia (Twelver and Ismaili), and Sufi representatives, with eight subsequent meetings taking place under the auspices of the King Abdulaziz Center for National Dialogue between 2004 and 2011.[46] The June 2003 meeting was the first time a dialogue of this nature had been held in Saudi Arabia, but the event resembled more of a stage-managed discussion than a genuinely interactive process of dialogue, even if the Secretary General of the King Abdulaziz Center for National Dialogue later expressed the hope that the meetings would convey the 'pulse of the Saudi street' to the King.[47]

Regime attempts to hold meetings on their own terms and not lose control of the agenda or the proceedings became strikingly visible in a separate event also held in Riyadh in 2003. This was a conference on human rights organized by the (state-linked) Saudi Red Crescent Authority, which was marred when security forces forcibly broke up a protest by demonstrators challenging officials over the slow pace of reform and arrested many of those involved.[48] The innate caution of Saudi leaders, probably shared by most or all of their Gulf counterparts, was encapsulated in a comment attributed to King Fahd: 'Why start fires on the inside, when there are fires on the outside?'[49]

A broadly similar dynamic was at play in Bahrain, where advocates of political opening in the 1990s and 2000s also made their case in terms of an evolutionary continuity of longstanding consultative custom, and regime efforts to manage a controlled process of dialogue did not go well. In 1996, a member of the political opposition noted that 'The elected assemblies that we are seeking are nothing but a natural development of the idea of consultation.'[50] Mansoor Al-Jamri, a prominent journalist who later founded the centrist *Al-Wasat* newspaper, argued that the 'open *majlis*' traditionally held by rulers and other figures of authority needed upgrading in the modern age as 'These open majlises have been unable to solve one single important problem (...) how can the emir, through the majlis, solve all the problems with each visitor (...) The British prime minister does not have enough time to receive 60 million Britons.'[51]

Part of the reason the subsequent process of political reform, initiated by King Hamad bin Isa Al Khalifa after he came to power in Bahrain in 1999, initially raised expectations was precisely because it was accompanied by what appeared at first a genuine round of consultation, which included opposition as well as clerical figures.[52] During the period between 1999 and 2001 in which it fleetingly appeared that liberalization might actually take place, the King held meetings with representatives of civil society and political groups, journalists, and former exiles who had returned to Bahrain.[53] The flurry of activity made the ensuing sense of disappointment when the King diluted the anticipated constitutional and political reforms, and concentrated authority in the executive branch of government, all the more acute.[54]

Chapters 4 and 6 include analysis of the decade separating the brief interlude of political opening in Bahrain, between 1999 and 2001, and the Pearl Roundabout uprising during the Arab Spring of 2011, in terms of the divergence in expectation between the regime and the spectrum of opposition groups. In 2011, demonstrators began their protest (which sparked the uprising) on 14 February, the tenth anniversary of the overwhelming approval of a National Action Charter in 2001 in a national referendum. The National Action Charter had symbolized the highpoint of the return to constitutional rule in Bahrain after twenty-seven years of national emergency and the suspension of the National Assembly, but its subsequent watering-down became a recurring flashpoint between government and opposition forces in the 2000s. The subsequent naming of the largely decentralized youth-led opposition movement as the February 14 Youth Coalition fused in the public mind the significance of the date ten years apart in modern Bahraini history.[55]

The Pearl Roundabout uprising of February 2011 was quelled by the deployment of Saudi national guardsmen and Emirati military police to Bahrain in mid-March and the imposition of three months of martial law that enabled the Bahraini security forces to restore a measure of control. The security crackdown began after negotiations between Crown Prince Salman bin Hamad Al Khalifa and members of the opposition failed to resolve the political crisis through consultation.[56] In June, the King called for a national dialogue to take place over the summer alongside a commission of inquiry.[57] Khalil Al-Marzouq, a former deputy speaker of the National Assembly who along with his seventeen Al-Wefaq (National Islamic Party) colleagues had resigned their seats in March 2011 in protest at the regime's crackdown on the protests, declared that 'this dialogue is not representative of the people. It is an ideas forum, rather than a people's representation.'[58] Having come under pressure to participate in the dialogue as a sign of good faith, the four Al-Wefaq representatives resigned a fortnight into the sessions as they felt the process was being stage-managed by the regime as a form of window-dressing.

Mansoor Al-Jamri, who by the time of the dialogue in July 2011 had been removed as editor of *Al-Wasat*, observed that much of the dialogue 'appeared to consist of a series of brief speeches more than a discussion' and that

> Each person speaks for a few minutes and it is usually not possible to speak again (...) There is no chance for give and take, as the number of people in each workshop is huge (...) Usually, pro-government speakers (around 85 percent of the attendants) dominate the start, middle and end of the talking. They will rise up against any person trying to cross what the government considers as red lines. Virtually all the opposition's demands are red lines.[59]

Elsewhere in the Gulf, it was little surprise that after the Emir of Kuwait suspended the National Assembly in 1986, the locus for (unofficial) political activity migrated to the *diwaniyas*, which were natural sites for the continuation of politics by other means. Their status as private spaces and the social networks created by the attendees at each of the *diwaniyas* enabled them to function as 'primary sites for private political activity when public political meetings and press freedom were banned.'[60] The movement for the restoration of the National Assembly was led by thirty-two of the fifty MPs from the parliament elected in 1985 and dissolved the following year, and was supported by the National Union of Kuwaiti Students and other associations in Kuwait, including women's groups, and by key members of the merchant community. In December 1989, a series of 'Monday *diwaniyas*' (*Dawawin al-Ithnain*) began to take place; these were public meetings involving several thousand people in some cases.[61] The first meeting was held at the home of Jasim Al-Qatami, a veteran advocate for political reform whose brother had been killed in a confrontation with the authorities during a campaign for a Legislative Council in 1938.[62]

The scale of the weekly meetings and their inherently political nature, at a time when parliament remained suspended and the media restricted, led to their being targeted by security forces, who initially sought to disrupt the entry of attendees and later, in January 1990, forcefully broke up a *diwaniya* using regular and riot police as well as the National Guard. This 'shocking display of force' ended the Monday *diwaniyas* and although it did not quell the movement to restore the National Assembly, it did prompt the Crown Prince to reach out to opposition and voluntary groups to initiate dialogue.[63] While the dialogue was consistent with informal regime outreach to key groups during periods of tension, it did not prevent many Kuwaitis from boycotting elections to a government-proposed but less powerful *Majlis al-Watani* (National Council) in June 1990.[64] After the Iraqi invasion, however, Kuwaiti *diwaniya* became important sites of resistance and served as meeting places for activists and community organizers.[65]

Gerd Nonneman has astutely observed that the memories of a past period of direct access to those in power is an inexact parallel to the size and complexity of modern bureaucratic states, even though 'ruling families have also consciously used these themes and instruments derived from them to build their legitimacy.'[66] To be sure, the growth in population and the increasing complexity of governance has created bureaucratic and institutional distance between rulers and other groups in society, but the legacies of consultation and access remain strong and have been appropriated both by governments and by oppositions either to defend a status quo rooted in the supposed maintenance of 'traditional values,' or to support calls for political reform for more formal representation. The Monday *diwaniyas* in Kuwait provide an example of how local customary practice has been used to frame and project political demands in the absence, at that time, of an institutional channel in the form of the (suspended) National Assembly.

Cases of 'informal' intervention to pre-empt or address potentially contentious issues continue to be utilized in a manner consistent with longstanding tribal expectations of consultation and mediation. Frequently these involve members of ruling families reaching out to tribal leaders or, in examples of individual rather than collective activism, to (male) relatives to try and resolve instances of (perceived or actual) dissidence before they trigger a state security or governmental response. Such cases can bring individuals or groups 'back into the fold' in ways that leave the honor and dignity of all parties intact. In the run-up to Kuwait's July 2013 elections to the National Assembly, the Emir, Sheikh Sabah al-Ahmad Al Sabah, met with prominent tribal leaders in a successful bid to peel them away from the unofficial coalition of political and tribal groups that had boycotted the previous elections in December 2012.[67] In Qatar in August 2021, two brothers of Emir Tamim bin Hamad Al Thani visited the *majlis* of the Al-Murrah and Al-Yefai tribes to soothe tensions after several days of anger at an electoral law that excluded many members of the tribes from voting in the first elections to the Shura Council that October.[68]

Petitions as an expression of grievance

Petitions have played an important role across the Gulf States in expressing and channeling social pressures and communicating them to ruling elites, especially during times of political or economic upheaval. In this context, Jessie Moritz has noted how petitions were but one of a variety of forms of political action that could be taken by citizens in Gulf States along a spectrum from quiescence to active opposition.[69] Petitions could have a mobilizing power that brought citizens together on specific issues that approximated a form of collective action, especially in a context where organized political activities, such as those arranged by political parties, were not permitted. The act of compiling and submitting a petition was thus a way of raising and sharing an issue of concern with the ruler, and as such was often seen by ruling elites as a form of activism that exceeded the permissible boundaries of political activity. As Madawi Al-Rasheed observed after the wave of petitions in Saudi Arabia in the 2000s, 'in the absence of independent forums, these petitions attract media attention and are an important means of testing the political atmosphere.'[70]

The late 1980s and early 1990s provide a case study of the ability of petitions to function as indicators of social dissent in times of political uncertainty. This period was one of retrenchment in the already meagre political openings that existed in the Gulf States, as the National Assemblies in both Kuwait and Bahrain had been suspended by their rulers, and it was also a moment of considerable external and internal vulnerability as well. The external threat was provided by the Iraqi invasion of Kuwait and the subsequent arrival of large numbers of Western forces in the Arabian Peninsula before and during the Gulf War in 1991. The sense of internal vulnerability was linked to the slump in oil prices (and therefore government revenues) that began in 1986 and which lasted throughout the 1990s until prices recovered in 2003.

In Kuwait, some 30,000 people signed a petition in March 1989 that was started by the above-mentioned former MPs from the (suspended) parliament as a way of expanding the reach of their campaign to restore the National Assembly. The group of former politicians quickly gained support from the long-established merchant elite as well as other segments of the business community and appeared to be morphing into a cross-community movement in support of a common political objective, which unnerved the authorities.[71] It was after the Emir refused to accept the petition that the organizers decided to begin the Monday *diwaniyas* noted in the previous section.[72] Shortly after liberation, in April 1991, another petition had more success as it increased the pressure on the Emir to implement the return to constitutional rule as promised at the October 1990 meeting-in-exile in Jeddah.[73]

Similar pressure in Bahrain was less successful in restoring the National Assembly, which had been suspended in 1975, despite three petitions in the mid-1990s that called for the resumption of parliamentary activity and free elections. A petition in October 1994 drew 23,000 signatories and was drawn up by prominent citizens and religious leaders from both the Sunni and Shia communities in Bahrain. This display of cross-sect cooperation unnerved the authorities who responded by arresting three of the Shia leaders who signed the petition, sparking widespread demonstrations among Shia communities and leading to the further arrest of hundreds of people by the security forces.[74] Undeterred, a second petition was sent to the Emir in April 1995 signed by 300 women, many of whom were members of professional associations, which also drew a severe response from the authorities. A third petition, in December 1995, indicated that the demands for an end to repression continued to resonate, despite the government crackdowns, as it was signed by a wide array of professionals and public figures.[75]

Political criticism of the Saudi leadership in the early 1990s, following the shock of the Iraqi invasion of Kuwait and the subsequent use of the Kingdom as a launching pad for the Gulf War, became manifest in a series of petitions to King Fahd that were accompanied by an upsurge in public demonstrations over domestic political issues in the Kingdom rather than support for Saddam Hussein or the Iraqi action.[76] A second wave of petitions in the early 2000s, after the equally seismic shock of the 9/11 attacks for the Saudi leadership, illustrated further the domestic impact of regional and international events.[77] Cumulatively, the petitions and open letters shook the hitherto largely closed political order and prompted a limited degree of opening that provided some breathing space for the Al Saud but did not quell the demands for reform or address some of the underlying social or economic points of grievance.

In the aftermath of King Fahd's decision in August 1990 to permit the stationing of U.S. and other mainly Western forces on Saudi soil and their use of the Kingdom as the launching pad for the Gulf War—reportedly the only decision Fahd took unilaterally, without seeking wider consensus, given the perceived urgency of the threat posed by Saddam Hussein to Saudi security—a wide variety of groups and individuals addressed a series of petitions and 'letters' to the authorities.[78] A first letter in early 1991 was signed by forty-three Saudis, including former Cabinet ministers, prominent businessmen, professors, and intellectuals, and was somewhat misleadingly described in Western media as a 'secular' petition, largely because its signatories were not religious clerics. Carefully couched in terms of constructive criticism, one of the ten reforms proposed by the signatories was 'the formation of a consultative council comprising the elite from among the qualified and knowledgeable decision makers.'[79]

Shortly afterward, a group of fifty-two religious figures issued a petition of their own, entitled 'Letter of Demands,' which made eleven proposals, including a request for an independent Consultative Council. More than 400 clerics signed this petition and thousands of copies were circulated, making it difficult for the King and the Al Saud to ignore it. The 'Letter of Demands' was followed in 1992 by a forty-six-page 'Memorandum of Advice' signed by 107 religious scholars which upped the ante as it made ten major demands on the authorities.[80] The 'Memorandum of Advice' caused special concern among the Saudi leadership at the potential erosion of support among one of their most important social bases because nearly three-quarters of the signatories were from the Najd region around Riyadh, the perceived heartland of the regime.[81] King Fahd subsequently removed seven of seventeen members of the Supreme Authority of Senior Scholars who declined to sign a statement that denounced the memorandum and its authors as 'misguided' and 'divisive.'[82]

A decade after the letters of 1991–2 (and the separate establishment of the Shura Council by King Fahd in August 1993[83]) came a second raft of petitions between 2003 and 2005 which again followed in the wake of a traumatic event which had external as well as domestic implications for Saudi Arabia. In this case the impact of the 9/11 attacks, masterminded by Osama bin Laden, a member of one of the most prominent business families in Saudi Arabia, and in which fifteen of the nineteen hijackers were Saudi citizens, converged with the lengthy absence from public life of King Fahd after his debilitating stroke in 1995, and the expectation that Crown Prince Abdullah would be more amenable to advocates of cautious reform.[84] Such feelings had been heightened by an 'Arab Charter' that Abdullah proposed in January 2003 which called (vaguely) for an end 'to the silence that has gone on for far too long' about the 'explosive situation in this area,' without going into detail or specifying any particular country.[85]

Like their 1990s' predecessors, the petitions in 2003 came from different groups in society and to the extent they agreed on one issue, it was the importance of better channels of consultation. The first petition, entitled 'The Vision,' emphasized the Islamic roots of citizenship, called for elections to the Shura Council, and declared that Islamic scripture required governments to consult with the people.[86] This was followed, several months later, by a second (separate) petition from representatives of Saudi Arabia's Shia communities, which, significantly, expressed their solidarity with the earlier petition and added their own call for structural change and equal representation in bodies such as the Shura Council.[87] A third petition in September 2003, entitled 'In Defense of the Nation,' was broader still, as it was signed by 306 people from a wide array of backgrounds, Shia as well as Sunni, and sought to cast its appeal to a wider social base than hitherto had been the case in the Kingdom.[88]

What became clear in the 2003 petitions is that they sought to build upon each other and widen the circle of signatories and adopted more of a confrontational tone in their list of demands than the 1991 letters. The 2003 petitions to the Saudi leadership also featured women among the signatories for the first time, with fifty-five women among the 306 signatories of the 'In Defense of the Nation' petition and 300 women signing a separate petition that requested that women be granted full and equal rights as citizens.[89] The potential convergence of advocates for reform will be examined more fully in Chapter 5. To forestall any such coming together, the Saudi authorities arrested twelve advocates of reform in January 2004, ironically one day after Crown Prince Abdullah delivered a speech in which he declared his support for 'gradual and well thought-out reform.' Three of those detained were subsequently tried and sentenced to terms of imprisonment in 2005 but were pardoned after Abdullah became King in August of that year.[90]

Another group of thirteen people were also arrested in March 2004, for signing the various petitions that had circulated over the previous year. Significantly, the authorities targeted a range of individuals from a variety of backgrounds in part to reinforce a message that social or political activism could not pay off. Those detained included non-Islamists and ideological leftists as well as

Islamists, including Abdullah Al-Hamed, one of the most renowned Saudi Islamist advocates of reform, who was still imprisoned when he died in 2020, and who had, in 2003, asserted that 'The main reason for the emergence of violence [in Saudi Arabia] is the absence of popular participation in decision-making (...) We say that political reform in an atmosphere of responsible freedom and dialogue is the best cure for extremism.'[91]

Even in Qatar, with its (relatively) more quiescent political landscape, petitions have been used periodically to raise and highlight issues of domestic concern. As in the other Gulf States in the 1950s and 1960s, there was an upsurge in workers' demands for political and economic rights as the first wave of oil revenues boosted state treasuries. In Qatar, these took the form of a petition in 1963 that contained thirty-five demands for reform, including for a fully elected Municipal Council in Doha.[92] One of the most vocal advocates of reform, Dr Ali Khalifa Al-Kuwari, who worked in Qatar's oil and gas sector as Vice-Chairman of the Qatar Liquefied Gas Company before joining Qatar University as a professor of economics, described what happened next:

> ... strikes, imprisonments and expulsions that preceded it and the subsequent pledge by the then ruler to enact reform and ratify the majority of the petition's demands. Demands for reform did not stop there, however, but continued at a lower intensity (...) before finally emerging into the light in 1992 in the form of two petitions. The most important of these petitions' demands was the election of a consultative council, appointed and tasked to draw up a permanent constitution. As a result of this, the signatories were punished with prison sentences, travel bans, the denial of their rights and the threat to rescind their Qatari citizenship.[93]

The signatories of the 1992 petition cast their demand for an elected council as 'in accordance with our Islamic faith, which directs us to adopt consultations and to abide by them.'[94] Notwithstanding the crackdown, the fact that the 1992 petitions were signed by fifty-four prominent (male) Qatari citizens reportedly played a significant role in convincing the then heir apparent, Sheikh Hamad bin Khalifa Al Thani, that a new approach (and ultimately, in 1995, a change of leader) was necessary.[95] Subsequently, as Emir, Sheikh Hamad proceeded to implement many of the requests made by the petitioners, although the first elections to the Shura Council had to wait a further twenty-six years before they finally took place in 2021.[96]

In the UAE, a petition submitted by 133 Emirati individuals and four professional organizations in March 2011 called for the election of all (rather than half) of the members of the forty-strong Federal National Council (FNC), as well as for a constitutional amendment that would grant the FNC full regulatory and supervisory power. These were modest demands compared with the political upheaval that was occurring contemporaneously in swathes of the Middle East and North Africa.[97] However, the petition appeared to strike a raw nerve with UAE authorities as they watched the Arab Spring unfold across the region, in part because the signatories came from a range of backgrounds that spanned the political spectrum. One of the signatories described to the political scientist Courtney Freer how the petition aimed 'to bridge the gap between different factions—to get liberals, Islamists, and nationalists together on a national course' and added that the organizers had deliberately limited the petition's scope 'to improvements of the FNC to get the maximum number of people to sign (…) We wrote the petition in very soft language, very diplomatic and fatherly language to attract more signatures.'[98]

Five of the signatories to the 2011 petition were subsequently arrested by the Emirati authorities and charged with 'publicly insulting' the leadership of the UAE. Although the 'UAE5' were later pardoned by the President, Sheikh Khalifa bin Zayed Al Nahyan, several of them, including human rights advocate Ahmed Mansoor and economist Nasser bin Ghaith, were rearrested in the mid-2010s and sentenced to lengthy terms of imprisonment. As bin Ghaith stated after his initial detention in 2011, 'I am politically neutral and well-connected, so it was surprising what happened to me—people were shocked. It shows the rising power of state security in our country.'[99] In the context of the restrictions of the already-limited spaces for political debate and societal mobilization, in the UAE as well as in other Gulf States in the years after the Arab Spring, the penalties for transgressing frequently unwritten 'red lines' became greater. Against the backdrop of a more sophisticated and intrusive system of state surveillance, the conduct of informal politics, even in private settings, became fraught with new levels of personal and political risk.

3

INSTITUTIONS

In a January 2016 interview with *The Economist* that made headlines for his announcement that a stake of Saudi Aramco would be listed in an initial public offering of shares, the then-Deputy Crown Prince of Saudi Arabia, Mohammed bin Salman Al Saud, declared that 'We are a country of institutions.'[1] In November the following year, Mohammed bin Salman, by now Crown Prince, surprised observers and members of his family by summoning dozens of businesspeople and royals to the Ritz-Carlton hotel in Riyadh and detaining them as part of an anti-corruption drive.[2] The detainees included many members of the Saudi business elite, such as the prominent 'royal businessman' Prince Alwaleed bin Talal Al Saud, as well as Adel Faqih, the Minister of Economy and Planning, and Ibrahim Al-Assaf, a former long-serving Minister of Finance who went on to become Minister of Foreign Affairs after his release.[3] A new anti-corruption body was established by King Salman just prior to the detentions, which replaced an existing committee, and was headed by Mohammed bin Salman himself.[4]

The Ritz-Carlton affair was described variously as a 'purge' and a power grab by Mohammed bin Salman as well as a 'shakedown' of the business elite, although it was also a populist move that appealed to Saudis who had long chafed at the perceived difficulties of breaking into deep-rooted vested economic interests.[5] The events at the Ritz-Carlton (and at other detention centers once those detainees who did not come to financial settlements were transferred into more conventional custody) nevertheless shook international investor confidence in Saudi Arabia, and levels of inward investment slumped in the aftermath.[6] Concerns focused on the opacity and seeming lack of due process in the detentions, the subsequent negotiations and agreements, and the eventual decisions to release or charge those involved.[7] In January 2019, the Royal Court stated that US$106 billion in cash, real estate, and other assets had been seized from the detainees, which, in Prince Alwaleed bin Talal's case, involved an undisclosed financial settlement after eighty-three days at the Ritz-Carlton, and wound up the anti-corruption body they had created in 2017.[8]

Mohammed bin Salman's actions illustrated several challenges that have faced and continue to face institutions and institutional processes in Saudi Arabia and the other Gulf States, and which are the subject of this chapter. These include the intermingling of personal interest with institutional process, as with the sudden creation of the new Supreme Committee to counter corruption under the chairmanship of Mohammed bin Salman, as well as a tendency to establish overlapping institutions that bypass existing structures and reflect a changed balance of power and authority—in the Ritz-Carlton case, the new anti-corruption body superseded an earlier Anti-Corruption Commission launched by King Abdullah in 2011.[9] The result was an outcome described (anonymously) by a senior U.S. official in the Trump administration as 'a shakedown operation and a power consolidation operation (…) to remind people going forward that their wealth and their well-being would depend on the Crown Prince and not on anything else.'[10]

In each of the Gulf States, the growth of institutions and other administrative and bureaucratic structures after the Second World War took place alongside the first influx of oil revenues into state treasuries. Institutions in theory and in functioning practice are designed to mediate between different power structures in society and are a form of regulation of the distribution of power among groups in the social hierarchy. As Mehran Kamrava has aptly noted, using examples from both sides of the Gulf as well as Egypt, the institutional landscape is reflective of the 'choices and bargains made early on by state leaders' in the formative era of state formation.[11] Faris Al-Sulayman, a Saudi analyst at the King Faisal Center for Research and Islamic Studies in Riyadh, has astutely observed (of China, but relevant to the Gulf monarchies as well), that political histories translate into institutional legacies and 'models' of development that are distinctive and hard to replicate.[12]

Processes of state formation across the six Gulf States were thus intertwined with the rentier aspects of economic development in the allocative states as they emerged in the second half of the twentieth century and continue to permeate state structures to varying degrees today. This synchronicity added another layer of distinctiveness to the processes of institutionalization (as well as to the political economies) in the region and illustrates the importance of analyzing institutions within the context of the political system in which they operate. This is especially the case where aspects of personalized decision-making operate and coexist, often uneasily, alongside institutional frameworks, as people, networks, and individual relationships remain significant to the accrual and projection of power and influence. At its heart is the sometimes-blurred distinctions between ruling families and the states they created and continue to lead in the twenty-first century.

Ruling families and the state

Any assessment of institutions and institutional resilience in Gulf settings must begin with Abdulhadi Khalaf's observation in 2003 that 'there is a distinct intertwining of state and the ruling families in a relation of indistinguishable organic unity.'[13] This is as much the case in the 2020s as it was in 2003 as any review of the links between Crown Prince Mohammed bin Salman Al Saud, the Public Investment Fund, and Saudi Arabia's Vision 2030 illustrates.[14] Furthermore, Khalaf noted that Gulf ruling families successfully managed to combine elements both of Michael Mann's description of the 'despotic power' of pre-modern states and the 'infrastructural power' of modern states. While despotic power flowed from the relative autonomy of the state in the Gulf from domestic social forces, infrastructural power rested on the control of institutions. It was this 'ability to combine both powers' that enabled ruling families to 'shape the domestic political processes in their countries, the contours of those processes, and the formal and informal structures they involve.'[15]

Scholarly and practical distinctions between 'state,' 'regime,' and 'government' are also applicable even if, in the context of the Gulf States, the dividing lines between them are less obvious than they would be in democratic or even in other non-monarchical authoritarian settings. Sheila Carapico and Stacey Philbrick Yadav have usefully described how a 'regime' is 'an intermediate stratum between the government (which makes day-to-day decisions and is easy to alter) and the state (which is a complex bureaucracy tasked with a range of coercive functions.)' Thus, 'a regime is understood by political scientists as a system of rules and norms by which power is distributed across and through state institutions.'[16] For all six of the Gulf monarchies, Russell Lucas added that the 'regime,' the ruling families which set the rules of the game, predated the emergence of the apparatus of the modern state in the twentieth century.[17]

While academic in nature, on occasion the differences between state, regime, and government have mattered in practice. One very public differentiation between 'regime' and 'state' that caused great alarm among U.S. partners in the Middle East, especially in the Gulf States, was the withdrawal of U.S. backing for the regime of embattled Egyptian President, Hosni Mubarak, in February 2011 and the transfer of that support to an interim military-led Supreme Council for the Armed Forces (and, in 2012, to Mohammed Morsi, the elected President who represented the Muslim Brotherhood).[18] Similarly, the Carter Doctrine of January 1980, seen by many as the linchpin of the web of U.S.-Gulf partnerships, was designed by the Carter administration in response to a perceived external challenge to state stability in the region (the Soviet invasion of Afghanistan) rather than an internal threat to regime security (the Iranian revolution). As Turki Al-Hamad, a Saudi political analyst, noted in 1997, the concept of 'state' security in all GCC states is defined 'in a very narrow, one-dimensional way, as the status quo continuity of the political regimes.'[19]

Although ruling families have maintained control over the apparatus of state structures, states are not unitary actors and are in fact an aggregation of many different institutions, agencies, and legal and bureaucratic regimes, just as they are in other settings around the world. As Mary Ann Tétreault and Haya Al-Mughni have observed in the case of Kuwait, formal and informal divisions within the overall rubric of the state can lead to a 'divergence in interests [which] results in a breakdown of unitary identification and behavior.'[20] This is as much a factor in the personalistic examples of the Gulf States as it is in the Weberian 'rational-legal' ideal type in which political authority is vested in the government of the day and is itself distinct from the regime and the bureaucratic 'state.' The difference is that in Gulf settings, it has frequently been different members of ruling families who carved out institutional 'fiefdoms,' which are examined in greater detail later in this chapter and which had the effect of creating sets of vested institutional interests which proved difficult politically to dislodge while incumbent heads were still alive.

Moreover, in the early years and in some cases until the 1960s, the individual ruler and members of his family who occupied ministerial positions functioned, in practice, as the institution, free to 'do much as they please, brooking little control from above.'[21] This was noted by Sir Rupert Hay, the British Political Resident in the Persian Gulf between 1946 and 1953, as he observed that members of ruling families who ran government departments did so 'with the minimum of financial or any other control by any central authority,' and added that 'each of these sheikhs is a law unto himself, and there is much in the administration which depends on their relations with each other, their presence or absence from the state or the willingness of the ruler to control their activities.'[22] Another British official, Reader Bullard, Minister in Jeddah between 1936 and 1939, described in 1938 how 'Ibn Saud has grown up with his state and has kept in many ways the methods of the Arab shaikh, who knows every person in the tribe and all their affairs. He still knows everyone of note personally and deals in person with every matter of importance.'[23]

Institutionalization and the creation of working bureaucracies were nevertheless essential components of the administrative state that emerged to receive and manage the redistribution of oil wealth, and which underpinned the creation of the all-encompassing welfare states in the Gulf. These distributive networks and processes are examined in more detail in Chapter 7, but broadly they included a wide range of benefits and services that were provided free or at heavily subsidized levels to the citizen population. Writing in 1987, shortly after the end of the first oil price boom, anthropologists Sulayman Khalaf and Hassan Hammoud listed the types of 'social welfare' which included 'a variety of free public services (education, health, housing, leisure and sport facilities) and the right of employment, as well as specific loans for marriage, home construction and renovations, and subsidies for certain foods, local telephone service, gas, electricity, and water.'[24] This was the case even in non-oil-rich emirates such as Dubai, where in 1999 some 10.4 percent of citizens' per capita income came from government transfers.[25] By 2009, one estimate put the average value of government support to male Emirati citizens at US$55,000 per year.[26]

Transitions away from personalized rulership

Saudi historian 'Abd Al-Aziz ibn 'Abd Allah Al-Khwaiter has described the nature of rulership in Saudi Arabia at the time of the creation of the modern Kingdom in 1932, a period in which Ibn Saud did not develop modern institutions but instead wielded power through personal decision-making and trusted advisors:

> ... the king was the source of power. He had the final word, which was bound solely by the power of the Sharia. He relied on no systematic administrative bodies other than the employees in his council, whose job was to submit to him the various matters that were raised in council, then to carry out his orders in addressing those matters. The king decided on administrative, political, military, economic, and social matters, and referred what concerned the Sharia to the relevant authorities.[27]

In her political and social history of the Trucial States, which became the United Arab Emirates in 1971–2, Rosemarie Said Zahlan added that, in the early twentieth century, the sheikhdoms':

> ... administrative infrastructure was so rudimentary as to be almost non-existent. The ruler had no civil service; no judges or law courts (...) no army, apart from his personal guards, and no police force. He could rarely, if ever, delegate authority to an appointed person or group of persons without risking his position.[28]

Aspects of personalized rulership were especially pronounced in the cases of 'strong' leaders who cast themselves (or were subsequently memorialized) as founding fathers in the still pre-statehood sheikhdoms. Examples of such leaders were Sheikh Jassim bin Mohammed Al Thani, Ruler of Qatar between 1878 and 1913, Sheikh Mubarak bin Jabir Al Sabah, Ruler of Kuwait from 1896 to 1915, and Ibn Saud, who ruled what became the modern Kingdom of Saudi Arabia between 1902 and 1953. More recent examples include Sheikh Zayed bin Sultan Al Nahyan in Abu Dhabi (1966–2004) and Sultan Qaboos bin Said Al Said in Oman (1970–2020), who, like their earlier counterparts, are referred to frequently as the 'father' of the contemporary nation. Writing on Dubai and the 'great man theory' in local narratives about the rule of Sheikh Rashid bin Saeed Al Maktoum (1958–90) Ahmed Kanna and Arang Keshavarzian observed that 'It is as if politics in "traditional" societies can be reduced to the will of the sheikh.'[29]

Oil concessions and the early distribution of royalties exemplified the conflation of ruler and state in the period before the Second World War and the lack of distinction between ruling family wealth and public finance. The concessions were signed in the name of the ruler, rather than with an institution of state such as a national oil company or energy ministry (which did not exist at the time), and royalties were paid to the ruler who retained discretion over how to distribute them.[30] In Bahrain, the ruler was allocated one-third of oil revenues in the 1930s, while in Qatar the allocation of one-quarter of oil revenues to the ruler continued into the 1960s.[31] In Saudi Arabia, Ibn Saud's financial advisor personally counted the 35,000 gold sovereigns delivered by Karl Twitchell, the Standard Oil Company of California's representative in Jeddah, after the concession was granted in 1933, and for several years thereafter Aramco had the sovereigns flown in from New York to Jeddah.[32] While the institutionalization of governing arrangements did introduce degrees of separation, at least on paper, issues around transparency, accountability, and opacity in decision-making came to characterize policymaking processes in the region.

The gradual mid-twentieth century transition away from purely personalized rulership was not without resistance from leaders accustomed to wielding untrammeled power (at least until the point they were deposed, most often by family members rather than from the buildup of social pressures). Ibn Saud reminded his subjects in the Najd, in the 1920s, not to 'forget that there is not one among you whose father or brother or cousin we have not slain (…) We took you by the sword, and we shall keep you within your bounds by the sword.'[33] A generation later, the Emirati businessman Easa Saleh Al-Gurg described how, in the late 1950s, the British Political Agent in Abu Dhabi persuaded Sheikh Sultan bin Shakhbut Al Nahyan, the son of the Ruler, to open a 'Government of Abu Dhabi—Municipal Office,' which was quickly closed after Sheikh Shakhbut visited the office and asked his son 'Do you imagine that there is another government in Abu Dhabi, apart from your father?'[34] As late as the 1980s, the Emir of Qatar, Sheikh Khalifa bin Hamad Al Thani, reportedly insisted on personally signing all checks over US$50,000 in value.[35]

Some of the earliest pressure on rulers to create new frameworks of governance came from the merchant elites who formed the strongest and most cohesive non-ruling family blocs in pre-oil societies on the Arabian Peninsula. Merchant families operated across transnational networks, with local agents and branches in coastal ports spanning the Indian Ocean littoral and extending in some cases to European cities, which introduced them to political ideas and economic developments in a world that was significantly wider than that available to many members of ruling families at the time.[36] In addition, merchants were significant sources of 'state' revenues in the pre-oil sheikhdoms, through customs duties and taxes on their trading activities and by acting as lenders to rulers and their families.[37] Most of the first (non-religious) schools and the earliest banks in the Arabian Peninsula were established by merchant families, whether in Kuwait, Bahrain, Dubai, or in the Hijaz before the Al Saud conquest.[38]

Merchants and other commercial elites, including members of ruling families, sought in the creation of institutional frameworks a degree of predictability and development to facilitate the conduct of their business affairs. Chambers of Commerce were among the earliest examples of institutionalization in Gulf States and in some cases their formation predated even the establishment of representative councils, although, like the councils, their membership initially was largely restricted to elite interests. The Jeddah Chamber of Commerce, for example, was formed in 1946 (and is the oldest of the twenty-eight chambers of commerce and industry grouped since 1980 in the Council of Saudi Chambers).[39] In Kuwait, merchant pressure in the 1920s and 1930s had pushed for the creation of representative institutions, and the Kuwait Chamber of Commerce and Industry was established in 1960, prior to independence the following year, the launch of the constitutional convention in 1962, and the formation of the National Assembly in 1963.[40]

Two broad 'meta-narratives' dominated the process of contemporary state creation in the Arabian Peninsula. The first encompassed the development of institutional capacities in the basic infrastructure of state, such as government departments, the armed forces, and functioning judicial and bureaucratic systems, and lasted from the 1920s and 1930s into the 1970s in the cases of Abu Dhabi and Oman. In the second, beginning in the 1980s but accelerating after the 1990s, the focus shifted to targeted policy interventions to (try and) strengthen domestic private sectors, address imbalanced labor markets, and diversify economies to create sustainable non-oil economic growth, often following multi-decade development plans such as Vision 2030 in Saudi Arabia (and other Vision 2030s in Bahrain and Qatar).[41] Parts of each of the periods occurred against the backdrop of rapid rises in international oil prices and government revenues (in the

1970s and 2000s) which further reinforced the need for greater institutional and bureaucratic absorptive capacity.

Formative periods of 'state-building' in the Gulf States, both before and after formal independence, were characterized by the growth of institutional structures which came into being largely to handle the more complex matters of administration, especially as significant oil revenues began to accrue. The creation of institutions—even where political authority remained centered firmly in rulers and their families—was part of a worldwide growth of the functions and capabilities of modern state structures. In the Gulf setting, processes of institutionalization were in large part the bureaucratic outgrowth of ruling family control which were—and to some extent remain—characterized by a reliance on personalized policymaking. To the extent that other factors shaped the institutions that developed, they included British interests in the protected states, the early influence of social groups such as the merchant families, the later impact of oil development, and what Fuad Khuri in his study of Bahrain labeled 'the tribal order of government.'[42]

The staffing of institutional structures and other state (and state-linked) agencies provided a means of appointing representatives of domestic social groups to key positions and achieving a workable balance among prominent tribes, merchant families, and religious constituencies.[43] As institutions and bureaucracies grew, they constituted additional pathways of co-optation and mechanisms for knitting such groups into the patronage networks that connected state and citizenry.[44] Networks of intermediaries managed these relationships, especially as the institutions of state grew more impersonal and created a distance between the ruler and the people, the continuation of the *majlis* notwithstanding.[45] Khaldoun Al-Naqeeb described an intermediary as 'someone with influence and/or leverage,' and Abdulhadi Khalaf added that, although they represented elite groups in society, modern intermediaries lacked the ability to become autonomous centers of power, as they sometimes had done in pre-oil settings, such as when leading merchants extended loans to members of ruling families.[46]

In her comparative study of Kuwait and Qatar, Jill Crystal noted that bureaucracies developed to manage and implement the distributive mechanisms which formed the basis of the welfare states that underpinned the transformation of regional political economies in the oil era. Writing in 1989, Crystal added that 'Bureaucrats have the potential for developing their own centers of power, social relationships, and political ideals and goals' especially as their size and administrative functions grew.[47] This has not in fact occurred, as across the Gulf States the growth of bureaucratic and administrative 'elites' provided a means of integrating the merchant class and other important social groups into the new structures of state that emerged, including in the oil and energy sector.[48] As Yasmine Farouk and Nathan Brown commented, in the context of Saudi Arabia but applicable elsewhere too, patterns of state-building and institutional development 'tended to build on past patterns rather than reverse them.'[49]

Canadian political scientist Robert Cox observed conceptually that 'institutions are particular amalgams of ideas and material power' which 'reflect the power relations at their point of origin' and may, eventually, 'take on their own life; they can become either a battleground of opposing tendencies, or stimulate the creation of rival institutions reflecting different tendencies.'[50] The practical evidence for this in the Gulf is that institutions followed (and reinforced) power relationships among their principals within the ruling families, more than that they presented any ideational or material challenge to the status quo. One reason for this is that bureaucracies have tended to function more as the implementing agency in a top-down decision making process rather than as a generator of policy proposals that reflect any form of bottom-up involvement in policymaking. Another is that 'traditional' familial and tribal ties became embedded within the emergent bureaucratic structures and formed the basis of the neo-patrimonial system that linked together new networks of patrons and clients headed by the ruler and his family.[51]

Separation (or otherwise) of power

The development of institutions in Saudi Arabia illustrates some of the challenges of moving from a personalized and patrimonial style of governance toward a functional process of government. This was critical as the onset of oil revenues made necessary the creation of mechanisms to administer the distributive welfare states that came to characterize the Gulf monarchies. The changes were fast-paced and far-reaching. Employment in the public sector was limited to a few hundred people when King Saud succeeded his father in 1953 but had risen to more than 100,000 when he was deposed eleven years later.[52] Such patterns of change did not occur uniformly or synchronously across the region and reflected an interaction between incoming resource abundance and political will on the part of the leadership. In cases where political will was not forthcoming, as in Abu Dhabi under Sheikh Shakhbut or in Oman under Sultan Said bin Taimur, meaningful institutionalization only started after they were replaced, in 1966 and 1970 respectively, just as in Saudi Arabia such changes had fully started with the passing of Ibn Saud.[53]

Ibn Saud created a Ministry of Foreign Affairs in 1930 and a Ministry of Finance the following year, as well as a Ministry of Defense in 1944, during the Second World War, but further institutionalization only took place toward the end of his life when power and responsibility was transferred to his sons. Thus, three ministries—Health, Interior, and the Saudi Arabian Monetary Agency—were established in 1951 and three more—Agriculture, Commerce and Industry, and Communications—in 1953, the year of Ibn Saud's death. Also in 1953, a Council of Ministers was created, and the following year the Ministry of Petroleum was established.[54] In the 1950s, six of the nine ministerial posts were held by members of the Al Saud, two by former advisors to Ibn Saud, and only one—the Minister of Commerce—by 'anyone other than a prince or someone dependent on a prince'—a leading member 'of a prominent Jeddah merchant family with international connections.'[55]

The bureaucratization of Saudi governing arrangements accelerated in the two decades after Ibn Saud's death albeit under the shadow of a competitive rivalry between King Saud and Crown Prince Faisal that ended in the former's abdication and the latter's accession to power in 1964. During this period, King Saud also moved the seat of government from Mecca to Riyadh.[56] As Sarah Yizraeli notes, the establishment of the Council of Ministers and the separation of the position of Prime Minister from that of King fed into the power struggle between Faisal (Prime Minister, 1954–60 and 1962–4) and King Saud.[57] As King (between 1964 and 1975), Faisal, for the first time in Saudi history, drew a distinction, at least on paper, between the state budget and Al Saud allowances, and also formalized the system of royal stipends.[58]

Separation of the posts of head of state (the King) and head of government (the Prime Minister) in Saudi Arabia ended after Faisal became King in 1964 and did not recur in the subsequent reigns of Ibn Saud's other sons Khalid, Fahd, Abdullah, and Salman, until Mohammed bin Salman was named Prime Minister (while still Crown Prince) in September 2022.[59] At the time of writing, the monarch continues to chair the Council of Ministers which has neither developed its own separate institutional authority nor been able to prevent individual members—always senior members of the royal family—from creating their own personal bases of power. There have been periods since 1964 when de-facto decision-making devolved from the King to the Crown Prince, notably when Abdullah acted as regent during the decade between King Fahd's stroke in 1995 and his death in 2005, and more recently when Mohammed bin Salman emerged as the driving force behind all aspects of Saudi policymaking with his appointment as Crown Prince in 2017.[60]

In the other Gulf States, there have been periods of tension between the sitting ruler and his Prime Minister which indicate that the head of government has at times functioned as, or been seen to pose, an alternative center of political authority. Examples included Tariq bin Taimur Al Said, the uncle of Sultan Qaboos who coexisted uneasily with his nephew in a short-lived, never-repeated spell as Prime Minister of Oman between 1970 and 1972; a much-longer but also contentious familial split in Bahrain between the Prime Minister of fifty years, Sheikh Khalifa bin Salman Al Khalifa, and his nephew, King Hamad bin Isa Al Khalifa, that only ended with Sheikh Khalifa's death in 2020; and, in Qatar, the premiership of Sheikh Hamad bin Jassim Al Thani from 2007 to 2013, a period characterized by a degree of tension between 'HBJ' and some of the circles around Qatar's powerful First Lady, Sheikha Mozah bint Nasser Al Missned.[61]

In Kuwait, the post of Prime Minister was held by the Crown Prince between 1965 and 2003 but the posts were split in 2003 due to the poor health of Crown Prince Saad Abdullah Al Sabah. Although the first post-2003 Prime Minister (Sheikh Sabah al-Ahmad Al Sabah) did become Emir, in 2006, the fact that the Prime Minister was no longer necessarily the ruler-in-waiting meant he became seen as a legitimate target for political criticism.[62] In the UAE, the position of Prime Minister was by convention reserved for the Ruler of Dubai as a counterpoint to the post of President held by the Ruler of Abu Dhabi. However, aside from the Abu Dhabi/Dubai division of responsibility in the UAE, Prime Ministers in Gulf States who posed a threat to the ruler did so because of a combination of seniority within the ruling family as well as their control of the machinery of government *per se*, and their power base was as much personal as institutional.

The frequency of Cabinet changes, including for the position of Prime Minister, in Kuwait indicates that governments are malleable and, in the Kuwaiti case with the far livelier parliamentary context, responsive to political and social pressures. More than a dozen governments came and went during the fourteen-year tenure of Emir Sabah al-Ahmad Al Sabah (2006–20) and the length of service of prime ministers steadily shortened. The turnover failed, however, to resolve the underlying tension in the Kuwaiti political system around what Michael Herb labeled the monarchical and electoral principles of political authority represented by the Cabinet (appointed by the Emir) and the National Assembly (of elected MPs).[63] In Oman, Sultan Qaboos resorted to reshuffling key ministers in 2011 to defuse public anger at perceived corruption among members of the economic and business elite, but without affecting the balance of political power.[64] This was seen as a safety valve to insulate the core of the ruling elite from popular discontent, but conversely, in Bahrain and Saudi Arabia the position of head of government was fused with that of Crown Prince in 2020 and 2022, making it harder to safely criticize a future head of state for his actions as Prime Minister.

Institutional weaknesses in practice

Once established, institutions could be undermined or bypassed, with several examples characteristic of contemporary developments in the Gulf States. These are a process of institutional fragmentation and the creation of parallel structures of governance, as well as the persistence of personalized 'fiefdoms' of control. In addition, the creation of an array of new bodies, such as Executive Offices and Executive Councils in Dubai and Abu Dhabi and an Executive Affairs Authority in Bahrain in the 2000s, and the centralization of much decision-making authority in the Royal Court in Saudi Arabia and the Emiri Diwan in Kuwait and Qatar in the 2010s, added layers of complexity to policymaking processes. So, too, did the formation of specialized cities and free zones, especially, but not only in the UAE, often with bureaucratic and legal carve-outs from national regulations.[65] While individual country experiences vary, a common thread that ties together the factors that weaken and undermine processes of institutionalization is the continuing importance of proximity and personal access to decision-makers.

A common tactic has been the creation of parallel, often overlapping institutions and agencies, especially in the military sphere and plethora of security forces, as covered in Chapter 8.[66] Such practice often related to an inability or an unwillingness to transfer decision-making responsibility through conventional means, such as removing or replacing a senior member of a ruling family. In such instances, it could be easier to create a new institution that over time would bypass the original entity and individual. A prominent example was the gradual sidelining of Petromin, Saudi Arabia's original 'national' oil company, in favor of Aramco, especially after the latter was nationalized in stages in the 1970s and 1980s. There were good reasons for concentrating technological expertise and national development in Aramco, but

Petromin was only formally dissolved in 2005, twenty years after it ceased to have any real functional responsibility.[67]

In Bahrain, King Hamad began to create a parallel decision-making structure almost as soon as he acceded to power in 1999. The following year, the Emir (as he was styled prior to 2001) established an Economic Development Board (EDB) chaired by his son and heir, Crown Prince Salman bin Hamad Al Khalifa. Over the course of the 2000s, the EDB 'increasingly appropriated decision-making functions formerly endowed to the cabinet' headed by the powerful Prime Minister, Prince Khalifa bin Salman Al Khalifa, the Crown Prince's great uncle who had been in post since 1970 and was seen as impossible to dislodge.[68] The EDB was one of multiple initiatives spearheaded by the Crown Prince as he jockeyed for position vis-à-vis his great-uncle in the 2000s, which also included labor market and educational reforms and a Vision 2030 process of strategic economic diversification.[69] In March 2009, the Secretary General of the oppositional Al-Wefaq National Islamic Society, Ali Salman, drew attention to this duality of control when he asked 'Who is running the country and coming up with its policies and strategies? Is it the Cabinet on Sunday or the EDB on Thursday? Two captains for one ship will certainly lead it to sink.'[70]

The formation in Qatar of Supreme Councils for Education and Health in the 2000s and their assumption of responsibilities from the Ministries of Education and Public Health in 2009 was viewed by some, including U.S. diplomats in Doha, as part of a tussle for authority among elite decision-makers. Specifically, a U.S. diplomatic cable in May 2009 (released by *WikiLeaks*) took the view that

> These developments are yet another round in the ongoing rivalry between Prime Minister/Foreign Minister Hamad bin Jassim Al Thani and the Amir's wife, Shaykha Mozah. The two ousted ministers were thought to have moved too close to the PM's camp in areas traditionally dominated by Shaykha Mozah. By ousting the two Ministers, replacing them with loyalists to her and [Heir Apparent Sheikh] Tamim, and moving the policymaking to the Supreme Councils, she has re-asserted her dominance in these two sectors. Observers feel that Mozah is better able to

manage them through Supreme Councils dominated by her and her supporters than allowing Prime Minister Hamad bin Jassim Al Thani to manage them through his ministries.[71]

The difficulty of replacing, rather than working around, key figures as noted above, illustrated the significance of personal 'fiefdoms,' as political scientist Steffen Hertog labeled them in the Saudi context, and the role of human agency in the formative period of institution-building. As state agencies were established between the 1950s and 1970s, many were headed by young members of ruling families who stayed in post for decades and carved out powerful spaces of personal control.[72] Key instances in Saudi Arabia were Prince Sultan, Minister of Defense for forty-eight years (1963–2011), Prince (later King) Abdullah, Commander of the National Guard for forty-seven years (1963–2010), Prince Saud al-Faisal, Foreign Minister for forty years (1975–2015), and Prince Nayef, Minister of Interior for thirty-seven years (1975–2012). As Hertog notes, the outcome of the intersection of family politics and administrative growth was an 'uncontrolled, patronage-based bureaucratic sprawl' rather than a legal-rational process of state-building.[73] Writing before King Fahd's death in 2005, Saudi academic Madawi Al-Rasheed identified five major 'circles of power' in the Al Saud that kept each other in check and placed real if informal constraints on decision-making processes.[74]

Other examples of centers of personal power in the Gulf States that had a significant bearing on the exercise of policymaking authority included, in Kuwait, Sheikh Sabah al-Ahmad Al Sabah's forty years as Foreign Minister between 1963 and 2003 and, in Bahrain, Prime Minister Khalifa bin Salman Al Khalifa's fifty-year tenure which ended in November 2020 with his death aged eighty-four. Sheikh Sabah dominated all aspects of Kuwait's regional diplomacy and foreign policy and continued to do so after he became Prime Minister (in 2003) and, in 2006, Emir. As Emir of Kuwait, Sheikh Sabah led efforts to defuse the Gulf crises in 2013–14 and again in 2017 when it was his shuttle diplomacy that played a key role in preventing the blockade of Qatar from escalating into potential military action.[75] In Bahrain, the Prime Minister, Sheikh

Khalifa, played an outsized role in every facet of economic and political decision-making that frequently overshadowed the formal power vested in his nephew, the King.[76]

Two examples from the United Arab Emirates and one from Qatar illustrate further the elasticity in practice of institutional arrangements on paper. Sheikh Mohammed bin Rashid Al Maktoum and his brother, Sheikh Hamdan bin Rashid Al Maktoum, were named the Minister of Defense and Minister of Finance in the first Cabinet after the formation of the UAE in December 1971, when they were twenty-two and twenty-six years old, respectively. The brothers were in the same positions as the UAE entered its half-centenary year in 2021, albeit with Sheikh Hamdan passing away in February of that year. Although the brothers remained the titular holders of the Cabinet rank, their ministerial responsibilities had long since been devolved to (non-royal) Ministers of State and, in the case of the Ministry of Finance, to other bodies such as the Ministry of Economy. A similar situation existed in Qatar until 2013 as the long-serving Minister of Interior, Sheikh Abdullah bin Khalid Al Thani, was hit by U.S. accusations over alleged sympathies with Al Qaeda in the 1990s.[77] While he remained in his titular post, his responsibilities were assumed by his Minister of State (and eventual successor as Interior Minister), Sheikh Abdullah bin Nasser Al Thani.[78]

Examples from the UAE illustrate also how institutional fragmentation, whether by personal design or through the creation of new authorities and jurisdictions, can also complicate the function of governance. In Dubai in the 2000s, Sheikh Mohammed bin Rashid put key lieutenants in charge of different state or state-linked agencies and fostered a degree of creative tension as each competed to develop the biggest or the most eye-catching project in the run-up to the financial crash that hit the emirate in 2008.[79] One of those close associates, Mohammed Alabbar, the chairman of the Emaar Properties real estate developer (in which the Investment Corporation of Dubai, a state investment fund, holds a 29 percent shareholding), described candidly in a 2015 interview with *Arabian Business* how:

I do not do anything without me talking to HH, he is the man who gave me unimaginable opportunities, and he gave me a chance to be who I am. And to trust me. And to create my career and my personality. And when I make mistakes he comes and pulls me up again. So I don't do anything without talking to him.[80]

Alabbar and the Chairmen of Dubai World and Dubai Holding worked side by side with Mohammed bin Rashid during the years of breakneck economic growth in the 2000s as they pioneered the developments that catapulted Dubai into global consciousness. As well as his position at Emaar Properties, Alabbar served also as the Director-General of the Dubai Department of Economic Development, illustrating the frequent crossover of positions across the state-business spectrum.[81] The 2009 crash saw the transfer of much decision-making authority in Dubai into the hands of Sheikh Ahmed bin Saeed Al Maktoum, the uncle of Mohammed bin Rashid and the founder of Emirates Airline who became head of both Dubai World and Dubai Holding in the 2010s. However, as Jim Krane noted in 2009, 'The institutions that make Dubai hum function in obscurity. Their power isn't codified in law. They are driven by individual personalities whose influence rises and falls on the sheikh's favor.'[82]

Dubai also led the way in carving out economic zones and specialized cities which have since been replicated across much of the region. This began with the construction of the Jebel Ali Port and free trade zone in the late 1970s which gave Dubai a 'first mover' advantage despite skepticism at the time that such a large-scale project was commercially necessary or economically viable.[83] The pace of development accelerated in the early 2000s with the launch of entities such as Dubai Internet City, Dubai Media City, and Dubai Healthcare City, with their own bespoke by-laws and legislative ordinances.[84] In addition, Dubai pioneered the creation of independent regulatory agencies which altered governance regimes in specific sectors, such as the Dubai Financial Services Authority, a move later replicated elsewhere in entities such as the Qatar Financial Center Regulatory Authority and the Abu Dhabi Global Market.[85]

Finally, individual policies may also get 'stuck' if decisions that are taken in a top-down manner fail to secure bureaucratic buy-in that impede their implementation in practice. An example of this occurred in Qatar in June 2009 when the Doha Center for Media Freedom shut down just eight months after it had been established. The center had been created in October 2008 as a partnership between the Qatar Foundation and Reporters without Borders, and had the support of Qatar's First Lady, Sheikha Mozah, the co-founder (with her husband, Emir Hamad bin Khalifa Al Thani) and chairperson of the Qatar Foundation. The Doha Center for Media Freedom marked the first creation of an international organization dedicated to the defense of media freedom in a non-Western setting and its credibility was boosted when Robert Ménard, one of the founders of Reporters without Borders and its then-Secretary-General, became the first Director-General of the Doha Centre.[86]

What happened next demonstrated the challenges of implementing policy in a context in which decisions which have (or had) personal top-down support got stuck farther down the bureaucratic chain. Tensions developed between Ménard and officials unused to dealing with local criticism of domestic Qatari policies. The feeling of mutual acrimony culminated in Ménard's resignation and the closure of the Doha Center for Media Freedom in June 2009 after less than one year of operation. In the public dispute that followed, Ménard claimed that his work had been 'suffocated' by middle-level bureaucrats (as opposed to the Qatar Foundation itself, or Sheikha Mozah), and asked 'How can we have any credibility if we keep quiet about problems in the country that is our host?'[87]

Institutional 'stickiness' such as that encountered by Ménard was not so much an expression of agency among lower-level bureaucratic actors but more symptomatic of the challenge in maintaining the political will of senior decision-makers as policies made their way through institutional channels. A broadly similar example was observable in Yemen after the Arab military intervention in 2015 divided much of the country not under Houthi control into Saudi and Emirati spheres of influence. Decisions on the conduct of operations taken at the most senior level by

Crown Princes Mohammed bin Salman and Mohammed bin Zayed passed down separate Saudi and Emirati chains of command for implementation so that they could look quite different by the time they filtered through to figures 'on the ground' in Yemen.[88] In other instances, policy implementation could be impeded by vested economic interests, as happened with attempts in Saudi Arabia and Bahrain to raise the cost of hiring expatriate workers over nationals.[89]

Finally, institutional arrangements can be bypassed. This was illustrated visibly in May 2009 when the UAE withdrew abruptly and without warning from the long-planned Gulf monetary union project less than a year before the single currency was due to come into effect. Plans for an eventual monetary union were included in the Unified Economic Agreement signed in 1981, shortly after the GCC was created, and a 2010 deadline was set at the GCC's annual summit in Muscat in December 2001.[90] Oman withdrew from the single currency project in 2006 out of concerns that the timeframe was too tight to achieve the convergence criteria but it was the Emirati withdrawal three years later which sounded the death knell of the plans. The UAE had campaigned to host the GCC Central Bank and believed it had received assurances to this effect; thus, Emirati officials responded negatively to the May 2009 decision to situate the bank in Riyadh where the GCC Secretariat was already based. Sheikh Abdullah bin Zayed Al Nahyan, the UAE Foreign Minister, left no doubt as to his country's displeasure as he declared that 'the UAE was the best choice for the headquarters. It is not about selecting Saudi Arabia, it is about not selecting the UAE.'[91]

4

REPRESENTATION

Writing in 1994, two years after the restoration of the National Assembly following its six-year hiatus either side of the Iraqi occupation of Kuwait, the political sociologist Mohammad Ghanem Al-Rumaihi observed of his native Kuwait that 'there is no single path to democracy (...) the machinery of implementation must be developed to reflect the tradition, history, and general social environment of each country. No one theory of democracy suits every situation in every country.'[1] There are indeed multiple 'models of democracy' which reflect a wide variety of participatory dynamics and underlying ideas which themselves have evolved significantly over time and place.[2] None of the six Gulf States can be classified as democracies, but if the principle of representation, rather than democracy as a political system, is taken as a building block of modern politics,[3] there is a spectrum of representative institutions in the Gulf. Indeed, for Al-Rumaihi, it is 'citizen participation in the affairs of society' that is significant.[4]

Analysis of representative processes, rather than just their outcomes, can shine a spotlight onto those aspects of participatory politics that do exist in GCC states and the extent to which they constitute a substantive pathway toward political reform or alternatively provide a veneer of pluralistic legitimacy to otherwise-unchanged ruling elites. Such an approach can also draw out the dynamics of political co-optation and contestation within and between factions at the elite level as well as among organized groups and other forms of professional associations. This is especially significant in non-democratic settings in which the power to affect political and policy outcomes is shaped by coalitions of interests that extend beyond the limited choices at the ballot box to encompass other representative forms, such as Chambers of Commerce and some civil society groups. As Tim Niblock observed in 1998, examining the representative and participative aspects of the systems already in place in the Gulf can shed valuable insight on the struggles for influence among competing factions within the state and society at large.[5]

A further point for examination is what different groups within the state and in society seek or expect from the institutionalization of representation. Just as no two councils or assemblies in the Gulf are the same, so there exists a variety of views over the form, scope, and extent of powers that the bodies should wield. In addition, since each of the institutions was established in a 'top-down' process that was designed to be qualified, measured, and controlled, there were differences among political and social groups as to whether participation was necessary or desirable. Friction over the 'rules of the game' has been a persistent point of tension between the government and political actors as well as among members of groups that define themselves in opposition to ruling circles. So, too, has been a degree of competition among political elites for the resources on offer as representative bodies took root and evolved.

Political arenas and electoral politics are not the only mechanisms through which forms of representative contestation can and do take place in Gulf settings. As Ellen Lust-Okar has observed of the wider region, 'Political participation is best understood through the interface of informal and formal politics.'[6] From the 1930s to the 1960s, clubs and societies, especially in Kuwait, Bahrain, and Dubai, provided spaces for an activist political culture that in many cases reflected the ideological strength of pan-Arab nationalism across the Gulf at the time.[7] Earlier chapters noted how Chambers of Commerce and Industry functioned as economic groups that represented political interests and acted as constraints, both formally and informally, on executive decision-making and, in some cases such as Saudi Arabia, provided rare examples of electoral accountability to their membership.[8] On a broader societal level, *diwaniyas* in Kuwait and the *majlis* elsewhere provide outlets for the discussion (and practice) of politics in informal settings, especially given the institutional weaknesses in the formal parameters of representative political bodies.[9]

This chapter begins with a section that analyzes elite perceptions of representation as expressed by members of the ruling elites in GCC states since the 1970s. These perceptions are significant because the creation of representative institutions has been a top-down initiative in every GCC case bar Kuwait and, to a lesser extent, Bahrain. Government expectations of the role that such bodies would play did not always align with those of the representatives that filled them, especially as the councils grew and evolved. The chapter goes on to examine the emergence of representative demands, the appearance of different forms of assemblies, and the degree to which each of the bodies was (or was not) able to influence executive action by rulers and governments. In addition, the chapter examines the ways in which political outcomes were limited by carefully drawn parameters of contestation which placed limitations on the exercise of genuinely autonomous forms of political power in practice.

Reluctant reformers

At the outset it should be noted that in most Gulf settings the demands for representative powers that emerged from societal and political groups during the twentieth century did not originate with members of ruling families, with the partial exception of Kuwait. Nor were rulers supportive of any move toward 'democracy' in the Western sense and made clear that representative powers were being delegated in a regionally specific way. In 1974, for example, Prince Fahd of Saudi Arabia, who later served as King between 1982 and 2005, told the Beirut-based newspaper *Al-Anwar* that there existed a 'common misperception that the Western democratic system is like an inevitable model that everyone has to follow.' Fahd added that the misperception existed because the parliamentary system in Western societies had arisen 'on the basis of "no taxation without representation".'[10]

In Qatar, Sheikh Khalifa bin Hamad Al Thani justified the decision to appoint, rather than elect, the twenty members of the Shura Council formed in 1972 as consistent with the longstanding principle of consultation. In a January 1973 interview with a Lebanese magazine, the Emir stated that 'the basic idea behind democracy is "participation" and that is what we are after here.' Sheikh Khalifa added that the men (and they were all men, across the Gulf, until the 2000s) appointed would, over time, acquire 'experience and parliamentary tradition' and that 'only when we master the democratic game, we can move to an advanced stage in this experiment.' Moreover, the Emir emphasized the need to carefully adapt and apply the representative principle to local social and cultural values, as he argued that 'Democracy is an advanced modern weapon. Like any other weapon, we have to be trained in its use. We have to understand democracy well in order to have it serve our ambitions for progress, and not to have it a liability to progress.'[11] The message that democracy was about participation was still being promulgated in Qatar thirty-five years later, when in 2008 Prime Minister Sheikh Hamad bin Jassim Al Thani declared that 'Democracy does not just mean voting or casting ballots. It ensures political participation.'[12]

The first chairman of the Shura Council established in Saudi Arabia in 1993 by King Fahd, Mohammed ibn Ibrahim ibn Jubair, was a former Minister of Justice and Hanbali jurist. In a December 2001 council debate shortly before his death the following month, ibn Jubair claimed that the Shura Council was advisory because 'Our duty is only to work out executive charters to implement legislation that had been revealed by the Almighty in the Holy Qur'an' and that 'the council does not legislate because laws exist in Shariah.'[13] Several years earlier, ibn Jubair had made it clear to a visiting delegation that 'the Shura is not a legislature, and it is not a step toward democracy. It is our own system, coming from our religion and habits and tradition.' Moreover, ibn Jubair justified

King Fahd's decision to appoint the membership of the Shura Council on the grounds that 'If we left it to voters, they would not choose members qualified to offer the King advice—they would elect tribal chiefs unable to read or write.'[14] One of the members of the first Shura Council in the 1990s declined a request by the British Consul-General for a meeting with the comment that 'my job as a member of this advisory council is to give advice to the king, not to you.'[15]

A somewhat different and at times contradictory approach was taken in Bahrain by Sheikh Khalifa bin Salman Al Khalifa, the world's longest-serving Prime Minister at the time of his death in November 2020. After an upsurge in domestic unrest in Bahrain in the mid-1990s, Sheikh Khalifa told a *New York Times* reporter that 'We are not afraid of democracy. We are afraid of the people who would misuse it.'[16] This was consistent with a comment attributed by British officials in Bahrain to Sheikh Khalifa in 1977, two years after the suspension of Bahrain's first assembly, that 'I have no intention whatsoever of holding elections or anything of the kind.'[17] And yet, in 1979, the Prime Minister told the Kuwaiti newspaper *Al-Siyasah* that 'We have known democracy since ancient times, before it assumed different shapes and was recorded in different forms (…) We knew democracy and practiced it through our direct contacts with the citizens without barriers and bureaucracy (…) We are practicing it in different ways.'[18]

Oman has taken a gradualist approach to development and this has been exemplified in statements by its Sultan of nearly half a century, Qaboos bin Said Al Said, as well as Badr Al Busaidi, a career official in the Ministry of Foreign Affairs who became Foreign Minister in August 2020. Speaking to journalist Judith Miller in February 1997, Sultan Qaboos argued that 'You can't push things too far or too fast in the Gulf' and that 'giving too much power too fast can still be exploited. Elections in many countries mean having the army prevent bloodshed. Is this democracy? Are these happy countries? Do such elections give people real choices? No. They are really just power struggles.'[19] Al Busaidi struck a broadly similar note a decade later when he suggested that 'Oman is not chasing some grand illusion of uniform modernity. There is no single model of what it is to be modern, which every nation and people must aspire to (…) Oman is building gradually upon structures and principles that have shaped its society for a very long time.'[20] In 2009, Sultan Qaboos also drew upon the notion of encouraging 'participation' in an address to the opening of the State Council which emphasized his own role in providing, in a top-down manner, the opportunities to do so.[21]

Emergence of representative demands

The development of representative institutions in the Gulf States—some elected, others appointed, or a mixture of the two—is best understood as an exercise in what Greg Power has termed 'managed reform' or 'controlled evolution' that accords with Daniel Brumberg's concept of 'guided pluralism' and Gerd Nonneman's notion of 'modernizing autocracy.'[22] Moreover, as Mehran Kamrava has observed of the Middle East more broadly, leaders sought to create institutions that were designed to enhance rather than supplant their political powers and privileges, and this has been the case in the Gulf context as well.[23] This has been evident in the ways in which rulers have sought to achieve 'balance' (in regional, tribal, and social groups, and, more recently, gender dimensions) in patterns of appointment to local and national councils in part to offset electoral outcomes and skew representative patterns in their favor.

All six GCC states have established representative bodies that have institutionalized older and previously more informal channels of consultation; indeed, the word *shura* appears in the titles of the councils in Saudi Arabia and Qatar as well as the lower chamber in Oman and the upper chamber in Bahrain. Historically, in the specific case of Oman, the Ibadi tradition of the *Imamate* required that the Imam be 'elected' albeit from a procedurally unrepresentative and very small group of peers.[24] Elections to national bodies have been introduced in five of the six Gulf States with the sole exception of Saudi Arabia where electoral contestation has been confined to the municipal level. And yet, limits imposed by executives on political participation have placed significant constraints on the representative process and ensured that, in practice, none of the 'modernizing autocracies' have evolved into fully constitutional monarchies.[25]

It should, however, be noted that social (and, to some extent, political) pressures on ruling elites to broaden the representative basis of decision-making long predated the creation of formal institutions in the 1960s and 1970s. These began at a sub-state level with the formation of councils of merchants, with one in Jeddah (then under Ottoman control) being established as early as the 1850s, and with Municipal Councils which were formed in towns across the Arabian Peninsula in the 1920s and 1930s.[26] Hijaz and Al-Ahsa also elected representatives to the Ottoman parliament prior to the First World War and to their later incorporation into the expanding Saudi state.[27] The first iteration of a Consultative Council (*Majlis Al Shura*) was established in Kuwait in 1921 and consisted of twelve men, all of whom were Sunni and most from Kuwait's merchant class, who were selected rather than elected.[28] Although the 1921 council was not representative of Kuwaitis of all backgrounds, was weakened by personal rivalries, and lasted only two months before it was dissolved, it was accompanied by a charter laying out its powers that Kuwaiti historian Abdulrahman Alebrahim has labeled 'the first written constitution in Kuwait's history.'[29]

The 1920s also saw the holding of an election to an eleven-member council in the Hijaz in December 1924 and the appointment in 1926 of Consultative Councils in the Hijazi cities of Mecca, Medina, Jeddah, Yanbu, and Taif, to represent the views of prominent families, religious clerics (*ulama*), and merchants in local governance, following their incorporation into the Kingdom of Hijaz and Najd by Ibn Saud.[30] Especially in the Hijaz, the Consultative Council, along with a Trade Council established in 1925 and dominated by members of Jeddah's powerful merchant community, was an especially strong counterpoint to Ibn Saud during the opening decade of Saudi state-building in the 1920s and 1930s, and was able to represent collective business interests and contest measures that harmed their economic power.[31] In the Eastern Province, which had been conquered by Ibn

Saud's forces in 1913, a council of local notables was appointed in Qatif in 1925 and again in 1927.[32]

Social and political pressures for representation in decision-making re-emerged in Kuwait in 1938 and spread to other emirates in the Gulf, including Bahrain and Dubai. Such pressures were in part an early reflection of growing Arab nationalist influence in Egypt and especially, in the case of Kuwait, across the border in neighboring Iraq. In addition, they were bolstered by the impact of newspapers and pamphlets and the first generation of students from the Gulf to study abroad.[33] As in 1921, the push for greater decision-making involvement came primarily from Kuwaiti merchants in reaction to economic losses during the Great Depression (and a decade-long commercial blockade of Kuwait by Ibn Saud) as well as political grievances against the Ruler and his perceived 'lack of attention to affairs of state.'[34] Many of the demands came from men who had, as children, been among the first to receive a 'modern' education at the Mubarakiyya School which had opened in 1912.[35]

Matters came to a head in March 1938 after a taxi driver and alleged oppositionist, Mohammed Al-Barrak, was flogged after he was found guilty of writing anti-ruler slogans in public places. Kuwaiti demands for a package of administrative reforms found their way into Iraqi media, and in June 1938 three prominent merchants in Kuwait met the Ruler and demanded he accede to an elected Legislative Council.[36] Merchants met that same evening at the house of Yusuf Al-Marzuq to draw up an electorate of the heads of 150 leading families which elected fourteen members to a Legislative Council presided over by Sheikh Abdullah al-Salim Al Sabah, the Ruler's cousin (and, in 1950, his eventual successor).[37] Article 1 of the law governing the powers of the council stipulated that the people were the source of power, as represented by the council, while Article 5 stated that the President was the source of executive authority.

These were meaningful powers to take control of, and the direction of the new Council alarmed British officials as well as the Ruler himself. One British official wrote that 'The law reads somewhat like the declaration of the French Assembly in 1791' while another added that 'we cannot deal with two conflicting authorities in Kuwait.'[38] Relations between the Council and the Ruler began to break down when the former approached the latter about handing over the annual payment of the oil concession agreed in the Ruler's name with the Kuwait Oil Company in 1934. The council also met with opposition from Kuwaitis who had been excluded from the process, including members of Kuwait's Shia communities, and the council was dissolved by the Ruler in December 1938 and several of its members imprisoned.[39]

Aside from Kuwait, demands for representative councils, also led by merchants, appeared in Dubai and Bahrain in 1938 as well. Merchant discontent in Dubai was similar in origin to that of Kuwait and arose out of the decade of economic hardship in the 1930s, which they contrasted to the Ruler's accrual of royalties from agreements with the British for an air base and oil concession. Just as in Kuwait, the payment of the oil concession upset the 'balanced relationship' between the Ruler and the merchant community which hitherto had provided him with revenue.[40] The (fleeting) success of Kuwait's elected council led Dubai's merchants to appoint a fifteen-member Consultative Council in October 1938 and set in motion practical steps to improve and expand the harbor, regulate the customs service, and as in Kuwait, take control of income and expenditure from the Ruler.[41] The Dubai council lasted little longer than its Kuwaiti counterpart as it was violently dissolved by the Ruler in March 1939 and replaced by a ruler-appointed council that included five of the merchants who had been selected in the more autonomous 1938 body.[42]

The reform movement in Bahrain in 1938 was less successful in demanding a full-fledged Legislative Council like the (short-lived) Kuwaiti model, in part because the Ruler and British officials held firm in the face of political demands in the wake of the activism witnessed in Kuwait and Dubai. As Rosemarie Said Zahlan observed, the demands for greater representation in Bahrain came in the wake of rising expectations following the expansion of local schools and the opening of a printing press as well as growing grievances against the lack of opportunities in the public and oil sectors.[43] Protestors' demands had earlier, in 1935, included a system of proportional representation for the Municipal Councils in the principal Bahraini towns of Manama and Muharraq, and several of the demonstrators went on to play a leading role in the far greater opposition movement in the 1950s, establishing a generational bridge across the pre/post-oil divide, just as they did in Kuwait as well.[44]

Merchant-led calls for greater representation in decision-making in Kuwait, Dubai, and Bahrain were interlinked as in each of the three emirates the onset of early oil revenues, in the form of concession payments, upset the delicate equilibrium of political and economic relationships between rulers and merchants. This was especially the case in these three examples where merchants had a more influential position in the pre-oil political economy than elsewhere in the Gulf, with the localized exception of the powerful Hijazi merchant class in and around Jeddah.[45] In the pre-oil period, rulers depended on the merchants as a source of revenue for public finance and merchants could threaten to relocate if they perceived taxes and duties to be unfair.[46]

While short-lived, Kuwait's brief Legislative Council of 1938 illustrates how continuities in the pressures for representation straddle the pre-oil and oil eras, as at least one of the members of the (elected) Constituent Assembly drawn up in 1962 to write Kuwait's post-independence constitution had been a member of the 1938 Council (and had been imprisoned as a result). Moreover, the President of the 1938 Council, Sheikh Abdullah al-Salem Al Sabah, was (by 1962) the Ruler of Kuwait and a supporter of the constitutional process.[47] Furthermore, the setback to representative decision-making in 1938 channeled political energies and demands for reform into clubs and societies that became prominent agents of change in Kuwait and other Gulf States in the 1940s and 1950s, as described in more detail in Chapter 5. The transition between the pre-oil and oil eras was far from a binary 'before/after' division but was instead a period of change that unfolded over the space of decades between the 1930s and the 1970s, with significant instances of civil activism and numerous linkages across the years.

Growth of representative institutions

Kuwait became a sovereign state in June 1961, followed a decade later by Bahrain (August 1971), Qatar (September 1971), and the UAE (December 1971). In Oman, the replacement of Sultan Said bin Taimur by his son, Qaboos bin Said, in July 1970, was the catalyst for accelerated economic and social development in the Sultanate while in Saudi Arabia, which unlike its smaller neighbors had never been a British protected state, the process of modern state formation really began after the death of Ibn Saud in November 1953.[48] Representative institutions were established in the immediate aftermath of independence in the cases of Kuwait, Qatar, and the UAE, more slowly in the Omani and Saudi cases, where their eventual introduction was framed as evolutionary measures that codified existing practices of consultation, and haltingly in Bahrain's case, where a 1973 assembly was suspended two years later.

The following table shows the representative institutions that exist (as of 2023) in the six Gulf States.

Name	Country	Formed	Elected/appointed
National Assembly	Kuwait	1963	50 elected; Cabinet are *ex officio* members
Consultative Council	Qatar	1972	20 appointed, now 30 elected and 15 appointed
Federal National Council	UAE	1972	40 all appointed initially, 20 elected since 2006
Consultative Council[49]	Oman	1991	86 elected members
Consultative Council	Saudi Arabia	1993	60 members initially, now 150, all appointed
Council of State	Oman	1997	83 members appointed by the Sultan
Council of Representatives[50]	Bahrain	2002	40 elected members
Consultative Council	Bahrain	2002	40 members appointed by the King

From the above, it will be seen that Kuwait's experience of elected representation predates by years its neighbors, with Qatar only holding its first election to a national body (as opposed to the Central Municipal Council, to which elections were first held in 1999) in 2021, and Saudi Arabia yet to do so. Even so, Kuwait experienced two lengthy periods in which the National Assembly was suspended, first between 1976 and 1981 and again from 1986 to 1992. In Bahrain, the Council of Representatives may have sat in four-year electoral cycles since 2002, but it is separated by a twenty-seven-year hiatus from its (more powerful) predecessor, a National Assembly of thirty elected members (and, as in Kuwait, fourteen *ex officio* Cabinet members) which sat from December 1973 until August 1975 when it was suspended indefinitely. The subsequent re-establishment of an elected representative institution in Bahrain was counterbalanced by an appointed second chamber, as was the case in Oman also.

The degree to which the councils were vested with meaningful powers was the outcome of a push-and-pull of factors that in part reflected the pre-oil balance of power between the ruling family, the merchant elites, and other social actors.[51] In Kuwait and Bahrain, there were other contingent factors specific to each country that led to the creation (albeit short-lived in Bahrain's case) of more directly influential bodies. These included a history of civil activism through participation in organized networks such as clubs and societies, mobilization in trades unions and labor strikes between the 1940s and the 1960s, and the comparatively greater spread of broader political ideologies in both countries.[52] As the Bahraini sociologist Abdulhadi Khalaf, who was himself elected to the 1973–5 National Assembly, observed, transnational coordination among Gulf activists, including from Iraq and Iran, also raised political expectations.[53] Another aspect of coordination, albeit at the official level, was the seconding, from Kuwait to Bahrain, of the legal advisor and constitutional expert Othman Khalil Othman to assist in the drafting of Bahrain's 1973 constitution, a decade after his work on Kuwait's 1962 Constituent Assembly and constitution.[54]

Kuwait and Bahrain were also distinct in that they faced an immediate external threat to national sovereignty, from Iraq and

Iran, respectively, at or around the time of formal independence in 1961 and 1971. The Iraqi military leadership of 'Abd al-Karim Qasim claimed Kuwait as part of Iraq on 25 June 1961, six days after Kuwait became an independent state, and appeared to send troops toward Iraq's southern border with Kuwait. The military (and diplomatic) threat posed to Kuwait by Iraq prompted the dispatch of British forces to Kuwait on 1 July, where they remained until they were replaced by an Arab League force in September.[55] In the case of Bahrain, twenty-six months of secret negotiations between British and Iranian officials culminated in the Shah abandoning a longstanding territorial claim to Bahrain and a subsequent United Nations' 'consultation' settling the matter in 1970, finding that 'the overwhelming majority of the people of Bahrain wish to gain recognition of their identity in a fully independent and sovereign State.'[56]

The historian Linda Colley has argued that there is a close correlation between warfare and armed violence and the spread of written constitutions around the world, including in non-democratic as well as democratic settings.[57] This is certainly true in the case of Kuwait where the political scientist Michael Herb has observed that 'No other explanation for Kuwaiti exceptionalism has such a close temporal relationship between the proposed cause and the actual writing of the 1962 constitution.'[58] Thus, within months of the Iraqi threat to Kuwait in June 1961, elections were held in December for a Constitutional Convention, which met for the first time in January 1962 and issued the Kuwaiti Constitution in November. Elections to the first National Assembly in Kuwait's history followed in January 1963.[59] Twenty of the thirty-one members of the Constitutional Convention were directly elected (the other eleven were government ministers) and their number included prominent opposition figures as well as one member of the 1938 Council.[60] Thirty years later, the Iraqi invasion of Kuwait in August 1990 and the subsequent seven-month occupation also catalyzed Kuwaiti political and social groups to come together, in Jeddah in October (as described in Chapter 2) to agree on the reinstatement of the National Assembly following liberation.

As Kuwaiti sociologist Haya Al-Mughni recalled in 1994, when looking back to 1990, 'The war acted like a volcano.'[61]

In the case of Bahrain, whose constitution was issued in 1973, the same year that elections to the National Assembly took place, Abdulhadi Khalaf suggested that the ruling family sought 'to acquire constitutional legitimacy' but that the subsequent twenty-seven-year suspension of the National Assembly two years later demonstrated that members of the elite 'did not accept the formal and informal political, administrative, and judicial consequences of that legitimacy.'[62] Instead, the ruling family constructed and defined the parameters of permissible political activity with considerations of regime security in mind, and in doing so, sought to 'adjust to some demands of modern governance while maintaining their traditional forms of rule.'[63] This included the creation, in 1992, of a wholly appointed Consultative Council (*Majlis Al Shura*) which was criticized by regime critics as a pale imitation of the suspended Assembly, and failed to placate members of the political opposition who continued their call for reform.[64]

Neither the Bahraini or, to a lesser but still meaningful extent, the Kuwaiti parliaments, have met what Herb has labeled the threshold of 'parliamentarism,' whereby monarchies realized that governments without parliamentary support or the backing of political parties could not govern.[65] Some of the similarities in the Kuwaiti and Bahraini experience may be attributable to the fact that both constitutions drew upon similar experts in their process of formation.[66] While political 'blocs' in Kuwait and political 'societies' in Bahrain (since the reinstatement of the National Assembly in 2002) have performed some of the functions of political parties, which remain disallowed across the region, Herb has identified multiple obstacles to parliamentarism which constrain the operation of representative institutions in practice. These include constitutional limitations, institutional barriers, electoral gerrymandering, and the weakness of safeguards against executive (ruling family) encroachment.[67] Set against this is the formalization of institutional channels of representation, including the creation of parliamentary committee systems with powers of oversight, as well as the socialization over time of representative bodies across the Gulf.

Cautious parameters of contestation

None of the representative institutions that have been created in the Gulf States since independence came about as a result of successful pressure 'from below' for political reform. Even the reinstatement of the National Assembly in Bahrain in 2002, which came after a period of sustained unrest in the 1990s and initially was welcomed by political opponents of the regime, was subsequently diluted by the addition of an upper chamber appointed by the King to counterbalance the assembly of elected MPs. The switch from the unicameral National Assembly of 1973–5 to the bicameral Council of Representatives and Consultative Council of 2002 angered many in Bahrain who accused the government of a breach of faith. The sense of disillusionment arose from the perception among oppositionists that King Hamad had promised that legislative power would rest with the elected chamber and that the appointed chamber would be advisory only in nature, and that, after 98 percent of Bahrainis had approved the government's National Action Charter roadmap for reform in February 2002, the leadership had reneged by vesting legislative authority in both chambers and giving the appointed body the power to reject bills from the elected assembly.[68]

The Bahraini example illustrated the power dynamic between a ruling family (and government) seeking to maintain political control and social groups attempting to expand representative and participatory openings. The committee that drafted the National Action Charter and the amendments to Bahrain's 1973 constitution was headed by the Minister of Justice, its forty-six members were appointed by Emiri decree, and it did not meet in public or accept any of the petitions submitted to it.[69] The executive made the rules and this has been a feature common to the experience of all representative institutions in the Gulf since the 1960s, starting with the National Assembly of Kuwait, where the sixteen-strong Cabinet sit as *ex-officio* MPs alongside the fifty elected members and vote as a bloc in support of government policy. This was an arrangement later followed by Bahrain's 1973–5 National Assembly and has on occasion made a significant difference to political outcomes, as in May 2005 when Cabinet *ex-officio* MPs were instrumental in overriding opposition to a bill allowing Kuwaiti women to vote and stand in elections.[70]

In Qatar, a new constitution drafted by Emir Hamad bin Khalifa Al Thani and ratified by 96 percent of voters in a 2003 referendum vested legislative authority in the Shura Council and stated that two-thirds of the forty-five council members would be elected. However, while the constitution went into force in June 2005, elections to the Shura Council failed to take place, and it remained a wholly appointed body, despite a public declaration by Emir Hamad in November 2011 that elections would take place in 2013.[71] Observers noted the lack of specific detail in the 2011 statement as well as the lack of consultation with domestic political or civil society figures before the announcement. By early 2013, however, there had been no further announcement either on the date of the national election or the mechanisms by which it would be conducted, despite the Shura Council's term coming to an end in June.[72]

Two op-eds in the same issue of *The Peninsula*, Qatar's English-language daily newspaper, in May 2013, both called for the elections to take place. The first article, entitled 'High Time for Shura Council Polls,' reminded the Emir of his numerous promises, going back to 1998, of political reform, including remarks at the fifty-ninth UN General Assembly meeting in September 2004, in which he said that 'Political reform and the participation of citizens in decision-making is no longer an optional thing that we can take or leave, but a necessity.'[73] The second op-ed, entitled 'Citizens Must Be Part of Decision-Making,' argued that 'our country and its leadership are negatively affected by the absence of public participation' and that

> Those opposing the idea of having a parliament are harming the stability of our country by wanting to do away with a basic pillar of the constitution approved by the citizens. Showing disrespect to one article of the constitution is disrespect to all the provisions of law, and it is just a matter of time before such people show

disrespect to the other articles of the statute and the nation's will (...) We only need citizens to be part of the decision-making process. This is what we hope for.[74]

A clause in the constitution permitted an extension of the appointed council's term 'if required by the public interest.'[75] However, in October 2019, Emir Tamim bin Hamad Al Thani ordered the creation of a committee to organize the elections to the Shura Council, and the first 'national' election took place in October 2021.[76] Both Emir Hamad's 2011 and Emir Tamim's 2019 statements on elections came at moments when Qatar was in the international spotlight for its support for Arab Spring uprisings in North Africa and Syria in 2011 and its tensions with regional neighbors during the blockade which began in 2017. A desire to bolster Qatar's international standing may therefore have factored into decision-making albeit in a controlled manner consistent with the top-down nature of widening participation elsewhere in the Gulf. In the event, the electoral law caused some controversy as it raised issues of citizenship and identity over which groups of citizens were eligible (or not) to take part, and a decision that voters would cast ballots in their district of origin meant that voting largely took place along tribal lines.[77] Several days of protests against the electoral law and exclusion of categories of Qatari citizens took place in August 2021, but subsided after two of the Emir's brothers engaged directly with tribal leaders to defuse tensions.[78]

In Oman, Sultan Qaboos engaged in a careful process of gradual opening-up that broadened representative participation to encompass key sectors of society, such as tribal groups and the newly educated, yet did not give away any meaningful political authority.[79] In a rare interview granted to the journalist Judith Miller in February 1997, later published in *Foreign Affairs*, the Sultan asserted that

We used to be governed in a very traditional way (...) I had promised on the first day of my rule to create a modern government. But I knew change had to be entered into slowly, very slowly. The level of education had to reach a certain point so that people would know what we were talking about (...) the Majlis' powers will expand with time, so there are no earthquakes. But we are still largely a tribal society, and it's still the government's job to defend the country. The man in the street often doesn't want or know how to deal with foreign governments or defend the country. He trusts me to do it.[80]

While the present Consultative Council in Oman dates from 1991, Sultan Qaboos established a predecessor, the State Consultative Council, by decree a decade earlier, in November 1981, which itself came after Qaboos initiated a twelve-member advisory Council on Agriculture, Fisheries, and Industries in April 1979.[81] The State Consultative Council consisted initially of forty-five members and was expanded to fifty-five in 1983; all appointments had to be confirmed by the Sultan and the council was advisory in nature.[82] The controlled nature of the council was evident in the allocation of its membership, with the forty-five (initial) seats in 1981 apportioned among representatives of government sectors and the different regions of Oman (which each had seventeen members), alongside eleven members who represented various private sector concerns.[83]

In 1991, the Consultative Council was created to better represent the fifty-nine districts of Oman, each of which had a representative chosen initially by the Deputy Prime Minister for Legal Affairs from three candidates who had been selected by local caucuses involving 'leading citizens.' Abdullah Juma Alhaj, a political scientist at United Arab Emirates University, observed how the Consultative Council aimed to combine 'Western concepts of political representation' with 'elements of the traditional majlis' and 'local Ibadi traditions of participation' in Oman.[84] Increases in the size of the Consultative Council saw the body expand from fifty-nine representatives in 1991 to seventy-nine in 1994, eighty-two in 1998, and eighty-six as of 2023. The 1997 and 2000 terms saw a significant growth in the 'electoral college' who selected the nominees for the council, with 51,000 and 175,000 eligible voters (including women), respectively, and in 2003 Oman became the first GCC state to adopt a system of universal suffrage for elections to a national body.[85] The 2003 election also saw the government permit for the first time (modest) campaigning by the candidates, but this was limited in practice to the circulation of biographies rather than policy manifestos or political promises.[86] The role of the council has remained consultative and advisory, with relatively low voter interest, and since 1997 it has been supplemented by an upper chamber, the Council of State, with eighty-three members appointed by the Sultan. Together, the Consultative Council and the State Council form the Oman Council (*Majlis Oman*).[87]

A broadly comparable process of cautious and gradual extension of representative participation occurred in the UAE after the creation of the federation in 1971. The Federal National Council (FNC) was established in 1972 as a forty-strong consultative chamber of appointed members by the leaders of each of the seven emirates, with eight seats for representatives from Abu Dhabi and Dubai, six for those from Sharjah and Ras al-Khaimah, and four for members from Ajman, Fujairah, and Umm al-Quwain. Membership of the FNC, especially when it was an all-appointed body (until 2006), tended to be drawn from the business community and prominent local merchant families in each of the seven emirates.[88] In this it had parallels with the Omani experience which also viewed the representative process as an exercise in balancing among various domestic constituencies and social groups.[89]

Although the FNC has the right to view all federal legislation and can propose, amend, or reject draft bills, it never threatened to shift decision-making away from the Council of Ministers (the Cabinet) or the Federal Supreme Council (of the seven rulers), which retains the power to pass bills over the opposition of the FNC. In the 1990s, Sheikh Fahim bin Sultan Al Qassemi, then the UAE Minister of Economy and Commerce and a member of the Ras al-Khaimah ruling family, asserted that

> ...we have developed without undermining the social, cultural, and political fabric of our society (...) Our system combines the best of the old with the best of the new. We have retained democratic Islamic traditions, foremost among which is the majlis, the open council in which national and local leaders meet regularly with citizens to discuss issues of concern.[90]

There were, nevertheless, times when members of the FNC raised and channeled broader concerns over sensitive issues to decision-makers. A prominent example occurred in 1986 when the FNC succeeded in amending a law on state security that had sparked widespread public debate.[91] Another example of a law that generated a rigorous debate at the FNC was the draft penal code, as:

> ... a number of stormy debates accompanied the article-by-article process of approving the country's penal code, making it the most debated legal document in the history of the UAE (...) objections were raised to an article providing for up to 10 years of imprisonment for membership in subversive organizations (...) a related article, proposing stiff penalties for the establishment of organizations without government consent, as well as for membership in any un-approved organization even while outside the country, was roundly attacked as abridging the personal rights and liberties of UAE citizens. Although the articles eventually were passed, they had been amended by the minister of justice, who had been present throughout the debates.[92]

While the FNC remained an appointed and consultative body for the first thirty-four years of its existence, a limited exercise in participation began after the passing of Sheikh Zayed in November 2004. In early 2006, the position of Minister of State for Federal National Council Affairs was created and Anwar Mohammed Gargash was appointed to oversee the first election in the UAE's history for half of the forty seats on the FNC. This took place in December 2006 with each of the seven emirate leaderships nominating potential electors. After security vetting of the electoral lists, a total of 6,595 people, including 1,162 women, eventually comprised the Electoral College that was eligible to vote for the 456 candidates (391 men and sixty-five women)—a figure that amounted to just 0.08 percent of the population. The voter pool consisted predominantly of university graduates and people aged between twenty-one and forty who were forbidden to form political parties and alliances or campaign on 'national' issues.[93]

Subsequent elections in the four-yearly cycle saw the Emirati authorities substantially expand the pool of eligible voters with a twentyfold increase from the 6,595 in 2006 to 129,000 in 2011, 224,000 in 2015, and 337,000 in 2019. Turnout remained within a band of between thirty and forty percent, and voting occurred largely along tribal lines, especially in the five 'Northern Emirates' beyond Abu Dhabi and Dubai. On occasion, FNC members expressed their disappointment at what they considered the 'slow pace' of sessions and regular ministerial absences from the council. One member from Dubai, Hamad Al-Rahoomi, summarized in 2015 the challenges he felt were undermining the performance of the FNC:

> … How can we tell people, 'Come and vote, the council is important, we monitor the Government?' How can we give ourselves to the people when it is no secret that we are struggling now to meet with the Government? This is unacceptable. We have a problem with low turnout during the elections and want to give the council value. One of the reasons why people are not getting involved in the elections is because no minister is available to attend the sessions. This affects the reputation of the FNC.[94]

After the 2015 FNC election, Amal Al-Qubaisi (who had been the first woman elected to the FNC in 2006) made history as she became the first female Speaker of any Arab parliamentary chamber.[95]

In Saudi Arabia, elections at the municipal level are the only (as of 2023) form of participatory engagement.[96] The restoration of municipal elections in 2005—in which men only could vote and run for office—were the first at any level in Saudi Arabia since the 1960s despite an electoral law having been formulated in 1977. Female voters and candidates were excluded not by the text of the 2004 electoral law but on the grounds that women did not possess their own identification cards.[97] Saudi officials moved slowly in enacting political reforms and often appeared to do so in response to internal or regional shocks; in early 1980, the Interior Minister, Prince Nayef bin Abdulaziz Al Saud, headed a committee that was appointed in the aftermath of the seizure of the Grand Mosque in Mecca by Sunni fundamentalists and unrest from Shia protestors in the Eastern Province to consider a Basic Law and a Consultative Council.[98] Ultimately, however, it took another moment of crisis— the Iraqi occupation of Kuwait and 1991 Gulf War—for King Fahd to formulate and adopt a Basic Law of Governance twelve years later, in January 1992.[99]

Periods of crisis can often be the 'push factor' for new ways of thinking about political organization, whether due to domestic or international pressure (or both), as seen in Kuwait in 1961 and in Saudi Arabia in 1979–80 and again in 1991. Writing in 2003, Khalid Al-Dakhil, a professor of political sociology at King Saud University in Riyadh, argued that the impact of the 1990–91 Gulf crisis was instrumental as:

> The fate of the Saudi nation was on the line and the fact that foreign, rather than national, troops were protecting the Kingdom created a sense of vulnerability and political failure that still lingers to this day. By exposing the Saudi government's inability to safeguard national security, the Gulf crisis made pressure for political reform unavoidable.[100]

The Basic Law unveiled by King Fahd in 1992 is perhaps best remembered for the fact that it empowered the King to select and remove the Crown Prince at his discretion and that 'grandsons of Abdulaziz were eligible to become King even if sons remained alive.'[101] The ramifications of the Basic Law for issues of royal succession would only become fully apparent a generation later when King Salman came to power in 2015. The other significant outcome of the Basic Law was the establishment of the Shura Council which first met in 1993 with sixty members, all appointed, and which was expanded to ninety members in 1997, 120 members in 2001, and its current membership of 150 in 2005, of whom thirty have been women since 2013. In 2003, the Shura Council was granted the right to initiate legislation and suggest amendments to existing regulations, although the King retains the final say should a difference arise between the Shura Council and the Council of Ministers (the Saudi Cabinet).[102]

There have been instances in which policy proposals which originated in the Shura Council received the support of the

Council of Ministers, such as a 2007 initiative to counter corruption which resulted in the creation of a ministerial-level committee answerable to King Abdullah.[103] While the council's powers did evolve, they did not begin to approach any form of active contestation of government policies; as a Saudi academic appointed by King Fahd to the inaugural Shura Council in 1993 observed, 'We were instructed to give our honest judgements on public issues, and we do. We provide information and analysis from outside the ministerial circle. In short, we are a body of advisors to the king, nothing more.'[104] Moreover, as noted by David Rundell, on major decisions—such as the launching of Saudi Vision 2030 by then Deputy Crown Prince Mohammed bin Salman in 2016, or measures such as the sale of shares in Saudi Aramco, or the introduction of Value Added Tax (VAT)—the Shura Council was not consulted at all.[105]

Limitations of power in practice

Exercises in representative institutions were top-down in nature albeit at times in part response to societal or regional pressures. They were, nevertheless, aimed at preserving the status quo insofar as none of the bodies that were established ever threatened to alter the structure or distribution of political power in any of the Gulf States. Regimes have utilized a range of tools to limit in practice the exercise of political power, such as shaping electoral outcomes through the gerrymandering of voter districts, deciding upon the 'rules of the game' for campaigning as well as for participating in elected or appointed bodies, utilizing alternative means such as decrees to push through controversial measures, and suspending representative institutions if they are seen to present a direct or perceived threat to regime security. This was the case even in Kuwait, whose National Assembly, by far the most vocal and assertive such body in the Gulf, was suspended by the Emir first in 1976 and again a decade later in 1986.

Kuwait's and Bahrain's National Assemblies illustrate several of the more common tactics deployed by regimes to enclose the boundaries of permissible political activities within clearly defined limits. The ability to control the process of creating electoral districts has led to charges by opposition figures in both countries of gerrymandering to secure favorable political outcomes. As the veteran Kuwaiti political scientist Ghanim Al-Najjar has observed, controversies over districting have been a perennial feature of the electoral landscape since the first National Assembly elections took place in 1963.[106] In 2006, as youth activists in Kuwait were mobilizing around the 'nabiha khamsa' ('we want five') campaign to reduce the number of electoral districts from twenty-five to five, on the grounds that having fewer (and larger) districts would make it more difficult to affect the outcomes, al-Najjar recalled that

> At the time of Kuwaiti independence in 1961, there was a division between popular support for a single electoral district for all of Kuwait, and a government desire for 20 constituencies. The struggle intensified to the point that a number of key political actors threatened to boycott elections if the government insisted on its position, leading to a compromise on ten districts. Four elections were held under that system, one of which was rigged (1967) and another of which led to an unconstitutional dissolution of the Assembly (1976). The government's displeasure with the ten-district system became clear in 1981 when it insisted on raising the number to 25 districts, which is the current system.[107]

In Bahrain, the sense of frustration felt in 2002 by political figures at King Hamad's previously noted dilution of his plan for political liberalization, through the addition of an appointed upper chamber above the reconstituted National Assembly, was magnified by discrepancies in the size of electoral districts. The (opposition-leaning) Bahrain Human Rights Society drew attention in 2003 to 'the imbalance of constituents in the electoral districts, with one predominantly Sunni district containing barely 400 voters while a Shia district could have up to 14,000.'[108] Seven years later, when analyzing the outcomes of the 2010 election (in which Al-Wefaq, the major Shia opposition group, won eighteen of the forty seats in the National Assembly), Claire Beaugrand estimated that Al-Wefaq's successful candidates required, on average, between two and three times the number of votes to win in their constituencies as compared with winning candidates in primarily Sunni electoral districts.[109]

Opposition anger also reflected the fact that, in the months immediately preceding the first session of the re-established National Assembly in Bahrain in December 2002, King Hamad issued fifty-six royal decrees, none of which could be amended by the bicameral legislature without both houses—elected and appointed—voting in favor.[110] And whereas, in the 2002, 2006, and 2010 elections, the drawing of electoral districts had sought to limit the number of seats that Shia (political opposition) societies could be competitive in, a new round of redistricting ahead of the 2014 election (in which Al-Wefaq did not run) appeared designed to reduce the electoral chances of organized Sunni Islamist groups instead.[111]

A separate tactic from districting is the limiting of political coordination both in campaigning and in the forming of parties although elements of the latter are evident in Kuwait and Bahrain in the form of political 'blocs' and 'societies,' respectively. Moves to atomize and depoliticize participation in representative bodies have been applied to varying degrees across the six GCC states. None of the Gulf States has allowed formal parties or ideological politics to operate or take root. Ibn Saud banned political parties upon the creation of the modern Kingdom of Saudi Arabia in 1932 partly in response to the Free Hijazi Party which had formed to resist the Al Saud takeover of the Muslim holy cities of Mecca and Medina.[112] Later attempts to provide organizational leadership came from leftist and (Arab) nationalist groups such as the Movement for Arab Nationalists in Kuwait and the National Union Committee in Bahrain in the 1950s.[113]

Writing in 2012 on the passing of Jassim Buhejji, one of the founding members of the National Union Committee in 1954, the Emirati writer Sultan Sooud Al Qassemi reflected on how the 'non-sectarian, pan-Arab independence movement' whose demands 'included a fully elected parliament, the legalization of workers' unions, and the establishment of a supreme court' in Bahrain:

> …was created in the wake of two significant developments: a strike in 1953 by the Arab employees of Aramco (…) when

many of the company's Bahraini workers returned to share tales of the popular activism that had swept the eastern province of their giant neighbor; and the escalation in 1953–54 of sectarian clashes in Bahrain, which highlighted the need for national unity if independence was to be achieved.[114]

Organized political demands were nevertheless deemed by regimes to pose a threat to their security and stability, whether they came from leftist and nationalist groups in the 1950s and 1960s or, later, from Islamist political movements from the 1970s onwards, as the next chapter analyzes more fully.[115]

Candidates for office found workarounds to the official restrictions, especially during electoral campaigns, and forged informal alliances and hosted meetings to discuss topical issues of the day. Jafar Al-Shayeb, a Saudi writer who was elected to the Qatif Municipal Council in 2005, described how 'Campaign programs were a sort of democratic wedding, with citizens invited to enormous tents to hear speakers invited by candidates discuss issues such as corruption, land distribution, state budgets, wealth distribution, and equal opportunities.'[116] However, Al-Shayeb also listed the electoral and structural factors that constrained the effectiveness of the representatives, such as low turnout and public awareness of their work and the limited authorities granted to them.[117] In one council elected in the March 2005 municipal elections, in Riyadh, it took fifteen months before the members held their first public meeting.[118]

The Saudi academic and women's rights advocate Hatoon Al-Fassi helped women prepare for participation in municipal votes.[119] After women were denied the opportunity to vote and run as candidates in the 2011 round of elections, Al-Fassi called for the creation of female-only councils to parallel the 'formal' male-only ones.[120] Al-Fassi attracted some support from male colleagues for her campaign and female participation was allowed for the first time in December 2015 when twenty-one women were elected. However, gender mixing during the campaign was banned and a new law issued after the results were declared required the council chambers to be completely segregated between male and female areas.[121] Speaking in response to the election of the twenty-one female candidates, Al-Fassi drew attention to the practical difficulties the women had faced in being unable to campaign and reach out to voters, but expressed optimism that

> Now you have women who are in the public eye for the first time, where they have to deal with real issues of their community (…) I believe that these local decisions are very important. Having women could change many discriminatory rules that deal with women's financial status, women's health, women's well-being.[122]

Regimes in the Gulf States also possess the ability to suspend representative institutions should they be perceived to have crossed 'red lines' (themselves not always clearly defined) or threatened to stray into sensitive or contested areas. This has been evident on the three occasions in which elected national assemblies have been suspended altogether, in Bahrain (between 1975 and 2002) and in Kuwait (between 1976 and 1981 and 1986 to 1992). In Bahrain, the Emir, Sheikh Isa bin Salman Al Khalifa, dissolved the National Assembly by decree in August 1975, during the summer recess when many of the MPs were out of the country.[123] This occurred after the success of 'opposition' candidates in securing nearly half of the thirty elected seats in the December 1973 elections prompted a wave of labor agitation in Bahrain which culminated in a series of large-scale strikes in the spring and summer of 1974. In response, the Emir issued a state security decree during the Assembly's summer recess which twenty-nine of the thirty elected MPs subsequently voted against. After another clash when twenty-nine MPs voted not to ratify an extension to an agreement to lease the base of Juffair to the U.S. Navy, the Emir dissolved the National Assembly citing its 'non-cooperative acts.'[124]

The two lengthy suspensions of the National Assembly in Kuwait further illustrate the ability of the executive to shut down parliamentary life if they felt it necessary for (often vague) definitions of national security. The 1976 dissolution took place at a time of regional tension in the aftermath of the start of the civil war in Lebanon the previous year and amid concern in the Kuwaiti leadership over potential overspill of political tension into the large Palestinian community resident in Kuwait. Members of parliament were vocally active at this sensitive time in passing a motion condemning the Syrian intervention in Lebanon and publicly criticizing Saudi 'intervention' in domestic Kuwaiti affairs.[125] However, there were also other moves by members of the National Assembly that seemed to cross the 'red lines' of permissible political activity. MPs voted to pass a law that would have strengthened judicial independence and, undeterred by an Emiri veto of the bill, sought to push it through a second time with a simple parliamentary majority, whereupon the Emir, Sheikh Sabah al-Salim Al Sabah, dissolved the National Assembly.[126] Just as in Bahrain the year before, the dissolution occurred during the summer recess, in August, and was accompanied by the suspension of the constitutional article that covered the National Assembly.[127]

In 1981 the Kuwaiti authorities reinstated the National Assembly—again at a time of regional turmoil after the Iranian revolution and the outbreak of the Iran-Iraq War when it was felt that citizen participation could strengthen regime security—albeit with a redistricting that increased the number of electoral constituencies from ten to twenty-five. Critics of the redistricting focused on the fact that candidates in the twenty-five districts would need fewer votes to secure election to the National Assembly and that 'vote buying' might therefore be facilitated.[128] Five years later, however, parliamentary life was suspended for a second time in July 1986, by Emir Jabir al-Ahmad Al Sabah, as the Kuwaiti leadership once again felt themselves buffeted by political and economic pressures arising from domestic and regional instability. These included the overspill of the Iran-Iraq War through the targeting of Kuwaiti shipping and energy infrastructure, a series of terrorist bombings and attacks on Kuwait which culminated in an assassination attempt on the Emir in May 1985, huge financial losses after the collapse of an illicit stock market (*Suq al-Manakh*) in 1982 which were made more acute by the subsequent sharp decline in oil prices in 1985, and, similar to 1976, attempts by parliamentarians to investigate sensitive issues, this time relating to state-business relations in Kuwait.[129]

A final barrier to (more than a limitation on) the exercise of genuinely autonomous political power is the role of regional influence, especially from Saudi Arabia, as the participatory openings unfolded elsewhere in the Gulf. Saudi pressure was applied on Kuwait at the time of the 1938 Legislative Council, lest the 'experiment' in representative politics, however limited, spark demands from Saudis for a similar body, and was applied again prior to the first dissolution of the National Assembly in 1976, especially after opposition MPs in the Kuwaiti assembly singled out Saudi leaders for criticism.[130] Similarly, in Bahrain, British officials attributed the growth in Saudi influence as one of the factors in the ruling family's shift away from political reform, culminating in the 1975 suspension of the National Assembly, which the Ambassador, Edward Given, suggested 'may be due to the influence of the Saudis, whom I believe greatly disapproved of the Bahrain experiment in democracy.'[131] In 1978, Ivor Lucas, a senior British diplomat who headed the Middle East Department at the Foreign Office (and who would be appointed Ambassador to Oman the following year) opined that 'all the traditional regimes in the Gulf are becoming increasingly dependent on Saudi support and that they must to a greater or lesser extent accept what goes with it.'[132]

Embedded concepts of representation

The parameters of contestation and limitations of participation have meant that none of the representative bodies in GCC states have substantively altered the balance of power away from ruling families in the Gulf. Limitations on the powers granted to representative institutions and their elected members have been a consistent feature of the regional landscape and been reflected in low (and declining) rates of participation.[133] That said, the concept of some form of institutionalized representation has become more deeply embedded in the political landscape and it is harder to imagine its suspension or outright dissolution in the manner of the Bahraini and Kuwaiti assemblies in the 1970s and 1980s, although the Saudi municipal elections, last held in 2015, appear to have been postponed indefinitely. A 'considerable degree of consolidation' has occurred, especially in Kuwait, where 'Elections have become an accepted part of the country's political life.'[134] Elsewhere, the fact that the Qatari leadership belatedly followed through with the elections to two-thirds of its Shura Council in October 2021, after a lengthy delay in finalizing the law governing the electoral and districting process,[135] is indicative of an underlying direction of travel, at least on the surface, even if, in practice, regimes continue to identify new ways to undermine political coordination by, for example, tacitly supporting independent candidacies.[136]

Representative bodies, including those that remain partly or wholly ruler-appointed, also function as a way of involving citizens in the decision-making process more directly, albeit in a carefully controlled manner designed to reinforce rather than challenge the existing balance of political power. The pattern of appointments to these bodies also enables the authorities to maintain a certain degree of social equilibrium in terms of which groups are represented and by whom. This includes the appointment of women not only to normalize the notion that women can and do play an active role in public life but also to counter the difficulties female candidates have faced in winning elections in the Gulf. In December 2018, for example, the UAE government decided that women would comprise half of the forty members of the next Federal National Council, a target made possible by the presence of the twenty appointed members after women won just seven of the twenty elected seats in October 2019.[137] The balancing of political appointees was also evident in the identity of the new members of the Saudi Shura Council announced (by royal decree) in October 2020 as well as the fifteen appointed members of Qatar's Shura Council in 2021.[138]

As the notion of at least some level of political participation has become normalized, lower voter turnouts notwithstanding, so other forms of representation within the existing institutional frameworks have started to increase in prominence. One example is the work of committees within the elected and appointed assemblies which provide opportunities for scrutinizing legislation and expanding input into, if not always influence over, policy outcomes.[139] After the restoration of the National Assembly in Kuwait in 1992, parliamentary committees launched multiple investigations into the events leading up to the Iraqi invasion, including whether the government was responsible for Kuwait's military defeat, the value of arms deals with Western partners, and, most sensitively, allegations of corruption and mismanagement in the Kuwait Investment Office. Looking back a decade later, Andrzej Kapiszewski observed that 'This was the first time in the GCC countries that such people [senior officials, including members of the ruling family] were publicly questioned, strongly criticized, and forced to take responsibility for their actions.'[140]

Another is the longer-standing influence wielded by Chambers of Commerce and other business associations, especially in settings such as Saudi Arabia where more formal avenues of representation are weaker. Elections to Saudi Chambers of Commerce and Industry have taken place nationwide and provided one of the few spaces for electoral contestation, including to women prior to the granting of female suffrage in the 2015 municipal elections.[141] In 2012, a female member of the Jeddah Chamber of Commerce stated, cautiously, that 'Change in my country does not work through protest but through dialogue with the state and the officials. We cannot force change; we can only reach change through working with the government and not against it. We have to lobby on a daily basis to achieve the change.'[142] In such settings where organized parties do not exist and where there is no openly competitive political landscape, professional associations—of jurists, lawyers, and journalists, for example, as well as women's groups and human rights associations—play a role in organizing and representing specific sets of interests and in negotiating for change, which may also explain why such groups and their networks were among the first to be targeted in security crackdowns in the UAE and Bahrain after the Arab Spring.[143]

Professional and business associations can exert influence on decision-making if they act as (often informal) pressure groups that conduct a form of politics away from the spotlight of the electoral cycle. Ian Skeet, a British consultant who worked extensively in Oman in the 1970s and 1980s, observed that the participatory aspect of the Oman Chamber of Commerce and Industry went 'far beyond' those of the State Consultative Council as a 'channel of information and opinion' and its active involvement in the preparation of policy proposals for labor market reforms and private sector job creation.[144]

In Kuwait, the Kuwait Chamber of Commerce and Industry has been powerful historically, including through its members' creation and control of the influential *Al-Qabas* newspaper, and was able to lobby the government for policy responses to issues such as the collapse of the *Suq al-Manakh* exchange in 1982.[145] In Bahrain, too, the business community has organized to defend entrenched interests from political interference or reform, especially in times of domestic unrest when their support has been needed to prop up regime stability. Economic and labor market reforms introduced in 2006 were significantly watered down in 2012 as the embattled Bahraini government sought to secure political support from the business community in the aftermath of the Arab Spring uprising the previous year.[146]

Unresolved push-and-pull

For all the advances in representation described in this chapter, there remains an unresolved tension between the qualified, measured, and controlled top-down approach toward granting political rights and the bottom-up demands for a greater and more meaningful extension of participatory power. Political openings have neither been especially incremental nor particularly successful in expanding or even safeguarding the elected and appointed bodies that have emerged since the 1960s. This reflects the fact that the assemblies that have been created have, from regime perspectives, been intended more to act as pressure valves rather than legislating chambers with power of their own. The friction between the 'push-and-pull' of demanding and conceding political rights has on occasion been most visible in Kuwait and Bahrain given their comparatively greater experience of representative institutions.

The push-and-pull and the gap between expectations and calls for reform came to the surface during the meeting of the Kuwaiti leadership-in-exile in Saudi Arabia in October 1990, and has been described in detail in Chapter 2. A generation later, some of the frustrations with the Kuwaiti concept of representation were later expressed by Ali Al-Rashed, a member of the National Assembly who served briefly as Speaker between December 2012 and June 2013. Speaking in 2008, Al-Rashed argued that 'The government does not know the meaning of democracy because in its view democracy means that the National Assembly approves everything that is presented to it; the government considers any disagreement a lack of cooperation.'[147] By contrast, Badr Al-Nashi, the Secretary General of the (Muslim Brotherhood aligned) Islamic Constitutional Movement between 2003 and 2009, suggested that political participation had yielded positive outcomes as the group widened its focus beyond issues of morality and social reform to encompass debates on educational policy, electoral redistricting, the formation of political parties, and dialogue with non-Islamist groups on judicial reform.[148]

A sense of frustration that the political 'rules of the game' were not only being set by ruling elites but also stacked against them prompted some groups to decide not to enter the game on the regimes' terms and others to withdraw at various junctures from electoral politics. Multiple political societies in Bahrain boycotted the 2002 and 2006 elections to the National Assembly while the 2012 and 2013 elections to Kuwait's National Assembly were also hit by electoral boycotts. Both in Bahrain and Kuwait the decisions by 'established' political groups to engage electorally left them vulnerable to being outflanked by more radical elements especially after the clampdowns that followed the regionwide protests in 2011. The dynamics among opposition figures and groups also crossed boundaries, as they had done throughout modern Gulf history, and the next chapter examines in detail the trajectories of oppositional power.

5

OPPOSITION

The previous chapter examined how representative processes gradually became embedded features in the six Gulf States and analyzed some of the unresolved tensions between top-down approaches to political reform and bottom-up demands for fairer and more equal participation. In this and the next chapter the focus shifts to those instances where groups and individuals refrained from following the 'rules of the game' set down by elites and moved into opposition to ruling families and national projects. These two chapters follow the pattern of previous chapters by focusing on thematic issues and cross-border linkages to draw out the variations in oppositional dynamics and regime responses. This chapter examines the oppositional cross-currents and the heavily transnational impulses that have run through the evolution of ideologies of opposition and connected groups and individuals in the Gulf to contemporaries across the Middle East, North Africa, and in some cases further afield. The following chapter then focuses on the range of regime responses to these manifestations of oppositional activity.

Several key themes run through the two chapters. One is that the causes of oppositional activity span a wide spectrum and can be political, economic, religious, or ideological in character, and another is that networks frequently had a transnational dimension that crossed state borders with ease. These characteristics retained their potency even as political economies in all Gulf States were transformed by the inflows of substantial oil- and gas-based revenues before, during, and after the 1970s. They further counter the notion inherent in much of the early literature of 'rentier state theory' that posited a reasonably direct relationship between economic distribution and political co-optation.[1] This chapter thus builds upon the work of Gwenn Okruhlik in the 1990s and, more recently, that of Jessie Moritz and Jim Krane, which critically re-examines the early conceptual underpinnings of rent-based political economies.[2]

A central point in this chapter is the centrality of cross-border dynamics 'from below' that characterized the emergence and growth of political and opposition movements across the Gulf States both before and after the transition into the oil era. These became manifest at specific times of regionwide action—1938, 1956, and 1963—as well as instances in the 1970s, 1980s, and 1990s as the epicenter of much ideological activity shifted from a focus on pan-Arabism toward Islamism. These ties reflected the intensely transnational links of settlement and exchange that connected the towns and cities of the Gulf with one another and, on both coastlines, with hinterlands such as western India and eastern Africa.[3] These societal linkages provided a powerful—and, to regimes, worrying—antidote to the 'top-down' dynamics of cross-border connections, such as dynastic linkages and political and security coordination among ruling elites, both before and especially after the creation of the Gulf Cooperation Council in 1981.

Oppositional cross-currents

One way in which opposition movements and individuals were able to exert influence on regime elites was through their ability to tap into regional cross-currents that were transnational in nature and had a resonance in the Gulf as much as they did elsewhere in the Middle East. A rich source of circulation of peoples and ideas was the Hajj, which created the conditions for a potent mixing of scholars, merchants, texts, and ideologies each year.[4] Literary circles flourished in Mecca, Medina, and Jeddah in the 1920s and in the pages of the *Sawt al-Hijaz* newspaper.[5] The annual movement of tens of thousands of pilgrims performing Hajj meant that, for many, including British officials in the 1930s, 'the Hijaz was seen as a place where radical ideological sentiments spread like wildfire' across a spectrum from pan-Arab nationalism to pan-Islamism.[6] Participation in the Hajj also contributed to the formation and maintenance of an Islamic consensus, and heightened awareness of belonging to a larger whole.[7] This had been a consistent concern for officialdom since the mid-nineteenth century, especially after the Indian Rebellion of 1857, and persisted into the twentieth century as research by Michael Christopher Low has demonstrated.[8]

In coming decades, as oil revenues began to transform the economic fortunes of the Gulf States, the region experienced waves of strikes between the 1940s and the 1960s, many originating among workers in the oil sector and exhibiting clear ideational and transnational dimensions. Although much of the unrest was about demands for better pay and conditions, there were also linkages to regional events as well as diffusion across national boundaries. Rosie Bsheer has drawn attention to the intensely political cross-currents that characterized Saudi Arabia during the reign of King Saud (1953–64), a period of 'various, and at times competing, progressive politics [which] point to the centrality of leftist movements and ideological struggles in the making of the state.'[9] Other scholars have filled gaps in the historical record by examining 'the role of anti-imperialism and nationalism in opposition to British involvement' in the Trucial States (later the UAE) but also in Bahrain and Kuwait as well as Oman.[10] Such scholarship describes a rich period in Gulf historiography which details the many areas of contestation that accompanied the transition into the oil era and documents a far bumpier process than rentier state theory would admit.[11]

Many of the first documented industrial actions in the Gulf involved workers of the Bahrain Petroleum Company (BAPCO) in 1938, when workers went on strike over recruitment policies, and, on a larger scale, in 1943, over salaries, working hours, and the right to establish an independent labor committee.[12] Initially, BAPCO employed mostly foreign workers—American personnel assisted by Iraqi rig operators and Sikh Indians—and by 1938 local anger at the small number of Bahraini employees as well as discontent with wages and working conditions sparked a strike that halted company operations for two days in November.[13] After the 1938 strike, BAPCO began to replace its workforce with Indian and Iranian laborers.[14] This attempt to reduce the mobilizing power of labor (especially organized labor) by importing foreign workers with fewer political (and, later, linguistic) connections to the domestic setting prefigured the much larger (and regionwide) moves between the 1970s and the 1990s to dilute the Arab workforce by turning to laborers from (multiple) Asian countries as a way of securing a disenfranchised and politically quiescent pool of workers who could be controlled (and deported) with ease should they prove troublesome.[15]

Saudi Arabia also saw significant labor and industrial unrest in the early years of the oil era. Robert Vitalis and others have noted that the first recorded strike in Saudi history took place in 1942 when 2,000 construction workers in Riyadh downed tools to demand a shorter working day, for which their ringleaders were beaten and imprisoned. Three years later, thousands of Saudi oil workers went on strike in July 1945 in protest at their conditions and were joined in their action by 1,700 Italian workers constructing the new refinery at Ras Tanura and 9,000 Arab laborers at Ras Tanura and Dhahran.[16] Employment at 'Saudi Camp' in Dhahran (and the conditions therein) exposed, for the first time, Saudi workers from all areas of the young country to one another as well as to political ideas and ways of organizing. As Saudi historian Madawi Al-Rasheed observed, Aramco 'not only facilitated the emergence of the first wave of Saudi administrators, technocrats, civil servants, and oil millionaires, but also the first political prisoners, dissidents, exiles, and opposition literary figures.'[17] In 1953, Saudi oil workers went on strike again after their demands for an end to segregation, better housing, and higher wages were refused by Aramco and forcefully suppressed by the Saudi state.[18] As much as 90 percent of the Saudi workforce at Aramco failed to report for work at the height of the strike in October 1953 and between 6,000 and 7,000 of Aramco's Saudi workers signed a petition to King Saud which urged him to recognize their demands.[19]

Just as BAPCO, which was Canadian-registered, and Aramco, which was American-owned, were the targets of many of the early strikers, so, too, in Qatar, was the (majority British-owned) Petroleum Development (Qatar)—the forerunner of Qatar Petroleum[20]—a point of disaffection for local workers who accused the company of discriminatory and unfair practices. Many of the early oil strikes were directed against the Western-owned companies, at times with some support from local elites as a way of putting pressure on the companies, and could assume political dimensions. Qatari oil workers laid off in 1942 after Petroleum Development (Qatar) halted wartime operations found jobs elsewhere in the Gulf, including in Sharjah and Kuwait but also with Aramco in Dhahran in Saudi Arabia and BAPCO in Bahrain, where production continued. Qatari workers in Bahrain took part in the strike of 1943 whereupon, one participant recalled, the police 'unceremoniously dumped us in boats and deported us to Qatar.'[21]

Qatari workers were politicized by the experience of their treatment by BAPCO in Bahrain during the 1943 strike, just as, a decade later, Bahrainis who had taken part in the Aramco strike in Saudi Arabia in 1953 returned 'to share tales of the popular activism that had swept the eastern province of their giant neighbor.'[22] The following year, they were among the founders of the National Union Committee as an inclusive, non-sectarian, pan-Arab movement that called for an elected parliament, judicial independence, and the legalization of workers' unions in Bahrain. The National Union Committee, which also went by the Higher Education Committee but was often known simply as 'The Committee' (Al-Hay'eh) by many Bahrainis, emerged after a short yet sharp increase in sectarian tension in September 1953 over the Ashura religious holiday. One of the movement's founders, Jassim Buhejji, received Gamal Abdel Nasser when the Egyptian President made a stopover in Bahrain on his way back from the Bandung Conference of (mostly) newly-independent Asian and

African states in May 1955, whereupon Nasser was 'carried on the shoulders of cheering Bahrainis—all despite the presence of Charles Belgrave, the British advisor to the island's Emir.'[23]

By 1954, Belgrave had been the right-hand man to successive rulers of Bahrain for nearly thirty years since his appointment in 1926 after the Political Resident in the Persian Gulf had recommended that 'Bahrain should not be left without a good Englishman in charge.'[24] Known to Bahrainis simply as 'The Adviser,' Belgrave effectively 'ran Bahrain's government, was the head of its police force and—in the absence of an organized legal code—personally operated its courts.'[25] Belgrave dismissed the National Union Committee and described one of its leaders, Abd al-Rahman Al-Bakir, as 'a fat, unhealthy, light-complexioned man, unreliable and excitable,' and believed that the opposition leaders were opportunistically appealing to the 'illiterate element in the population.'[26] Belgrave shared a sense of entitlement with the Ruler, Sheikh Salman bin Hamad Al Khalifa, encapsulated by an exchange the Ruler in the 1950s had with Bernard Burrows, the Political Resident. Upon hearing that Burrows had deputed a junior colleague to meet with members of the committee leading the demonstrations, Sheikh Salman summoned Burrows and declared that 'I hear that the young men in your Residency are hob-knobbing with my opposition. I won't have it! If you want to know what's going on in my island, you come and ask me!'[27]

Belgrave's dim view of Al-Bakir contrasted with that of British officials in Bahrain who took a more nuanced position that Al-Bakir was a moderating influence in the calls for political evolution on the island. As such, British officials met with reform-minded Bahrainis against the advice (and the wish) of Belgrave, who was employed by the Ruler rather than the British Political Residency.[28] Such a division of opposition into 'moderates' and 'extremists' proved to be another trope of elite circles—whether indigenous or external—that would recur at regular intervals throughout the decades that followed. It relates to a weak-point of opposition movements in the Gulf, namely a tendency to split into factions, which provided opportunities for regimes to selectively co-opt and coerce to widen these fractures, consistent with Ellen Lust-

Okar's observations about structures of contestation arising from their partial inclusion in the political process.[29] When Belgrave was finally relieved of his duties, in 1957, the Foreign Office stated that he had lost the confidence of British officials 'and is regarded as a liability by people in London with interests in the Gulf.'[30]

A final spasm of oil-related opposition took place in 1963, when disturbances among striking offshore and oil terminal workers in Abu Dhabi (which had discovered oil a generation later than Bahrain and Saudi Arabia) caused deep alarm among both British officials, who dispatched a squadron of the Trucial Oman Scouts to secure the oilfields, and the ruling family, as striking workers called for far-reaching political changes in the sheikhdom.[31] Many of the oil workers were nationals of other Arab states who brought with them political ideologies, to the alarm of British authorities and rulers alike.[32] The same year also saw significant protests in Qatar which assumed a political dimension as pan-Arabists engaged in demonstrations and formed a National Unity Front which 'demanded limitations on the power of the ruling Al Thani family, the establishment of a state budget and a representative council.'[33] As in Abu Dhabi, the unrest in Qatar alarmed British officials who authorized the Political Resident (in Bahrain) to intervene if necessary to secure British interests and placed a battalion of the Parachute Regiment on standby.[34]

The history of early activism across all the Gulf States, but especially in Abu Dhabi and Qatar which later was largely written out of historical accounts of state development, illustrates that entities which today are seen as relatively depoliticized were not always so. As Farah Al-Nakib observes, the political activism of the 1950s spanned the entire region as 'oil worker strikes, Arab nationalist demonstrations, and anti-British protests and boycotts unleashed a wave of political agitation never seen before, or since, on the streets and in the markets of Gulf cities.'[35]

Transnational and pan-regional linkages

Labor activism and other forms of political mobilization also responded to international developments, especially during the period of regional turbulence in the wider Middle East that spanned the Suez Crisis and the Arab-Israeli wars of 1948, 1956, 1967, and 1973. The fusion of regional issues with domestic politics gave opposition movements a potency especially during the turbulent mid-century decades. As Fred Halliday observed in his study of the Middle East in international relations, 'the history of the spread of political ideas in the Middle East—of nationalism, socialism, Marxism, Islamism—has been a trans-national one.'[36] Recent scholarship on the Gulf has rightly situated the Arabian Peninsula within a much broader geographical framework connected by intellectual and commercial currents to communities which span the Red Sea and much of the western Indian Ocean littoral.[37] Moreover, the port towns and littoral communities on both the Arab and the Persian coastlines of the Gulf historically had more connections with each other, through trade and migration, than they did with towns in the interior, such as Teheran or Riyadh, with further links to the east coast of Africa and the west coast of India.[38]

Ideas and ideologies not only crossed political boundaries but also made regimes and governments vulnerable to external events beyond their borders and their capacity to control. Early examples of this came in the 1920s when students in Kuwait protested at the rise in Jewish immigration to mandate-era Palestine in some of the first recorded political demonstrations in the Gulf.[39] In Dubai in 1923, '[Arab] nationalist and literary celebrations, held by members of the ruling family and the wealthy merchants' took place on the occasion of the visit to the sheikhdom of a prominent Arab nationalist from Tunisia, Tha'alibi, who had been introduced to Rashid bin Mani, later the head of the Dubai reform movement in 1938, in Bombay.[40] In 1929, students at two boys' schools in Bahrain joined their teachers in a strike called by their Syrian headmaster in protest at British policies and took part in days of demonstrations.[41]

The first generation of Arab nationalists in Kuwait in the 1930s were heavily influenced by intellectual and political connections in neighboring Iraq, an epicenter of early pan-Arabism, and received sympathetic coverage and support in Iraqi media for their endeavors.[42] Other links were forged through education; seven Kuwaitis were awarded scholarships to study in Iraq in 1924, and that number included Khalid bin Sulaiman Al-Adsani who later played a major role in the short-lived Legislative Council of 1938 as its Secretary.[43] Many of those involved in the Legislative Council went into exile in Iraq, and also in India, after its forced dissolution in December 1938.[44] A Palestinian educational mission arrived in Kuwait in 1936 and played an additional significant role in advancing and expanding the Kuwaiti educational system hitherto dominated by the several schools established by merchant families in the 1910s and 1920s.[45]

Also significant was the transregional network of Al-Falah Schools established by the Jeddah merchant Mohammed Ali Alireza after 1905, with the initial school in Jeddah followed by later ones in Mecca (1912), Dubai (1928), Bahrain (1930), and Bombay (1931), with many of the early teachers and teaching materials coming from Egypt.[46] Alireza had made the money which he used to finance the schools from business operations out of Bombay with links to Gulf markets in Dubai, Kuwait, and Bahrain.[47] Muhammad Morsy Abdullah, an early historian of the UAE, noted that the Al-Falah School in Dubai was an epicenter for the spread of pan-Arab sentiments from Iraq (from where many of the teachers hailed), and that in about 1930 a boy scout troop was established at the school which 'paraded frequently in the narrow streets of the town, carrying flags and chanting Arab nationalist songs, applauded by their parents and citizens.'[48] In Saudi Arabia, teachers from Palestine, Syria, and Lebanon 'spread leftist and pan-Arab ideas' in the 1940s and 1950s in schools established by Aramco, some of whose students later took part in demonstrations.[49]

Saudi employees at Aramco installations in the Eastern Province city of Dammam organized protests in 1953, and again in 1955 and 1956, and petitioned King Saud to seek an end to Saudi military cooperation with the United States.[50] The outbreak of the Six-Day War in June 1967 saw 'Arab mobs' attack the American Camp in Aramco's enclave, stone cars, and target the home of Aramco's President, Tom Barger.[51] Worryingly (from the perspective of the Saudi authorities), the 1953 strike was led by a labor committee of seven Saudis who had studied abroad in Lebanon and in the U.S.[52] Large crowds greeted Nasser when he visited Riyadh and Dhahran in 1956 and gave him 'a hero's welcome' while 'virtually ignoring King Saud.'[53] Workers at Kuwait's main oil port of Ahmadi physically disrupted the transportation of oil and the loading of British and French tankers during the war over Suez in 1956, and significant protests against British involvement at Suez also took place in Doha, where disgruntled oil workers made common cause with Arab nationalists and dissident members of the ruling family.[54] The protests in Abu Dhabi and Qatar in 1963 took place against the backdrop of Ba'athist coups in Iraq in February and Syria in March. Kuwaiti labor unions called a general strike during the Six-Day War in 1967 and orchestrated a three-day suspension of oil exports during the Yom Kippur War in October 1973.[55]

After the creation of the State of Israel in 1948 and the Arab-Israeli wars that followed, tens of thousands of Palestinians migrated to the Gulf States, with two notable spikes in 1948 and 1967. The flow of Palestinian refugees was in part a function of labor supply and demand as Palestinians possessed the educational and professional skills to staff the new bureaucracies in the rapidly-developing Gulf oil states. This was particularly significant in health and education as Palestinians and other Arab expatriates plugged shortfalls in the pool of skilled indigenous manpower to meet the transformative needs of rapid modernization.[56] In Kuwait, for example, the number of Palestinian and Jordanian workers rose from 14,000 in 1957 to 78,000 by 1965—a figure that, by comparison, would have exceeded the entire population of the sheikhdom in 1938.[57] A second wave of Palestinian migrants arrived after the 1967 Six-Day War, including the future leader of Hamas, Khaled Mishaal, whose family settled in Kuwait where he first became active in Palestinian politics.[58]

The influx of Palestinians, Egyptians, Syrians, Jordanians, and Yemenis also acted as a transmitter of ideological and pan-Arab sentiments that fused local and regional political currents. Many of the first generation of Palestinians who arrived in Kuwait after 1948 were members of the intelligentsia, and they played an important role in staffing academic and professional positions as

Kuwaiti institutions developed. The General Union of Palestinian Students was active in Kuwaiti student politics, especially after the establishment of Kuwait University in 1966, and in the 1970s the University was the setting for some of the first duels between Fatah—which had been founded in Kuwait by Yasser Arafat in 1959—and the Palestinian Islamist movement led by Khaled Mishaal.[59] Also influenced by regional currents were the first generation of students from the Gulf, especially from Kuwait, Bahrain, and the Trucial States, who pursued higher education at Arab centers of learning across the Middle East.[60] Demands for political reform in Bahrain in the 1950s, for example, were led by students—female as well as male—returning from study in Baghdad, Beirut, Cairo, and also Kuwait.[61]

In a description of the Trucial States, which is applicable to the other coastal sheikhdoms (Kuwait, Bahrain, Qatar, and Oman) in the mid-twentieth century as well, Kristi Barnwell observed that

> As men from the Trucial States left to work in oil fields in such places as Bahrain, Iraq, and Saudi Arabia, they would eventually come into contact with other Arabs who were well versed in anti-imperialist and nationalist ideologies. Similarly, as the Trucial States began to require outside expertise in the areas of education, health care, and construction, Arabs from Egypt, Syria, Palestine, and elsewhere would take up jobs in the Trucial States and bring with them their perspectives on Britain's involvement in the region.[62]

Illustrative of this trend, Ahmad Al-Khatib, who was to become one of the most significant political figures in Kuwait in the second half of the twentieth century, left for Lebanon to study at the International College and then the American University of Beirut in 1942 where he was introduced to Arab nationalist leaders and thinkers from Palestine (George Habash) and Syria (Hani Al-Hindi), with whom he later co-founded the Movement of Arab Nationalists (MAN). A medical student who became the first physician in Kuwait, Al-Khatib helped treat patients in the Palestinian refugee camps that were established in Lebanon after the 1948 Nakba; as Abdel Razzaq Takriti has observed, this was a formative experience in Al-Khatib's life:

As he was witnessing the tragedies around him, Al-Khatib shared his own small income with his two Palestinian classmates, and the bonds of their friendship grew. It was in this context that they began to think of responding to the 1948 war, convinced that it required the formation of an organized group.[63]

In 1949, while still in Lebanon, Al-Khatib co-founded The Arab Nationalist Youth, which 'became the nucleus out of which the MAN emerged' in Kuwait in 1958 and, after he returned to Kuwait in 1954, established clubs, such as the Nationalist Cultural Club, cultural committees, and a magazine, *al-Imam* ('Conviction'), forming an 'infrastructure for intellectual dissemination and political organization.'[64] Al-Khatib benefited from, and worked closely with, members of Kuwait's merchant community, including those who had been at the forefront of the 1938 reform movement discussed in Chapter 4, as well as more reform-minded members of the ruling family, including the Chairman of the short-lived 1938 Legislative Council, Sheikh Abdullah al-Salim Al Sabah, who succeeded as Ruler of Kuwait in 1950. Such connections became evident after Kuwait became an independent state in 1961 when Al-Khatib was elected the Vice-Chair of the Constituent Assembly alongside its Chair, 'Abd al-Latif Al-Ghanim, scion of one of Kuwait's oldest and most prestigious merchant families and a member of the 1938 Council who had spent more than four years in prison after its forced dissolution a generation earlier.[65]

Pan-Arabism ascendant

Cosmopolitan merchant elites in Kuwait, Bahrain, and Dubai were at the forefront in developing local support for pan-Islamic and Arab nationalist movements in part through their links with peoples and ideas that included networks in India as well as in the rest of the Arab world.[66] As the Kuwaiti historian Abdulrahman Alebrahim has observed, the 'historical links between emirates, states, and trading ports' are critical nodes of inquiry, albeit ones that have frequently been overlooked in the literature.[67] In the period before the opening of the first Arabic printing press in the Gulf, the Dubai merchants imported Arab books and nationalist magazines from Cairo for onward transmission to subscribers across the Gulf, while Kuwaiti merchants were strongly influenced by political and intellectual developments in late-nineteenth and early-twentieth century India.[68]

The transnational connections among the circles of regional intelligentsia were especially strong in Bahrain where a Literary Club, established on the island of Muharraq around 1919, 'began hosting icons of the Al-Nahda literary renaissance during their visits to Bahrain,' with the ideas (and *Al-Manar* journal) of Rashid Rida, the Lebanon-born, Cairo-based Islamic reformer, particularly influential in 'creating a transnational network of followers and participants' that connected Bahrain to the more-established centers of intellectual and political activity in the Arab world.[69] The proliferation of literary, cultural, and sports clubs and professional associations in Manama and neighboring Muharraq 'played a crucial role in the articulation and circulation of political opinions' in Bahrain and 'raised the banner of Arabism.'[70] The members of clubs such as *Nadi Al-'Urubah* ('The Arab Club') and *Nadi Al-Bahrayn* ('The Bahrain Club') also played key roles in the creation of independent media such as *Sawt Al-Bahrain* ('The Voice of Bahrain').[71]

Pan-Arabism was particularly strong in Kuwait and Bahrain and gathered momentum following the Suez Crisis. The Egyptian government assisted Kuwaiti authorities as they expanded the system of public education in the sheikhdom and by 1956, the year of Suez, Egyptians accounted for forty-four of the sixty-four secondary school teachers at boys' schools in the country.[72] Kuwaiti historian Talal Al-Rashoud has noted of the Department of Education during this period that its 'director, Abdulaziz Husain, was an Egyptian-educated Kuwaiti and an ardent Nasserist,' and that 'Kuwait's 1956 national curriculum made the fostering of Arab national awareness a primary goal of education' not only in Kuwait but also in other sheikhdoms, such as Sharjah, which were in receipt of Kuwaiti educational assistance.[73] Support for Arabism was not confined to opposition movements and became enshrined in aspects of foreign policy. After Kuwaiti independence in 1961, its educational and developmental support was institutionalized in a Permanent Committee for Gulf Assistance overseen by the Minister of Information (and future Emir), Sheikh Sabah al-Ahmad Al Sabah. Sheikh Sabah began his forty-year stint as Foreign Minister in 1963 and in 1966 the Ministry of Foreign Affairs assumed responsibility for an expanded General Authority for the Arabian South and the Gulf.[74]

Suez finally claimed the resignation of the Emir of Bahrain's previously-noted British advisor, Belgrave, in 1957, and followed a celebrated incident the previous year when thousands of Bahraini protestors blocked the path of a vehicle carrying the British Foreign Secretary, Selwyn Lloyd, across the causeway from the island of Muharraq to the capital, Manama, chanting 'Selwyn go home' as they did so.[75] In Saudi Arabia, anger over Suez led King Saud to implement an oil embargo for the first time as he ordered Aramco to suspend oil exports to Britain and France, leading to petrol rationing in both countries and foreshadowing the larger and far more impactful Arab oil embargo initiated by Saud's brother and successor, King Faisal, against select Western states in 1973.[76] The Saudi leadership (under Faisal) also joined Kuwait, Iraq, and Algeria in suspending oil shipments to the U.S. and Britain during the 1967 Arab-Israeli war, although this 'embargo' had a minimal impact because the U.S. was still largely self-sufficient in oil and not yet heavily reliant on imported supplies, as it would be just six years later.[77]

Pan-Arab movements posed a threat to ruling elites in myriad ways that relate to the issues already examined in this chapter, not least in their ability to imagine and project a different political future than that presented by the status quo, and in their fusion of local and regional drivers of mobilization. Many of the first waves of returning students and incoming Arab workers raised awareness of the ideologies they brought with them. Palestinian and Yemeni workers spread 'revolutionary ideas' at Aramco camps in Dhahran against the backdrop of the regional pan-Arab ascendancy in the 1950s.[78] So, too, on Saudi Arabia's western coastline, did the Hijazi intelligentsia who returned to Saudi Arabia in the 1930s and 1940s after study in Egypt and the Levant and took jobs in nascent state institutions, the media, and the oil and education sectors.[79] Elsewhere, Iraqis working in Kuwait in the 1960s and early 1970s tried to recruit Kuwaitis to join the Ba'ath Party, while the 1971 elections for the National Assembly returned fifteen MPs who either were members of or considered sympathetic to the Movement of Arab Nationalists.[80]

Transnational opposition in action—the Popular Front for the Liberation of Oman and the Arabian Gulf

Before the remainder of this chapter explores the shift from Arabism to Islamism as the center of oppositional gravity in the final third of the twentieth century, this section focuses on the Popular Front for the Liberation of the Occupied Arabian Gulf (PFLOAG) in the 1960s and 1970s.[81] The PFLOAG emerged from the Movement of Arab Nationalists in 1968 and became an epicenter for political resistance from across the Gulf until it too split into factions in 1974 and faded into obscurity. Britain's withdrawal from Aden in 1967 and the establishment of the (Marxist) People's Democratic Republic of Yemen (PDRY) facilitated and accelerated the radicalization of elements of the Arab nationalist movements in the Gulf and their mobilization around a more openly ideological banner. For several years, PFLOAG posed a sustained challenge both to the British, as they prepared to withdraw from the Gulf, and to the circles of ruling families and associated elites as they navigated the political turbulence of the decolonization era.[82] Both the Movement of Arab Nationalists and the Dhofar Liberation Front, which also evolved into PFLOAG, labeled the attempts which began in 1968 to form a nine-member Union of Arab Emirates (which, minus Bahrain and Qatar, became the UAE in 1971) as 'a false federation which serves neo-imperialist plans.'[83]

From its inception, PFLOAG drew on transnational political and financial support as well as a cross-regional mobilizational reach, which made it an especial threat to the conservative ruling regimes in the Gulf as they emerged from the umbrella of British protection between 1968 and 1971. Aden provided PFLOAG with a base and funding as the organization subsumed the Dhofar Liberation Front (formed in the Omani governorate of Dhofar across the border from South Yemen in 1964) and exerted greater and far more direct political and military influence over the rebellion in Dhofar against the Omani government which began in 1965.[84] Ideological and material support for PFLOAG also came from the Soviet Union and China and the Ba'athist regime in Iraq, while elsewhere in Dhofar support for the separatist rebels came from the Yemeni Socialist Party across the border in PDRY.[85]

The mobilization over Dhofar is a case study that illustrates the intensely strong connections, both practical and ideational, among activists across the Arabian Peninsula in support of a common regional cause. Recruits for PFLOAG came from Kuwait, Qatar, and the Trucial States in addition to Oman and Bahrain, and Kuwait and Dubai became particularly significant centers of activism and political activity.[86] Young men from the easternmost Yemeni governorate of Al-Mahra, which borders Dhofar and has many cross-border tribal, social, and cultural links, embraced Marxist ideals while living in Kuwait in the 1960s and some returned home to join revolutionary groups including PFLOAG.[87] In 1964, 140 Dhofari men traveled to Basra from across the Gulf States to participate in guerilla warfare training overseen by members of Iraqi military intelligence, after which they became the military core of the newly-created Dhofar Liberation Front, the precursor to PFLOAG.[88] The Ba'athist regime in Iraq supported PFLOAG until its defeat in Oman in 1975, and by the early 1980s the remnants of PFLOAG consisted only of a tiny group of exiles based in Muammar Qaddafi's Libya.[89]

Political and economic conditions in Dhofar (and the rest of Oman) in the 1960s created a receptive base for the ideological messaging of PFLOAG and other revolutionary movements. The lack of economic development and opportunities in Imamate Oman in the mid-twentieth century meant that many Omanis left in search of work elsewhere, where they often performed the types of unskilled and menial jobs later filled by South Asian workers.[90] Flows of migrant labor took place within the Gulf as workers from comparatively less developed countries moved to Kuwait and Bahrain in large numbers that set them apart from the later nationalization of labor markets for citizens. Men from

Dhofar moved to other Gulf States in the 1950s and 1960s and many found jobs in security roles as well as in the police and armed forces in Qatar, Bahrain, Saudi Arabia, Kuwait, and Sharjah where 'they were lifted by the rising tide of pan-Arabism and "warmed up" by the Suez events,' after which they began to form organized groups.[91]

Writing in his classic 1974 account, *Arabia without Sultans*, Fred Halliday noted that 'the dominant political experience of many Dhofaris had been their period as *émigré* workers in the Gulf.'[92] As Dale Eickelman observed, 'even when not directly involved in overt political actions' in their host countries, the Omani emigrants in the 1950s and 1960s:

> ... became aware of political movements elsewhere in the Arab world and of the open attitude toward development of the rulers of some neighboring states. The large number of these emigrants, some of whom were able to return periodically to their villages in Oman, accelerated the transformation in popular conceptions of what a just ruler should do.[93]

Up to 50,000 Omanis were employed in the other Gulf States (excluding Saudi Arabia) by the 1960s and the rate of emigration accelerated with the start of the Jabal Akhdar war in the interior of Oman in 1954, which also served as a mobilizing tool of pan-Arabism in opposition to British-supported rule.[94] Nearly 20,000 Omanis worked in Kuwait in 1965 and by 1971 the 10,000 Omanis in Bahrain constituted 28 percent of Bahrain's expatriate workforce. Even four years later, after the pace of economic and social development in Oman had started to accelerate under Sultan Qaboos, nearly one-third of the overall Omani labor force was still employed abroad.[95] Among the many who left Dhofar in this period was a teenage Yusuf bin Alawi bin Abdullah who traveled to Kuwait to complete his education and then, inspired by Nasser's pan-Arabist radio broadcasts, joined the Dhofar Liberation Front and spent the 1960s in Iraq, Syria, and Egypt, where he became the DLF representative in Cairo.[96] When the majority of the DLF was subsumed into PFLOAG in 1968, bin Alawi formed a breakaway moderate faction and later worked with Oman's new Sultan, Qaboos bin Said Al Said, paving the way for bin Alawi's political rehabilitation and decades-long spell as Oman's Minister Responsible for Foreign Affairs until he retired in August 2020.[97]

Two additional points of significance arise from the experience of Oman and Dhofar. The first is that, in Oman, political opponents of the regime, such as bin Alawi, were later rehabilitated and reintegrated into society. Sir Donald Hawley, British Ambassador to Oman between 1971 and 1975, during the first years of Qaboos's rule, noted the significance of the appointment of 'former rebels' to senior government posts.[98] One of Hawley's successors in Muscat, during the Gulf War in 1991, recollected that he had met Sultan Qaboos's 'right-hand man' in the 1960s when the former was an Assistant Political Officer in Dubai, and the latter was there in exile.[99] Something similar was observable in Qatar as well, as close relatives of several of the leaders of the 1963 protests became extremely prominent in state institutions under the leadership of Sheikh Hamad bin Khalifa Al Thani in the 1990s and 2000s. Their experience differed greatly from the lengthy prison sentences meted out to later generations of political activists in Gulf States, especially in Bahrain, Saudi Arabia, and the UAE.

The second point of significance, which builds upon the earlier sections on pan-Arabism in the Gulf, is that Kuwait became a haven for political dissidents from neighboring states in the 1960s and 1970s as opposition figures from Bahrain, Saudi Arabia, and Oman all sought refuge there.[100] The fact that Kuwait provided financial aid to, and was the only Gulf state to retain air links with, PDRY after 1967 caused tension with Saudi leaders, who felt that Kuwait was too close to unfriendly regimes, and also with Oman, which expelled Kuwait's attaché from Muscat in 1974.[101] Kuwaiti officials later resisted Saudi attempts to take measures to rein in 'subversive' acts by dissidents. Kuwait was also the only Gulf country not to sign a bilateral security agreement with the Kingdom in the early 1980s and blocked a GCC initiative in 1982 to create a unified security pact.[102]

Arabism to Islamism

The Arabian Peninsula is the historic 'cradle of Islam' and the ruling regimes in all six of the Gulf States draw legitimacy from Islam as a basis for law and aspects of governance. Ibn Saud used the religious title of Imam for two decades after he reconquered Riyadh for the Al Saud in 1902, but in 1921 he assumed the secular title of Sultan and, after the conquest of Hijaz in 1925, that of King. Ibn Saud used religion as a powerful tool for securing political control and territorial expansion as he conquered the territories that became the Kingdom of Saudi Arabia in 1932.[103] After the crushing of the *Ikhwan* as a rival power base in 1929 and especially after the transition to an oil economy, Ibn Saud ensured that changes occurred in consultation with (and with the consent of) the *ulama*.[104] While regime survival across the Arabian Peninsula was rooted in the exercise of political power, rather than religious authority, the former could be threatened if the latter was seriously contested. As Fred Halliday observed in a valedictory lecture in 2009 that looked back on his academic career, the category 'Islam' by itself lacks explanatory meaning in the absence of analysis of the ways religion is interpreted, used, and adapted, by whom and to what end.[105]

An illustration of how tightly Islam was woven into the fabric of state and society in the region was given by Jamal Khashoggi, the Saudi journalist whose brutal murder by agents of the Saudi state in 2018 shocked the world. Writing in 2004, Khashoggi recalled how, in the 1930s, Ibn Saud rejected a request by Hassan al-Banna, the founder of the Muslim Brotherhood, to establish a branch in the newly-unified Saudi Arabia, and declared that 'The entire Kingdom is a branch for the Brotherhood and all Saudis are Muslim brothers.'[106] This underscored the fact that while Saudi Arabia and the other Gulf States were rooted firmly in religious values it was the expectation of rulers that political authority rested with them. On occasions when religion and politics clashed, it was the latter which prevailed in instances such as when Ibn Saud's forces took on and decisively defeated the religious-tribal *Ikhwan* at the Battle of Sabilah in 1929.[107] Ibn Saud was, nevertheless, careful to reintegrate and co-opt the defeated *Ikhwan* into Saudi state institutions, including (and especially) the National Guard as they emerged in and after the 1930s.[108]

Multiple reasons account for the fading of pan-Arabism and its replacement as a mobilizing force by various strands of political Islamism. These include the eclipse of Nasserism, following Egypt's resounding defeat in the Six-Day War with Israel in June 1967, and tacit decisions by ruling elites in the Gulf to support Islamist groups, in part to counter and weaken the political influence of organized Arab nationalism.[109] In Kuwait, for example, Arab nationalist control over labor and educational unions weakened as pro- and anti-Nasser factions emerged after 1967, and many of their strongholds were banned by the government after they protested the decision to suspend the National Assembly in 1976. Three years later, candidates affiliated with the Muslim Brotherhood won the student elections at Kuwait University for the first time, and turned the powerful National Union of Kuwaiti Students into a bastion of Islamist control.[110] The redistricting of electoral constituencies ahead of the restoration of the National Assembly in 1981 also worked to the benefit of Islamist candidates who subsequently entered parliament for the first time.[111]

Other reasons also accounted for, and facilitated, the growth of Islamism as a set of political ideologies in the Gulf, as elsewhere in the Arab and Islamic world, where religious principles were fused into every aspect of life.[112] One was transnational and another was more material in nature. While pan-Arabism had in part spread through the exchange of ideas and encounters between citizens and residents in the Gulf and other Arab states in the early twentieth century, members of the Muslim Brotherhood who fled political crackdowns in Egypt and Syria found refuge and employment in the Gulf in the 1950s and 1960s. Two notable waves of persecution of the Muslim Brotherhood in Egypt occurred in 1954, after an attempt on the life of President Gamal Abdel Nasser, and a decade later, in 1965. Thousands of members were imprisoned, others were executed, and many fled and found refuge in the Gulf States.[113] Arrivals in the Gulf included Yusuf al-Qaradawi, the Egyptian-born cleric and 'spiritual leader' of the Muslim Brotherhood whose six-decade-long presence in Qatar, until his death in September 2022, later caused controversy.[114]

Many of the *émigrés* were skilled professionals and formed the nucleus of the generation of civil servants who staffed the bureaucracies which emerged in the oil-era period of institution- and state-building in the 1960s and 1970s. This trend was pronounced in the education and judicial sectors in Saudi Arabia, Qatar, and the UAE, in which many of the new arrivals found employment.[115] The Saudi government never recognized the Brotherhood, but many of its members took jobs in state entities in the 1970s, splitting into factions which followed the writing of Sayyid Qutb or Hassan al-Banna, and coexisting alongside other Islamist movements such as the Salafi group.[116] In Qatar, al-Qaradawi established and led the College of Sharia at Qatar University while other scholars with ties to the Muslim Brotherhood took up positions in the Ministry of Education with oversight over schools' curricula and textbooks.[117] A similar trajectory was evident in the UAE, the major difference being that the Brotherhood-aligned officials who assumed senior positions were Emirati citizens rather than expatriate residents, as they were in Qatar. An Emirati offshoot of the Brotherhood (*Jam'iat al-Islah wa-l-Tawjih al-Ijtima'i*, the Reform and Counselling Association), formed in 1974, and members held several Cabinet positions in the 1970s, including Minister of Education and Minister of Justice and Islamic Affairs.[118]

Beyond the Muslim Brotherhood, Islamists primarily from South Asia played an instrumental role in the creation of the Islamic University of Medina, which opened in 1961 and became a central part of what Michael Farquhar has labeled a 'transnational religious economy consisting of flows—both within and across national borders—of material capital, spiritual capital, and religious migrants.'[119] (Juhayman Al-Utaybi, the ringleader of the seizure of the Grand Mosque in Mecca by Islamic militants in 1979, studied at the Islamic University of Medina and, like numerous other participants in the siege and to the consternation of the Saudi authorities, had served in the National Guard.[120]) In establishing an Islamic University, one of the aims of the Saudi state was precisely to 'counter the transnational extension of leftist republican projects by advancing a competing program grounded in claims to [the] historical and religious authenticity' of its Saudi-Wahhabi backers.[121] The 1970s additionally saw King Faisal create a series of pan-Islamic organizations, including the Muslim World League, in a bid to reclaim for Saudi Arabia the mantle of religious authority that groups such as the Muslim Brotherhood appeared to challenge.[122] Islamists—Shia as well as Sunni—across the region formed transnational networks of their own in the 1970s and 1980s which included *émigrés* from political repression and conflict in Iraq and Iran, with a notable focus on links that connected groups and individuals in Saudi Arabia, Kuwait, and Bahrain.[123]

Material reactions to the rapid modernization of Gulf States' societies and disquiet over the pace and direction of change in the 1970s also contributed to a growing backlash among more conservative groups. The fact that opposition, expressed this time in Islamist terms, emerged at a time of unprecedented accumulation of wealth as oil revenues soared after the Arab oil embargo is an important corrective to rentier state theory which, as Pascal Ménoret observes, ought to 'have made it possible for the state to buy off any budding revolt and to trade social prosperity for the tranquility of the royal family.'[124] Especially (but not only) in Saudi Arabia, many individual and collective responses to the socio-economic transformation focused on a re-centering around religion and a growing willingness to react politically. Social and political dissent, expressed in religious terms, also assumed a tribal dimension in many instances, such as in Saudi Arabia in the 1970s and Kuwait in the 2000s, and gave a voice to groups which perceived themselves to be in disfavor with official policies and decisions.[125] The assassination of King Faisal in March 1975 and the seizure of the Grand Mosque in Mecca by Islamist extremists in November 1979 were two of the most violent expressions of emerging opposition to Al Saud rule.[126]

By 1979, which also saw the toppling of the Shah of Iran and his replacement by a revolutionary theocratic regime as well as sustained protests in the Eastern Province of Saudi Arabia, Islamism superseded pan-Arabism as the main perceived source of threat to the political status quo in the Gulf.[127] Fouad Ibrahim, a political activist who played a significant role in mobilizing Saudi Shia communities, observed that while it had been pan-Arabism that had attracted many Saudis, especially in the oil sector, in the 1950s, by 1979 it was Islam to which they turned in opposition to state policies.[128] While couched in religious rather than nationalist terms, many of the underlying causes of oppositional politics in the 1970s and 1980s were rooted in perceived and actual cases of discrimination, marginalization, and unequal access to state resources, as in the protests in the Eastern Province in late 1979.[129] The ideological challenge to regime security from the politicization of Islam took Saudi officials largely by surprise, just as they had initially misread the Islamic nature of the revolution in Iran, with Crown Prince Fahd stating in January 1980 that 'the new regime in Iran is working under the banner of Islam, which is our motto in Saudi Arabia.'[130]

The early 1980s witnessed a spate of incidents which put ruling elites on notice that domestic and regional developments could come together to pose a threat to regime security and regional stability. As the struggle for control of post-Shah Iran swung in favor of Ayatollah Khomeini, the new regime quickly sought to export its brand of revolutionary political Islam and foment unrest in regional Arab states.[131] Iranian state radio announced in January 1980 a plan to create a force to export the revolution and the following month broadcast a call for revolt against the Saudi royal family.[132] In late 1981, an Iranian-linked group, the Islamic Front for the Liberation of Bahrain, was accused of plotting a failed coup to overthrow the Al Khalifa ruling family.[133] A series of terror attacks and mass-casualty bombings occurred in Kuwait, which also came under missile fire during the early stages of the Iran-Iraq War, culminating in an attempt to assassinate the Emir in May 1985.[134] The aftermath of the attack on the Emir saw the purging of Kuwaiti Shia from the military and security forces, a highly-charged political atmosphere in the National Assembly which had been elected earlier that year, and its dissolution on security grounds by the Emir in 1986.[135]

Islamist groups appropriated language and terms to fit the domestic context within which they operated, especially in the specific circumstances of Saudi Arabia. As Madawi Al-Rasheed observed in 1996, for the Al Saud 'to use Islam to legitimize a political system is to invite opposition groups to debate the degree to which Islam has been incorporated in politics.'[136] One group which emerged was the *Sahwa* ('Awakening') movement led by prominent Sunni clerics such as Salman Al-Awdah who functioned as 'the figureheads of underground networks comprised of academic and professional elites.'[137] The *Sahwa* emerged as a mix of Muslim Brotherhood ideology and Saudi Wahhabism and did not adopt a rejectionist attitude toward the Al Saud, unlike the militants who seized the Grand Mosque in 1979.[138] The movement gained popularity in the 1980s, especially on university campuses and in intellectual circles in Saudi Arabia, and moved into open political opposition after the Iraqi invasion of Kuwait in 1990 when Al-Awdah and other clerics associated with the *Sahwa* refused to support the stationing of U.S. and coalition forces in the Kingdom and vocally criticized those 'state clerics' who provided religious cover for King Fahd's decision.[139]

The diversity of Saudi Islamist groups and the fact that they were rooting their demands for greater involvement in a more transparent decision-making process in Islamic concepts posed a challenge to the religious and political authority claimed by the Al Saud.[140] In petitioning for political reform, Abdullah Al-Hamid, one of the co-founders of the Committee for the Defense of Legitimate Rights (CDLR) in the 1990s, and, later, the Saudi Civil and Political Rights Association (ACPRA) in the 2000s, emphasized the centrality of the principle of consultation, as laid down in the Quran, as he stated that 'Shura cannot be achieved in a practical sense until the following conditions are met: a nation of institutions and of constitutionality.'[141]

Formed after the ferment of the Gulf War and the petitions which followed, the CDLR and later the ACPRA framed their demands in a 'language of rights' based on the interpretation of Islamic texts and terms.[142] This made their ideological, as well as theological, challenge the more potent even if they did not call into question the political legitimacy of existing regimes but merely called for reforms. As Al-Rasheed observes of Al-Hamid, who spent much of the last two decades of his life in prison prior to his death in detention in 2020, what made him such a (perceived) threat to the Saudi political elite was the way in which he 'framed rights in a religious language rather than [as] imported concepts' and 'fused tradition with new meanings' as when he 'proved that the Islamic concept of *rahat*, the peaceful crowd which assembles in the public sphere demanding rights and exposing injustice, is a central right in Islam.'[143] Another regional commentator, Fatma Al-Sayegh, noted that disquiet at the retention of Western forces after 1990 was a spur to 'organized Islamist criticisms of the political systems' in the UAE and other Gulf States.[144]

Calls for political openings in other Gulf States in the 1990s were also made within the framework of Islam, including in Qatar and Bahrain.[145] In Kuwait, an 'Islamic revival' had taken shape in the 1980s, with the entry of Muslim Brotherhood-affiliated and other Islamists into National Assembly politics, and the process gathered pace after the Iraqi invasion in 1990.[146] Many Kuwaiti Salafi relocated to Saudi Arabia, where they drew upon personal and kinship networks to integrate into Saudi Salafi circles and participate in the *Sahwa* movement as it engaged in 'debates over the obedience to the ruler and the necessity to enact political reforms' both in Saudi Arabia and, when they returned home after liberation in 1991, in Kuwait.[147] Associational and voluntary networks, many run by Islamist organizations, Shia as well as Sunni, played important coordinating roles in the resistance movement in Kuwait.[148] As Mary Ann Tétreault observed, mosques were 'protected by religious values from the degree of surveillance and interference that governments—including Iraqi occupying forces—exercise in other gathering places.'[149]

A series of arrests in Oman in 1994, which culminated in terms of imprisonment being handed down to 135 individuals, shone a murky spotlight onto levels of regime nervousness at the potential, still less actual, reach of oppositional Islamist activity.[150] News of the arrests, which in some accounts numbered more than 400, shook Oman as they amounted to the first indication of potentially large-scale internal dissent since the ending of the Dhofar War and the fading of PFLOAG in the 1970s. In a National Day speech,

Sultan Qaboos 'accused those arrested of being Islamic extremists' and there were suggestions that some of those detained were linked to the Muslim Brotherhood or even to Al Qaeda, and that they had been accused of plotting to overthrow the government.[151] Little actual evidence was produced to support such allegations, although some reports suggested that the network had focused on cultural and educational matters as part of 'the Islamic revival in the Gulf' and had issued a 'political statement' that criticized Omani policy toward Israel.[152] After the detainees were sentenced in November 1995, Sultan Qaboos issued a pardon to all Omanis involved in political activities in an attempt to allow all concerned to save face and bring an end to the matter. The policy response nevertheless illustrated the security-first approach of the authorities who may have been alarmed by suggestions that the detainees represented a significant cross-section of Omanis from a wide variety of socio-economic and regional backgrounds.[153]

Regimes in the Gulf responded to the religious zeitgeist by seeking to re-emphasize the centrality of Islam after years of freewheeling economic development and rapid urban and spatial modernization, illustrating the degree to which Islamist movements reshaped some of the boundaries of political discourse.[154] In 1978, a year before the Shah fell but two years after the suspension of the National Assembly, the Emir of Kuwait, Sheikh Jabir al-Ahmad Al Sabah, called publicly for a national 'renewal' focused on 'the Islamization of the state' and 'changing the present order into a new order.'[155] The 'religious turn' in Saudi policymaking included King Fahd's decision in 1986 to adopt the title of 'Custodian of the Two Holy Mosques' as the Al Saud became more attentive to the conservative Wahhabi establishment after the shocks of the Grand Mosque siege and the Islamic revolution in Iran.[156] Nearly four decades later, Mohammed bin Salman blamed the events of 1979, and the policy responses, for the subsequent problems of religious militancy in Saudi Arabia and the Gulf region, leading Jamal Khashoggi to accuse the Crown Prince of 'peddling revisionist history.'[157] At the time, officials had made suggestions of Iran's involvement in seizing the Grand Mosque, but produced no evidence to support their assertion.[158]

Attempts by ruling elites to 'manage' opposition therefore oscillated between support for, or suppression of, various groups—be they pan-Arab, merchant-led, or Islamist-focused—at different times, depending on the type and level of risk they were perceived to pose to regime interests.[159] While officials initially had given some tacit support to political Islam and the Muslim Brotherhood to offset and weaken pan-Arab currents, over time, they came to be seen by regimes, especially the Al Saud, to pose a challenge to their own religious and political authority. In pursuing this strategy, the overriding objective was to make it harder, in practice, for oppositional forces to come together and present a united front that could jeopardize the political survival of the dynastical regimes. Islamists and merchants worked together in Kuwait after the National Assembly was suspended in 1986. Ironically, while regime elites resisted their campaign to restore parliamentary life, such coordination laid the foundation for the resistance to the Iraqi occupation in 1990 as well as the political negotiations with the Al Sabah in exile in Jeddah.[160]

The next chapter examines how ruling elites responded to opposition groups in ways that sought to hinder coordination and forestall the creation of unified movements which might meaningfully threaten the structure and balance of political power. There were times, as with the National Union Committee in Bahrain or with the mobilization of workers during the early oil era, when it appeared as if a mass-based opposition could take root and become a counterforce in domestic political landscapes. Even after the creation of redistributive mechanisms which altered the parameters of relations between state and society, there were attempts to coordinate, usually on issue-specific rather than ideological grounds. In 1990, Saudi Shia groups tried, unsuccessfully, to bridge the theological divide and reach out to Sunni Salafis deeply critical of the government's decision to host non-Muslim troops in the Kingdom.[161] After parliamentary politics resumed in Bahrain in the 2000s, Sunni and Shia Islamist groups cooperated on occasion on issues such as the reform of land ownership or opposition to the sale of alcohol.[162] In 2011, the sight of Bahrainis of all social and religious backgrounds converging on the Pearl Roundabout and chanting 'No Shia, no Sunni, only Bahraini' represented a determination by demonstrators to reject the regime's efforts to divide its opponents and present instead a united front in support of calls for change.[163]

6

RESPONSES

In this chapter, the focus shifts to the various ways in which regimes across the Gulf States responded to the manifestations of opposition described in Chapter 5. The chapter begins with an analysis of 'securitization' and the framing of oppositional demands (by regimes) in terms of 'red button' issues calculated to appeal to an external audience in primarily Western capitals, especially Washington, D.C. A second section refocuses on domestic responses as splits and factions emerged within opposition groups, in part over whether or not to engage politically on terms so clearly set by the regimes themselves. This became very apparent during the Arab Spring upheaval in 2011 when youthful new movements less willing to accept the 'rules of the game' challenged and outflanked the 'established' opposition groups which struggled to define and articulate their own response. The chapter ends with an assessment of the narrowing of oppositional spaces since the Arab Spring as regimes unveiled measures that expanded the authoritarian tools of control and significantly restricted the conduct of 'permissible' activities. One result has been the growing diaspora communities of political exiles outside the Gulf States which while not necessarily new, as in the case of Bahrain, are different in size and scale this time around.

Regime securitization responses

For decades, a favored tactic by ruling authorities in the Gulf States has been to frame political opposition in terms that are likely to resonate externally among key audiences of policymakers and opinion-formers in Western capitals and provide cover as they crack down internally. Over the years, the labeling may have evolved—from linking opponents to communism, Islamism, and terrorism—but the underlying messaging, that the existing regimes are holding the line against disruptive, transnational forces, has remained broadly consistent. In responding so, ruling circles in Gulf capitals sought to create common threat perceptions with international, primarily Western, partners as they engaged, largely successfully, in strategies of securitization that reframed narratives around political opposition on terms favorable to their interests. Especially in the context of the Gulf States, in which decisions frequently are taken by relatively small circles of elite policymakers, analyzing how and why people act sheds important light on the relationships between power, knowledge, and the interests they seek to project and preserve.[1]

Securitization refers to the processes by which specific issues become constructed as threats to security, by whom, and for what reason. If an issue is successfully securitized, and accepted as such by the relevant audience, the principal actor may feel empowered to take extraordinary measures to combat it. Such measures may exceed the rules-based systems that otherwise regulate the conduct of normal behavior, and they demonstrate the importance of agency in defining and shaping responses to specific issues.[2] An example of securitization at the global level was the 'war on terror' pursued by George W. Bush in the United States after the 11 September 2001 terrorist attacks. The Bush administration constructed the challenge it faced from Al Qaeda as a threat to (Western) civilization that required military action to respond to it and therefore legitimized (at least temporarily) the adoption of extraordinary measures that rested on a special interpretation of international law and the norms of the global system.[3]

Ruling elites in Gulf States consistently have framed domestic and regional challenges to their leadership in terms calculated to win international support, and to deflect and distract from local wellsprings of political or economic discontent. Over time, the object of the narrational zeitgeist has evolved from an initial focus on communism and left-wing ideological mobilization during the Cold War to a later emphasis on the threats to regime security posed by Islamism in the 1980s and 1990s and terrorism in the 2000s.

During the Cold War, the (perceived) challenge to regional stability from communism was used by Gulf officials, particularly in Saudi Arabia, to bind the West, namely the U.S., into supporting a geopolitical status quo that was rooted in the conservative monarchies as a bulwark against (radical) change and upheaval.[4] Such an approach was facilitated by the fact that U.S. officials tended to view the Middle East, as they did many other parts of the world, 'almost entirely through the global Cold War prism.'[5] Odd Arne Westad has observed that this dominant worldview gave agency to regional actors, on both sides of the ideological divide, as they framed political agendas 'in conscious response' to the broader superpower rivalry.[6] Gulf rulers were adept at maneuvering to secure their interests during the Cold War just as they had earlier done when playing off British and Ottoman rivalries in the nineteenth and early twentieth centuries.[7]

In the 1950s, Aramco (under American ownership) undermined protests at its labor practices in Saudi Arabia by seeking to link local activism with the communist bogeyman as the Cold War took shape, and as U.S. officials involved in military training urged their Saudi counterparts to deploy security forces to the Eastern Province to protect Aramco's facilities.[8] This occurred as it was the Saudi (largely Shia) workforce that organized the strike at Aramco in 1953, and another in 1956, when their demands included the right for industrial representation amid signs of support for elements of Nasser's pan-Arabism.[9] As Toby Matthiesen and Rosie Bsheer have documented, socio-economic and (in the case of Saudi Shia), identity-based grievances intersected with the impact of transnational networks (of migrants and ideology) and existing networks to create the conditions for a radicalized public sphere and leftist mobilization in the Kingdom as well as in the neighboring sheikhdoms.[10] One of the reasons these class- and ideological-based groups posed a threat to rulers and to the status quo was the way in which they worked to overcome social divisions (between Sunni and Shia, in the Saudi and Bahraini context) and present a unified front in support of political change, whether radical or progressive.[11]

Oil company officials, diplomats, and rulers played up the threat, as they saw it, from destabilizing regional movements, which included the challenge to the status quo from Nasser and Arab nationalism, especially in the highly-charged and politicized aftermath of the Suez Crisis in 1956.[12] Saudi Arabia was included in the Eisenhower Doctrine policy, laid out by President Dwight D. Eisenhower, in January 1957, which extended American economic and military assistance to Middle Eastern countries threatened by 'international communism.' The U.S. Ambassador to Saudi Arabia, George Wadsworth, declared that 'Saudi Arabia is a stabilizing force in the region' and that 'we want to build up something strong which will resist this nebulous force of aggression which we sense building up.'[13] Eisenhower's Under Secretary of State, Herbert Hoover Jr. (son of the eponymous president), added that King Saud's influence would be 'important in moderating both extreme nationalist and pro-Soviet views among the Arabs.'[14]

This was a view that persisted across successive U.S. presidencies during the Cold War, with Henry Kissinger repeating the mantra of enlisting Saudi moderation against forces of regional radicalism after the turmoil of the 1973 Arab-Israeli war and Arab oil embargo. President Lyndon B. Johnson earlier had told the visiting King Faisal in 1966 that 'As long as I am in office, I will not permit your country to be gobbled up by the communists,' to which Faisal responded that Saudi Arabia was 'just as anticommunist as the United States.'[15] Johnson's successor as president, Richard Nixon, recalled in his memoirs how Faisal 'saw Zionist and Communist conspiracies everywhere around him' and 'even put forward what must be the ultimate conspiratorial notion: that the Zionists were behind the Palestinian terrorists.'[16]

Soon after Faisal's assassination in March 1975, the new Crown Prince, Fahd, played the Cold War card as he sought to pressure British officials to adopt a more pro-Arab position vis-à-vis Israel, stating that otherwise the Soviet Union would 'appear to be the only power working for peace, for the restoration of Palestinian Arabs and for the withdrawal of Israel to its pre-1967 boundaries' and warning that, in any new war with Israel, 'Arabs would align themselves en masse with the Soviet Bloc' and 'the West would lose all influence in the area which would be regarded by the rest of the world as yet another Indo-China.'[17] In 1978, Fahd warned the U.S. Ambassador to Saudi Arabia that 'If you don't reassert your position as the leader of the free world, we here in Saudi Arabia had better be preparing to greet the Russians with rose petals as they cross the Red Sea and the Gulf.'[18] During the 1980–1 presidential transition, one of the few policy decisions that Jimmy Carter asked Ronald Reagan to maintain was an arms sale of F-15 fighter jets and Airborne Warning And Control System (AWACS) planes to Saudi Arabia.[19]

Carter's request illustrated how 'red button' issues gradually moved from the purported threat to regimes' security from communism toward a new perceived threat from Iran, especially as it became conflated with radicalizing and transnational trends. This conflation was not without merit, as the new Khomeini regime did initially support the extension of its revolutionary fervor to the Gulf States.[20] In January 1980, Iranian state radio announced a plan to create a force to export the revolution and the following month broadcast a call for a revolt against the Saudi royal family.[21] An Organization of Islamic Revolution formed among Saudi Shia communities in the Eastern Province in 1980, established an information office in Teheran 'to coordinate political activities,' and became 'a focal point' for Shia in other Gulf States, especially Bahrain, Kuwait, and the UAE.[22] Khomeini himself declared in a speech that 'The Iranian revolution is not exclusively that of Iran, because Islam does not belong to any particular people (...) we will export our revolution throughout the world because it is an Islamic revolution.'[23]

Rulers in Gulf capitals quickly disabused themselves of their initially cautious approach to the new political landscape in Iran and proclaimed that revolutionary Iran had superseded communism as the most urgent source of ideological threat that they faced.[24] A series of incidents in the early and mid-1980s illustrated how domestic opponents could fuse with the post-revolutionary fervor to create new challenges to the political status quo. After the Iran-Iraq War began in September 1980, and Kuwait and Saudi Arabia began visibly to assist Iraq, Ayatollah Khomeini warned Gulf leaders that they would face 'measures' in response. Saudi officials were unnerved by the fact that thirteen Saudi citizens were among the alleged perpetrators of the failed plot in Bahrain in 1981, which also included one Kuwaiti and one Omani and was first uncovered in Dubai.[25] Later in the decade, in 1987, Saudi Shia advocates of armed struggle against the Al Saud, who had been given refuge in Iran after the revolution, founded Hezbollah al-Hijaz and participated in a series of acts of political violence against regime targets.[26]

Faced with signs of a new transnational threat to their own conceptions of national security and regional stability, ruling elites responded with their own creation of structures designed to enhance (top-down) inter-state cooperation and cross-border assistance. Rulers' perception of shared threats was most evident in the strengthening of Saudi-Bahrain relations even as the Saudis were unable to generate a Gulf-wide consensus over a common military or security strategy.[27] In November 1979, as the revolution in Iran was unfolding and in the wake of weeks of unrest in the Eastern Province of Saudi Arabia that Saudi authorities ascribed to Iranian 'meddling,' Saudi officials took the decision to proceed with the construction of a road link to Bahrain, which opened in 1986 as the King Fahd Causeway. The bridge had been under consideration since the 1960s when it triggered a row with the Shah of Iran who cancelled a planned visit to the Kingdom in 1968 to protest a Saudi pledge of support for its construction.[28]

After 1979, the Saudi and Bahraini leadership converged around a view that they faced a joint challenge from Iran, a state that Prince Nayef, the Saudi Interior Minister, labeled 'the terrorist of the Gulf.'[29] Rory Miller observed that while the causeway was 'publicly presented as an investment in deeper GCC integration,' the fact that 'the four-lane highway was wide enough to accommodate tanks and was designed to withstand bombing from the air was rarely mentioned.'[30] The revolution in Iran and the signs that the Khomeini government would try to export its revolutionary brand of politicized (Shia) Islam meant that, in the words of one Saudi commentator in 1979, 'it is now essential to put a tail on Bahrain so it doesn't float away to Iran.' For emphasis that would resonate with a *New York Times* audience (to whom the comments were made), the commentator added that 'The Saudi government does not want a Cuba 15 miles off its shores.'[31] Bahraini officials publicized Saudi military patrols in the Eastern Province in a bid to draw Western attention to the threat they faced from the revolutionary leadership, which restated Iran's territorial claim to Bahrain in September 1979.[32]

The strategic and security value of the link between Saudi Arabia and Bahrain became visibly apparent during the political uprising that shook Bahrain in the mid-1990s, when Saudi forces crossed the causeway in a display of strength and the Saudi Minister of Interior, Prince Nayef, declared that the security of Bahrain was inseparable from the security of Saudi Arabia, and again in 2011, when detachments of the Saudi Arabian National Guard and military police from the UAE deployed to Bahrain to assist the Bahraini government as it restored order following the Pearl Roundabout uprising.[33] Bahrain's Foreign Minister, Sheikh Khalid bin Ahmed Al Khalifa, claimed, in 2011, without providing any evidence, that Gulf forces were in Bahrain 'to deter an external threat' and added that 'We have never seen such a sustained campaign from Iran on Bahrain and the Gulf as we've seen in the past two months.'[34]

Attempts by officials in Gulf capitals to link regional developments to Iran did not always succeed in deflecting attention and attributing blame for specific issues and incidents, especially after the shock of the 9/11 attacks in which seventeen of the nineteen hijackers were citizens of Saudi Arabia and the UAE. The longstanding Saudi Ambassador to the U.S., Prince Bandar bin Sultan Al Saud, initially appeared to place indirect causal attribution for the radicalization of Al Qaeda on Iranian targeting of shipping in the Gulf during the Iran-Iraq War in the 1980s which, he argued, prompted the U.S. military presence in the region which so galvanized Osama bin Laden in the 1990s. As a scholar of contemporary Gulf politics put it, 'such denial, diversionary tactics, and tortuous arguments pointed to the sheer magnitude of the crisis that the 9/11 attacks, bin Laden, and Al Qaeda represented for the Saudi elite.'[35]

The appeal to 'red button' issues continued nevertheless to attract international partners especially after the immediate shock of 9/11 began to wane. In 2008, a former U.S. Ambassador to Saudi Arabia asserted that 'The alternative to Saudi Arabia's royal family today is not some Arabic-speaking version of the Swedish parliament, but a Sunni version of Iran's Shia theocracy.'[36] As Toby Craig Jones, an American political scientist who has written extensively on Saudi Arabia and Bahrain, observed, in 2012, rulers in the Arab Gulf monarchies 'have summoned the specter of an Iranian threat' ever since the 1979 revolution, and 'appear to have calculated correctly, for to date Washington has paid far more attention to Iranian maneuvering, real and imagined, than to the excessive force used to grind down pro-democracy and human rights activists on the Arab side of the Gulf.'[37] This became evident during the Arab Spring in 2011. Secretary of State Hillary Clinton responded to allegations of U.S. inconsistency in supporting anti-regime protestors in Libya but not in Bahrain by stating candidly that 'There will be times when not all of our interests align (…) that is just reality. That is our challenge in a country like Bahrain.'[38]

In the 2010s, and especially after the rise of the Islamic State of Iraq and Syria (ISIS) became an issue of global concern, new threats from terrorism, which in several Gulf States was conflated with Islamism, became objects of regime securitization strategies. This became a feature of officials' responses to the challenges not only to regional stability (from ISIS) but also to regime security (from Arab Spring unrest) and was manifest in the formulation of sweeping new counter-terrorism laws and the designation of the Muslim Brotherhood as a terrorist organization in Saudi Arabia and the UAE in 2014.[39] Regimes sought to ride the wave of international concern about Islamist militancy in Iraq and Syria to stigmatize opposition groups and their political demands. The hardline Saudi and Emirati stance toward the Brotherhood caused a dilemma for the Bahraini government, which was, by 2014, reliant on Riyadh and Abu Dhabi for financial and political support. The influence of sectarian politics in Bahrain, encouraged by the regime to divide the opposition, meant that the Bahraini offshoot of the Brotherhood had been a part of the loyalist camp, rather than a mainstay of the opposition, as in Kuwait.[40] Bahrain's Foreign Minister, Sheikh Khalid bin Ahmad Al Khalifa, sought to square the circle by differentiating between the international Muslim Brotherhood (based in Egypt) and its local affiliates, just as the Kuwaiti branch had done in 1990 when it cut ties with the Brotherhood in Cairo after the latter supported Iraq's invasion of Kuwait.[41]

Divisions and factionalism in opposition circles

This section examines some of the ways in which oppositions were 'neutered' by factional splits which in certain cases were exacerbated by regime strategies to divide and rule and thereby prevent the formation of a unified alternative center of political power. As noted in Chapter 5, the cross-class (and cross-sectarian) cooperation in the National Union Committee in Bahrain in the mid-1950s and the ideological potency of Arab nationalism across the Gulf in the 1960s indicated how opposition movements could mobilize and generate a mass appeal that presented a significant threat to the status quo. However, splits within opposition movements also served to undermine their impact and created openings for regimes to 'pick off' individuals and factions, especially in times of crisis, such as the aftermath of the Gulf War in 1991 and the Arab Spring upheaval in 2011.

Participation in representative institutions, such as those analyzed in Chapter 4, could also amount, in practice, to drawing opposition groups into a carefully-controlled political landscape, splitting them over issue-specific policies, and creating wedges between those choosing to engage and those remaining outside the political arena.[42] Writing about Jordan and Morocco, the two other monarchies in the Arab world, Ellen Lust-Okar noted that when ruling elites were able to divide oppositions into 'loyalist' and 'radical' (or 'illegal') camps, coalition movements were far less likely to unify around common demands, and that access to 'the formal political system' was one way in which groups could be divided, especially as 'Authoritarian elites determine which opponents may or may not participate.'[43] Sami Atallah has suggested that in the cases of both Kuwait (in 1963) and Bahrain (in 1973), the creation of National Assemblies (short-lived, in Bahrain's case) served to contain opposition movements in part by bringing them into a process of participation on terms set largely by the regimes as a valve to regulate pressure.[44]

Oppositions could split in multiple ways that in part reflected the contextual issues at hand. Tensions in Kuwait surfaced after liberation in February 1991 between Kuwaitis (and foreign residents) who remained in the country during the seven months of Iraqi occupation and those who either were out of the country at the time of the Iraqi invasion or chose to leave Kuwait in the months that followed. Less than a third of the Kuwaiti population stayed in Kuwait throughout the occupation and up to 350,000 found refuge in Saudi Arabia, along with the Emir and other senior Al Sabah members who based themselves at a repurposed Sheraton hotel near the south-western Saudi city of Taif.[45] Many of those who remained in Kuwait formed the backbone of local resistance groups, including hitherto politically marginalized groups of women as well as Kuwaiti Shia communities whose loyalty had at times been called into question during the Iran-Iraq War. A 2007 study of political attitudes in Kuwait since 1991 observed that

> During the invasion and occupation, the opposition groups rallied and became leaders of the resistance. These members of the Islamic and nationalist movements, their voluntary associations and other groups that had been the most politically marginalized since the dissolution of parliament in 1986—the Shias and the commercial class—manifested the most loyal support of Kuwait's sovereignty and the emir as its legitimate ruler, willing to fight and die for their nation.[46]

After liberation, tensions emerged between 'outsiders'—those who returned from exile—and 'insiders'—those who stayed and resisted the occupation, especially as ruling family and government officials sought to control the process of political reconstruction.[47] Some of these tensions were described by a Kuwaiti healthcare official who told a reporter on the first anniversary of liberation that when some of those who had been in exile returned to Kuwait, 'they had a very negative attitude to those of us who had stayed behind. You can see a feeling of guilt in some of their actions since liberation (...) Those of us who stayed are accused of all sorts of things (...) some people even try to hint that we might have been collaborators.'[48] Another activist stated in 1991 that 'we want [government] ministers from the people who were in Kuwait during the Iraq time.'[49] From the other direction, hostility from many government officials toward Kuwaitis who had remained *in situ* during the occupation was a characterizable feature of the post-liberation landscape in the run-up to the 1992 elections for the restored National Assembly.[50]

Opposition in Kuwait was also fueled by and linked with bouts of factional infighting within the ruling family, especially in times of political tension such as the contested nature of the 2006 succession to Emir Jabir al-Ahmad Al Sabah and the turbulent early years of Emir Sabah al-Ahmad's subsequent rule. This period saw Kuwait go through six elections to the National Assembly (and more than a dozen governments come and go) in the seven years between 2006 and 2013. Feuds between senior members of the Al Sabah as they jockeyed for position in the ruling hierarchy intersected with oppositional dynamics as rival sheikhs sought to build coalitions of support within the National Assembly. Statements ahead of the May 2008 election illustrated this, as an Islamist candidate, Khaled Sultan, told a campaign rally that 'The main problem in the domestic political arena is the feud among members of the family' while a former Minister of Oil, Abdulmohsen Al-Mudej, declared separately that 'What has been happening lately is a struggle among some members of the ruling family, and they have made parliament the arena of this infighting.'[51]

For Kuwaiti political analyst Saleh Al-Saeedi, ruling family infighting changed the concept of political opposition after 2006, as 'Now it is one group of MPs siding with one wing and the other group loyal to another wing,' and 'stability does not depend on parliament because it does not govern. It depends on the ruling family.'[52] Ali Zaid Al Zu'abi, a Kuwaiti professor of anthropology, added that the 'overlapping interests of political alliances within and outside the family' became an entrenched and destabilizing feature of Kuwaiti politics.[53] This trend culminated in months of unrest in 2011 which brought about the resignations first of Kuwait's Deputy Prime Minister, in June, and then the Prime Minister, in November; both senior members of the ruling family who were engaged in a bitter years-long rivalry that drew in parliamentary factions on both sides.[54] Links between one of the Al Sabah protagonists and members of Kuwait's tribal opposition also contributed to political fragmentation after 2011 as some parliamentary blocs chose to boycott National Assembly elections in 2012 and 2013 while others did not.[55]

Choosing whether to participate in electoral politics in Kuwait and Bahrain, especially when the 'rules of the game' were seen by many in opposition circles to favor regime interests and not offer a way to challenge the structure or balance of political power, has been another source of division for oppositions in both countries. Questions of inclusion or exclusion were not only matters for regimes (in drawing up the parameters of permissible contestation) but also issues that caused debate and discord among oppositions over the extent to which taking part would merely 'window-dress' and legitimize regimes' electoral systems. Members of Kuwait's political opposition split over participation in National Assembly elections as early as the third parliamentary vote in 1971 in response to the widespread perceptions of governmental 'manipulation' of outcomes in the previous electoral cycle in 1967.[56]

Splits among oppositional groups over participation in regime-led strategies of what Daniel Brumberg labeled 'controlled liberalization' (careful openings that fall short of democratization) and, in the view of Steven Cook, were 'tactical political openings,' were especially prevalent in Bahrain in the decade of 'regime reform' in the 2000s.[57] Fundamental differences of opinion over whether to engage with the regime or stand outside the political framework first appeared during the initial, short-lived National Assembly in Bahrain that operated between 1973 and 1975. On that occasion, Bahraini members of the (Arab nationalist) Popular Front for the Liberation of Oman and the Arabian Gulf advocated a continuation of armed struggle against the regime, while members of the National Liberation Front chose to participate in the electoral process and saw eight of their candidates elected to the short-lived assembly, which the regime shut down after just two years.[58]

The fact that the Bahraini government suspended political and civil liberties for twenty-seven years after 1975 meant that opposition groups responded very cautiously to the Emir's reinstatement of parliament in 2002, especially after backtracking on initial promises of farther-reaching reform, as Chapter 4 noted.[59] It was therefore of little surprise that the question of participation in the 2002 National Assembly election split the various opposition groups just as had happened a generation earlier. Al-Wefaq, the largest Shia Islamist political society joined the leftist Wa'ad (the National Democratic Action Society, whose Popular Front predecessor had also refused to participate in 1973) and two other societies to boycott the 2002 vote while two groups formed a progressive platform and won several seats in the lower chamber.[60] Four years later, it was Al-Wefaq's turn to diverge over the issue of electoral participation, as divisions emerged within the movement over whether to continue the election boycott or engage in the political process.[61]

Al-Haq's breakaway from Al-Wefaq in 2006 highlighted the difficulties that faced opposition groups as they sought to justify participation in electoral politics where the 'rules of the game' meant they could not realistically hope to alter the structure or balance of political power. Al-Wefaq duly emerged as the largest bloc after the 2006 election with seventeen of the forty parliamentary seats, but all seventeen MPs walked out of the National Assembly in May 2008 in protest at statistics that showed a 42 percent jump in the population, from the previous figure of 740,000 to a new total of 1.05 million.[62] Allegations that the regime had engaged in large-scale 'political naturalizations' to alter the demographic makeup of Bahraini society had overshadowed the 2006 election and provided the context to the acute sensitivity around the sudden increase in population numbers.[63] Their decision to engage in the political process cost Al-Wefaq more in credibility among opposition circles than it yielded in tangible policy outcomes.[64]

On the eve of the Arab Spring which rocked Bahrain (and, to a lesser extent, Kuwait) in 2011, Bahraini academic Omar AlShehabi observed how the Bahraini government 'seemed to be in a very comfortable commanding position' after the three parliamentary elections of 2002, 2006, and 2010, which had divided the opposition over the issue of whether (or not) to take part, as:

> ... The formal opposition was effectively contained within a lame-duck parliament, and the more radical elements outside of the official institutions were strongly curtailed by a slew of trials and imprisonment, on charges of terrorism and plotting to overthrow the regime.[65]

In a similar vein, French academic Laurence Louër referred to this period as 'the era of tame opposition' in which 'the most important opposition force had resigned itself to play by the rules of the game imposed by the king.'[66] The events of 2011 exposed the fractures within the opposition in Bahrain as well as in Kuwait. In both countries, the 'established' groups which had engaged in the political process found themselves outflanked by primarily youth-led calls for more radical and far-reaching change. Ellen Lust observed of the Arab Spring upheaval more broadly (but applicable to the Bahraini and Kuwaiti examples as well) that the uprisings were led by new coalitions with less regard for state co-optation mechanisms.[67]

Close observers of Bahrain noted that Al-Wefaq, as the 'established' opposition, was caught off guard, just as the regime was, when demonstrators occupied the Pearl Roundabout in Manama in February 2011, and that hardliners on all sides gained in influence the longer the standoff continued. In 2012, a report co-written by a Bahraini academic and reform advocate described the youth movement, which called itself the February 14 Youth

Coalition (both for the date of the first protests in 2011 and the date of the National Action Charter exactly ten years earlier, which, as noted, many felt was later watered down by the regime), as:

> ... a confederation of loosely organized networks (...) faceless, secretive, and anonymous (...) thousands of supporters [who] have abandoned the failed leadership of the country's better established, but listless, political opposition.[68]

A report compiled by the International Crisis Group in 2011 observed that Al-Wefaq and other licensed opposition groups were 'shocked' when Al-Haq and two other unlicensed groups declared a 'Coalition for a Bahraini Republic' in March 2011 and announced plans to march on the royal palace.[69] Moreover, in trying to regain credibility among the youth-led, grassroots movements camped at the Pearl Roundabout, Al-Wefaq found itself adopting 'more far-reaching demands' in its dialogue with Crown Prince Salman bin Hamad Al Khalifa.[70] In May 2011, two months after the negotiations collapsed and forces from other Gulf States entered Bahrain to assist in the restoration of order, a representative of Al-Wefaq reflected that 'One of our mistakes might have been that we were too soft with the masses. We should have led them.'[71]

A similar tension between established political opposition and new youth entrants—those inside and outside the system—was observable in Kuwait when street protests, which were some of the largest in the country's history, erupted in 2011 and continued into 2012. The demonstrations remained non-violent although they were broken up by security forces and did result in a political confrontation with the authorities that dominated the period between 2012 and 2014. Elections to the National Assembly in February 2012 swept in a wave of opposition MPs who won thirty-five of the fifty seats and promptly organized themselves into a majority bloc led by Musallam Al-Barrak.[72] Tensions emerged between the opposition in parliament and those engaged in the protest movement (again primarily youth-led, as in Bahrain) when the former gave in to the Kuwaiti government's refusal of their demand for more representation in Cabinet posts. This caused anger among many demonstrators who criticized the MPs' failure to press hard enough on issues such as the legalization of political parties and an elected (not appointed) government.[73]

The new youth groups pressured the established opposition to maintain a hardline stance and in April 2012 merged into a Civil Democratic Movement which called for an elected Cabinet with a non-royal Prime Minister.[74] As in Bahrain, the demands from 'the street' outflanked those from the political class and illustrated a greater willingness of those outside the system to challenge the regime and its institutions, as both countries struggled to absorb the entrance of new political participants less willing to observe the (mostly unwritten) boundaries of political participation and intent on rewriting some of the rules of the game. The use of innovative new tactics had been seen in 2006 when youth-led advocates of reform to the electoral districts used blogs and wore orange in imitation of the color revolution in Ukraine that had captured international attention the previous year.[75] In July 2012, an account of three nights of meetings between the youth activists and opposition politicians by Elizabeth Dickinson, the UAE-based reporter for Abu Dhabi's *The National* newspaper, captured the tensions between the groups over the speed and scale of the demands for change: 'many of the MPs have been in politics longer than Kuwait's politically active youth have been alive but it was these young men and women who set the tone at the meetings.'[76]

In responding to the events of 2011–12, the Bahraini and Kuwaiti governments adopted a series of measures which aimed to divide opposition movements and to dilute their ability to disrupt the political arena. The authorities in Bahrain banned most political societies associated with the opposition, including Al-Wefaq, and jailed their leaders after convicting them on spurious charges such as inciting hatred and promoting disobedience, and sought to weaken organized political actors across the board.[77] Post-2011 elections to the National Assembly in 2014, 2018, and 2022 were notable for the success of independent candidates, rather than those affiliated with political blocs, including Sunni Islamists linked to Salafi groups or the Muslim Brotherhood, who saw their parliamentary representation and political influence decline. With organized political groups fractured and largely outside parliament, the government faced little opposition as it introduced stringent new anti-terrorism measures in 2014.[78]

The authorities in Kuwait pursued a mixed approach of 'carrots and sticks' in weakening and dividing the opposition forces that had built up in 2011 and 2012. After the Constitutional Court annulled the results of the (opposition-dominated) February 2012 elections in July, swathes of opposition politicians from liberal, Islamist, and tribal backgrounds, boycotted the two subsequent elections to the National Assembly, in December 2012 and June 2013. Turnout in the December 2012 vote fell from 60 to 40 percent as many groups stayed away in protest at the annulment of the old Assembly and a new electoral law.[79] In response, members of the ruling family, led by the Emir, reached out to leaders of the major tribes that had taken part in the electoral boycott and secured their pledge to return to the political arena, driving a wedge into the broader oppositional faction.[80] Other instances of targeted dialogue and outreach to select groups resulted in the return of liberal and Salafi blocs to the political fold ahead of the July 2013 election, which saw the splintering of the boycott movement.[81] During the subsequent 2013–16 parliament, the Kuwaiti government nevertheless passed legislation that banned those convicted of insulting the Emir from standing in future elections, thereby targeting a wave of senior opposition figureheads such as Al-Barrak, who left Kuwait for exile in Turkey after his own conviction.[82]

One final example from Saudi Arabia illustrates how oppositions could fracture even in the absence of the question of whether to participate in representative institutions, as in Bahrain or Kuwait. Both Shia and Sunni Islamist groups split in the 1980s and 1990s over strategy and tactics of engagement with a regime based upon the politics of exclusion and selective co-optation. In both cases, key distinctions which emerged were approaches that emphasized non-violence in seeking and achieving political objectives as well as differences over whether the Saudi regime could be engaged in good faith at all.[83] In 1989, a group within the Saudi Shia community co-led by Hasan Al-Saffar published a list of their demands for an agreement with the state; these included an end to political and religious discrimination against Saudi Shia as well as the granting of freedom of expression and religious worship. Al-Saffar had been one of the founders of the Organization for the Islamic Revolution in the Arabian Peninsula after the Iranian revolution, but by 1989 he had moved from a policy of rejection of the state to a call for dialogue with it.[84]

Exiled Shia leaders who opted for dialogue with the state and for gradual reform rather than revolution, began a dialogue with Ghazi Al-Gosaibi, the Saudi Ambassador to the United Kingdom, in the early 1990s.[85] This resulted in a reconciliation agreement in 1993 in which the government released (some) political prisoners, made pledges of investment in the Eastern Province, and relaxed the ban on building Shia mosques and marking Shia religious festivals and mourning periods. Those such as Al-Saffar who took advantage of the amnesty for political opponents and returned from exile met personally with King Fahd on their return to Saudi Arabia, and later supported Crown Prince Abdullah's national dialogue initiative in 2003 and participated in Municipal Council elections in and after 2005.[86] However, the pact caused deep divisions among Shia political communities, including several of Al-Saffar's former colleagues as well as more militant organizations who advocated for direct action against the Saudi state and who observed that the 1993 agreement did not lead to the ending of discriminatory practices against Saudi Shia.[87] Such differences added to the existing socio-political and theological diversity within Saudi Shiism.[88]

A broadly similar (if largely unconnected) dynamic was observable in Sunni Islamist circles in Saudi Arabia in the 1990s. Here, too, splits emerged over whether and how to engage with the regime, and arguments focused later over whether the decision to engage had been the right one, given that cycles of state repression continued, apparently unabated and, over time, at an even greater intensity. The decision by King Fahd in August 1990 to invite U.S. forces onto Saudi soil led to a three-way split among the *Sahwa* movement and lay behind several of the subsequent open letters and petitions to the Saudi authorities.[89] Among the 'rejectionist' camp which moved into outright opposition was the influential *Sahwa* cleric, Salman Al-Awdah, who condemned the entry of non-

Muslim forces into the Kingdom. In his Friday sermons, Al-Awdah refused to endorse the King's decision, and argued that it was un-Islamic to fight one evil with the aid of a greater evil.[90] Many of the clerics who opposed the Saudi authorities in 1990–1 spent much of the 1990s in prison, a period which Osama bin Laden later claimed was critical to the radicalization of an element of their number in favor of armed confrontation with the Saudi state.[91]

Narrowing oppositional spaces

Post-Arab Spring crackdowns severely restricted the ability of opposition groups to function within the political system in Bahrain and, to a lesser degree, in Kuwait, and to exist without the threat of arrest and long imprisonment elsewhere in the Gulf, especially in Saudi Arabia and the UAE. Regimes across the region responded to the fallout from the 2011 uprisings by deepening their own authoritarian structures and narrowing still further the spaces permitted for legitimate political activities. New counter-terrorism legislation was unveiled in several of the Gulf States which included expansive and vague definitions meaning that virtually any form of protest could be labeled a terrorist act. A new counter-terrorism law in the UAE in 2014 defined a 'terrorist outcome' as any action 'antagonizing the state' and included specific sentencing provisions for those convicted of acting with intent to 'undermine national unity or social peace' or publicly declaring 'lack of allegiance to the State or the regime.'[92] In Saudi Arabia in 2022, a young female student pursuing a PhD at the University of Leeds in the U.K. was sentenced to thirty-four years' imprisonment, under the Counter-Terrorism Law, after being charged with 'supporting those who seek to disrupt public order' by liking and retweeting posts on Twitter.[93] Even Qatar, which was the first state in the Gulf to criminalize the spreading of 'fake news' in 2014 but which was seen as less draconian in pursuing political opponents, sentenced two brothers to life in prison in 2022 for taking part in demonstrations over the new electoral law ahead of the 2021 Shura Council vote.[94]

A 'political diaspora' of exiled communities has long existed, with waves of Bahrainis seeking refuge in primarily Western capitals over the decades and a nascent Saudi opposition taking shape in London in the 1990s where the presence of exiled activists became a flashpoint in bilateral British-Saudi relations.[95] London had long been host to Muslim opposition groups from across the Middle East and North Africa and provided an 'Islamic infrastructure' for the incoming dissidents.[96] For one of the founders of the Committee for the Defense of Legitimate Rights, his base in London enabled him to print and send newsletters to up to 300,000 recipients in Saudi Arabia by fax and, later, by email.[97] However, in 1996, a split in the Saudi opposition based in London meant that the *émigré* community lost a degree of credibility just as the internet was taking off, which could otherwise have magnified manifold its reach and penetrability.[98] While the first regional connections to the internet had existed since the 1970s in select research institutions and university laboratories, broader access was carefully restricted through the use of national servers and constant monitoring of users' online behavior.[99] Nevertheless, the advent of highspeed DSL internet connections in 2001 transformed access to the online information sphere, as did the rapid advances in broadband speeds a decade later.[100] Different groups of Bahraini exiles also established themselves in London and Copenhagen, as well as Damascus, with the British- and Danish-based exiles becoming especially vocal critics of conditions in Bahrain in the 1990s and 2000s.[101]

What was different about the new waves of diaspora exiles in the 2010s, after the post-Arab Spring security crackdowns, was their size as well as the fact that they encompassed figures from additional countries such as Kuwait and the UAE. One internal study attributed to the Royal Court in Saudi Arabia reportedly estimated that 50,000 Saudis could be seeking political asylum abroad by 2030, the totemic year which marks the milestone of Mohammed bin Salman's vision to transform the Kingdom.[102] An increase in asylum applications from Kuwaiti citizens was notable for the inclusion of several senior members of the Al Sabah who had been caught up in political power-plays, while Emiratis who escaped the post-2011 crackdown on political opposition and human rights advocates found their way to London via Doha, where their initial presence had contributed to the friction between the UAE and Qatar.[103] In addition, Turkey became a haven for many of the newer generation of Gulf exiles in the 2010s, including the Kuwaiti political opposition leader, Musallam Al-Barrak, and the Saudi columnist, Jamal Khashoggi, who was murdered in the Saudi Consulate in Istanbul by agents of the Saudi state in October 2018.[104]

Officials in Gulf capitals, especially Riyadh, have been mindful to the prospect of the larger (and more vocal) groups of citizens abroad mobilizing politically, lobbying international institutions, linking hitherto geographically separate networks, and building support in Western media for their cause. In her study of Mohammed bin Salman, *The Son King*, Madawi Al-Rasheed compiled evidence that this was beginning to happen among Saudi exiled communities as they came together to plan a structured approach to their advocacy.[105] Jamal Khashoggi was a node in this network and his communications with other Saudi exiles were intercepted and monitored by Saudi officials. One such event 'that attracted many voices in the diaspora' took place in London in December 2018, two months after Khashoggi's murder, attended by a wide range of exiles from diverse backgrounds and geographical locations.[106] Not for nothing did members of the Shura Council urge the Saudi government in 2016, two years before the killing of Khashoggi, to 'investigate this phenomenon and its causes before it becomes a security threat or a social dilemma.'[107]

International outrage over Khashoggi's grisly death and dismemberment drew global attention to the increase in repression in the Saudi Arabia of Mohammed bin Salman, as did later allegations of a plot to target a Saudi dissident living in Canada and the detention of female Saudi advocates in 2018. The latter had been associated with campaigns to expand women's rights, including the right to drive, which was a reform announced by Mohammed bin Salman in September 2017, taking effect in May 2018. Their arrest, and subsequent claims of mistreatment in custody, generated further negative coverage but suggested that

Saudi authorities did not wish to appear to give any credence to any notion that advocacy might work, or that rights are anything other than granted to the populace by the ruler of the day. Similar international damage was done to the reputation of the UAE, in 2018, by the arrest and sentencing to life imprisonment of a British doctoral student on spurious allegations of spying. Although the student was later released after an outcry in the United Kingdom, the incident had an impact on calculations of risk in approving the conduct of scholarly fieldwork in the UAE as well as much of the broader region. In both countries, and in Bahrain, where groups such as Al-Wefaq have been banned and their leaders imprisoned, the squeezing of spaces for legitimate political activities will continue to resonate internally and externally.

7

DISTRIBUTION

This chapter examines the distributive processes that have tied states and regimes in the Gulf to societies before, during, and after the transformative economic impact wrought by the discovery, extraction, and export of oil and gas reserves. Control of economic resources and decisions on how (and to whom) to distribute the proceeds have affected (and reflected) relationships of power within Gulf societies and represented the outcome of intensely political choices over the allocation of accrued wealth. In the specific setting of the Gulf States, with the strong overlap between ruling families and state institutions and the sometimes blurred lines between the two, social and economic considerations have, in practice, been significant in shaping the nature of the distinctive political economies which have emerged.

The analysis in this chapter builds upon the work of Jill Crystal, Michael Herb, and others which has documented how the contours of pre-oil economic and political arrangements has had an impact on the political and economic tradeoffs which accompanied the transition into the oil era across the Gulf. There are underlying points of continuity which connect pre- and post-oil trajectories even as broader contextual conditions have changed almost beyond recognition. An opening section explores the salient features of pre-oil economies in the Gulf and the economic and social power wielded by merchant communities as a practical counterweight to the political control of ruling families. This leads into a second section which describes how the advent of the oil era changed the balance of economic power and analyzes the political choices which determined the shape and structure of the allocation of revenues. Subsequent sections assess critiques of rentier state theory, analyze methods of distribution (and contestation), and examine whether changes were evolutionary rather than revolutionary in scale and impact.

Pre-oil economies

Oil was first discovered in the Gulf in Bahrain in 1932 and after a hiatus caused by the Second World War, exports commenced in significant volume in 1946, in the cases of Bahrain, Kuwait, Saudi Arabia, and Qatar, and two decades later, in the 1960s, in Abu Dhabi, Dubai, and Oman. Pre-oil conditions were characterized by a combination of precarity and thin margins of subsistence for many in the Arabian Peninsula and a more equitable division of economic and commercial power at the apex of societies. Examples of 'traditional' economic activities included pastoralism and small-scale oasis agriculture, fishing, shipbuilding and maritime trade, and pearl diving.[1] Control of these economic sectors was the basis for economic and social, if not political, power and far from being monopolized by rulers and members of their families, it was shared among a class of merchants (*al-tujjar*) of Arab, Persian, and Indian origin. This merchant elite contributed to rulers' treasuries through payment of taxes and duties and used the threat of taking their business elsewhere to exercise a subtle yet real constraint on political decision-making.[2]

There was no monolithic 'merchant community' across the Gulf and their strength, size, and cohesiveness as a bloc varied from place to place. As Michael Herb has noted, this in part reflected whether the merchants were primarily of Najdi Arab origin, as they were in Kuwait, where they were more powerful and often linked through intermarriage, or whether their number included significant merchants of 'external' origin, either Persian as in Dubai, or Yemeni as in the Hijaz under Ottoman rule and in the Saudi Arabia taking shape after 1932, or Indian as in Oman and Bahrain.[3] The greater diversity of origin of the merchant class in Bahrain and Oman meant they lacked the social cohesion of their counterparts in Kuwait and were less able to assert a collective political or economic interest.[4]

Relations between the merchant community and ruling elites in this period were not always cordial. The political power vested in the ruler extended to (and was augmented by) their ability to set, impose, and collect taxes, grant exemptions to favored allies, and 'ensure that no one person, family, or tribe became more powerful than them.'[5] The equilibrium between economic and political interests was prone to disruption as, for example, in 1910, when the Ruler of Kuwait, Sheikh Mubarak, doubled taxes to finance military expenditure and as part of his campaign to consolidate the power of the nascent 'state' under his control and weaken the influence of the merchants.[6] (One of the first administrative institutions Mubarak had created, in 1899, three years after seizing power in Kuwait, was a Customs Department.[7]) As documented in Chapter 1, several leading merchants left Kuwait for Bahrain and Al-Ahsa, taking the economic and pearling resources they controlled with them, until Mubarak relented and backed down.[8]

In other circumstances, rulers borrowed money from the merchant elite as it was the latter, rather than the former, who had access to comparatively greater resources, and both Ibn Saud in the 1930s and the Omani Sultanate were often in debt, in the Omani case to the Indian merchant community in Muscat.[9] As late as 1949, shortly before oil began to be exported in large quantities, the new Ruler of Qatar opted to borrow money from the Darwish merchant family rather than the oil company, Petroleum Development Qatar, as that carried fewer political conditions. In Bahrain, merchants, many of Indian or Persian origin, developed considerable influence in the pre-oil political economy of the archipelago as they were granted large tracts of land as well as control over tax collection and other services in return for cash advances to the Ruler.[10] The strength of the merchant class in pre-oil Kuwait was to some extent counterbalanced by the fact that the ruling Al Sabah family had built up substantial landholdings in date plantations in southern Iraq which Farah Al-Nakib estimates provided the Ruler with no less than 27 percent of his annual earnings in 1906.[11]

Merchants wielded social as well as economic power in the pre-oil Gulf and lay behind the creation of some of the first modern schools, libraries, and financial institutions as well as the first push for organized political representation in the form of the movements for elected councils described in Chapter 4. In addition to the network of Al-Falah Schools established after 1905 by the Jeddah merchant Mohammed Ali Alireza, merchants established the first 'modern' schools in Dubai in 1903 and Kuwait in 1910 and financed a school in Muharraq in Bahrain which opened in 1919, shortly after a son of the then Ruler had visited the United Kingdom for the Peace Day celebrations at the end of the Great War.[12] Hafiz Wahba, the Egyptian educator and diplomat who later became a senior advisor to Ibn Saud and the first Saudi Ambassador to the United Kingdom, taught in the al-Mubarakiya and al-Ahmadiya schools in Kuwait and became head of the al-Hidaya school in Bahrain, which met for its first three years in the *majlis* of Ali bin Ibrahim Al-Zayyani, a leading Bahraini merchant, while its school building was under construction.[13]

During the period of comparative resource scarcity on the Arabian Peninsula, the merchants' close involvement in the import, export, and transport of goods placed them within an intensely transnational sphere and connected them with counterparts across the Gulf, the wider Indian Ocean, and beyond. This encompassed international networks of credit in which Indian Hindu merchants, and, in Bahrain, Persian financiers played central roles in connecting ports and centers of commerce across the Indian Ocean littoral.[14] The Kuwaiti historian Fahad Bishara has described how, during the economic peak of the pre-oil boom (which, in the case of the pearling economy, peaked in the decade before the First World War):

> ... the merchants and mariners of the Gulf had established sizeable communities in a number of western Indian ports,

including Karachi, Bombay, Goa, and Calicut, with some venturing further into the interior and taking up residence in such trading centers as Hyderabad and Poona. Western India quickly became a cornerstone of the Indian Ocean world of Gulf merchants, providing them with access to foodstuffs such as rice, sugar, tea, and spices as well as textiles, building materials such as Indian teak and other types of timber, which were vital to the burgeoning dhow-building industry in the Gulf.[15]

Merchants' networks were transnational and multilingual and fully integrated into international networks of trade and exchange.[16] In his memoir *The Wells of Memory*, published in 1998, the Emirati merchant (and, later, diplomat) Easa Saleh Al-Gurg recalled how the networks of merchant families crossed national and regional boundaries, especially in the period before oil and the formalization of modern borders:

> My family's connection with the family of Shaikh Mustafa bin Abdul Latif [in Bahrain] is a good example of the way in which prominent families in different parts of the Gulf kept in touch with each other and exchanged services, and, when necessary, help. Shaikh Mustafa (...) a substantial merchant in the pearl trade, spent most of his time in Bombay where there was a large and prosperous Gulf community (...) The family, which was Iranian in origin, maintained a large office in Dubai.[17]

Writing about Bahrain's most prominent merchant family of the nineteenth century, the Safar, James Onley provides an evocative description of a relentlessly trans-regional family hailing from Hillah in modern-day Iraq but putting down deep roots across Bahrain, Iran, and India:

> Hajji Mirza Muhammad Ali Safar (1778–1845) was born in Bushehr; lived in Hillah, Mochah, Bahrain, Bushehr and Bombay; was a Persian, Ottoman and possibly British Indian subject; wrote his letters in Farsi and Arabic (...) His brother, Hajji Muhammad Jafar, was born in Bombay to a Persian mother from Shiraz, lived in Bombay and Bushehr, was a British Indian subject, dressed in the style of an Indian merchant in Bombay, and probably spoke Farsi, Arabic and Hindi.[18]

In what became Saudi Arabia, the merchant families of the Hijaz (including the Ali-Rida, Zainal, Shobokshi, and Jamjum) constituted the mainstay of economic power in the Arabian Peninsula, together with immigrant merchants, many of whom came from Hadramawt in Yemen (the Bin Mahfuz, Bin Ladin, Bin Sakr, and Ka'aki families being prominent examples). The merchant community in Jeddah had organized itself into a Commercial Council (*majlis tijari*) as early as 1853 which served to represent their interests in urban politics in the Hijaz prior to Ibn Saud's takeover in 1925.[19] These early economic elites operated from East Africa to India and were cosmopolitan in their outlook and connections to international economic interests. In his seminal study of the major Gulf merchant families, Michael Field described how one of the scions of the Alireza family, Mohammed Ali, visited Paris for the first time in 1920, and:

> Drawing on the help of business friends, he opened an office at 62 rue La Fayette, on the edge of the main shopping area of Paris (…) From the early 1920s, Mohamed Ali made it his habit to spend several months at a stretch in Paris each year—he bought a house on the Champs Elysees (…) During the height of his career in pearls, he lived almost permanently in Bombay and Paris.[20]

Such movement (and opportunity) was restricted to elites and was not generally available to most of the inhabitants of the Arabian Peninsula, many of whom were ensnared in unequal relationships of economic power based on hierarchical stratification of work, debt, and bondage, especially in the pearling sector.[21]

While there was wide variation across the Gulf, and significant differences between the coastal and inland ecosystems of commerce and trade, the pre-oil dependence on pearl fishing mirrored the later reliance on oil as a commodity with volatile external swings in demand and price. As early as 1841, British officials estimated that, across the sheikhdoms, between 30,000 and 40,000 people were employed in the pearl sector during the annual 'season.'[22] In his *Gazetteer of the Persian Gulf, Oman and Central Arabia*, published by the Government of India between 1908 and 1915, J.G. Lorimer stated that more than 22,000 men left the ports along the Trucial Coast in 1,215 boats, and that taxes and dues on the sector accounted for up to 70 percent of revenues for the Rulers of Sharjah and Ras al-Khaimah.[23] Guillemette Crouzet has estimated that, between 1860 and 1914, 'the Gulf provided more than half the pearls sold on the global market and almost 80 percent of finer, high-value pearls.'[24]

Pearling structured social relationships and hierarchies within a segmented labor force, broken up into merchant-moneylenders, the ship captains (*nakhodas*), and the divers and haulers who undertook the dangerous tasks of collecting the pearls from the seabed, and spawned a derivative service economy that supported and sustained it. However, this mainstay of the pre-oil economy, which integrated the Gulf economic elite with the epicenters of the pearl trade in Bombay and Paris, was decimated by two external events in quick succession. The demand for luxury goods fell away during the Great Depression while the Gulf could no longer compete on cost with new competition from cheaper and mass-produced cultured pearls from Japan. By 1931, pearl prices were up to 75 percent lower than their pre-crash level in 1929.[25]

While discussion of 'pre-oil' and 'oil' economies can imply a binary division of Gulf economic history into 'before' and 'after,' there was no immediate or quick transition from one to the other, rather a process which unfolded over the 1930s and 1940s and lasted into the 1950s and 1960s in Abu Dhabi and Oman. Even then, it was only in the 1970s, after the renegotiation of relationships with foreign oil companies and the nationalization of (or, in the case of Abu Dhabi in the UAE, the assumption of national control over) the energy sector, coupled with the sharp rise in oil prices after 1973, that the 'oil age' fully took shape.[26] The collapse of the market for Gulf pearls in the 1930s did nevertheless have immediate socio-economic consequences and contributed to a period of significant hardship before the oil era began. One chronicler of the Gulf described the decimation of the pearl sector as 'a disaster which almost overnight removed the one export on which the people of the Gulf could rely to bring in foreign earnings.'[27]

Qatar was among the hardest hit as its pre-oil economy was less diversified than those in Kuwait, Bahrain, Dubai, and the Hijaz in Saudi Arabia with fewer alternative sources of commercial or trading activity. During the 'years of hunger' in the 1930s and 1940s, between one-third and a half of the population temporarily left the Qatari peninsula in search of work elsewhere.[28] This included nearly all merchants, except for two families who stayed behind, meaning that the non-ruling family business community in Qatar entered the subsequent oil age in a comparatively weaker position than their regional peers.[29] The advent of the Second World War caused further economic disruption and dislocation of trade relationships across the Gulf States and with their hinterland in India and South Asia, and led to a pause in the development of the nascent oil sectors as well as delaying the start of petroleum exports until 1946.[30]

Once the oil era commenced, 'traditional' pre-oil economic activities declined rapidly. The last large fleet of pearling ships left Dubai in 1949 while 1955 was the first annual season that saw no pearling boats leave Qatar.[31] In Kuwait, the size of the pearling fleet, which had peaked in 1912 with 812 boats, dwindled rapidly as it fell from forty-eight boats in 1948 to twenty in 1955 and just eleven in 1958.[32] On land, the last camel caravan left the central Saudi city of Unayzah, a historical stopping point for pilgrims and traders crossing the Arabian Peninsula, in 1945.[33] The merchant class lost its control of the 'means of production' and their economic and social power declined still further as oil revenues freed emerging state institutions from reliance on the taxes and duties that hitherto had been mainstays of rulers' treasuries.[34] In Saudi Arabia, the erosion of pre-oil structures of power was linked to state policies implemented by Ibn Saud, such as the abolition of grazing rights for Badu tribes which curtailed their ability to exist independently of the centralizing authority with its emphasis on sedentary rather than nomadic settlement.[35] Some of the guilds of professional groups in Jeddah (as in other cities in the Ottoman Empire) lasted into the 1960s before the final vestiges of their collective economic power faded along with the crafts they represented.[36]

Kuwaiti merchants' transnational investments and landholdings in India, Iraq, and other parts of the Arabian Peninsula enabled many to survive the 1930s' depression and the collapse of the pearling market in a comparatively better state than their peers elsewhere in the Gulf. The previously-mentioned Hilal Al-Mutairi, who had led the 1910 protest at the Ruler's imposition of new duties in Kuwait, 'invested his pearling income in real estate in both Bahrain and Bombay as well as date plantations in Basra.' Such investments provided Kuwaiti merchants with an economic base to continue to challenge the political elite, as seen in the 1938 Legislative Council and, later, in the give-and-take negotiations in the Constitutional Convention after Kuwaiti independence in 1961.[37] While the variation in merchants' pre-oil standing did have an impact on their own transition into the oil era, there were regionwide characteristics to the 'ruling bargain' which emerged between the 1950s and the 1970s.

The oil transitions

The transformative impact of oil revenues on the Gulf States is immediately apparent to anyone who spends time in the gleaming cityscapes of Dubai, Abu Dhabi, Doha, or, in recent years, the sprawling new urban and development projects associated with Mohammed bin Salman in Saudi Arabia. Oil in commercial quantities was first struck in Bahrain on 31 May 1932, followed six years later by the discovery of two of the largest fields ever found, at Burgan in Kuwait and at Ghawar in Saudi Arabia, within the space of nine days of each other in March 1938, and at Jebel Dukhan in Qatar a year later.[38] The Second World War meant that exports did not begin until 1946. In the other Gulf States, oil discoveries did not occur until well into the post-war period, in 1958 (in Abu Dhabi) and the early 1960s in Dubai and Oman, with policy decisions in Abu Dhabi and Oman to fully exploit the oil being delayed by a further decade.[39] Already by 1960, the Gulf States were producing 15 percent of the world's oil, and this proportion doubled to 30 percent just a decade later, on the eve of the Arab oil embargo of 1973–4.[40]

Revenue from the export of oil (and, later, natural gas) elevated ruling dynasties above competing economic interests and provided emerging state structures with substantial, though not complete, autonomy from domestic social forces. American oil executives at Aramco, for example, made extensive use of the networks, connections, and local knowledge of the Saudi merchant elite in the early years of the oil industry, 'for advice what to do, which approach to take, and whom to turn to when trying to do business the right way in an unfamiliar environment.'[41] A distinctive set of distributive mechanisms gradually took shape across the Gulf States within a more stratified economic framework that came to encompass layers of 'rentiers' flowing downward from the state at its apex.[42] Oil 'rents'—and the political decisions on how to use them—became intertwined with the creation of modern state structures and the often-uneasy processes of institutionalization, as described in Chapter 3. This took shape between the 1950s and the 1970s as the incoming revenues from oil enabled ruling elites to create distributive or 'rentier' states in which, as Khaldoon Al-Naqeeb put it, the 'national economy (…) does not depend directly on oil but indirectly on the state expenditure' as 'public spending becomes the primary channel through which oil revenues are distributed to society' and 'the central role of the state becomes evident.'[43]

Rulers first received oil-related income as royalties from the concessions they granted to foreign oil companies in the 1930s which, in some cases such as Dubai, preceded by three decades the eventual discovery of oil.[44] However, the concession payments, while significant in the context of the difficult economic conditions of the 1930s and 1940s, were dwarfed by the exponential increase in revenue once oil began to be produced on a commercial scale after the Second World War. In Oman, they enabled the Sultan, Sa'id bin Taimur, to 'judiciously (…) strengthen his ties with the leading sheikhs of the interior' which proved valuable as the Sultan 'sought to facilitate the safe passage of oil exploration teams in the northern part of the interior not effectively under imamate control.'[45]

Oil revenue in Saudi Arabia rose from US$10.4 million in 1946, the year the first cargo of oil was exported, to US$169.8 million in 1953.[46] Government revenues then increased exponentially after the renegotiation (and nationalization) of relationships with the Western-controlled oil companies and the surge in prices after the Arab oil embargo. Between 1960 and 1980, Saudi annual oil income rose from US$333 million to a hitherto barely unimaginable US$104 billion.[47] In Kuwait, oil revenues soared from US$760,000 in 1946 to US$169 million in 1953, and rose again to US$9.8 billion in 1973.[48] Qatar exported its first oil shipment in 1949 and by 1955 oil accounted for 97.5 percent of state revenues in the sheikhdom.[49] A decade later, the population of Abu Dhabi doubled in the four years after Sheikh Zayed's fast-tracked development of the emirate's oil reserves when he seized power from his brother, Sheikh Shakhbut, in August 1966.[50]

Revenues from the export (rather than the mere extraction) of oil ultimately transformed the economic structures and development patterns in the Gulf States. As the pre-existing patterns of administration that still held sway across large parts of the Arabian Peninsula until the 1930s and 1940s were incapable of absorbing or utilizing the enormous sums that began to flow into rulers' treasuries, the following decades saw the rapid creation of institutional frameworks that often coexisted uneasily alongside the more traditional measurements of power and authority, as noted in earlier chapters in this book. Oil revenues were intertwined from the start with the processes of modern state creation as ruling elites reformulated traditional tribal structures into more recognizably contemporary forms of governance.[51] Qatari economist Ali Khalifa Al-Kuwari examined the patterns of allocation of oil revenues in the smaller Gulf States (excluding Saudi Arabia) between the 1940s and the 1970s. Al-Kuwari observed that 'the public revenue in all the Emirates in the pre-oil period was either considered as the private income of the ruler (Qatar, Abu Dhabi, and Dubai) or a considerable part of it was reserved for the ruling family (Bahrain and Kuwait).'[52] Through the early 1970s, Al-Kuwari calculated that about one-third of total oil income received in Bahrain and Qatar and one-quarter in Abu Dhabi was allocated to ruling families, with a smaller proportion in Kuwait which was the first to institute a clear separation between ruler and state in 1964.[53]

Writing four decades later and looking back at a far longer period of oil (and gas) income, Bahraini academic Omar AlShehabi documented persistent shortcomings in budgetary transparency and fiscal accountability especially around allocations to ruling families, military spending, and foreign transfers. As with Al-Kuwari in the 1970s, AlShehabi in the 2010s noted that Kuwait was the regional outlier with (relatively) 'publicly and independently audited, transparent final accounts of its budget.'[54] AlShehabi argued that disclosure and auditing of government accounts declined after the 1970s' oil boom as new channels for 'appropriation and enrichment' appeared. By comparing estimates of the value of oil and gas exports with publicly declared government figures for oil and gas revenues for four Gulf countries (Oman, Qatar, Saudi Arabia, and the UAE) between 2002 and 2011, AlShehabi found a difference of US$772 billion, amounting to about 26 percent of total oil and gas revenues for the period; a proportion, he noted, that had not significantly altered from Al-Kuwari's findings in his 1970s study of the early oil years.[55]

Rentier theory and its critics

Rentier state theory originated in the 1970s and 1980s as a tool of analysis to examine the impact of rents such as revenues from oil on the nature of states such as Saudi Arabia and their interaction with society. Hazem Beblawi argued that a rentier economy developed when the creation of wealth was centered on a small fraction of society, while in a rentier state the government is the principal recipient of the external rent, and plays the central role in distributing this wealth to its citizenry.[56] Giacomo Luciani extended this analysis of rentierism by distinguishing between allocative and productive states, in which the income derived from the export of oil frees allocation states from their productive economic base.[57] State autonomy from domestic taxation and other forms of wealth extraction was expected to change the political 'rules of the game,' as the absence of a taxation/representation link would, it was believed, lessen the incentive for mobilization around demands to change political institutions or government policy.[58]

Much of the early literature on rentier state theory seemed to suggest that the advent of oil effectively 'froze' political development and institutional arrangements and enabled ruling elites to do away with traditional socio-economic constraints on the arbitrary exercise of political power. It is the case, as Anh Nga Longva noted of Kuwait (but applicable elsewhere as well), that historically 'porous categories' of social and economic identification became less fluid and more rigid in the second half of the twentieth century.[59] Against this, Uzi Rabi has posited the notion of the state as a 'political field' (rather than an independent or autonomous political actor) 'within which different actors compete for influence and resources.'[60] Such an approach enables consideration of the questions of political will, policymaking priorities and choices, and societal responses, informal as well as formal, which were vital to shaping (and, over time, reshaping), the lived reality of the oil era in the Gulf States and the distinct characteristics in each country's case.[61]

There were, to be sure, key elements of the oil economies as they emerged which conformed to aspects of rentier state theory, although these did not take effect immediately and only became pronounced after oil prices and government revenues surged following the Arab oil embargo in 1973–4. It was this later period, the 'first' oil boom in the 1970s, which saw the lifting of many of the remaining taxes in Saudi Arabia and the other Gulf States as well as the final dismantling of the vestiges of the extractive mechanisms that had existed in the pre-oil era. In her study of Saudi Arabia, Kiren Aziz Chaudhry noted that most taxes and fees on Saudi citizens were withdrawn together with nearly all indirect taxes, the government stopped collecting private-sector social security payments and rescinded 'the mainstays of the old treasury, pilgrim fees and taxes on services in the holy cities of Mecca and Medina,' cancelled the imposition of personal income tax on foreign workers, and offered renewable five-year tax holidays to foreign companies.[62] Chaudhry noted also that 'oil royalties and a greater ability to borrow abroad eased the state's dependence on the revenues and administrative expertise' of the Hijazi merchant elite, which also enabled a shift in the balance of power within

Saudi Arabia as a new political and economic class more closely associated with the Najd region around Riyadh (and with the Al Saud) grew in power.[63]

When the elements of the distributive mechanisms that came to characterize the political economies of the Gulf States in the oil era first emerged, they did so at a time of relatively small populations and seemingly limitless resources.[64] Qatar had a population of about 20,000 at the end of the 1940s while fewer than 100,000 people lived in the seven Trucial States that later became the UAE.[65] Kuwait had a population of 160,000 in 1952 which itself had more than doubled from the total of 75,000 in 1937, the year before the first oil was struck.[66] Even Saudi Arabia had a population of only about 3.5 million in the early 1960s, a figure that rose tenfold in the next half century.[67] While much of the subsequent increase in the combined population of the six Gulf States from 4 million in 1950 to over 40 million by 2005 (and an estimated 56 million in 2022) came from inward migration, the number of citizens rose steadily to reach 23 million in 2022, the majority of whom, nearly 18 million, were Saudi nationals.[68]

Population growth altered the per capita balance of resource revenues, in some cases significantly, as new discoveries of oil and gas reserves failed to keep pace, other than in Qatar, even if some of the pessimistic predictions about 'peak oil' did not materialize.[69] (Indeed, the true extent of GCC states' energy reserves remains a matter of conjecture, as stated oil reserves in several of the countries registered sudden leaps in the mid-1980s around the time of OPEC's adoption of country production quotas; the UAE's stated reserves for 1986 were nearly three times higher than those for 1985, while Saudi Arabia added nearly 100 billion barrels to its stated reserves between 1987 and 1988.)[70] Across the GCC, the level of oil exports per capita declined from an average of US$15,000 in 1980 to US$6,000 in 2000 while in Saudi Arabia alone the level of oil income per capita fell from US$16,650 to US$7,239 in the same twenty-year period.[71]

Since the 1990s, critiques of rentier state theory have moved beyond the 'no taxation without representation' argument to focus on local agency and decision-making in the creation and continual remaking of contemporary Gulf polities. In the case of Saudi Arabia, Steffen Hertog has traced the dynamic interplay among elite politics, royal family factionalism, and patronage networks alongside the growth of administrative structures.[72] Herb's examination of Kuwait and the UAE has shown how two states with outwardly similar 'rentier mentalities' could nevertheless have completely different political and economic outcomes in practice.[73] Justin Gengler has shown how, in the specific case of Bahrain, rather than attempting to use the (limited) resource rents to try and secure 'a universal rentier social contract,' political authorities concentrated instead on directing economic benefits to 'a finite constituency [of citizens] whose support is sufficient to ensure the continuity of the regime.'[74] Differing speeds of economic liberalization in the 2000s reflected the diversity of calculations about policy priorities and the balance of domestic interests even, in the case of Dubai and Abu Dhabi, by decision-makers in the same country.[75]

As Gwenn Okruhlik observed in 1999, it is 'not the simple receipt of oil revenue, but the choices made on how to spend it' which are critical. Okruhlik emphasized the importance of political choice (and who makes those decisions) and the interaction between structural rentier state theory and personal rulership in analyzing the political economy of the oil states which emerged in the Gulf. She observed that rentier theory alone could not explain the persistence of oppositional dissent, especially in Saudi Arabia, Bahrain, and Kuwait, since the 1960s. Consequently, the state's apparent financial autonomy did not, in practice, translate into immunity from societal pressures, as some early advocates of the 'ruling bargain' would have.[76] More recently, a 2019 study produced by the Project on Middle East Political Science (POMEPS) examined in detail the politics of 'rentier states' in the Gulf. Contributors, especially Andrew Leber and Jessie Moritz, illustrated the significance of the 'who gets what, why, and how' political choices about revenue distribution as well as the complicated relationship between rent, distribution, and co-optation of societal forces in examining allocation policies and desired (as well as actual) policy outcomes.[77]

Distribution and contestation

With the full advent of the oil era, following the nationalization of oil companies and the surge in oil prices in the 1970s and the belated acceleration of energy development in Abu Dhabi and Oman, the relationship between states and economic actors evolved in significant ways. Incoming revenues facilitated and funded the growth of the bureaucratic apparatus of statehood and the ruling families across the Gulf asserted control over natural resources in the name of the states they led. The role and structure of the 'oil states' which emerged transformed Gulf societies and gave the Gulf States the distinct characteristics that distinguished them from political economies elsewhere in the region.[78] Government monopoly over the receipt and use of revenues created new path dependencies as mechanisms emerged to manage the distribution of the (primarily oil) rent from state to society. In this context, questions over oil, investment, and distribution came to form key pillars of public policy discourse, practice, and periodic contestation.[79]

The importance of economic distribution to political survival was evident in the palace coups in Abu Dhabi in August 1966 and Oman in July 1970 which brought to power two of the most consequential and longest-serving regional leaders, Sheikh Zayed bin Sultan Al Nahyan and Sultan Qaboos bin Said Al Said. In Abu Dhabi, Sheikh Zayed's older brother, Shakhbut, had been in power since 1928 while in Oman, Sultan Said bin Taimur, Qaboos's father, had ruled since 1932. Both men had ruled during the years of hardship in the 1930s and witnessed first-hand the economic difficulties that left an indelible impression on their styles of rule. Shakhbut, in particular, was judged by British officials to have developed 'a reputation for being extremely reluctant to spend more money than was absolutely essential.'[80] The first inflows of oil revenues in the early 1960s highlighted Shakhbut's resistance to economic development that might lead to social or political change. The British Political Agent in Abu Dhabi, Hugh Boustead, observed that 'It is clearly no easy task for a Ruler, after a lifetime of poverty, to accustom himself to the idea that his income will henceforward be counted not in hundreds of pounds but in millions.' He added, condescendingly, that 'Shakhbut is finding the mental adjustment much more difficult than have any other Rulers of oil states and it is questionable whether he wishes to make the adjustment at all.'[81] The Political Agency's annual report for 1965 went so far as to label Shakhbut an autocrat 'whose insistence on personal control of even the minutest details of government would make Louis XIV look like a constitutional monarch.'[82]

Oil exports in Oman had commenced in 1967 but the Sultan, Said bin Taimur, was even more cautious than Sheikh Shakhbut about carefully controlling the pace and scale of economic and social development. John Townsend, a British official who later served as Economic Advisor to the Government of Oman in the 1970s, recalled how Said 'made all decisions on oil matters himself, without advice.'[83] The Sultan wished to strike a balance between development and modernization which achieved the former but not the latter, and lived a frugal life that was reflected in his desire to keep public expenditure as low as possible.[84] Matters were not helped by the fact that Said retreated permanently to the southern city of Salalah in 1958 which made policy coordination with officials in Muscat more difficult, or by the fact that he tried to isolate his son, Qaboos, upon his return from the United Kingdom, where Qaboos had spent time studying the workings of local government by observing Suffolk County Council.[85] On 23 July 1970, Qaboos toppled his father, with British assistance, in a largely bloodless coup which saw the ousted Sultan accidentally shoot himself in the foot.[86] In a statement issued after he seized power, Sultan Qaboos justified his decision to assume power in distributional terms as he declared that

> I have watched with growing dismay and increasing anger the inability of my father to use the newfound wealth of this country for the needs of its people. That is why I have taken control (...) I promise you all that my immediate task will be to set up as quickly as possible a forceful and modern government.[87]

Both Sheikh Zayed and Sultan Qaboos accelerated domestic development and oversaw the creation of comprehensive welfare states that had started to emerge elsewhere in the Gulf in the 1960s. Citizens of Gulf States became the beneficiaries of numerous measures that channeled the oil windfall into virtually every facet of socio-economic life. Examples included the expectation of (male) employment in the rapidly-expanding public sector and state-owned enterprises, the provision of free or heavily subsidized utilities and services such as education and healthcare, and the right to a plot of land and access to low-interest loans to develop it.[88] In Qatar and the UAE, male citizens received stipends if their choice of marriage partner was also a citizen.[89] One study of the UAE in the 2000s calculated the annual value of subsidies and state handouts to Emirati citizens at US$55,000, as a government minister acknowledged that 'People don't see it as the government giving them something. They see it as a right.'[90] Kuwait subsidized and supplemented the wages and benefits of citizens who worked in the private sector, with the value of state 'allowances' to male, married private sector employees exceeding US$3,000 a month in 2012.[91]

Miriam Lowi observed that many of the distributive measures were regressive in nature and tended to 'favor the concentration of wealth within ruling elites and their closest allies, to placate strategically important groups.'[92] Kuwait initiated a land acquisition scheme in the 1950s whereby the government purchased land at inflated prices which served to further enrich the already-wealthy landowning class of merchants and, in many cases, ruling family members. Mary Ann Tétreault calculated that 'about a quarter of Kuwait's total revenues from oil were distributed directly to individuals through this program' between 1946 and 1971, while Ali Al-Kuwari estimated that expenditure on land purchases peaked at 42 percent of total government spending in 1959 and remained more than 20 percent throughout the 1960s.[93]

Distributive measures also sharpened debates over inclusion and exclusion in Gulf societies as political boundaries solidified and as classes of citizenship were defined along patrilineal descent and tribal lineage that emphasized historical membership of the pre-oil polity.[94] Chapter 1 noted the political and economic benefits of belonging and these became more pronounced in the

1960s and 1970s as citizenship became a tool of rent allocation.[95] Moreover, as Longva observed, since citizenship gave access to the welfare state and distributive benefits, it imparted significant social and economic privileges to those in society with 'national membership.'[96] Decisions over citizenship and related issues, such as naturalization, gave rulers the power to restrict who was in or out, and established a connection between expressions of political loyalty and the receipt of economic benefits.[97] The power of existing elites was also bolstered as they worked with British and oil company officials to codify the measures that covered the sponsorship and employment of non-citizen workers (collectively known as the 'kafala' system), starting in Bahrain in the 1930s, Kuwait in 1949, Saudi Arabia in 1952, and Qatar in 1955.[98]

Members of ruling families continued to assert themselves in the business landscape of the Gulf although pre-oil trajectories did shape subsequent developments. The small size of the pre-oil merchant community in Qatar, and the fact that many of the merchants had temporarily left the peninsula during the years of hardship in the 1930s, meant that there was more space for Al Thani members to move in to. By contrast, merchants' strength in Kuwait ensured their dominant position in business post-oil, while in Dubai and Abu Dhabi the ruling dynasties remained reliant on merchant expertise as they developed. In Oman, the size of the ruling family was far smaller than its regional counterparts, while in Saudi Arabia and Bahrain, the business community preserved their positions of leadership until at least the 1970s.[99] The most successful merchants transformed into diversified conglomerates and often cemented their ties to ruling families through intermarriage and renewed older networks of interpersonal relationships that ran alongside the personalization of key decision-making in the decades of post-oil state consolidation.[100]

The existing economic elite also benefited disproportionately from measures which required foreign companies and individuals seeking to do business in the Gulf to work through local partners. Both the agency and the sponsorship system provided ample opportunities for intermediaries to profit from business relationships; the difference between them was that whereas foreign companies needed an agent to export to the Gulf States, a sponsor was required if a company wished to operate locally.[101] The assignment of these rights by state officials was one of the most significant ways in which state-business relations were reconfigured in the oil era. Cut out from direct ownership or control of the energy sector, prominent merchants pursued business opportunities in other industries that were either derivative to the oil sector or were initiated with state assistance from accrued oil revenues. A new relationship evolved whereby merchant families were granted the most lucrative concessions to import goods or operate franchises, as a way of assuring loyalty and giving them an economic stake in the status quo. In the words of Jill Crystal, a 'ruling bargain' emerged as 'merchants renounced their historical claim to participate in decision-making, [and] in exchange the rulers guaranteed them a large share of the oil revenues.'[102]

In his memoir of his early fieldwork in Kuwait in the 1950s, the social anthropologist Peter Lienhardt recalled the surge in applications for agency rights for manufactured imports and consumer goods—a process replicated in all other Gulf States. Lienhardt observed that 'Many of the most valuable agencies had been acquired by the leading families who had been prominent in the pearl industry. They started with various advantages over others: an established position, experience of large-scale business, a reputation for reliability and financial integrity, and wide connections and influence.' Lienhardt added that 'Partnerships with foreign companies were "gold mines," and here it certainly looked as if the ruling family had some influence in deciding who the local partners would be.'[103] Mohamed Al-Rumaihi saw a similar dynamic in Bahrain as he noted, in the 1970s, that 'the granting of import licenses and the setting up of agencies were rigidly controlled by the Government for the benefit of the big merchants. Any newcomer wishing to enter a particular field faced a monopoly situation which was almost impossible to break.'[104]

Many of the 'traditional' merchant families also played leading roles in the creation of the first local banks in the Gulf in the 1950s and 1960s as the influence of the British Bank of the Middle East

(BBME), which had been granted concessionary rights in Kuwait, Dubai, and Oman by British officials and had opened branches in Qatar, Saudi Arabia, and Bahrain, began to wane.[105] A group of Kuwaiti merchants established the National Bank of Kuwait in 1952, after they were 'angered when required to provide a guarantor for a loan from the BBME,' while the Bin Mahfouz family created the National Commercial Bank in Saudi Arabia a year later.[106] Merchant interests were also represented in the Al Watani Bank in Saudi Arabia (1958), the Commercial Bank of Kuwait and Gulf Bank (1960), the Al Ahli Bank (1967), and the Commercial Bank of Qatar, the first private bank in the country opened by members of the Al-Fardan family in 1975.[107] In the UAE, and especially in Dubai, local merchants were instrumental in the creation of the banking and financial sector with the powerful Al-Ghurair family, some of whose members had been active in the Dubai reform movement in 1938 and Arab nationalist politics in the 1950s, establishing the Mashreq Bank.[108]

Maintaining the welfare states and navigating the volatility in oil markets and economic cycles were key political objectives for ruling elites, especially in times of prolonged downturns as in the 1980s and 1990s. This was illustrated starkly in Saudi Arabia, where the challenge was more acute owing to the much larger population vis-à-vis the smaller Gulf States, after oil prices fell sharply after 1981, plunged by two-thirds in 1986, and remained low for the remainder of the century. Oil revenues fell from US$186 billion in 1982 to US$42 billion in 1986 by which time central bank assets were shrinking, the current account deficit was soaring, and there was growing pressure on the currency peg with the dollar.[109] And yet, even though government expenditure halved in the 1980s and state revenues did not fully recover until the early 2000s, spending on wages and allowances increased significantly in absolute and relative terms, rising from 13 to 49 percent of the national budget between 1981 and 1990 and to 60 percent by 1999.[110]

Cutbacks to capital projects and curbs on discretionary spending were hallmarks of policymakers' responses to the economic slowdowns in both the 1980s and the 2010s. Officials across the Gulf States considered these areas to be less politically sensitive than those that directly affected the distributive aspects of the welfare states, and the presence of substantial numbers of foreign workers meant that expatriates often would be the first to be affected by job losses. Caution was reinforced by the fallout after Qatar introduced an austerity budget in 1983 and imposed charges for some government services where even these modest changes generated noticeable societal pushback from political and business elites as well as ordinary Qataris.[111] In March 1986, Kuwait's Deputy Prime Minister (and future Emir), Sheikh Sabah al-Ahmad Al Sabah, announced plans to slash the budget by 25 percent but added that 'the standard of living of ordinary people would not be affected.'[112]

Hesitant responses in the 1980s appeared therefore to conform with early literature on rentier state theory. In 1988, Saudi authorities issued a royal decree which reimposed income tax on foreign workers only for King Fahd to order its cancellation within forty-eight hours amid concerns that the tax 'was expected to lead to a mass exodus of the more highly paid foreigners in the country.'[113] A generation later, when oil prices crashed again after 2014 and ushered in a new period of budget deficits that lasted until 2021, governments similarly slashed capital and infrastructure spending as a first response. On this occasion, they went considerably farther than they had done in the 1980s and unveiled a range of measures that rolled back subsidies in key areas and introduced a variety of new fees and indirect taxes.[114] The difference in response in the 2010s was part a recognition that distributive systems designed when recipient populations were far smaller were no longer sustainable, with the six GCC states collectively spending US$70 billion a year on energy subsidies alone by 2015, and also followed the uneasy discovery that not even a period of record oil prices and government revenues in the 2000s rendered the Gulf States fully immune from the political upheaval of Arab Spring unrest in the Middle East and North Africa in 2011.[115]

Evolution or revolution

Regimes' self-interest in political survival meant that officials began to express more vocally the need to reform their economies and specifically to address issues of subsidies which they began to describe as unsustainable. In 2013, with oil prices still high, Kuwait's Prime Minister, Sheikh Jaber Mubarak Al Sabah, stated bluntly that 'Everyone must understand that the existing welfare state that Kuwaitis are used to cannot continue.'[116] Also in 2013, Oman's Minister of Oil and Gas, Mohammed Al-Rumhi, warned that 'We are wasting too much energy in the region and the barrels we are consuming are becoming a threat (...) What is really destroying us right now is subsidies' which encouraged wasteful consumption and ate into the amount of oil that had to be diverted for domestic use rather than earmarked for export.[117] The most memorable intervention was by Saudi Arabia's then deputy Crown Prince, Mohammed bin Salman, who authorized his financial advisor, Mohammed Al Sheikh, to tell Bloomberg in 2016 that between 2010 and 2014 there had been '80 to 100 billion dollars of inefficient spending' each year and that Saudi Arabia would have gone 'completely broke' by 2017 had expenditure remained at pre-2015 levels.[118] To be sure, there was an element of the new Saudi leadership seeking to blame its predecessor, under King Abdullah, for the economic woes it faced as Salman assumed power in January 2015. That said, Saudi Arabia posted a US$98 billion budget deficit (equivalent to about 15 percent of its GDP) in 2015, was drawing on foreign reserves at an alarming rate, and was facing additional military spending commitments as it became bogged down in an unwinnable war in Yemen.[119]

With the exception of Kuwait, where the populist political landscape and constant tussle between elected MPs and the appointed Cabinet held back austerity measures, officials across the Gulf enacted cost-cutting and revenue-raising initiatives after 2014.[120] For the most part, these sought to trim, rather than dismantle, the distributive mechanisms, and officials backtracked on occasions where new charges threatened to trigger a political backlash. MPs in Bahrain protested loudly against rises in fuel prices in 2016 while the inability of parliament and government to reach consensus on subsidy reform led the Bahraini authorities to scrap a planned streamlining of subsidies in 2019.[121] Mooted hikes in prices of meat and fish in Bahrain and Kuwait were scaled back after public backlash in 2015, while in Kuwait the National Assembly was dissolved in 2016 after MPs opposed a unilateral government decision to reduce fuel subsidies and raise petrol prices by up to 80 percent.[122] Saudi citizens openly protested sudden sharp increases in electricity bills in 2016 and King Salman abruptly removed the Minister of Water and Electricity in an effort to defuse public anger over the issue.[123] In April 2017, King Salman issued a royal decree that reinstated 'all allowances, financial benefits, and bonuses' for public sector workers, seven months after they had been cut, and after calls for demonstrations in four Saudi cities.[124]

The cautious approach to economic reform was evident in that many of the new charges hit expatriates and businesses before they targeted citizens and that new taxes were indirect rather than direct. Value Added Tax (VAT) was introduced in 2018 in Saudi Arabia and the UAE, 2019 in Bahrain, and 2021 in Oman, although plans for a GCC-wide application of VAT foundered. Officials in Saudi Arabia and Bahrain later raised the rate from the initial 5 percent to 15 and 10 percent, in 2020 and 2022 respectively, while in the UAE plans were finalized to introduce a corporate income tax in 2023.[125] However, Omani officials put on hold plans for an income tax on citizens, which would have been a milestone in the Gulf, after oil and gas prices soared following the full Russian invasion of Ukraine in February 2022, providing budget relief after years of deficits.[126] And yet, the fact that taxes were introduced without unmanageable public backlash could embolden officials to take further measures to reformulate aspects of the welfare systems that hitherto many had considered untouchable.[127]

Citizens' attachment to the notion that subsidies have become a right of citizenship, over the five decades since the oil era began in earnest in the 1970s, is therefore more nuanced and malleable, as research by Jim Krane and Steffen Hertog has found.[128] There is also awareness across Gulf capitals that the economic windfall from oil and gas will not last forever, and that greater global emphasis on climate action and the energy transition will generate new pressures on oil and gas producers. The risk of being left with stranded assets has prompted Gulf States' energy officials, especially in Riyadh and Abu Dhabi, to monetize reserves while the oil still commands value, and to transfer the revenues to investment funds.[129] Thus, an initial public offering of 1.5 percent of the shares in Saudi Aramco in 2019 raised US$29.4 billion which was transferred to the Public Investment Fund (PIF), the sovereign fund earmarked by Mohammed bin Salman as the vehicle for the 'giga-projects' (such as Neom) associated with his Vision 2030 to transform the Saudi economy.[130] In 2022, an additional 4 percent of Aramco shares, worth about US$80 billion, were moved to the PIF as part of the fund's plan to raise its assets under management to US$1 trillion by 2027.[131]

PIF emerged at speed from relative obscurity within the Ministry of Finance and was transformed into a global investor once control of its operations was transferred to the Council of Economic and Development Affairs, chaired by Mohammed bin Salman, in 2015.[132] Equally rapid, in Abu Dhabi, was the growth of conglomerates, such as Royal Group and the International Holding Company, linked to Sheikh Tahnoon bin Zayed Al Nahyan, the powerful brother of UAE President Mohammed bin Zayed Al Nahyan.[133] Their startling rise in the late 2010s and early 2020s was indicative of a new breed of investment funds in the Gulf which mixed commercial and strategic considerations far more closely and took on greater risks in pursuit of higher returns to support programs of national economic diversification.[134] It remains to be seen whether such strategies will succeed in creating genuinely competitive non- or post-oil sectors or generating sufficient jobs needed to absorb large numbers of new labor market entrants. The scope and scale of investments worldwide nevertheless gives the Gulf States, primarily Saudi Arabia and the UAE as well as Qatar, new forms of economic leverage and infrastructural power, especially in the post-February 2022 global energy (and energy security) landscape, and is consistent with Matthew Gray's theory of 'late rentierism' in which economic actors in Gulf States respond to 'globalization, new technologies, freer trade and investments, social changes, and development imperatives.'[135]

For all the headline-grabbing initiatives of the PIF and of the groups linked to Sheikh Tahnoon, the fact remains that these entities are controlled by senior members of ruling families, similar to other investment funds in the UAE such as Mubadala or the Kuwait and Qatar Investment Authorities.[136] The convergence of business and strategic opportunities is part of a new phase of Gulf economic statecraft which, as Karen Young has observed, more closely aligns aid, development, and investment policies.[137] It is less clear that they can address the structural imbalances in the economies of the Gulf States and succeed where previous efforts to diversify and expand beyond the energy sector have failed. An estimated 20 percent of Saudi families are believed to live at or near the poverty line, and the Kingdom, with its larger population, and Bahrain and Oman, with their smaller reserves of oil and gas, face economic headwinds that are more imminent and urgent than their counterparts in Kuwait, Qatar, and the UAE.[138] Protests in Oman in 2021 over high unemployment and economic pressures illustrated the continuing mobilizational power of discontent with perceived and actual failings in distributive and welfare processes, as demonstrations spread rapidly to cities and towns across the Sultanate.[139]

Policy responses to blunt or contain the impact of the Arab Spring upheaval in 2011 indicated a clash between considerations of political stability in the short-term and economic sustainability over the longer-term as regimes unveiled measures which prioritized the former over the latter. These included hand-outs of cash (Kuwait, Bahrain, and the UAE), creating jobs in already saturated public sectors (Saudi Arabia, Bahrain, Oman), and raising workers' wages and benefits (Qatar, Saudi Arabia, Oman). The scale of the additional government spending was enormous as state spending in the six GCC states soared by 20 percent during 2011 alone as the measures came into effect.[140] Hertog observed, at the time, how a lasting legacy of the regional upheaval for the Gulf States was likely to be the legacy of the economic, rather than political responses to counter the unrest, because 'expectations are easy to raise but difficult to curb, creating a ratchet effect that demands ever larger outlays during every political crisis.'[141] Many of the subsequent measures outlined in this final section aimed to provide substance and depth to economic reforms, but only time may tell whether they contribute to or are cast aside for interests of regimes' political survival.

8

MILITARIES

The final chapter in this book examines the role of 'hard' power in enabling regimes in the Gulf to respond to threats and challenges in both internal and external affairs and assesses how the monarchies have navigated and survived the wars and revolutions that toppled so many of their regional peers. Securing the state has taken myriad different forms in each of the six Gulf States but a number of general patterns are discernible. These include the conflation of national and regime security, the role of external security partners, initially Britain and then the United States, the emergence of multiple and often overlapping security forces, and threat perceptions which did not always align with conditions 'on the ground.' While the Gulf States have certainly not avoided exposure to domestic instability and regional insecurity, their durability marks them as the great political survivors in the Arab world and repays close attention.

There are four sections to this chapter, which begins with an overview of the role of external partnerships which have provided a near constant backdrop to the conduct of security and defense affairs for most of the modern history of the Gulf, with the limited exception of the period after British withdrawal in 1971. A second section explores how regimes assess the internal and external threats that they face and how this informs their view of what the concept of 'security' means. The third section analyzes how rulers and the elites around them have maintained control of the defense and security apparatus, including through the construction of sophisticated systems of surveillance, and details instances where this has gone wrong as ruling elites misread the nature of threats on occasion. The chapter, and the book, ends with a final section that examines how several of the Gulf States have augmented their 'hard' power capabilities with varying arrays of 'soft' power as they have emerged as significant regional and international actors in the opening decades of the twenty-first century.

Evolution of external partnerships

A search for security against internal rivals and external threats has been a longstanding feature of the political entities which emerged in the Arabian Peninsula before and after the discovery of oil. In the 'traditional' sheikhdoms and emirates before modern political boundaries took shape, the fluidities of belonging to shifting tribal alliances made control of local resources an important element of 'hard' power. Rulers maintained retinues of armed guards but remained reliant on the support from the Bedouin belonging to 'loyal' tribes for use in conflict and provided protection in return.[1] This relationship was based around an unwritten agreement which recognized the sheikhs as the political authority with the ability to exert coercive powers such as the collection of tax or the enforcement of justice.[2] The Saudi-Wahhabi rulers in central Arabia and the Qawasim in Ras al-Khaimah and Sharjah stood out in the late eighteenth and early nineteenth centuries for their control and deployment of, respectively, military, and naval resources.[3]

Ibn Saud's campaigns of conquest which underlay the creation of the modern Kingdom of Saudi Arabia in 1932 offer the closest approximation to the Weberian principle of the monopoly over the legitimate use of force as a marker of statehood. The 'unification' of Saudi Arabia through the conquest of al-Ahsa in 1913, the Hijaz in 1924–5, and the southern regions of Asir, Najran, and Jizan in 1930 was accomplished by military force albeit, as Cronin notes, using pre-modern, traditional tribal techniques of warfare.[4] In

1929, Ibn Saud turned on the *Ikhwan*, the tribal militias he had mobilized but which had become a threat to his consolidation of political authority and control, and defeated them decisively in a battle that David Rundell described as, in some ways 'a thoroughly medieval scene and in others it reflected the Al Saud's ability to move with the times' as 'an *Ikhwan* charge ran straight into well-concealed British machine guns that Saudi merchants had obtained in Kuwait.'[5] Many of the defeated *Ikhwan* fighters were subsequently integrated into the tribally-based National Guard by Ibn Saud which still later became a power base for the future King Abdullah as he assumed control of the force, and its patrimonial largesse, in 1963.[6]

For the small sheikhdoms on the eastern coastline of the Arabian Peninsula, their durability as distinct political units was safeguarded by a series of agreements with British officials which marked them as 'protected states' (rather than the more intrusive 'protectorates' in place in southern Yemen).[7] This first iteration of an external security structure in the Gulf began in 1809 when the Royal Navy bombarded Qawasim strongholds of Ras al-Khaimah and Lingah, on the Arabian and Persian shores of the Gulf, in response to attacks on British Indian shipping, and extended an offer of protection to the Sultan of Muscat, who had provided maritime support for the expedition.[8] Incidents of what the British, controversially, labeled acts of 'Arab piracy' against commercial shipping continued, however, and prompted a larger intervention in 1819, again with support from the Sultan of Muscat, which culminated in the razing of Ras al-Khaimah and other fortified ports at Ajman and Umm al-Quwain and the sinking of 184 Qawasim ships.[9]

Beginning in 1820, a regional security architecture emerged which was based on two key principles—external intervention in regional affairs and the provision of protection to local partners—which played a defining role in structuring relations with, first, the United Kingdom, and, later, the United States. (The gap which separated the British military withdrawal from the Gulf in 1971 and the gradual increase in the U.S. role in Gulf security in the 1980s illustrated some of the dangers facing the Gulf States in the interim.) British officials imposed a General Treaty of Maritime

Peace on local rulers in January 1820 immediately after the cessation of operations against Ras al-Khaimah, and the following year the government of Bombay established a naval Gulf Squadron and created the Residency system of Political Agents and Political Officers.[10] The Political Resident of the Persian Gulf was located in the Persian port city of Bushehr until 1946 when it was switched to Bahrain while responsibility for the Residency system in the British protected states was transferred from the Indian Political Service to the Foreign Office in 1947–8.[11]

Political and security relations between the Trucial leaders and British (and British Indian) officials deepened again in 1835 with the signing of a Maritime Truce which was intended to end the sporadic maritime skirmishes that the General Treaty of 1820 had failed to completely eradicate. The Maritime Truce extended British protection to Abu Dhabi, Ajman, Dubai, Ras al-Khaimah, and Sharjah, and after several extensions it was converted into a Perpetual Maritime Truce in 1853.[12]

The provision of external security facilitated rulers' consolidation of internal power, but British residents and agents also wielded significant influence. Glencairn Balfour Paul, who served as Political Agent in Dubai in the 1950s, recalled that, while the powers of the political agents were informal on paper, in practice 'the boundary between offering advice and enforcing it may have been as narrow as a vocal inflection.'[13] Balfour Paul added that 'attempts by jurists to define the nature of a British Protected State have a somewhat *ex post facto* look' as 'Britain may be said to have made up the rules of the game as she went along, with the result that no-one really knew what they were.'[14] An earlier generation of British officials had evinced similar confusion over the extent of the political geographies they were agreeing to protect. Lord Lansdowne, the Foreign Secretary at the turn of the twentieth century, commented of the Ruler of Kuwait after the 1899 Anglo-Kuwaiti Agreement that 'no one knows where his possessions begin and end, and our obligations towards him are as ill-defined as the boundaries of his Principality.'[15]

British 'interests,' as framed by the network of political agents operating within the Political Residency, took precedence in any clash with the actions of the local rulers, in a manner that sharply distinguished the 'Pax Britannica' in the Gulf from the U.S.-led security umbrella which eventually replaced it. For example, British officials in the Trucial States had long suspected that arms were being smuggled through the port of Dubai to Persia and Baluchistan in the period before the First World War. In 1910, officials implemented strict searches of incoming shipping, engaged in an armed clash with suspected traffickers, and banned all foreign visitors to the Trucial sheikhdoms for a period that lasted nearly a decade.[16] During the war, British forces which had invaded and incrementally occupied Mesopotamia imposed a blockade on Kuwait in 1917 to prevent the flow of goods to Ottoman-controlled enemy territory in modern Iraq. British perceptions that the Ruler of Kuwait was unwilling to take on the domestic merchant and tribal interests which controlled the illicit Ottoman trade led to the unusual position, as John Slight has observed, of Kuwait becoming 'a British protectorate that was treated as an enemy power.'[17]

Although the focus of the Political Residency system was nominally on external and regional affairs, British officials also played critical roles in the creation of the early police and, later, armed forces which provided the sheikhdoms with the coercive capabilities associated with successful patterns of state-building.[18] These forces superseded the rulers' traditional reliance on armed guards, retainers, and loyal tribesmen for local security arrangements in the towns and localities under their control, and drew upon experiences of colonial policing in settings such as India, Sudan, Palestine, and Aden.[19] Bill Edge, the incoming head of Abu Dhabi Police in 1961 had, for example, worked for the Palestine Police during the British mandate era and then for the Kuwait Police, and in 1963, after a spike of unrest among oil workers, he was reinforced by a British officer who arrived from the Bahrain Police to set up a riot squad for Abu Dhabi.[20] Jill Crystal has, however, noted a variation in styles of early policing which largely mirrored their later evolution:

> Bahrain had a very forceful police, Qatar's was intermittently so, Kuwait's was far less violent. When Arab Nationalist

demonstrations swept the Gulf in 1956, Qatar consequently called out the police; in Bahrain a state of emergency was declared and tribal levies recruited into a special riot squad, while in Kuwait the police chief resigned rather than fire on Kuwaitis.[21]

Sir Anthony Parsons, who later served as British Ambassador to Iran at the time of the revolution which toppled the Shah, served as Political Agent in Bahrain between 1965 and 1969 and recalled the range of his powers:

> I was not only the mini ambassador to the mini State, but I was also, I suppose, the Ruler's Foreign Minister and Defence Minister, because we were responsible for conducting Foreign Affairs and Defence. So I was seeing the Ruler, his brothers and top people literally every day (...) in 1967 we had the Israeli War and my Political Agency was besieged for the whole period and very nearly sacked at the end. It was saved by the Ruler himself coming down, unescorted, alone and personally dispersing the crowd.[22]

As the sheikhdoms approached the end of the Pax Britannica in 1971, British influence in their police forces declined rapidly as they recruited heavily among Jordanians, Yemenis, and Dhofaris from Oman.[23]

British officials also established the Trucial Oman Levies in 1951. Based in Sharjah, and renamed the Trucial Oman Scouts in 1956, the force was created with a mixture of policing and more militarized functions in mind. Many of the initial recruits came from local tribes, especially in Abu Dhabi. They were augmented later by the recruitment of Omanis, including a squadron comprised entirely of Dhofaris, and were employed to maintain internal order, which included the interdiction of tribal raiding parties.[24] The force was tasked with protecting the Trucial States against external attack, and 'routinely rotated around the Trucial States, known as "Operation Roundabout"' and also took part in military operations in Oman.[25] In October 1955, two detachments of the Levies intervened in the Buraimi dispute to end the standoff caused by Saudi claims on the eponymous oases and surrounding villages which belonged to Abu Dhabi and Oman. They were supported by two RAF heavy bombers as well as aircraft based in Aden and Bahrain, which flew low over the Saudi-held positions while the Levies cleared the villages of occupying forces.[26]

The long phase of British protection gave way to a more uncertain era, from the perspective of the Gulf rulers, in the 1960s and 1970s. This was the period in which British arrangements ended with Kuwait, in 1961, and with Qatar, Bahrain, and the Trucial States a decade later, in 1971, and in which the Dhofar War and the strength of pan-Arab movements shook the political foundations of the regional order. Rulers' concern for what might come after the British withdrawal was magnified by developments in June 1961 which saw British forces return to the emirate just six days after Kuwait became fully independent. In practice, Kuwait had operated as a sovereign state since 1959, but the termination of its British protected status only occurred on 19 June 1961 in a statement made by the future Prime Minister, Edward Heath.[27] The Political Agent, John Richmond, became Britain's first Ambassador to Kuwait, and commented condescendingly that independent Kuwait would have to prove 'that she was more than a collection of oil wells sheltering under a new form of British Imperialism.'[28]

Six days after Kuwait's formal independence, Iraq's Prime Minister, 'Abd al-Karim Qasim, laid territorial claim to Kuwait, on the basis that the sheikhdom had been attached to the Ottoman *vilayet* of Basra prior to the 1899 and 1914 agreements with Britain, and moved troops toward the southern border.[29] The claim foreshadowed a similar one put forward twenty-nine years later, in August 1990, when Saddam Hussein framed his annexation of Kuwait in terms of redressing 'the pen of colonialism and the scissors of the evil ones.'[30] An article in the exchange of notes between the British and Kuwaiti governments of 19 June 1961 that pledged British assistance to Kuwait, should the latter request it, was activated on 30 June, and 7,000 British troops were dispatched to Kuwait to forestall a potential Iraqi invasion.[31] Operation Vantage drew on British military reserves from across the Gulf and further afield, including Aden and Kenya in addition to forces stationed in Sharjah, Bahrain, and Oman, and British soldiers remained in Kuwait until October 1961 when they were replaced by an Arab League force.[32] (Interestingly, the retention of most British government records under the 'thirty-year rule' meant that the 1961 papers covering the Iraqi threat to Kuwait were released to the public in January 1991, just as the Gulf War was about to get under way.[33])

The immediacy of the threat posed by one of the large regional states and the scrambling of military resources served to focus attention on Britain's commitments to the Gulf sheikhdoms, especially after Indian independence in 1947 removed the main historical reason for British presence in the region. By the 1960s, the value of the Gulf sheikhdoms to Britain lay in the security of supply of up to 40 percent of oil imports as well as an outsize contribution to the financial stability of investments in sterling.[34] Disruption to the flow of sterling-denominated oil from Kuwait in the Suez Crisis and subsequent closure of the Canal had put pressure on the pound and provided an early indication of Britain's post-war economic weakness.[35] Economic and financial challenges and the political unease of a Labour government at the seemingly anachronistic maintenance of colonial-era protected relationships lay behind a precipitate announcement in January 1968 that Britain would withdraw from all positions 'east of Suez' by the end of 1971. The decision took the rulers by surprise because a Foreign Office minister had toured the Gulf in the aftermath of the chaotic British withdrawal from Aden in November 1967 to provide reassurance to local partners.[36]

Sir Stewart Crawford, Britain's Political Resident at the time of the 1968 announcement of withdrawal, did not believe the rapid toppling of the British-supported leaders in the Aden Protectorate and the short-lived Federation of South Arabia held any resonance to the Gulf sheikhdoms, as he argued that in the Gulf:

> ... we do not have, as we have had in Aden, to constitute a new government, the Rulers are all firmly in their saddles and can be counted on to show much more sense, guts and leadership than the Aden Amirs (...) Instead of a Yemen next door, there is a reasonably solid and pretty inert Saudi Arabia.[37]

Such optimism notwithstanding, the Rulers of Abu Dhabi, Dubai, Bahrain, and Qatar raised the possibility of contributing financially to underwriting the cost of a continued British military presence in the Gulf. However, the Foreign Office in London informed the Ruler of Dubai that the British Government did not wish 'to tie themselves either to staying indefinitely or to making their withdrawal subject to the veto of the Rulers,' while the Secretary of State for Defence in Harold Wilson's Labour government, Denis Healey, stated bluntly that 'it would be a great mistake if we allowed ourselves to become mercenaries for people who would like to have a few British troops around.'[38] Negotiations began for a nine-state Union of Arab Emirates of the seven Trucial States plus Bahrain and Qatar, but this foundered on the inability to reach agreement on a division of political power and executive authority that would satisfy the leaders of the four major protagonists in Abu Dhabi, Dubai, Doha, and Manama.[39] In the event, the Rulers of Abu Dhabi and Dubai met in July 1971 and agreed to form the United Arab Emirates which duly came into existence on 2 December with six members and the seventh, Ras al-Khaimah, joining belatedly in February 1972.[40]

Internal and external threats

Nearly two decades separated the withdrawal of British protection from the smaller Gulf States in 1971 and the emergence of the United States as a direct and major contributor to regional security in the latter stages of the Iran-Iraq War and particularly after the Iraqi invasion of Kuwait in 1990. What amounts to the present security architecture in the Gulf—the six states of the Gulf Cooperation Council (GCC) in close partnership with the U.S., and Iran and Iraq excluded—evolved during the 1980s and early 1990s. Its emergence was not a foregone conclusion, developed in fits and starts over a period of many years, was in response to specific events rather than part of any underlying plan, and it was far from axiomatic that the U.S. would ultimately fill the void created by the departing British forces. Both at the time, and especially when viewed retrospectively, this was a period of internal and regional uncertainty for all the Gulf States, including Saudi Arabia, where King Faisal was assassinated by a family member in 1975.[41]

Challenges to the political order and regional status quo began immediately. On 30 November 1971, the day before Britain's withdrawal from the Trucial States, Iranian forces occupied Abu Musa and the Greater and Lesser Tunbs, three islands in the Strait of Hormuz claimed by Sharjah and Ras al-Khaimah. Four policemen from Ras al-Khaimah were killed during a skirmish on Greater Tunb, and the Iraqi government cut diplomatic relations with Britain in protest at London's failure to prevent the Iranian move.[42] Two (entirely separate) palace coups in quick succession resulted in the killing of the Ruler of Sharjah in January 1972 and the ousting of the Emir of Qatar the following month.[43] Unresolved boundary disputes and lingering emirate-level attachments marred the process of state formation in the UAE, with three different military forces, the Abu Dhabi Defense Force, the Dubai Defense Force, and the newly-created Union Defense Force (the successor to the Trucial Oman Scouts) intervening in the Sharjah coup.[44] As late as 1978, the Rulers of Dubai and Ras al-Khaimah threatened to secede after Sheikh Zayed issued a decree abolishing the emirate-level forces and placing them under the Federal Military Command in Abu Dhabi.[45]

British service personnel stayed behind in many of the Gulf States in advisory and training capacities rather than commanding roles, with the exception of Oman where they continued to provide military leadership throughout the Dhofar War and significantly beyond.[46] Bahrain also employed British officials in senior positions in the police and state security into the 1990s with one remaining in post until 1998 despite a past that included controversial service as a colonial policeman during the Mau Mau rebellion in Kenya.[47] The scale of assistance to Oman that enabled Sultan Qaboos to turn the tide in the Dhofar War and declare victory in December 1975 belied any notion of a precipitous cut-off in British military support, even if it was the dispatch of an Iranian brigade and air force detachments to Dhofar in 1974 that was decisive.[48] Some Iranian forces remained in Oman until they were withdrawn after the 1979 revolution and the Shah's officials reportedly drew up contingency plans in the mid-1970s to secure the Musandam Peninsula to safeguard maritime traffic through the Strait of Hormuz should Sultan Qaboos's hold on power falter.[49]

Neither the British advisory presence after 1971 nor Iran's (temporary) role in Oman approximated for anything like a regional security guarantor. Prior to their withdrawal, many of the Arabists in the Foreign Office in London, such as Sir William Luce, a former Political Resident, had believed that Saudi Arabia was the 'keystone of any solidarity between the Gulf States and the Arabian Peninsula.'[50] Indeed, a Cabinet Committee on Defence and Oversea Policy had, in 1965, asserted that 'Geography is the basic reason for thinking of Saudi Arabia as, in a sense, our eventual heir in the Persian Gulf some time after 1970.'[51] And yet, as a study of Saudi policymaking, at the time of the British withdrawal, by Prince Faisal bin Salman Al Saud makes clear, a variety of reasons meant that the Kingdom was impractical as a security alternative. Chief among these were the fact that Saudi Arabia had unresolved territorial disputes with its newly-independent neighboring states and the weak state of the Kingdom's own military capabilities.[52]

A major point of complication for considerations of security arrangements was (and to some extent remains) the imbalance in the regional system between three large and conventionally far more powerful states, Iran, Iraq, and Saudi Arabia, and the five other Gulf States of varying degrees of smallness. Indeed, as Rory Miller has observed, Saudi Arabia is seven times larger in territory than Oman which itself is bigger than the other four Gulf States put together.[53] Iran was bigger still, and presented an ideational and material challenge to regional security as did Iraq under Saddam Hussein's Ba'ath Party rule, especially (but not only) after the revolutionary toppling of their monarchies in 1958 and 1979, respectively. Moreover, at various points in modern Gulf history, all three larger powers have posed territorial claims over their smaller neighbors: Iraq on Kuwait in 1961 and 1990, in addition to territorial claims in the 1930s and boundary incursions in the 1970s; Iran to Bahrain and the three occupied UAE islands; and Saudi Arabia to Kuwait in the 1920s, Qatar in the 1930s, and Abu Dhabi and Oman in the 1950s and 1970s.[54]

The legacy of boundary disputes and cross-border rivalries, many of a tribal or commercial nature, ran deep, especially in a context of such intense transnational connectivity, and against the backdrop of Saudi Arabia having developed a reputation for using its size as leverage over its smaller neighbors.[55] Nicholas Cocking, a British officer posted to the Trucial Oman Scouts as part of a career spent mostly in various postings across the Middle East, later related how:

> Saudi Arabia has always claimed suzerainty over all the minor states of the periphery of the Gulf in one way or another; a suzerainty which is vigorously rejected by the various Emirs and Sheikhs, but they are very much conscious of their big brother sitting in the middle of the Peninsula (...) there were some fairly tense negotiations between the British and the Saudis over what should be left behind in terms of what should be given to the United Arab Emirates and what could rightly be claimed for the Saudis.[56]

It was to counter the threat, perceived and actual, posed by Saudi Arabia to the significantly less powerful sheikhdoms as they approached the end of British protection which led to the formation of national military forces in what became the UAE. In Abu Dhabi, the Ruler, Sheikh Shakhbut, 'was adamant that he required an armed force of his own, predicating this need on the threat from Saudi Arabia.' This threat assessment was shared by the commander of the Trucial Oman Scouts, who was 'directed to prepare his forces to forestall a Saudi advance into the western part of Abu Dhabi—with support from the RAF—for four days, allowing time for British troops to assemble and defeat the Saudi forces in a land battle.'[57] The formation of the Abu Dhabi Defense Force in 1964 set off a chain reaction as the Ruler of Dubai, Sheikh Rashid, created the Dubai Defense Force in 1967 and Sheikh Saqr formed the Ras al-Khaimah Mobile Force in 1969, while the Rulers of Sharjah and Umm al-Quwain set up their own National Guards.[58] The existence of these five separate forces considerably complicated the amalgamation of military units into the Union Defense Force after 1971 and was a process that was not completed until 1996.[59]

Concerns at potential Saudi hegemony in the Arabian Peninsula were not fully allayed by the formation of the Gulf Cooperation Council which brought together the six Gulf hereditary states. Various proposals for a regionwide organization had been tabled since 1976 and, on occasion, had included Iran and Iraq as well as Saudi Arabia and its five smaller neighbors, although never Yemen. Discussions for an eight-member organization (incorporating Iran and Iraq) took place in Jeddah in 1975 and Muscat in 1976 but had failed to make any further progress prior to the revolution in Iran and the start of the Iran-Iraq War.[60] However, the geopolitical shocks of revolution and war meant that what became the GCC came together at speed in little more than three months between February and May 1981.[61] Kuwaiti political scientist Abdul-Reda Assiri observed, nearly a decade later, that the GCC was born from 'the exigencies of realpolitik, to shield the member states, as well as their societies from unconventional threats.'[62] In the UAE, Abdulkhaleq Abdulla went farther and argued that the speed with which the GCC came together indicated that it was 'a panic response to a situation of profound uncertainty' between 1979 and 1981.[63]

Saudi Arabia apart, the other five states in the GCC were still in formative state-building periods in the 1980s, and wary of the potential for Saudi dominance within the new organization, whether through population, size of armed forces, intra-regional trade flows, or geostrategic importance.[64] This was illustrated in the attempt in the 2000s to create a regional gas pipeline network that would bypass Saudi Arabia, as well as the UAE's abrupt withdrawal from the Gulf monetary union project. Saudi Arabia was unable to prevent the construction of the Dolphin pipeline from Qatar to the UAE and Oman but succeeded in blocking its northward extension to Kuwait by refusing to grant transit rights.[65] In 2009, the UAE left the planned single currency after an announcement that the GCC Central Bank would be located in Riyadh. Abu Dhabi had campaigned hard to host the bank in part to offset concerns at the Saudi-heavy structure of the GCC with its Secretariat in Riyadh, and Emirati officials made their displeasure very clear.[66]

To obviate the imbalance in power and deficit of trust, the GCC presented itself as a cautious status quo entity designed to shield its member states and societies from the transnational threats of spillover of regional instability from Iran and Iraq. Member governments retained responsibility for almost all aspects of political and economic policy and resisted any putative limitations on their sovereignty.[67] Sensitivities over sovereignty contributed to the failure of a GCC initiative in 2006 to examine a regional nuclear energy initiative as the UAE chose to pursue and develop their own national nuclear energy program instead.[68] A similar caution was evident in the trajectory of the Peninsula Shield Force after its formation at the third GCC leaders' summit in 1983; as Rory Miller has noted, 'competition and suspicion, as well as diverging national interests, conspired to reduce the value and effectiveness of the unit.'[69]

Areas of disagreement included whether and how to cooperate on matters of internal security and intelligence sharing that could be used by one member state against targets and individuals in another.[70] Both in 1982 and again in 1994, Kuwait opposed plans for an internal security agreement on the basis of a clause which would have enabled GCC security forces to pursue suspects 20 kilometers into the territory of a neighboring state.[71] On the one occasion when Kuwait did seek security assistance, at the height of the Tanker War phase of the Iran-Iraq War in 1986, the GCC turned down its request to station a contingent of Peninsula Shield Forces on Bubiyan Island, just across from the Iranian-occupied Iraqi Faw peninsula, as there was no consensus among member states, especially from Oman and the UAE, to adopt a more confrontational approach to the war.[72]

This record meant it was of little surprise that Kuwaiti leaders first contacted U.S. officials for assistance as Iraqi forces invaded in August 1990 rather than any of their GCC counterparts, although Gulf States' forces subsequently participated in the multinational coalition to liberate Kuwait.[73] Until the 1980s, the U.S. military and security footprint in the Gulf had been small and low-profile, with an emphasis on 'over-the-horizon' capabilities during the Cold War rather than a direct regional presence. A small U.S. naval force had been stationed in Bahrain since 1947, leasing facilities within the British base at Juffair, and in Saudi Arabia, the United States Air Force constructed an airbase in Dhahran and maintained a Strategic Air Command there until 1962.[74] U.S. forces withdrew from Saudi Arabia in 1962 and did not return to the Arabian Peninsula until 1990 but a web of energy and security interests bound the Kingdom and the U.S.[75]

The Gerald Ford and Jimmy Carter presidencies began the process of expanding the level of U.S. military and naval resources devoted to the region, filtered primarily through the Cold War lens. The U.S. acquired the airbase at Masirah in Oman from Britain in 1975 and signed a ten-year access to facilities agreement with Sultan Qaboos in 1980.[76] The Carter administration created a Rapid Deployment Joint Task Force in 1977, renamed the U.S. Central Command in 1983.[77] Carter also articulated a policy proclamation in his State of the Union address in January 1980, known as the Carter Doctrine. Reacting to the Soviet invasion of Afghanistan the previous month and reflecting concerns that this might be the prelude to a move to try and gain a foothold in the Gulf or the Indian Ocean, Carter declared that 'Any attempt by an outside force to gain control of the Persian Gulf region will be regarded as an assault on the vital interests of the United States of America, and will be repelled by any means necessary, including military force.'[78]

The trigger for the more visible U.S. military posture in the Gulf was the escalation of attacks on international merchant shipping and regional oil and gas facilities as the Iran-Iraq War progressed. The number of attacks on merchant shipping jumped from seventy-one incidents in 1984 to 111 in 1986 and then surged to 181 the following year, when targeted vessels came from Kuwait, Saudi Arabia, Qatar, and the UAE.[79] And yet, U.S. officials initially rebuffed a request from Kuwait for assistance in protecting its shipping, as officials were anxious to avoid a potentially open-ended commitment, and reversed course only after Kuwait approached the Soviet Union instead. The subsequent internationalization of Gulf waters occurred as the U.S., the U.K., France, Italy, and the Soviets all sent warships to conduct convoy operations that protected Kuwaiti vessels during the 'Tanker War' phase of the Iran-Iraq War in 1987 and 1988.[80] The U.S. Navy also attacked Iranian naval ships in the Persian Gulf in Operation Praying Mantis, a sharp retaliatory strike in April 1988 after a U.S. frigate was damaged by an Iranian-placed mine.

Two years later, the Iraqi invasion of Kuwait on 2 August 1990 and the U.S. assembly of a thirty-four-nation coalition to liberate Kuwait in the 1991 Gulf War cemented the U.S. as a permanent feature of the regional security landscape. After the war, and contrary to an initial condition set by King Fahd that all U.S. forces would withdraw from Saudi Arabia once Kuwait was liberated, several thousand remained in the Kingdom once the bulk of the coalition presence was withdrawn in May 1991.[81] The U.S. also signed additional defense cooperation agreements with Kuwait and Bahrain in 1991, Qatar in 1992, and the UAE in 1994, and returned 36,000 troops to Kuwait and Saudi Arabia in September 1994 after Saddam Hussein again massed forces on the Iraq-Kuwait boundary.[82] These agreements and response to the new threat from Iraqi aggression prompted the Clinton administration to expand its naval and military assets in the Gulf as part of a policy of 'Dual Containment' of Iraq and Iran as the 1990s gave way to the 2000s.[83]

The contours of the contemporary regional security structure therefore took shape before the further shocks of the terrorist attacks on 11 September 2001, in which seventeen of the nineteen hijackers were citizens of Saudi Arabia and the UAE, and the U.S.-led 'war on terror' which followed. The U.S. role in the Gulf was transformed from an 'over-the-horizon' posture in the 1980s into an embedded feature of the Gulf States' defense and security calculus, which further inhibited GCC-wide initiatives.[84] These developments did not, however, contribute to the creation of a security community in the Gulf or even to a semblance of a viable or stable regional order. Moreover, the backlash against the more visible presence of Western forces in the Arabian Peninsula, especially but not only in Saudi Arabia, generated new sources of grievance and discontent against regime elites and their policy choices. This ranged from the radicalization of Osama bin Laden and his jihadi followers to more widespread (and non-violent) anxieties at the 'smothering embrace' of the perceived U.S. role in Gulf affairs. Hussein Al-Qallaf, a Shia Islamist MP in Kuwait articulated the feelings of many across the region in 1996 as he stated that 'If America defends its interests, then we have every right also to defend our beliefs and our principals.'[85]

Reading (and misreading) threats

External security and defense relationships have enabled regimes in the Gulf to focus their own coercive capabilities on the maintenance of domestic order, even if the distinction between internal and external (in)security has always been blurred. Unlike many postcolonial states, including elsewhere in the Middle East and North Africa such as Syria, Iraq, Libya, or Algeria, the Gulf regimes did not rely upon or inherit mass armies that had emerged during a struggle for independence or in the years that followed.[86] The link between war- and state-making did not exist, with the partial exception of the early twentieth century unification through conquest of Saudi Arabia under Ibn Saud and Oman during the Dhofar War and the early years of Sultan Qaboos, largely due to the fact that the passage of sovereignty was not accompanied by regime change or the appearance of a new set of dominant social classes or political arrangements.[87]

The configuration of 'hard' military power reflected the ruling elites' perceptions of the concept of 'security' and the conflation of national security interests with the survival of the regimes they headed. 'Regime security' could be narrowed still further to mean the safeguarding of the position of the ruler as much against members of his own family as against any societal or regional threat. Chapter 1 noted the preponderance of internal coups in many of the Gulf States throughout the twentieth century, and this shaped rulers' views of risk and threat. As an example, five of the seven rulers of the emirates which formed the UAE in 1971–2 had seized power from a relative, and their preoccupation was the maintenance of their own political control above all else.[88] In a book published in 1994, Bahrain's then Crown Prince, Sheikh

Hamad bin Isa Al Khalifa, wrote that 'Instead of having to face a large fire after it has spread, it is better to extinguish the small sparks which can cause it.'[89] A zero-sum approach to addressing putative threats to security also guided attempts to 'coup-proof' regimes against challenges from within the military as with the uncovering of plots inside the Saudi armed forces in the 1950s and 1960s.[90]

Institutional fragmentation was a common feature of state security structures across the Middle East and North Africa, in republics and monarchies alike, as a key element of a 'coup-proofing' strategy in which a proliferation of agencies kept watch on each other as well as the population at large.[91] In the specific context of the Gulf States, Laurence Louër has also observed that 'competing dynastic factions' within the ruling families compounded the multiplication of security agencies.[92] The previous section documented this in the case of the UAE for two decades after the creation of the federation. In Bahrain, in early 1997, the aforementioned Crown Prince Hamad created a new National Guard under his authority while his uncle, the powerful Prime Minister, Prince Khalifa bin Salman Al Khalifa, was 'on an extended trip abroad,' in an apparent bid to dilute the Prime Minister's control over the internal security forces.[93]

A similar pattern of fragmentation was evident in Saudi Arabia in the decades after the death of Ibn Saud in 1953 and the growth of powerful institutional 'fiefdoms' under the control of senior figures in the royal family, notably the Ministry of Defense under Prince and, later, Crown Prince Sultan (1963–2011); the Ministry of Interior, under Prince, and later Crown Prince Nayef (1975–2012); and the National Guard, under Prince, and later King Abdullah (1963–2010, and under Abdullah's son, Prince Miteb, until 2017). As Steffen Hertog has noted, the forces they controlled grew into 'large, passive, and dependent clienteles of individual regime figures' in what he labeled 'rentier militaries' rooted in princely interest rather than military expediency.[94] The Saudi Arabian National Guard additionally became a mechanism to wield patronage to a tribal base which served to tap into and mobilize tribal networks in return for their loyalty and allegiance, albeit to some extent to an individual (Abdullah) within the broader royal ecosystem.[95] The fact that leaders of the religious fundamentalists who seized the Grand Mosque in Mecca in 1979 were themselves former members of the National Guard illustrated how such loyalty could not be taken for granted, and may have been a reason why the significance of the threat they posed, from a perceived 'loyalist' base, was missed.[96]

The chaotic aftermath of the capture of the Grand Mosque in November 1979 by extremist militants who held the compound for two weeks left deep scars in Saudi Arabia that have resonated through to the present day. Mohammed bin Salman himself has claimed the events and legacy of 1979 set the Kingdom on a path away from moderation that only he, as Crown Prince four decades later, has been able to challenge and reverse.[97] It is certainly the case that the takeover of the Grand Mosque profoundly shook the circles of power in Saudi Arabia which responded with greater displays of religiosity in public and policy spaces, as noted in Chapter 5. However, the shock was magnified because it called into question, in the most existential way, the reliability of a group hitherto seen as a bedrock of regime loyalty, as well as one of the strategies of aligning tribal solidarities with national institutions, as Cronin relates:

> This was the first serious action in which the National Guard had been involved and its manifold practical weaknesses became rapidly apparent. Chaos resulted from unserviceable vehicles, shortages of weapons and faulty ammunition (…) The tribal structure of the Guard, believed by Saudis to be its primary political strength, was soon shown to be a serious military weakness, with Guardsmen refusing to obey orders from senior officers unless they came from those in their own unit.[98]

Saudi control over the Grand Mosque was eventually restored by Jordanian and French special forces. In the aftermath, one of the authorities' responses was to draft in a contingent of 10,000 Pakistani troops who were attached to the 12th Armored Brigade stationed near Tabuk.[99] The military relationship with Pakistan was deep-rooted and had been used to provide air cover for the

Kingdom in the 1960s, especially during the civil war in Yemen which periodically spilled across the border into Saudi Arabia.[100] Saudi officials also reportedly expressed an interest in Pakistan's nuclear weapons program in the 1990s and Prince Sultan, the Defense Minister and Crown Prince, visited Pakistani uranium enrichment and ballistic missile facilities in 1999, shortly after Pakistan had conducted its first successful nuclear test.[101] General expenditure on military and security budgets also increased significantly in the aftermath of 1979, with Jean-François Seznec estimating that a total of US$432 billion was spent between 1984 and 2001 alone, albeit likely on weapons systems and other 'hardware' rather than force training and development.[102]

Concerns about the loyalty of military personnel surfaced also in Kuwait after the shock of the Iraqi invasion in August 1990. The '*bidun*' community (stateless residents of Kuwait) had formed the backbone of the army and police force in the 1970s and 1980s with Claire Beaugrand estimating that as much as 80 percent of regular army personnel (who did not and could not hold officer rank) were *bidun* before 1990.[103] Against the backdrop of regional insecurity stemming from the Iran-Iraq War and the aftermath of a series of terrorist attacks in Kuwait, as well as an economic crisis caused by sharply falling oil prices in the mid-1980s, the Kuwaiti government reclassified the *bidun* as 'illegal residents' in December 1986 and recommended that they be gradually replaced in the armed forces.[104] However, the systematic exclusion of *bidun* from the Ministries of Defense and Interior only gathered pace after Kuwait's liberation in 1991 as they were made scapegoats for the Kuwaiti military's capitulation in the face of the Iraqi advance, and stigmatized as 'traitors' thereafter, despite the failings at senior political and military leadership levels.[105]

One of the tools used by regimes across the Gulf States to minimize the risk of threats emerging from within the military has been the employment of foreign service personnel, as illustrated by the Saudi recruitment of the Pakistani units noted above. Zoltan Barany has observed that foreign contract soldiers 'generally have no political interests to pursue and seldom participate in attempts to overthrow the regime' while their lack of connections to local communities meant that 'the state can deploy them with confidence against citizens in domestic contingencies.'[106] Most of the foreign soldiers were Sunni Muslims recruited from other Middle Eastern states, such as Jordan, Syria, and Yemen, or from South Asia, including Pakistan, especially in Bahrain, which embarked on a recruitment spree in 2011 as protests in the country intensified.[107] Writing after the security forces had crushed the uprising, Barany reminded readers that Bahrain's military was not a national army but 'a fighting force of Sunni Muslims who are charged with protecting a Sunni ruling family and Sunni political and business elites.'[108] In the UAE, officials took a different approach to ward off any potential spread of Arab Spring volatility, as the *New York Times* obtained documents which indicated that Erik Prince, the founder of Blackwater, the private military contractor, had been engaged to:

> … put together an 800-member battalion of foreign troops (…) intended to conduct special operations missions inside and outside the country, defend oil pipelines and skyscrapers from terrorist attacks and put down internal revolts (…) in recruiting the Columbians and others from halfway around the world, Mr. Prince's subordinates were following his strict rule: hire no Muslims.[109]

The use of non-Muslim soldiers, reportedly from countries such as Columbia and South Africa, was intended not only to utilize their combat-hardened expertise but also because, the *New York Times* claimed, 'Muslim soldiers, Mr. Prince warned, could not be counted on to kill fellow Muslims.'[110] The pace of recruitment from Columbia was such that the country's deputy Defense Minister told the *Financial Times* in 2013 that 'We are worried that very good people are abandoning our forces' as 'These are soldiers with a lot of experience, and it took great effort to train them well.'[111]

Rulers and ruling elites have also been caught flat-footed on occasion in their assessment of the balance of risk and threat. Sir Anthony Parsons, the British Ambassador to Iran during the Iranian revolution, visited Arab Gulf capitals in 1979 and 'discovered that the principal source of anxiety was not the spread of the Iranian revolutionary message but Iraqi attempts to dominate the smaller Gulf states.'[112] Just as Iraq was seen by some as the more urgent challenge in 1979 than Iran, so a decade later there was another misreading of the balance of threat assessments to regional security in the Gulf. The British Ambassador to Saudi Arabia in 1990 acknowledged that one reason that Western intelligence agencies did not pick up the threat that Saddam Hussein posed to Kuwait was because their focus was trained on Iran, from 'whence the main threat to stability in the Gulf was considered to come.'[113] Officials in Kuwait and other GCC capitals also failed to appreciate the full significance of the Iraqi military buildup on the Kuwaiti border in part because Iraq had a record of border violations going back to the 1960s, which fed into political assessments that 'at the most, the Iraqis might go for a limited objective consistent with their demands, such as the Rumaila oilfield along the frontier or a repetition of previous border incursions.'[114]

Moving ahead another decade, Saudi security and intelligence forces missed the threat posed by returning Saudis from Afghanistan after the toppling of the Taliban regime in 2001 and a decision by bin Laden in early 2002 to turn his fighters against the Kingdom. After instructing Saudi fighters in Afghanistan to return home and begin preparing for a campaign of terrorism, between 300 and 1,000 recruits returned to Saudi Arabia via third countries and formed the nucleus of two Al Qaeda networks that largely (though not completely) escaped the notice of Saudi officialdom.[115] However, the significance of their return was underappreciated in the run-up to the launch of Al Qaeda's terror campaign in Saudi Arabia in May 2003, which lasted until 2006, in part because the Saudi security community failed to believe they faced a jihadist threat and remained focused instead on the perceived vulnerability of the Shia population to acts of Iranian 'meddling' in domestic Saudi affairs.[116]

In 2011 and 2012, the outbreak of political upheaval across much of the Middle East and North Africa led many in the Gulf to attribute the demonstrations to foreign interference rather than domestic root causes of discontent. The fact that protests initially swept through Bahrain and the Eastern Province of Saudi

Arabia led Saudi, Bahraini, and other Gulf officials to accuse Iran of involvement in fomenting the unrest.[117] 'Securitizing' the demonstrations by linking them to destabilizing Iranian activity served as a way to deny them credibility and to press the right buttons to Western audiences, especially in Washington, D.C. and London, and was not unsuccessful in the Bahraini and Saudi cases, as Simon Mabon has illustrated.[118] The Bahraini uprising led to the deployment of Peninsula Shield Forces not to defend regional interests against an external aggressor but rather to assist a regime in restoring domestic order against an internal threat.[119] In an interview with the Saudi-owned, London-based *Asharq al-Awsat* newspaper published two weeks after Peninsula Shield Forces deployed to Bahrain in March 2011, the commander, Major General Mutlaq bin Salem Al-Azima, stated that

> ... our mission is to secure Bahrain's vital and strategically important military infrastructure from any foreign interference. Everybody knows that when a state becomes preoccupied with its internal security, this increases its need to secure its international borders (...) This is an emergency force, and so it has special forces, rapid response troops, as well as support troops.[120]

When large-scale demonstrations spread to Sunni-majority areas in the Gulf, such as Kuwait in 2012, it became harder to ascribe them to Iranian-linked or pan-Shia sectarian motivations. Instead, the Director-General of Dubai Police, Dhahi Khalfan Tamim, asserted that the Muslim Brotherhood was planning to 'take over' the Gulf monarchies and added, without providing supporting evidence, that 'My sources say the next step is to make Gulf governments figurehead bodies only without actual ruling. The start will be in Kuwait in 2013 and in other Gulf states in 2016.'[121] Khalfan also appeared to suggest that the Muslim Brotherhood were 'secret soldiers for America and they are executing plans to create tension;' language which echoed that of Bahrain's Foreign Minister, Prince Khalid bin Ahmed Al Khalifa, who had in 2011 claimed that the U.S. was implicated in 'a conspiracy involving Iran' to weaken the Arab world through protest.[122]

The aftermath of the Arab Spring protests which occurred in Gulf States saw the assertion of control over public space as well as narratives. Charles Tripp drew attention to the significance of public spaces as performative sites for the politics of resistance in 2011 with Tahrir Square in Cairo and the Pearl Roundabout in Manama becoming focal points for the uprisings in Egypt and Bahrain, respectively.[123] In March 2011, the graceful pearl monument at the heart of the roundabout was bulldozed to erase the symbolic heart of the protest movement, with Bahrain's Foreign Minister, Prince Khalid declaring that 'It is a removal of a bad memory.'[124] Its destruction, days after Peninsula Shield Forces had entered Bahrain, was ironic since the monument had been erected to commemorate the first GCC Summit to take place in Manama, in 1982, its six sails marking each of the GCC member states.[125] Across the causeway, in 2017, Saudi authorities stood accused of ordering the destruction of the historic quarter of Awamiya, a town in the Eastern Province long an epicenter of anti-government protests, 'to prevent militants using the narrow streets to evade capture' by security forces.[126] A generation earlier, Iraqi forces in Kuwait had sought to harness the control of space in a different manner, as they renamed streets, buildings, and even entire neighborhoods 'to create an illusion of support for the occupation.'[127]

Regimes also responded to the Arab Spring era with measures which sought to establish control over narratives and public debate. This in part took the form of updated counter-terrorism and cyber-crime regulations in several of the Gulf States which included vaguely-worded clauses and expansive definitions which gave officials broad power to go after critics accused of acts as anodyne as spreading 'fake news.'[128] Governments, especially but not only in Saudi Arabia and the UAE, also invested heavily in developing a sophisticated surveillance apparatus which consisted both of deeper local capabilities and the procurement of spyware and other technologies from abroad, including from companies based in Israel.[129] Campaigns of deception and disinformation additionally became far more targeted and offensive in nature and were prominent features of both the 2013–14 and 2017–20 iterations of the 'Gulf crises' which pitted Qatar against three of its fellow GCC states, namely Bahrain, Saudi Arabia, and the UAE. What Marc Owen Jones has labeled 'digital authoritarianism' involved the 'weaponization' of social media that belied early assumptions that the rise of Twitter and related platforms might have an empowering effect rather than offering regimes powerful opportunities to establish new tools of social control.[130]

Two of the most active figures in the appearance of a far more controlled and authoritarian political landscape in the Gulf in the decade which followed the Arab Spring were the Crown Princes of Abu Dhabi and Saudi Arabia, Mohammed bin Zayed Al Nahyan and Mohammed bin Salman Al Saud. Although separated by nearly a quarter-century in age, the two were, together with Emir Tamim bin Hamad Al Thani of Qatar, part of a new generation of leadership who emerged in the Gulf. Both Mohammed bin Zayed, who became Ruler of Abu Dhabi and President of the UAE in 2022, and Mohammed bin Salman, who added the role of Prime Minister to his many roles as undisputed decision-maker in Saudi Arabia, also in 2022, centralized power around them in ways that differed significantly from their predecessors.[131] Their distinctive assumption of authority gave some credence to an oft-discussed prediction by Christopher Davidson in 2012 that some of the monarchies might soon cease to exist 'in their current form.'[132] Rather than collapsing, Saudi Arabia under Mohammed bin Salman and the UAE of Mohammed bin Zayed instead saw the consolidation of military and security functions as a key element in their centralization of power, through the creation of the Presidency of State Security and the Presidential Guard, respectively.[133] The war in Yemen provided a chastening lesson to both leaders of the limitations in their ability to project military power beyond their borders, but the loyalty of these praetorian guards has yet to be fully tested.

What is next?

Saudi Arabia, the UAE, and Qatar all developed more potent combinations of 'hard' and 'soft' power in the 2000s and 2010s which meshed with a greater willingness to project these types of 'smart' and 'subtle' power beyond their borders, on a regional and, in some cases, an international level. 'Smart' power, 'the combination of the hard power of coercion and payment with the soft power of persuasion and attraction,' was coined by Joseph Nye to go beyond his earlier conception of 'soft' power as 'getting others to want the outcomes that you want' and being able to 'co-opt (rather than coerce) and set the agenda in world politics.'[134] Mehran Kamrava further delineated the notion of 'subtle' power, drawing upon insights gained from living in the Gulf and working in the Middle East, as 'the ability to exert influence from behind the scenes,' a characteristic he suggested was evident in Qatari foreign policymaking during and immediately after the Arab Spring.[135] These manifestations of different forms of power were (mostly) exercised externally rather than internally, and were a feature of Gulf States' foreign rather than domestic policy responses to the changing regional and international context before and after the Arab Spring.

Processes of globalization since the 1990s and periods of high energy prices since the 2000s opened new opportunities for states to project themselves in the international arena and to assert influence at the regional level, where the Gulf increasingly became a center of gravity for the Middle East. Conventional metrics of power, such as extent of territorial mass or size of population, were supplemented by new global flows, of investment, information, and changing patterns of trade among others, which began to rebalance power relations across the world.[136] GCC states became active participants in the reshaping of geoeconomic influence as they developed financial centers, aviation hubs, and greater visibility in the architecture of international governance after the global financial crisis in 2008.[137] The emergence of at least three of the Gulf States as assertive actors which aligned their growing capabilities (in the political, economic, and security arenas) with a more expansive policy intent was not without its challenges.[138] The most direct impact of power projection after the Arab Spring was felt regionally, in Gulf States' interventions in Libya, Syria, and Yemen, and in the political transitions in Egypt. Within the region, the Gulf crises of 2013–14 and 2017–20 set Gulf States against each other in a manner that placed considerable strain on many of the transnational cross-border linkages described in this book.[139]

The hosting of the 2022 FIFA World Cup in Qatar and the extraordinary array of sporting events taking place across the Gulf States, together with the greater visibility of entities and individuals from the Gulf in international sporting institutions, in governing capacities and as owners and participants, has focused attention as never before on the rise of the Gulf States as assertive actors in a changing global order.[140] Terms such as 'sportswashing' have emerged to describe the phenomenon whereby countries and companies tap into the global appeal of sport (and culture[141]) to burnish their international image and change narratives away from more negative issues, such as human rights violations, the (mis) treatment of migrant workers and marginalized communities, and the lack of political freedoms. The term does not only apply to the Gulf States and has been used for the 2018 FIFA World Cup in Russia, the 2022 Winter Olympics in Beijing, and Israel Start-Up Nation's sponsorship of a professional cycling team.[142] However, the frequency with which sportswashing is applied to the Gulf (Bahrain and the UAE also sponsor professional cycling teams, which brought UAE-Team Emirates victory in the Tour de France in 2020 and 2021, and Saudi Arabia's Public Investment Fund generated global attention in 2023 with its foray into professional men's golf through the LIV Tour and in the majority acquisition of four leading Saudi football teams) has generated critical attention on the use of sport as a tool of soft power by Gulf States.[143]

Broader issues relating to the increasing global urgency of climate action and greater focus on the multiple sets of energy transitions are likely to cause additional changes in the way the Gulf States engage externally, even as they navigate their own sensitive (and halting) pathways toward post-oil economies. The fallout from the full-scale Russian invasion of Ukraine in February 2022 generated significant benefit for ruling elites in the major Gulf energy exporters as oil and gas price rises reversed years of budget deficits and fiscal pressures, even in smaller producers such as Oman which returned to surplus in 2022. In addition, the rush to secure alternative oil and gas supplies as European states scrambled to reduce reliance on imports from Russia re-stated the centrality of the Gulf in global energy security considerations and gave figures such as Mohammed bin Salman renewed importance on the international stage. The rehabilitation of Mohammed bin Salman (as he received visits in 2022 from Emmanuel Macron, Boris Johnson, Joe Biden, and Olaf Scholz) was a side effect of the Western campaign to isolate Vladimir Putin.[144]

It may be that the rise in oil and gas prices as a result of the Russia-Ukraine war is the last significant 'windfall' for hydrocarbon producers before the energy transitions set in, including transformative developments in small modular reactors and the electrification of transportation systems. If this is the case, it is an open question whether Gulf States' attempts to diversify and build genuinely non- or post-oil economies can succeed this time around, when previous efforts have fallen short. The progress of Saudi Arabia's Vision 2030 and associated 'giga-projects' will be worth watching for signs of whether, and how, the promise of transformational economic (and social) change feeds into, or tries to wall off, any evolution in political or governance structures. The UAE, which hosts the COP28 international Climate Change Conference in Dubai in 2023, seeks both to expand oil production and focus on decarbonization in the expectation that it (and other Gulf producers) will be the 'last man standing' and able to produce oil more cheaply and with less carbon intensity than any competitor. Qatar has made its bet on natural gas being the bridging fuel in the energy transition as it embarks on a massive expansion of liquefaction capacity that will lock its Liquefied Natural Gas (LNG) into world energy markets for years, if not decades, to come.

Looking comparatively at the durability of other political systems, one of the characteristics of the Chinese Communist Party that has explained its longevity has been its ability to adapt to changing times and circumstances, although Xi Jinping's authoritarian turn and unprecedented third term may test this.[145] Other non-Western states, such as Singapore, have long been viewed in the Gulf as a successful example of a model of a 'development state' which combined elements of state guidance and private initiative but remained politically authoritarian as it diversified into an advanced, knowledge-based economy.[146] Ruling elites in the Gulf States, however, remain wedded to neo-patrimonial forms of rule and political economies based on the redistribution of wealth as described in this book. The failure of initiatives to pool together within the GCC indicates that rulers (and ruling families) remain reluctant to share political resources with each other, still less to devolve meaningful governing responsibilities to their own citizens. The resolution, if any, to this logjam, will determine whether the next phase of economic and social development amounts to more of the same in attempts by rulers to effect change on their own terms and continue to be the most distinct political survivors in a rapidly altering global landscape.

NOTES

INTRODUCTION

1. See, for example, Jim Krane, *Energy Kingdoms: Oil and Political Survival in the Persian Gulf* (New York: Columbia University Press, 2019) and the collection of essays in Michael Herb and Marc Lynch (eds.), *The Politics of Rentier States in the Gulf*, POMEPS Studies 33, 2019. See also Jessie Moritz, 'Rentier Political Economies in the Gulf Oil Monarchies,' in Mehran Kamrava (ed.), *Routledge Handbook of Persian Gulf Politics* (Abingdon: Routledge, 2020), p.163.

2. Paul Dresch, 'Societies, Identities and Global Issues,' in Paul Dresch and James Piscatori (eds.), *Monarchies and Nations: Globalisation and Identity in the Arab States of the Gulf* (London: I.B. Tauris, 2005), p.3.

3. Nicolas Pelham, 'The Precarious Rise of the Gulf Despots,' *London Review of Books*, 40(4), 22 February 2008.

4. Farah Al-Nakib, 'Modernity and the Arab Gulf States: The Politics of Heritage, Modernity, and Forgetting,' in Mehran Kamrava (ed.), *Routledge Handbook of Persian Gulf Politics* (Abingdon: Routledge, 2020), pp.58–9. Al-Nakib proposes a slightly different timeframe for the 'in between' period in Kuwait, namely the period from the end of the Second World War to the mid-1980s.

5. Fred Halliday, 'In a Time of Hopes and Fears,' *British Journal of Middle Eastern Studies*, 36(2), 2009, p.173.

6. Isaac Chotiner, 'A Middle Eastern-Studies Professor on his Conversations with Mohammed bin Salman,' *The New Yorker*, 8 April 2019.

7. Madawi Al-Rasheed, 'Saudi Arabia Post 9/11: History, Religion and Security,' *Middle Eastern Studies*, 43(1), 2007, p.156.

8. See, for example, Nadav Samin, *Of Sand or Soil: Genealogy and Tribal Belonging in Saudi Arabia* (Princeton: Princeton University Press, 2015); Uzi Rabi (ed.), *Tribes and State in a Changing Middle East* (London: Hurst &

Co., 2016); Alanoud Al-Sharekh and Courtney Freer, *Tribalism and Political Power in the Gulf: State-Building and National Identity in Kuwait, Qatar and the UAE* (London: I.B. Tauris, 2022); and Scott Wiener, *Kinship, State Formation and Governance in the Arab Gulf States* (Edinburgh: Edinburgh University Press, 2022).

9. W.G. Runciman, *A Treatise on Social Theory. Vol. II: Substantive Social Theory* (Cambridge: Cambridge University Press, 1989).

10. W.G. Runciman, 'The Old Question,' *London Review of Books*, 9(4), 19 February 1987.

11. Michael Mann, *The Sources of Social Power. Volume 1: A History of Power from the Beginning to A.D. 1760* (Cambridge: Cambridge University Press, 1986).

12. Turki Al-Hamad, 'Will the Gulf Monarchies Work Together?,' *Middle East Quarterly*, 1997, pp.49–50.

13. Sulayman Khalaf, 'Camel Racing in the Gulf: Notes on the Evolution of a Traditional Cultural Sport,' *Anthropos* 94, 1999, p.102.

14. Madawi Al-Rasheed, 'Durable and Non-Durable Dynasties: The Rashidis and Sa'udis in Central Arabia,' *British Journal of Middle Eastern Studies*, 19(2), 1992, p.151.

15. Khalid Al-Azri, 'Change and Conflict in Contemporary Omani Society: The Case of Kafa'a in Marriage,' *British Journal of Middle Eastern Studies*, 37(2), 2010, pp.123–5.

16. Mehran Kamrava, 'Politics in the Persian Gulf: An Overview,' in Mehran Kamrava (ed.), *Routledge Handbook of Persian Gulf Politics* (Abingdon: Routledge, 2020), p.1.

1.   RULERS

1. Khalid Al-Dakhil, 'Abdullah Streamlines Saudi Succession Plans but Limits the Power to Choose,' in Joshua Craze and Mark Huband (eds.), *The Kingdom: Saudi Arabia and the Challenge of the 21ˢᵗ Century* (London: Hurst & Co., 2009), p.74.

2. Michael Herb, *All in the Family: Absolutism: Revolution, and Democracy in Middle Eastern Monarchies* (New York: SUNY Press, 1999).

3. John Duke Anthony, 'The Union of Arab Amirates,' *Middle East Journal*, 26(3), 1972, p.278.

4. Two good studies of factionalism in ruling families are Mehran Kamrava, 'Royal Factionalism and Political Liberalization in Qatar,' *Middle East Journal*, 63(3), 2009, pp.401–20; and Justin Gengler, 'Royal Factionalism, the Khawalid, and the Securitization of "the Shi'a Problem" in Bahrain,' *Journal of Arabian Studies*, 3(1), 2013, pp.53–79.

5. J.E. Peterson, 'The Emergence of Post-Traditional Oman,' *Working Paper No.5*, Durham Middle East Papers, Sir William Luce Publication Series, 2005, p.1.

6. Madawi Al-Rasheed, *A History of Saudi Arabia* (Cambridge: Cambridge University Press, 2010 edition), p.24.

7. A useful look at succession patterns is Russell Lucas, 'Rules and Tools of Succession in the Gulf Monarchies,' *Journal of Arabian Studies*, 2(1), 2012.

8. Youssef Ibrahim, 'Saudi King Issues Decrees to Revise Governing System,' *New York Times*, 2 March 1992.

9. Joseph Kéchichian, *Legal and Political Reforms in Sa'udi Arabia* (Abingdon: Routledge, 2013), pp.137–8.

10. Askar Al-Enazy, *The Creation of Saudi Arabia: Ibn Saud and British Imperial Policy, 1914–1927* (Abingdon: Routledge, 2010), p.10.

11. Nasir Al-Huzaimi, *The Mecca Uprising: An Insider's Account of Salafism and Insurrection in Saudi Arabia* (London: I.B. Tauris, 2021), pp.46–7.

12. The first letter, written by 'One of the grandsons of the Founder King Abdul Aziz' and dated 4 September 2015, included the assertion that 'A fool, on the other hand, is one who does not heed the events and experience of history. History taught us how King Abdul-Aziz overcame the challenges of Sabilla and Umm Radh'ma, how the family reunited effectively after the dispute between the late Saud and Faisal, and how the family withstood the storms of Nasserism and the Kuwait crisis. But history also taught us how the first state did not withstand the Egyptian invasion, and how the second state was torn apart by disputes.' See Hugh Miles, 'Saudi Royal Calls for Regime Change in Riyadh,' *The Guardian*, 28 September 2015.

13. Sultan Alamer, 'The Saudi "Founding Day" and the Death of Wahhabism,' *Arab Gulf States Institute in Washington*, 23 February 2022.

14. Frauke Heard-Bey, 'Conflict Resolution and Regional Cooperation: The Role of the Gulf Cooperation Council 1970–2002,' *Middle Eastern Studies*, 42(2), 2006, p.211.

15. Rosemarie Said Zahlan, *The Creation of Qatar* (Abingdon: Routledge, 2016 edition), p.86.

16. Ibid. p.88.

17. John Bulloch, *The Gulf: A Portrait of Kuwait, Qatar, Bahrain and the UAE* (London: Century Publishing, 1984), p.29.

18. Zainab Fattah, 'Bahrain Left Out of World Cup's Show of Middle East Unity,' *Bloomberg*, 30 November 2022.

19. Sultan Sooud Al Qassemi, 'Tribalism in the Arabian Peninsula: It's a Family Affair,' *Al Arabiya*, 3 February 2012.

20. Christopher Davidson, *Abu Dhabi: Oil and Beyond* (London: Hurst & Co., 2009), p.5; Christopher Davidson, *Dubai: The Vulnerability of Success* (London: Hurst & Co., 2008), p.13.

21. Michael Quentin Morton, *Buraimi: The Struggle for Power, Influence and Oil in Arabia* (London: I.B. Tauris, 2013), p.3.

22. Frauke Heard-Bey, *From Trucial States to United Arab Emirates* (Dubai: Motivate Publishing, 2004 edition), pp.50–2.

23. The Qawasim (sing. Al Qassemi) ruled Sharjah as well as Ras al-Khaimah and were the paramount maritime power in the Gulf during the eighteenth and early nineteenth centuries.

24. Davidson, *Vulnerability of Success*, p.15.

25. Abdullah Omran Taryam, *The Establishment of the United Arab Emirates 1950–1985* (London: Croon Helm, 1987), p.234.

26. Mishaal Al-Gergawi, 'Emirates plus Etihad Equals Neo-Federal UAE,' *Gulf News*, 13 December 2009.

27. Niklas Haller, 'A Labyrinth in the Sand: British Boundary-Making and the Emergence of the Emirati Territorial State,' *PhD Dissertation*, University of Exeter, 2019, p.335 and p.347.

28. James Onley, 'Britain and the Gulf Shaikhdoms, 1820–1971: The Politics of Protection,' Georgetown School of Foreign Service in Qatar: *Center for International and Regional Studies Occasional Paper*, 2009, p.5.

29. Paul Rich, *Creating the Arabian Gulf: The British Raj and the Invasions of the Gulf* (Lanham: Lexington Books, 2009), p.71.

30. Lisa Anderson, 'Absolutism and the Resilience of Monarchy in the Middle East,' *Political Science Quarterly*, 106(1), 1991, p.5.

31. Frederick Anscombe, *The Ottoman Gulf: The Creation of Kuwait, Saudi Arabia, and Qatar, 1870–1914* (New York: Columbia University Press, 1997), p.3.

32. David Rundell, *Vision or Mirage: Saudi Arabia at the Crossroads* (London: I.B. Tauris, 2020), p.45.

33. Quoted in Marc Owen Jones, *Political Repression in Bahrain* (Cambridge: Cambridge University Press, 2020), p.57.

34. Staci Strobl, *Sectarian Order in Bahrain: The Social and Colonial Origins of Criminal Justice* (Lanham: Lexington Books, 2018), p.17.

35. For the authoritative account of the rise of Mohammed bin Zayed and Mohammed bin Salman, see Christopher Davidson, *From Sheikhs to Sultanism: Statecraft and Authority in Saudi Arabia and the UAE* (London: Hurst & Co., 2021). Mohammed bin Zayed became Ruler of Abu Dhabi (and President of the UAE) on the death of his older brother, Khalifa bin Zayed Al Nahyan, in May 2022. Mohammed bin Salman became head of government (Prime Minister) in September 2022, but remains the Crown Prince of Saudi Arabia as of August 2023.

36. H.E. Chehabi and Juan Linz, *Sultanistic Regimes* (Baltimore: Johns Hopkins University Press, 1998).

37. See, for example, Davidson, *From Sheikhs to Sultanism*.

38. C.A. Bayly, *The Birth of the Modern World 1780–1914* (Oxford: Blackwell Publishing, 2004), p.248 and p.253.

39. J.P. Bannerman, 'The Impact of the Early Oil Concessions in the Gulf States,' in R.I. Lawless (ed.), *The Gulf in the Early Twentieth Century: Foreign Institutions and Local Responses* (Durham: Centre for Middle East and Islamic Studies, 1986), pp.76–7.

40. Haifa Alangari, *The Struggle for Power in Arabia: Ibn Saud, Hussein and Great Britain, 1914–1924* (Reading: Ithaca Press, 1998), p.247.

41. Waleed Al-Munais, 'Social and Ethnic Differentiation in Kuwait: A Social Geography of an Indigenous Society,' *PhD dissertation*, School of Oriental and African Studies, University of London, 1981, p.321.

42. Strobl, *Sectarian Order in Bahrain*, p.6.

43. M. Talha Çiçek, 'Negotiating Power and Authority in the Desert: The Arab Bedouin and the Limits of the Ottoman State in Hijaz, 1840–1908,' *Middle Eastern Studies*, 52(2), 2016, p.269.

44. Peter Lienhardt, *Disorientations: A Society in Flux: Kuwait in the 1950s* (Reading: Ithaca Press, 1993), p.55.

45. Ibid.

46. J.E. Peterson, 'Rulers, Merchants and Shaikhs in Gulf Politics: The Function of Family Networks,' in Alanoud Alsharekh (ed.), *The Gulf Family: Kinship Policies and Modernity* (London: Saqi Books, 2007), p.30.

47. James Onley and Sulayman Khalaf, 'Shaikhly Authority in the Pre-Oil Gulf: An Historical-Anthropological Study,' *History and Anthropology*, 17(3), 2006, pp.204–5.

48. Mohammed A.J. Althani, *Jassim the Leader: Founder of Qatar* (London: Profile Books, 2012), p.169.

49. Muhammad Al-Atawneh, 'Is Saudi Arabia a Theocracy? Religion and Governance in Contemporary Saudi Arabia,' *Middle Eastern Studies* 45(5), 2009, p.721; Ulrike Freitag, 'Helpless Representatives of the Great Powers? Western Consuls in Jeddah, 1830s to 1914,' *Journal of Imperial and Commonwealth History*, 40(3), 2012, p.362.

50. Al-Atawneh, 'Is Saudi Arabia a Theocracy?,' p.722.

51. George Joffe, 'Boundary Delimitation: The Role of History,' in George Joffe and Richard Schofield (eds.), *Geographic Realities in the Middle East and North Africa: State, Oil and Agriculture* (Abingdon: Routledge, 2021), pp.81–2.

52. Joseph Kostiner, *The Making of Saudi Arabia 1916–1936: From Chieftaincy to Monarchical State* (Oxford: Oxford University Press, 1993), pp.114–15.

53. See, for example, Peterson, 'Emergence of Post-Traditional Oman.'

54. Fuad Khuri, *Tribe and State in Bahrain: The Transformation of Social and Political Authority in an Arab State* (Chicago: University of Chicago Press, 1980), p.35.

55. Gerd Nonneman, 'Political Reform in the Gulf Monarchies: From Liberalization to Democratization? A Comparative Perspective,' in Anoushiravan Ehteshami and Steven Wright (eds.), *Reform in the Middle East Oil Monarchies* (Reading: Ithaca Press, 2008), p.6.

56. Max Weber, 'Politics as a Vocation,' in H.H. Gerth and C. Wright Mills (translated and edited), *From Max Weber: Essays in Sociology* (New York: Oxford University Press, 1946), available online at: http://fs2.american. edu/dfagel/www/Class%20Readings/Weber/PoliticsAsAVocation.pdf

57. Cf. Fred Halliday, *Arabia without Sultans* (London: Saqi Books, 2012 edition).

58. These core institutions have been labeled 'sovereign ministries,' traditionally the Ministries of Interior, Defense, and Foreign Affairs, as well as the titular position of Prime Minister, which have been held mostly by senior members of ruling families, although there has been some variation in this pattern since 2010.

59. Fred Halliday, *The Middle East in International Relations: Power, Politics and Ideology* (Cambridge: Cambridge University Press, 2005), p.278.

60. Martin Hvidt, 'The Dubai Model: An Outline of Key Development-Process Elements in Dubai,' *International Journal of Middle East Studies*, 41(3), 2009, p.400.

61. Dania Thafer, 'Obstacles to Innovation in Rentier Economies: States, Elites, and the Squandering of the Demographic Dividend,' *PhD dissertation*, American University, 2020, p.101.

62. Eran Segal, 'Merchants' Networks in Kuwait: The Story of Yusuf al-Marzuk,' *Middle Eastern Studies*, 45(5), 2009, pp.715–16.

63. Herb, *All in the Family*, pp.87–8; John Townsend, *Oman: The Making of the Modern State* (London: Croom Helm, 1977), pp.90–2; Calvin Allen and W. Lynn Rigsbee, *Oman under Qaboos: From Coup to Constitution 1970–1996* (London: Frank Cass, 2000), p.36.

64. Al-Rasheed, *History of Saudi Arabia*, p.83. The other three non-Saudi members of the political committee were Khalid Al-Hakim, a Syrian, Khalid Al-Ghargini, a Libyan, and H. St. John Philby, a British citizen and father of the future spy, Kim Philby.

65. The British Diplomatic Oral History Programme, Churchill College, University of Cambridge, 'Recollections of Sir John Thomson GCMG,' recorded and transcribed by Catherine Manning, 20 July 2016, available online at: https://www.chu.cam.ac.uk/archives/collections/bdohp/#H

66. Jörg Matthias Determann, *Historiography in Saudi Arabia: Globalization and the State in the Middle East* (London: I.B. Tauris, 2021 edition), p.41.

67. Tancred Bradshaw, *The End of Empire in the Gulf: From Trucial States to United Arab Emirates* (London: I.B. Tauris, 2021), p.166.

68. Samuel Huntingdon, *Political Order in Changing Societies* (Yale: Yale University Press, 1968); Halliday, *Arabia without Sultans*.

69. Al-Rasheed, *History of Saudi Arabia*, p.73.

70. 'Qatar: The Emir's Dilemma,' *Gulf States Newsletter*, 25(662), 28 May 2001, p.1; 'PM's Son Weds, Former CP to Marry,' *Gulf States Newsletter*, 30(778), 24 March 2006, p.6; 'Qatar: Another Top Al-Thani Wedding,' *Gulf States Newsletter*, 30(783), 9 June 2006, p.4; 'Cabinet Members in Tamim's Latest Government,' *Gulf States Newsletter*, 45(1136), 11 November 2021, p.7.

71. Malise Ruthven, 'The Saudi Trillions,' *London Review of Books*, 39(17), 7 September 2017.

72. Rundell, *Vision or Mirage*, p.128.

73. Andrea Rugh, *The Political Culture of Leadership in the United Arab Emirates* (New York: Palgrave Macmillan, 2007), pp.220–1.

74. Ibid. p.176.

75. Anastasia Nosova, 'The Merchant Elite and Parliamentary Politics in Kuwait: The Dynamics of Business Political Participation in a Rentier State,' *PhD dissertation*, London School of Economics and Political Science, 2016, p.82.

76. Kristian Coates Ulrichsen, *Qatar and the Gulf Crisis* (London: Hurst & Co., 2020), pp.22–3; Shohei Sato, *Britain and the Formation of the Gulf States: Embers of Empire* (Manchester: Manchester University Press, 2016), pp.110–15.

77. 'High-Level Marriage Reflects Personal Element in Saudi-Bahraini Relationship,' *Gulf States Newsletter*, 35(903), p.3.

78. Frank Kane, 'UAE and Saudi Arabia Send Forces to Bahrain,' *The National*, 14 March 2011.

79. Elham Manea, *Regional Politics in the Gulf: Saudi Arabia, Oman, Yemen* (London: Saqi Books, 2005), p.28.

80. Rundell, *Vision or Mirage*, p.88; Joseph Kostiner, 'On Instruments and Their Designers: The *Ikhwan* of Najd and the Emergence of the Saudi State,' *Middle Eastern Studies*, 21(3), 1985, p.303.

81. Abdel Razzaq Takriti, *Monsoon Revolution: Republicans, Sultans, and Empires in Oman, 1965–1976* (Oxford: Oxford University Press, 2016 edition), pp.84–5.

82. Uzi Rabi, 'Oman's Foreign Policy: The Art of Keeping All Channels of Communication Open,' *Orient* 46(4), 2005, p.551.

83. John Beasant, *Oman: The True-Life Drama and Intrigue of an Arab State* (Edinburgh: Mainstream Publishing, 2002), p.130.

84. J.E. Peterson, 'Oman's Diverse Society: Southern Oman,' *Middle East Journal* 58(2), 2004, p.259. A ceasefire was negotiated in March 1976 but it was not always respected or even acknowledged by rebel groups; see James Worrall, *Statebuilding and Counterinsurgency in Oman: Political, Military and Diplomatic Relations at the End of Empire* (London: I.B. Tauris, 2014), p.217.

85. The Bayt al-Ma'shani.

86. Marc Valeri, *Oman: Politics and Society in the Qaboos State* (London: Hurst & Co., 2009), pp.138–40.

87. Peterson, 'Oman's Diverse Society,' p.267.

88. Dawn Chatty, 'Rituals of Royalty and the Elaboration of Ceremony in Oman: View from the Edge,' *International Journal of Middle East Studies*, 41(1), 2009, p.46.

89. Dawn Chatty, *Mobile Pastoralists: Development Planning and Social Change in Oman* (New York: Columbia University Press, 1996), p.9; 'Abd al-Fattah

Hasan Abu 'Aliyya, 'Early Roots of Projects to Settle the Bedouins in the Arabian Peninsula,' in Fahd al-Semmari (ed.), *A History of the Arabian Peninsula* (London: I.B. Tauris, 2010), pp.209–10.

90. Richard Schofield, 'International Boundaries and Borderlands in the Middle East: Balancing Context, Exceptionalism and Representation,' *Geopolitics*, 23(3), 2018, p.614.

91. Strobl, *Sectarian Order in Bahrain*, p.9.

92. J.E. Peterson, 'Sovereignty and Boundaries in the Gulf States: Settling the Peripheries,' in Mehran Kamrava (ed.), *International Politics of the Persian Gulf* (New York: Syracuse University Press, 2011), p.23.

93. Ash Rossiter, 'Survival of the Kuwaiti Statelet: Najd's Expansion and the Question of British Protection,' *Middle Eastern Studies*, 56(3), 2020, p.381.

94. S.B. Kelly, *Desert Dispute: The Diplomacy of Boundary-Making in South-Eastern Arabia, Volume 1* (Berlin: Gerlach Press, 2018), p.1.

95. Zahra Babar, 'The "Enemy Within": Citizenship-Stripping in the Post-Arab Spring GCC,' *Middle East Journal*, 71(4), 2017, p.530.

96. Anh Nga Longva, 'Nationalism in Pre-Modern Guise: The Discourse on Hadhar and Badu in Kuwait,' *International Journal of Middle East Studies*, 38(2), 2006, pp.183–4.

97. Mary Ann Tétreault, 'A State of Two Minds: State Cultures, Women, and Politics in Kuwait,' *International Journal of Middle East Studies*, 33(2), 2001, p.216; Haya Al-Mughni, 'The Politics of Women's Suffrage in Kuwait,' *Arab Reform Bulletin*, 2(7), 2004, published by the Carnegie Endowment for International Peace; Justin Gengler, *Group Conflict and Political Mobilization in Bahrain and the Arab Gulf: Rethinking the Rentier State* (Bloomington: Indiana University Press, 2015), p.45.

98. Abdulhadi Khalaf, 'GCC Rulers and the Politics of Citizenship,' *Al-Monitor*, 26 December 2012.

99. Khaldoun Al-Naqeeb, 'Loyalty and Opposition in Kuwaiti Politics,' paper presented at Brown University, October 1998, p.3, available online at: The Khaldoun Alnaqeeb Archive, https://www.khaldounalnaqeeb.com/en/index.jsp

100. 'Tribal Expulsions Raise Questions of Human Rights,' *Gulf States Newsletter*, 29(755), 15 April 2005, pp.6–7.

101. Noora Lori, 'Time and Its Miscounting: Methodological Challenges in the Study of Citizenship Boundaries,' *International Journal of Middle East Studies*, 52(4), 2020, p.724.

102. For an example of how the early concessions operated in practice, see Kamal Osman Salih, 'The 1938 Kuwait Legislative Council,' *Middle Eastern Studies*, 28(1), 1992, pp.89–90.

103. J.E. Peterson, *Saudi Arabia under Ibn Saud: Economic and Financial Foundations of the State* (London: I.B. Tauris, 2018), p.50.

104. Andrew Rathmell and Kirsten Schulze, 'Political Reform in the Gulf: The Case of Qatar,' *Middle Eastern Studies*, 36(4), 2000, p.56.

105. For more on this process, see the chapters in this book on Institutions (Chapter 3) and Distribution (Chapter 7).

106. Jill Crystal, *Oil and Politics in the Gulf: Rulers and Merchants in Kuwait and Qatar* (Cambridge: Cambridge University Press, 1990), p.4; Courtney Freer, 'Exclusion-Moderation in the Gulf Context: Tracing the Development of Pragmatic Islamism in Kuwait,' *Middle Eastern Studies* 54(1), 2018, pp.4–5.

107. Michael Field, *The Merchants: The Big Business Families of Saudi Arabia and the Gulf States* (Woodstock: The Overlook Press, 1985), p.108.

108. Salwa Alghanim, *The Reign of Mubarak Al-Sabah: Shaikh of Kuwait 1896–1915* (London: I.B. Tauris, 1998), pp.139–40; Farah Al-Nakib, *Kuwait Transformed: A History of Oil and Urban Life* (Stanford: Stanford University Press, 2016), pp.30–1.

109. Nelida Fuccaro, *Histories of City and State in the Persian Gulf: Manama Since 1800* (Cambridge: Cambridge University Press, 2009), p.57.

110. Gregory Gause, 'The Persistence of Monarchy in the Arabian Peninsula: A Comparative Analysis,' in Joseph Kostiner (ed.), *Middle East Monarchies: The Challenge of Modernity* (Boulder: Lynne Rienner Publishers, 2000), p.186.

111. Mahdi Abdalla Al Tajir, *Bahrain 1920–1945: Britain, the Shaikh and the Administration* (London: Croom Helm, 1987), p.206.

112. Elham Fakhro, 'Land Reclamation in the Arabian Gulf: Security, Environment, and Legal Issues,' *Journal of Arabian Studies*, 3(1), 2013, pp.48–9.

2. CONSULTATION

1. Suzi Mirgani, 'An Overview of Informal Politics in the Middle East,' in Suzi Mirgani (ed.), *Informal Politics in the Middle East* (London: Hurst & Co., 2021), pp.5–6.

2. Ellen Lust-Okar, 'Taking Political Participation Seriously,' in Ellen Lust-Okar and Saloua Zerhouni (eds.), *Political Participation in the Middle East* (Boulder: Lynne Rienner Publishers, 2008), p.2.

3. James Bill, 'The Plasticity of Informal Politics: The Case of Iran,' *Middle East Journal*, 27(2), 1973, pp.131–3.

4. Jeremy Jones and Nicholas Ridout, *A History of Modern Oman* (Cambridge: Cambridge University Press, 2015), p.198.

5. Joseph Kéchichian, *Legal and Political Reforms in Sa'udi Arabia* (Abingdon: Routledge, 2013), p.114.

6. William Rugh, 'The United Arab Emirates: What Are the Sources of Its Stability?,' *Middle East Policy*, 5(3), 1997, p.19.

7. Jill Crystal, *Oil and Politics in the Gulf: Rulers and Merchants in Kuwait and Qatar* (Cambridge: Cambridge University Press, 1990), p.56.

8. Rosemarie Said Zahlan, *The Making of the Modern Gulf States* (Reading: Ithaca Press, 1998 edition), pp.28–9.

9. Fatma Al-Sayegh, 'Merchants' Role in a Changing Society: The Case of Dubai, 1900–90,' *Middle Eastern Studies,* 34(1), 1998, p.91.

10. Giacomo Luciani, 'Democracy vs. Shura in the Age of the Internet,' in Abdulhadi Khalaf and Giacomo Luciani (eds.), *Constitutional Reform and Political Participation in the Gulf* (Dubai: Gulf Research Centre, 2006), p.277.

11. Lindsey Stephenson, 'Women and the Malleability of the Kuwaiti Diwaniyya,' *Journal of Arabian Studies,* 1(2), 2011, p.184. In Oman, the gatherings were known as *Siblah.* See Abdullah Juma Alhaj, 'The Political Elite and the Introduction of Political Participation in Oman,' *Middle East Policy,* 7(3), 2000, p.184.

12. 'Qatari Activists Publish Blueprint for Reform,' *Al-Monitor,* 13 October 2012.

13. Mary Ann Tétreault, 'Civil Society in Kuwait: Protected Spaces and Women's Rights,' *Middle East Journal,* 47(2), 1993, p.279.

14. Rivka Azoulay, *Kuwait and Al-Sabah: Tribal Politics and Power in an Oil State* (London: I.B. Tauris, 2020), p.120 and p.124; Clemens Chay, 'Dissecting the Spatial Relevance of the Diwaniyya in Kuwait,' in Suzi Mirgani (ed.), *Informal Politics in the Middle East* (London: Hurst & Co., 2021), p.72.

15. Clemens Chay, 'Parliamentary Politics in Kuwait,' in Mehran Kamrava (ed.), *Routledge Handbook of Persian Gulf Politics* (Abingdon: Routledge, 2020), p.335.

16. Farah Al-Nakib, *Kuwait Transformed: A History of Oil and Urban Life* (Stanford: Stanford University Press, 2016), p.68.

17. David Rundell, *Vision or Mirage: Saudi Arabia at the Crossroads* (London: I.B. Tauris, 2020), pp.29–30.

18. Christopher Davidson, *Dubai: The Vulnerability of Success* (London: Hurst & Co., 2008), pp.31–2.

19. William Rugh, 'Emergence of a New Middle Class in Saudi Arabia,' *Middle East Journal,* 27(1), 1973, p.20. On 25 March 1975, a nephew shot King Faisal dead during one of the *majlis* sittings.

20. Summer Scott Huyette, *Political Adaptation in Sa'udi Arabia: A Study of the Council of Ministers* (Abingdon: Routledge, 2019 edition), p.94.

21. Tawfic Farah and Faisal Al-Salem, 'Political Efficacy, Political Trust, and the Action Orientations of University Students in Kuwait,' *International Journal of Middle East Studies,* 8(3), 1977, p.327.

22. Dawn Chatty, 'Rituals of Royalty and the Elaboration of Ceremony in Oman: View from the Edge,' *International Journal of Middle East Studies,* 41(1), 2009, p.50.

23. Ibid. pp.51–2.

24. Calvin Allen and W. Lynn Rigsbee, *Oman under Qaboos: From Coup to Constitution 1970–1996* (London: Frank Cass, 2000), pp.47–8.

25. Youssef Ibrahim, 'Kuwaiti Exiles Reunite in an Imperfect Harmony,' *New York Times*, 13 October 1990.

26. 'Democracy within Limits,' *Gulf States Newsletter*, 15(397), 29 October 1990, pp.8–11.

27. Youssef Ibrahim, 'Exiles from Kuwait Debate Looser Rule by the Emir's Family,' *New York Times*, 10 October 1990.

28. Fred Halliday, 'A Military Solution Will Destroy Kuwait,' *Middle East Report 168*, January/February 1991.

29. Hassan Al-Ebraheem, 'The Gulf Crisis: A Kuwaiti Perspective: An Interview with Hassan Al-Ebraheem,' *Journal of Palestine Studies*, 20(2), 1991, p.99.

30. 'Democracy within Limits,' *Gulf States Newsletter*, 15(397), 29 October 1990, pp.9–10.

31. Hussein Ghubash, *Oman: The Islamic Democratic Tradition* (Abingdon: Routledge, 2006), p.200, and Torgeir Fjaertoft, 'The Saudi Arabian Revolution: How Can it Succeed?,' *Middle East Policy*, 25(3), 2018, p.136. See also Mordechai Amir, 'The Consolidation of the Ruling Class and the New Elites in Saudi Arabia,' *Middle Eastern Studies*, 23(2), 1987, p.154.

32. Milton Viorst, 'The Storm and the Citadel,' *Foreign Affairs*, 75(1), 1996, p.101.

33. Madawi Al-Rasheed, *A History of Saudi Arabia* (Cambridge: Cambridge University Press, 2010 edition), p.82.

34. Tim Niblock, 'Social Structure and the Development of the Saudi Arabian Political System,' in Tim Niblock (ed.), *State, Society and Economy in Saudi Arabia* (London: Croom Helm, 1982), p.89.

35. Gregory Gause, 'Saudi Arabia Over a Barrel,' *Foreign Affairs*, 79(3), 2000, p.83.

36. Chay, *Spatial Relevance*, p.74; Pete Moore, 'Guilty Bystanders,' *Middle East Report 257*, 2010, available online at: https://merip.org/2011/01/guilty-bystanders/

37. Gerd Nonneman, 'Saudi-European Relations 1902–2001: A Pragmatic Quest for Relative Autonomy,' *International Affairs*, 77(3), 2001, p.634.

38. Anoushiravan Ehteshami, *Globalization and Geopolitics in the Middle East: Old Games, New Rules* (London: Routledge, 2007), p.119.

39. This process began in the pre-oil era with the formation, in Bahrain, of a *Majlis al-'Urf* in 1919 which by 1935 had evolved into a twenty-two-member *Majlis al-Tijarah*; see Mahdi Abdalla Al-Tajir, *Bahrain 1920–1945: Britain, the Shaikh and the Administration* (London: Croom Helm, 1987), p.22 and pp.231–3.

40. Hend Al Muftah, 'Is Qatar's Shura Election a Step Towards "Western Democracy"?,' *Doha News*, 26 September 2021.

41. Alain Gresh, 'The Most Obscure Dictatorship,' *Middle East Report 197*, November/December 1995, available online at: https://merip.org/1995/11/the-most-obscure-dictatorship/

42. Ibid.

43. Raed Abdulaziz Alhargan, 'Saudi Arabia: Civil Rights and Local Actors,' *Middle East Policy*, 19(1), 2012, p.132.

44. Quoted in Pascal Ménoret, *Graveyard of Clerics: Everyday Activism in Saudi Arabia* (Stanford: Stanford University Press, 2020), p.90.

45. Toby Craig Jones, 'Seeking a "Social Contract" for Saudi Arabia,' *Middle East Report 228*, 2003, available online at: https://merip.org/2003/09/seeking-a-social-contract-for-saudi-arabia/

46. Mark Thompson, 'Assessing the Impact of Saudi Arabia's National Dialogue: The Controversial Case of the Cultural Discourse,' *Journal of Arabian Studies*, 1(2), 2011, pp.164–5.

47. Jones, 'Seeking a "Social Contract";' Thompson, 'Saudi Arabia's National Dialogue,' p.165.

48. Toby Craig Jones, 'Violence and the Illusion of Reform in Saudi Arabia,' *Middle East Research and Information Project*, 13 November 2003, available online at: https://merip.org/2003/11/violence-and-the-illusion-of-reform-in-saudi-arabia/

49. Frederick Wehrey, 'Saudi Arabia: Shi'a Pessimistic about Reform, but Seek Reconciliation,' *Arab Reform Bulletin*, 5(5), 2007, published by the Carnegie Endowment for International Peace.

50. Louay Bahry, 'The Opposition in Bahrain: A Bellwether for the Gulf?,' *Middle East Policy*, 5(2), 1997, p.52.

51. Ibid. p.52.

52. Edward Burke, 'Bahrain: Reaching a Threshold,' *FRIDE Working Paper No.61*, 2008, pp.2–3.

53. J.E. Peterson, 'Bahrain: Reform—Promise and Reality,' in Joshua Teitelbaum (ed.), *Political Liberalization in the Persian Gulf* (London: Hurst & Co., 2009), p.162.

54. Neil Quilliam, 'Political Reform in Bahrain: The Turning Tide,' in Anoushiravan Ehteshami and Steven Wright (eds.), *Reform in the Middle East Oil Monarchies* (Reading: Ithaca Press, 2008), pp.84–5.

55. Toby Craig Jones and Ala'a Shehabi, 'Bahrain's Revolutionaries,' *Foreign Policy*, 2 January 2012.

56. Justin Gengler, 'Royal Factionalism, the Khawalid, and the Securitization of "the Shi'a Problem" in Bahrain,' *Journal of Arabian Studies*, 3(1), 2013, p.75.

57. Ala'a Shehabi and Marc Owen Jones, 'Bahrain's Uprising: The Struggle for Democracy in the Gulf,' in Ala'a Shehabi and Marc Owen Jones (eds.), *Bahrain's Uprising* (London: Zed Books, 2015), pp.6–7.

58. Anon., 'Popular Protests in North Africa and the Middle East (VIII): Bahrain's Rocky Road to Reform,' *International Crisis Group Middle East/North Africa Report No.11*, 28 July 2011, p.19.

59. Ibid.

60. Stephenson, 'Women and the Malleability of the Kuwaiti Diwaniyya,' p.189.

61. Shafeeq Ghabra, 'Voluntary Associations in Kuwait: The Foundation of a New System?,' *Middle East Journal*, 45(2), 1991, p.212.

62. Mary Ann Tétreault, *Stories of Democracy: Politics and Society in Contemporary Kuwait* (New York: Columbia University Press, 2000), p.70.

63. Ibid. pp.70–2.

64. Ghabra, 'Voluntary Associations in Kuwait,' pp.212–13.

65. Katherine Meyer, Helen Rizzo, and Yousef Ali, 'Changed Political Attitudes in the Middle East: The Case of Kuwait,' *International Sociology*, 22, 2007, p.292.

66. Gerd Nonneman, 'Political Reform in the Gulf Monarchies: From Liberalization to Democratization? A Comparative Perspective,' in Anoushiravan Ehteshami and Steven Wright (eds.), *Reform in the Middle East Oil Monarchies* (Reading: Ithaca Press, 2008), pp.4–5.

67. 'Kuwait Emir Courts Tribal Leaders as Parliament Dissolved—Again,' *Gulf States Newsletter*, 37(949), 20 June 2013, p.6.

68. 'Qatar Prepares for Shura Election Amid Dispute with Tribes over Citizenships,' *Gulf States Newsletter*, 45(1132), 2 September 2021, p.9.

69. Jessie Moritz, 'Oil and Societal Quiescence: Rethinking Causal Mechanisms in Rentier State Theory,' in Michael Herb and Marc Lynch (eds.), *The Politics of Rentier States in the Gulf*, POMEPS Studies 33, 2019, p.42.

70. Madawi Al-Rasheed, 'Royal Rule in a Time of Change,' in Joshua Craze and Mark Huband (eds.), *The Kingdom: Saudi Arabia and the Challenge of the 21st Century* (London: Hurst & Co., 2009), p.19.

71. Anastasia Nosova, 'The Voice and Loyalty of Business in Kuwait: Merchant Politics in Times of Contestation,' *British Journal of Middle Eastern Studies*, 45(2), 2018, p.178.

72. Anastasia Nosova, 'The Merchant Elite and Parliamentary Politics in Kuwait: The Dynamics of Business Political Participation in a Rentier State,' *PhD dissertation*, London School of Economics and Political Science, 2016, pp.167–8.

73. Kristian Coates Ulrichsen, 'Studious Silence Falls on Arab Spring,' *Open Democracy*, 25 April 2011.

74. Munira Fakhro, 'The Uprising in Bahrain: An Assessment,' in Gary Sick and Lawrence Potter (eds.), *The Persian Gulf at the Millennium: Essays in Politics, Economy, Security, and Religion* (London: Palgrave Macmillan, 1997), p.181.

75. Ibid. p.187.

76. Shibley Telhami, 'Arab Public Opinion and the Gulf War,' *Political Science Quarterly*, 108(3), 1993, p.449.

77. Gwenn Okruhlik, 'Understanding Political Dissent in Saudi Arabia,' *Middle East Research and Information Project (MERIP)* online commentary, 24 October 2001.

78. Fred Lawson, 'Keys to the Kingdom: Current Scholarship on Saudi Arabia,' *International Journal of Middle East Studies*, 43(4), 2011, p.742; Rundell, *Vision or Mirage*, p.174.

79. Al-Rasheed, *History of Saudi Arabia*, p.163.

80. Kéchichian, *Legal and Political Reforms*, pp.170–2.

81. Gresh, 'Most Obscure Dictatorship.'

82. Youssef Ibrahim, 'Saudi King Ousts 7 Senior Clerics for Acts of Criticism by Omission,' *New York Times*, 15 December 1992.

83. R. Hrair Dekmejian, 'Saudi Arabia's Consultative Council,' *Middle East Journal*, 52(2), 1998, p.206.

84. Khalid Al-Dakhil, '2003: Saudi Arabia's Year of Reform,' *Arab Reform Bulletin*, 2(3), 2004, published by the Carnegie Endowment for International Peace.

85. Peter Baker, 'Saudi Prince Calls for Arab Reforms,' *Washington Post*, 16 January 2003.

86. Jones, 'Seeking a "Social Contract".'

87. Ibid.

88. Jones, 'Violence and the Illusion of Reform.'

89. Ebtisam Al Kitbi, 'Women's Political Status in the GCC States,' *Arab Reform Bulletin*, 2(7), 2004, published by the Carnegie Endowment for International Peace.

90. Andrew Hammond, *The Islamic Utopia: The Illusion of Reform in Saudi Arabia* (London: Pluto Press, 2012), p.80.

91. Ibid. p.126.

92. Louay Bahry, 'Elections in Qatar: A Window of Democracy Opens in the Gulf,' *Middle East Policy*, 6(4), 1999, p.119.

93. 'Interview with Dr. Ali Khalifa Al Kuwari, Author of "The People Want Reform…in Qatar, Too",' *Heinrich Boll Stiftung*, October 2012, available online at: http://www.lb.boell.org/web/52-1170.html

94. Youssef Ibrahim, '54 Qatar Citizens Petition Emir for Free Elections,' *New York Times*, 13 May 1992.

95. Anoushiravan Ehteshami and Steven Wright, 'Political Change in the Arab Oil Monarchies: From Liberalization to Enfranchisement,' *International Affairs*, 83(5), 2007, p.921.

96. Mehran Kamrava, 'Royal Factionalism and Political Liberalization in Qatar,' *Middle East Journal*, 63(3), 2009, p.419.

97. Anon., 'No Sheikh-Up Here,' *The Economist*, 17 March 2012.

98. Courtney Freer, *Rentier Islamism: The Influence of the Muslim Brotherhood in Gulf Monarchies* (Oxford: Oxford University Press, 2018), p.133.

99. Ibid.

3. INSTITUTIONS

1. 'Transcript: Interview with Muhammad bin Salman,' *The Economist*, 6 January 2016, available online at: https://www.economist.com/middle-east-and-africa/2016/01/06/transcript-interview-with-muhammad-bin-salman

2. Michael Jansen, 'Saudi Arabia Shaken by Crown Prince's High-Stakes Crackdown,' *Irish Times*, 6 November 2017.

3. 'Saudi Arabia Princes Detained, Ministers Dismissed,' *Al Jazeera*, 5 November 2017; 'Saudi Purge Will Quell Critics but Worry Investors,' *Oxford Analytica*, 10 November 2017.

4. David Kirkpatrick, 'Saudi Arabia Arrests 11 Princes, Including Billionaire Alwaleed bin Talal,' *New York Times*, 4 November 2017.

5. 'Uncertainty Follows After Al-Salman Purge Establishes a New Model Saudi Autocracy,' *Gulf States Newsletter*, 41(1048), 20 November 2017, p.1; Dan De Luce, Ken Dilanian, and Robert Windrem, 'How a Saudi Royal Crushed His Rivals in a "Shakedown" at the Ritz-Carlton,' *NBC News*, 3 November 2018.

6. Dominic Dudley, 'Saudi Arabia Suffers Shock Collapse in Inward Investment,' *Forbes*, 7 June 2018.

7. Simeon Kerr and Andrew England, 'Wealthy Saudis Sit on Cash as Purge Casts Shadow over Investment,' *Financial Times*, 23 July 2018; Martin Chulov, 'Night of the Beating: Details Emerge of Riyadh Ritz-Carlton Purge,' *The Guardian*, 19 November 2020.

8. Tom DiChristopher, 'Saudi Arabia Says It Raised $106 Billion from "Anti-Corruption" Drive that Swept Up Royals,' *CNBC*, 30 January 2019; 'Saudi Prince Alwaleed Reached Secret Agreement with Government: BBG,' *Reuters*, 19 March 2018.

9. 'MBS Blends Anti-Graft Crackdown with a Very Political Purge,' *Gulf States Newsletter*, 41, Special Report, 7 November 2017, p.1; 'Saudi Crown Prince to Head New Committee to Combat Corruption,' *Al Arabiya*, 4 November 2017. The anti-corruption council established at short notice in 2017 was later disbanded in 2019 having been deemed to have completed its work.

10. De Luce, Dilanian, and Windrem, 'How a Saudi Royal Crushed His Rivals.'

11. Mehran Kamrava, 'Preserving Non-Democracies: Leaders and State Institutions in the Middle East,' *Middle Eastern Studies*, 46(2), 2010, p.251.

12. Faris Al-Sulayman, 'Rethinking State Capitalism in the Gulf States: Insights from the China-Focused Literature,' *King Faisal Center for Research and Islamic Studies,* Special Report, 2021, p.10.

13. Abdulhadi Khalaf, 'What the Gulf Ruling Families Do When They Rule,' *Orient*, 44, 2003, p.544.

14. Joey D'Urso, 'Newcastle Takeover: Why PIF and the Saudi State Are the Same Thing,' *The Athletic*, 13 October 2021. See also Alexis Montambault Trudelle, 'The Public Investment Fund and Salman's State: The Political Drivers of Sovereign Wealth Management in Saudi Arabia,' *Review of International Political Economy*, 30(2), 2022.

15. Khalaf, 'What the Gulf Ruling Families Do When They Rule,' p.541.

16. Sheila Carapico and Stacey Philbrick Yadav, 'The Breakdown of the GCC Initiative,' *Middle East Report 273*, Winter 2014, available online at: https://merip.org/2014/12/the-breakdown-of-the-gcc-initiative/

17. Russell Lucas, 'Monarchical Authoritarianism: Survival and Political Liberalization in a Middle Eastern Regime Type,' *International Journal of Middle East Studies*, 36(1), 2004, p.106.

18. See H.A. Hellyer, *A Revolution Undone: Egypt's Road Beyond Revolt* (London: Hurst & Co., 2016) for an authoritative account of the revolution in Egypt in 2011 and its aftermath and consequences through to 2016.

19. Turki Al-Hamad, 'Will the Gulf Monarchies Work Together?,' *Middle East Quarterly*, 1997, p.47.

20. Mary Ann Tétreault and Haya Al-Mughni, 'Gender, Citizenship and Nationalism in Kuwait,' *British Journal of Middle Eastern Studies*, 22(1), 1995, p.64.

21. Rupert Hay, 'The Impact of the Oil Industry on the Persian Gulf Shaykhdoms,' *Middle East Journal*, 9(4), 1955, p.368.

22. Rupert Hay, *The Persian Gulf States* (Washington, D.C.: Middle East Institute, 1959), p.101.

23. Reader Bullard and E.C. Hodgkin (ed.), *Two Kings in Arabia: Letters from Jeddah 1923–25 and 1936–39: Reader Bullard* (Reading: Ithaca Press, 1993), p.220.

24. Sulayman Khalaf and Hassan Hammoud, 'The Emergence of the Oil Welfare State: The Case of Kuwait,' *Dialectical Anthropology*, 12(3), 1987, p.355.

25. Christopher Davidson, *The United Arab Emirates: A Study in Survival* (Boulder: Lynne Rienner Publishers, 2005), p.89.

26. Jim Krane, *Dubai: The Story of the World's Fastest City* (London: Atlantic Books, 2009), p.267.

27. 'Abd Al-Aziz ibn 'Abd-Allah Al-Khwaiter, 'King Abdul Aziz: His Style of Administration,' in Fahd Al-Semmari (ed.), *A History of the Arabian Peninsula* (London: I.B. Tauris, 2010), pp.204–5.

28. Rosemarie Said Zahlan, *The Origins of the United Arab Emirates: A Political and Social History of the Trucial States* (London: Macmillan, 1978), p.57.

29. Ahmed Kanna and Arang Keshavarzian, 'The UAE's Space Race: Sheiks and Starchitects Envision the Future,' *Middle East Report 248*, 2008.

30. Kamal Osman Salih, 'The 1938 Kuwait Legislative Council,' *Middle Eastern Studies*, 28(1), 1992, p.87; Andrew Rathmell and Kirsten Schulze, 'Political

Reform in the Gulf: The Case of Qatar,' *Middle Eastern Studies*, 36(4), 2000, p.56; Marc Owen Jones, *Political Repression in Bahrain* (Cambridge: Cambridge University Press, 2020), p.60.

31. Rathmell and Schulze, 'Political Reform in the Gulf,' p.56; Owen Jones, *Political Repression in Bahrain*, pp.60–1.

32. J.E. Peterson, *Saudi Arabia under Ibn Saud: Economic and Financial Foundations of the State* (London: I.B. Tauris, 2018), p.50; William Mulligan, 'A Kingdom and a Company,' *Aramco World*, May/June 1984.

33. Rosie Bsheer, *Archive Wars: The Politics of History in Saudi Arabia* (Stanford: Stanford University Press, 2020), p.49.

34. Easa Saleh Al-Gurg, *The Wells of Memory: An Autobiography* (London: John Murray, 1998), p.67.

35. Rathmell and Schulze, 'Political Reform in the Gulf,' p.59.

36. Eran Segal, 'Merchants' Networks in Kuwait: The Story of Yusuf al-Marzuk,' *Middle Eastern Studies*, 45(5), 2009, p.710; James Onley, 'Transnational Merchants in the Nineteenth Century: The Case of the Safar Family,' in Madawi Al-Rasheed (ed.), *Transnational Connections and the Arab Gulf* (Abingdon: Routledge, 2005), pp.68–9; Fahad Ahmad Bishara, 'The Many Voyages of Fateh Al-Khayr: Unfurling the Gulf in the Age of Oceanic History,' *International Journal of Middle East History*, 52(3), 2020, pp.407–8.

37. Mary Ann Tétreault, *Stories of Democracy: Politics and Society in Contemporary Kuwait* (New York: Columbia University Press, 2000), p.36; Peterson, *Saudi Arabia under Ibn Saud*, p.10.

38. Khalaf and Hammoud, 'Emergence of the Oil Welfare State,' p.348; Fatma al-Sayegh, 'Merchants' Role in a Changing Society: The Case of Dubai, 1900–90,' *Middle Eastern Studies*, 34(1), 1998, p.91; Pete Moore and Bassel Salloukh, 'Struggles under Authoritarianism: Regimes, States, and Professional Associations in the Arab World,' *International Journal of Middle East Studies*, 39(1), 2007, p.57; Bsheer, *Archive Wars*, p.38.

39. Hendrik Kraetzschmar, 'Associational Life under Authoritarianism: The Saudi Chamber of Commerce and Industry Elections,' *Journal of Arabian Studies*, 5(2), 2015, p.190.

40. Pete Moore, *Doing Business in the Middle East: Politics and Economic Crisis in Jordan and Kuwait* (Cambridge: Cambridge University Press, 2004), pp.46–8.

41. The first multi-decade development plan was Vision 2020, unveiled in Oman in 1995. See also Matthew Gray, 'A Theory of "Late Rentierism" in the Arab States of the Gulf,' *Georgetown University School of Foreign Service in Qatar, Center for International and Regional Studies Occasional Paper No.7*, 2011.

42. Fuad Khuri, *Tribe and State in Bahrain: The Transformation of Social and Political Authority in an Arab State* (Chicago: University of Chicago Press, 1980), p.85.

43. J.E. Peterson, 'Tribe and State in the Arabian Peninsula,' *Middle East Journal*, 74(4), 2021, p.513.

44. Steffen Hertog, 'The Political Decline and Social Rise of Tribal Identity in the GCC,' *London School of Economics Middle East Centre blog*, 25 July 2018.

45. Davidson, *Study in Survival*, p.73.

46. Khaldoun Al-Naqeeb, 'Loyalty and Opposition in Kuwaiti Politics,' paper presented to a workshop at Brown University, October 1998, p.4, available online at the *Khaldoun Al-Naqeeb Archive*, https://www.khaldounalnaqeeb. com/en/book-conference.jsp; Abdulhadi Khalaf, 'Rules of Succession and Political Participation in the GCC States,' in Abdulhadi Khalaf and Giacomo Luciani (eds.), *Constitutional Reform and Political Participation in the Gulf* (Dubai: Gulf Research Center, 2006), p.42.

47. Jill Crystal, 'Coalitions in Oil Monarchies: Kuwait and Qatar,' *Comparative Politics*, 21(4), 1989, p.438.

48. Paul Aarts, 'Oil, Money and Participation: Kuwait's Sonderweg as a Rentier State,' *Orient, 32*, 1991, p.212.

49. Yasmine Farouk and Nathan Brown, 'Saudi Arabia's Religious Reforms are Touching Nothing but Changing Everything,' *Carnegie Endowment for International Peace*, 7 June 2021.

50. Robert Cox, 'Social Forces, States and World Orders: Beyond International Relations Theory,' *Millennium: Journal of International Studies*, 10(2), 1981, pp.136–7.

51. Stephanie Cronin, 'Tribes, Coups and Princes: Building a Modern Army in Saudi Arabia,' *Middle Eastern Studies*, 49(1), 2013, p.2.

52. William Rugh, 'Emergence of a New Middle Class in Saudi Arabia,' *Middle East Journal*, 27(1), 1973, p.10.

53. John Townsend, *Oman: The Making of the Modern State* (London: Croom Helm, 1977), p.63; Helene von Bismarck, *British Policy in the Persian Gulf, 1961–1968: Conceptions of Informal Empire* (Basingstoke: Palgrave Macmillan, 2013), p.167; Ragaei El Mallakh, 'The Challenge of Affluence: Abu Dhabi,' *Middle East Journal*, 24(2), 1970, p.137.

54. Abdulrahman Al-Sadhan, 'The Modernization of the Saudi Bureaucracy,' in Willard Bening (ed.), *King Faisal and the Modernization of Saudi Arabia* (London: Croom Helm, 1980), pp.77–8.

55. Rugh, 'Emergence of a New Middle Class,' p.12.

56. Bsheer, *Archive Wars*, p.69.

57. Sarah Yizraeli, *The Remaking of Saudi Arabia: The Struggle between King Sa'ud and Crown Prince Faysal, 1953–1962* (Tel Aviv: The Moshe Dayan Center for Middle Eastern and African Studies, 1997), pp.103–4.

58. David Rundell, *Vision or Mirage: Saudi Arabia at the Crossroads* (London: I.B. Tauris, 2020), p.57.

59. Samer Al-Atrush, 'Saudi Crown Prince Mohammed bin Salman Appointed Prime Minister,' *Financial Times*, 27 September 2022.

60. Madawi Al-Rasheed, 'Mystique of Monarchy: The Magic of Royal Succession in Saudi Arabia,' in Madawi Al-Rasheed (ed.), *Salman's Legacy: The Dilemmas of a New Era in Saudi Arabia* (London: Hurst & Co., 2017), pp.46–7.

61. Mehran Kamrava, 'Royal Factionalism and Political Liberalization in Qatar,' *Middle East Journal*, 63(3), 2009, p.403.

62. Mohammad Alwuhaib, 'Kuwait: The Crisis and its Future,' *Arab Reform Brief*, 63, 2012, published by the Arab Reform Initiative.

63. Michael Herb, 'A Respite in Kuwait?' *Foreign Policy*, 21 December 2012.

64. Marc Valeri, 'Towards the End of the Oligarchic Pact? Business and Politics in Abu Dhabi, Bahrain, and Oman,' in Kristian Coates Ulrichsen (ed.), *The Changing Security Dynamics of the Persian Gulf* (London: Hurst & Co., 2017), p.95.

65. Christopher Davidson, 'The Impact of Economic Reform on Dubai,' in Anoushiravan Ehteshami and Steven Wright (eds.), *Reform in the Middle East Oil Monarchies* (Reading: Ithaca Press, 2008), pp.160–2.

66. Cf. Steffen Hertog, 'Rentier Militaries in the Gulf States: The Price of Coup-Proofing,' *International Journal of Middle East Studies*, 43(3), 2011, pp.400–2.

67. Steffen Hertog, 'Petromin: The Slow Death of Statist Oil Development in Saudi Arabia,' *Business History*, 50(5), 2008, pp.647–8.

68. Katja Niethammer, 'Opposition Groups in Bahrain,' in Ellen Lust-Okar and Saloua Zerhouni (eds.), *Political Participation in the Middle East* (Boulder: Lynne Rienner Publishers, 2008), p.150.

69. Kristian Coates Ulrichsen, *Insecure Gulf: The End of Certainty and the Transition to the Post-Oil Era* (London: Hurst & Co., 2011), p.100.

70. Mohammed Al-A'ali, 'Budget Rejected Again by MPs,' *Gulf Daily News*, 6 March 2009.

71. 'Qatar's Leading Lady Shows Clout in Ouster of Two Female Ministers,' Confidential cable dated 14 May 2009, available online at the Public Library of U.S. Diplomacy: https://wikileaks.org/plusd/cables/09DOHA315_a.html

72. Steffen Hertog, *Princes, Brokers, and Bureaucrats: Oil and the State in Saudi Arabia* (Ithaca: Cornell University Press, 2010), pp.47–9.

73. Ibid. p.49.

74. Madawi Al-Rasheed, 'Circles of Power: Royals and Society in Saudi Arabia,' in Paul Aarts and Gerd Nonneman (eds.), *Saudi Arabia in the Balance: Political Economy, Society, Foreign Affairs* (London: Hurst & Co., 2005), p.189.

75. Kristian Coates Ulrichsen, 'Kuwait as a Mediator in Regional Affairs: The Gulf Crises of 2014 and 2017,' *The International Spectator*, 56(4), 2021, p.128.

76. Marc Valeri, 'Oligarchy vs. Oligarchy: Business and Politics of Reform in Bahrain and Oman,' in Steffen Hertog, Giacomo Luciani, and Marc Valeri

(eds.), *Business Politics in the Middle East* (London: Hurst & Co., 2012), p.22.

77. Brian Ross and David Scott, 'Qatari Royal Family Linked to Al Qaeda,' *ABC News*, 7 February 2003.

78. Kamrava, 'Royal Factionalism and Political Liberalization,' p.414. Something broadly similar had happened in Qatar in the late-1970s and the early-1980s after the titular Foreign Minister, Sheikh Suhaim bin Hamad Al Thani, fell out with his brother, Emir Khalifa bin Hamad Al Thani, whereupon a Minister of State for Foreign Affairs took on most of the duties, but not the titular position, of Foreign Minister until Sheikh Suhaim's death in 1985.

79. Martin Hvidt, 'The Dubai Model: An Outline of Key Development-Process Elements in Dubai,' *International Journal of Middle East Studies*, 41(3), 2009, p.402.

80. Anil Bhoyrul, 'Exclusive: Mohammed Alabbar—Uncensored,' *Arabian Business*, 12 April 2015.

81. 'Mohammad Alabbar: All You Need to Know,' *AMEinfo.com*, 8 February 2017.

82. Krane, *Dubai*, p.138.

83. Christopher Davidson, *Dubai: The Vulnerability of Success* (London: Hurst & Co., 2008), p.106.

84. Arang Keshavarzian, 'Geopolitics and the Genealogy of Free Trade Zones in the Persian Gulf,' *Geopolitics*, 15(2), 2010, pp.274–5.

85. Mark Thatcher, 'Governing Markets in the Gulf States,' in David Held and Kristian Ulrichsen (eds.), *The Transformation of the Gulf: Politics, Economics and the Global Order* (Abingdon: Routledge, 2012), pp.129–31.

86. 'The Limits to Liberalisation: A Press Row in Qatar,' *The Economist*, 14 May 2009.

87. Kristian Coates Ulrichsen, 'Rebalancing Global Governance: Gulf States' Perspectives on the Governance of Globalization,' *Global Policy*, 2(1), 2011, p.69.

88. Peter Salisbury, 'Risk Perception and Appetite in UAE Foreign and National Security Policy,' *Chatham House Research Paper*, 2020, p.32.

89. Hasan Tariq Alhasan, 'Bahrain's New Labour Scheme: One Step Forward, Two Steps Back?,' *Open Democracy*, 5 August 2012.

90. Alexis Antoniades, 'The Gulf Monetary Union,' in Mehran Kamrava (ed.), *The Political Economy of the Persian Gulf* (London: Hurst & Co., 2012), pp.177–8.

91. 'The Door to Monetary Union Not Entirely Shut,' *Khaleej Times*, 22 May 2009.

4.   REPRESENTATION

1. Mohammad Al-Rumaihi, 'Kuwait: Oasis of Liberalism?' *Middle East Quarterly*, 1994, available online at: https://www.meforum.org/150/kuwait-oasis-of-liberalism

2. David Held, *Models of Democracy* (Cambridge: Polity Press, 2006 edition), pp. 7–8.

3. As argued by David Runciman, *Politics* (London: Profile Books, 2014), pp. 30–1.

4. Al-Rumaihi, 'Oasis of Liberalism.'

5. Tim Niblock, 'Democratization: A Theoretical and Practical Debate,' *British Journal of Middle Eastern Studies*, 25(2), 1998, p. 226.

6. Ellen Lust-Okar, 'Taking Political Participation Seriously,' in Ellen Lust-Okar and Saloua Zerhouni (eds.), *Political Participation in the Middle East* (Boulder: Lynne Rienner Publishers, 2008), p. 2.

7. Toby Matthiesen, 'Migration, Minorities, and Radical Networks: Labour Movements and Opposition Groups in Saudi Arabia, 1950–1975,' *International Review of Social History*, 59(3), 2014, pp. 475–7.

8. Hendrik Kraetzschmar, 'Associational Life under Authoritarianism: The Saudi Chamber of Commerce and Industry Elections,' *Journal of Arabian Studies*, 5(2), 2015, p. 185.

9. Eran Segal, 'Political Participation in Kuwait: Diwaniyya, Majlis and Parliament,' *Journal of Arabian Studies*, 2(2), 2012, p. 139.

10. Victor McFarland, *Oil Powers: A History of the U.S.-Saudi Alliance* (New York: Columbia University Press, 2020), pp. 155–6.

11. Letter from M.S. Buckmaster (British Embassy, Beirut) to P.J.F. Mansley (British Embassy, Qatar), 19 January 1973, London: The National Archives, file FCO 8/2080—'Political Situation in Qatar.'

12. 'Democracy Should be Built on Accountability: Qatari PM,' *The Peninsula*, 10 June 2008.

13. Badr Al-Khoraif and Obeid al-Ansari, 'Ibn Jubair Dies at 76,' *Arab News*, 25 January 2002.

14. Milton Viorst, 'The Storm and the Citadel,' *Foreign Affairs*, 75(1), 1996, p. 100.

15. The British Diplomatic Oral History Programme, Churchill College, University of Cambridge, 'Recollections of Stuart Laing MA Mphil,' recorded and transcribed by Moira Goldstaub, 15 March 2018, available online at: https://www.chu.cam.ac.uk/archives/collections/bdohp/#H

16. Douglas Jehl, 'Bahrain Rulers Say They're Determined to End Village Unrest,' *New York Times*, 28 January 1996.

17. Report from Edward Given (British Ambassador to Bahrain) to Ivor Lucas (Middle East Department, Foreign and Commonwealth Office), 20 June

1977, London: The National Archives, file FCO 8/2872—'Bahrain Internal Political Situation.'

18. Louay Bahry, 'The Opposition in Bahrain: A Bellwether for the Gulf?,' *Middle East Policy*, 5(2), 1997, p.52. The original citation for Sheikh Khalifa's quote was an interview in *al-Siyasah* on 8 August 1979.

19. Judith Miller, 'Creating Modern Oman,' *Foreign Affairs*, 76(3), 1997, pp.14–15.

20. Badr Al Busaidi, 'Oman's Approach to Development,' in Anoushiravan Ehteshami and Steven Wright (eds.), *Reform in the Middle East Oil Monarchies* (Reading: Ithaca Press, 2008), pp.129–132.

21. Nawra Al Lawati and Gail Buttorf, 'Working Women in the Oil Monarchies,' in Mehran Kamrava (ed.), *Routledge Handbook of Persian Gulf Politics* (Abingdon: Routledge, 2020), p.251.

22. Greg Power, 'The Difficult Development of Parliamentary Politics in the Gulf: Parliaments and the Process of Managed Reform in Kuwait, Bahrain and Oman,' in David Held and Kristian Coates Ulrichsen (eds.), *The Transformation of the Gulf: Politics, Economics and the Global Order* (Abingdon: Routledge, 2012), p.29; Daniel Brumberg, 'Democratization in the Arab World? The Trap of Liberalized Autocracy,' *Journal of Democracy* 13(4), 2002, p.56; Gerd Nonneman, 'Political Reform in the Gulf Monarchies: From Liberalization to Democratization? A Comparative Perspective,' in Anoushiravan Ehteshami and Steven Wright (eds.), *Reform in the Middle East Oil Monarchies* (Reading: Ithaca Press, 2008), p.30.

23. Mehran Kamrava, 'Preserving Non-Democracies: Leaders and State Institutions in the Middle East,' *Middle Eastern Studies*, 46(2), 2010, p.252.

24. John Wilkinson, *The Imamate Tradition of Oman* (Cambridge: Cambridge University Press, 1987), pp.170–1.

25. Nonneman, 'Political Reform,' p.30.

26. Ulrike Freitag, *A History of Jeddah: The Gate to Mecca in the Nineteenth and Twentieth Centuries* (Cambridge: Cambridge University Press, 2020), p.61.

27. Toby Matthiesen, 'Centre-Periphery Relations and the Emergence of a Public Sphere in Saudi Arabia: The Municipal Elections in the Eastern Province, 1954–1960,' *British Journal of Middle Eastern Studies*, 42(3), 2015, p.323.

28. Abdulrahman Alebrahim, *Kuwait's Politics before Independence: The Role of the Balancing Powers* (Berlin: Gerlach Press, 2019), p.80.

29. Ibid. p.95; Mohammad Salameh and Mohammad Al-Sharah, 'Kuwait's Democratic Experiment: Roots, Reality, Characteristics, Challenges, and Prospects for the Future,' *Journal of Middle Eastern and Islamic Studies* (in Asia), 5(3), 2011, p.61.

30. Toby Matthiesen, 'Centre-Periphery Relations,' p.323.

31. Kiren Aziz Chaudhry, *The Price of Wealth: Economies and Institutions in the Middle East* (Ithaca: Cornell University Press, 1997), pp.70–2.

32. Ibid. pp. 323–4.

33. Ibrahim Al-Marashi, 'Iraq's Gulf Policy and Regime Security from the Monarchy to the Post-Ba'athist Era,' *British Journal of Middle Eastern Studies*, 36(3), 2009, p.451.

34. Mary Ann Tétreault, *Stories of Democracy: Politics and Society in Contemporary Kuwait* (New York: Columbia University Press, 2000), p.63.

35. Peter Lienhardt, *Disorientations: A Society in Flux: Kuwait in the 1950s* (Reading: Ithaca Press, 1993), p.62.

36. Kamal Osman Salih, 'The 1938 Kuwait Legislative Council,' *Middle Eastern Studies*, 28(1), 1992, p.76.

37. Eran Segal, 'Merchants' Networks in Kuwait: The Story of Yusuf al-Marzuk,' *Middle Eastern Studies*, 45(5), 2009, p.715.

38. Salih, '1938 Legislative Council,' p.78.

39. Khaldoun Al-Naqeeb, 'The Shia of Kuwait and Minority Politics,' Conference paper delivered in Kuwait, 1996, p.11, PDF available online at: The Khaldoun Alnaqeeb Archive, https://www.khaldounalnaqeeb.com/UploadedFiles/conference/152/152.pdf. A short-lived attempt to create a new council in Kuwait was made in March 1939 but was quashed by the ruler through the use of force.

40. Fatma Al-Sayegh, 'Merchants' Role in a Changing Society: The Case of Dubai, 1900–90,' *Middle Eastern Studies*, 34(1), 1998, p.94.

41. Ibid. p.95.

42. Christopher Davidson, *Dubai: The Vulnerability of Success* (London: Hurst & Co., 2008), pp.33–4.

43. Rosemarie Said Zahlan, *The Making of the Modern Gulf States* (Reading: Ithaca Press, 1998 edition), pp.64–5.

44. Hamad Ebrahim Abdulla, 'Sir Charles Belgrave and the Rise and Fall of Bahrain's National Union Committee, January 1953 to April 1957,' *PhD dissertation*, University of East Anglia, 2016, p.9.

45. J.E. Peterson, 'Rulers, Merchants and Shaikhs in Gulf Politics: The Function of Family Networks,' in Alanoud Alsharekh (ed.), *The Gulf Family: Kinship Policies and Modernity* (London: Saqi Books, 2007), pp.28–31.

46. Farah al-Nakib, *Kuwait Transformed: A History of Oil and Urban Life* (Stanford: Stanford University Press, 2016), pp.31–2.

47. Shafeeq Ghabra, 'Voluntary Associations in Kuwait: The Foundation of a New System?,' *Middle East Journal*, 45(2), 1991, p.201.

48. David Commins, *The Gulf States: A Modern History* (London: I.B. Tauris, 2012), pp.184–94.

49. The Consultative Council in Oman that was created in 1991 was an evolutionary move that replaced the wholly appointed State Consultative Council which had been established in 1981. See Jeremy Jones and Nicholas Ridout, 'Democratic Development in Oman,' *Middle East Journal*, 59(3), 2005, p.385.

50. A previous National Assembly had sat in Bahrain between 1973 and 1975.

51. Sulayman Khalaf and Hassan Hammoud, 'The Emergence of the Oil Welfare State: The Case of Kuwait,' *Dialectical Anthropology*, 12(3), 1987, p. 348.

52. Ghabra, 'Voluntary Associations in Kuwait,' p. 211.

53. Abdulhadi Khalaf, 'Labor Movements in Bahrain,' *Middle East Report* (published by the Middle East Research and Information Project), 4 May 1985.

54. Abdullah Alhajeri, 'Citizenship and Political Participation in the State of Kuwait: The Case of the National Assembly (1963–1996),' *PhD dissertation*, University of Durham, 2004, p. 169.

55. Taylor Fain, 'John F. Kennedy and Harold Macmillan: Managing the "Special Relationship" in the Persian Gulf Region, 1961–63,' *Middle Eastern Studies*, 38(4), 2002, pp. 102–3.

56. Roham Alvandi, 'Muhammad Reza Pahlavi and the Bahrain Question, 1968–1970,' *British Journal of Middle Eastern Studies*, 37(2), 2010, p. 159 and p. 175.

57. Linda Colley, *The Gun, the Ship, and the Pen: Warfare, Constitutions, and the Making of the Modern World* (London: Profile Books, 2021), pp. 10–11.

58. Michael Herb, *The Wages of Oil: Parliaments and Economic Development in Kuwait and the UAE* (Ithaca: Cornell University Press, 2014), p. 90.

59. Ibid. p. 91.

60. Ghabra, 'Voluntary Associations in Kuwait,' p. 211.

61. Chris Hedges, 'Three Years after Gulf War, Sense of Siege Grips Kuwait,' *New York Times*, 8 October 1994.

62. Abdulhadi Khalaf, 'What the Gulf Ruling Families Do When They Rule,' *Orient*, 44, 2003, p. 546.

63. Ibid. p. 542.

64. Douglas Jehl, 'Sheikh Isa, 65, Emir of Bahrain Who Built Non-oil Economy,' *New York Times*, 7 March 1999.

65. Michael Herb, 'Princes and Parliaments in the Arab World,' *Middle East Journal*, 58(3), 2004, pp. 372–3.

66. Alhajeri, 'Citizenship and Political Participation,' p. 169.

67. Ibid. p. 373.

68. Edward Burke, 'Bahrain: Reaching a Threshold,' *FRIDE Working Paper No. 61*, 2008, p. 3.

69. J.E. Peterson, 'Bahrain: Reform—Promise and Reality,' in Joshua Teitelbaum (ed.), *Political Liberalization in the Persian Gulf* (London: Hurst & Co., 2009), p. 161.

70. Mary Ann Tétreault, 'Kuwait: Slouching towards Democracy?,' in Joshua Teitelbaum (ed.), *Political Liberalization in the Persian Gulf* (London: Hurst & Co., 2009), p. 112.

71. Allen Fromherz, *Qatar: A Modern History* (Washington, D.C.: Georgetown University Press, 2012), p.126.

72. Kristian Coates Ulrichsen, *Qatar and the Arab Spring* (London: Hurst & Co., 2014), p.164.

73. Hassan Abdelrehim Al Sayed, 'High Time for Shura Council Polls,' *The Peninsula*, 23 May 2013.

74. Lahdan bin Isa Al Mohannadi, 'Citizens Must Be Part of Decision-making,' *The Peninsula*, 23 May 2013.

75. Justin Gengler, 'Qatar's First Elections Since 2017 Reveal Unexpected Impact of GCC Crisis,' *Al-Monitor*, 24 April 2019.

76. Isabel Debre, 'Qatar's Emir Promises Shura Council Elections Next Year,' *Associated Press*, 3 November 2020.

77. 'Establishment Figures Prevail in First Shura Council Election,' *Gulf States Newsletter*, 45(1135), 14 October 2021, p.5.

78. 'Qatar Prepares for Shura Election amid Dispute with Tribes for Citizenships,' *Gulf States Newsletter*, 45(1132), 2 September 2021, pp.9–10.

79. Abdullah Juma Alhaj, 'The Politics of Participation in the Gulf Cooperation Council States: The Omani Consultative Council,' *Middle East Journal*, 50(4), 1996, p.97.

80. Miller, 'Creating Modern Oman,' pp.14–15.

81. Marielle Risse, *Community and Autonomy in Southern Oman* (London: Palgrave Macmillan, 2019), pp.49–50.

82. Alhaj, 'Politics of Participation,' pp.560–1.

83. 'State Advisory Council Formed,' *Gulf States Newsletter*, 7(174), 2–15 November 1981, p.3.

84. Ibid. p.559.

85. Uzi Rabi, 'Oman: "Say Yes to Oman, No to the Tribe!",' in Joshua Teitelbaum (ed.), *Political Liberalization in the Persian Gulf* (London: Hurst & Co., 2009), pp.213–15.

86. Jones and Ridout, 'Democratic Development in Oman,' p.386.

87. Abdullah Juma Alhaj, 'The Political Elite and the Introduction of Political Participation in Oman,' *Middle East Policy*, 7(3), 2000, pp.105–6.

88. Shahid Jamal Ansari, *Political Modernization in the Gulf* (Delhi: Northern Book Center, 1998), p.116.

89. Jones and Ridout, 'Democratic Development in Oman,' p.389.

90. Fahim bin Sultan Al Qassemi, 'A Century in Thirty Years: Sheikh Zayed and the United Arab Emirates,' *Middle East Policy*, 6(4), 1999, p.2.

91. Herb, *Wages of Oil*, p.52.

92. Ansari, *Political Modernization*, pp.116–17.

93. May Al-Dabbagh and Lana Nusseibeh, 'Women in Parliament and Politics in the UAE: A Study of the First Federal National Council Elections,' *Dubai School of Government / Ministry of Federal National Council Affairs paper*, February 2009, p.22.

94. 'Some FNC Members Unhappy with Pace of Current Term,' *The National*, 17 March 2015.

95. 'UAE Elects First Female Parliamentary Speaker,' *Gulf News*, 18 November 2015.

96. Mark Thompson, 'Societal Transformation, Public Opinion and Saudi Youth: Views from an Academic Elite,' *Middle Eastern Studies*, 53(5), 2017, p.843.

97. Rasheed Abou-Alsamh, 'Saudi Municipal Elections Raise Hopes,' *Arab Reform Bulletin*, 3(2), 2005, published by the Carnegie Endowment for International Peace.

98. 'Consultative Council Proposed,' *Saudi Arabia Newsletter*, 16, 28 January–10 February 1980, p.9.

99. McFarland, *Oil Powers*, pp.201–2.

100. Nimrod Raphaeli, 'Demands for Reforms in Saudi Arabia,' *Middle Eastern Studies*, 41(4), 2005, p.527.

101. David Rundell, *Vision or Mirage: Saudi Arabia at the Crossroads* (London: I.B. Tauris, 2020), p.61.

102. Ibid. pp.124–5.

103. Saad Sowayan, 'Top-down Fight against Corruption Leaves Saudis Wondering Who Will Watch the Watchdogs,' in Joshua Craze and Mark Huband (eds.), *The Kingdom: Saudi Arabia and the Challenge of the 21st Century* (London: Hurst & Co., 2009), pp.83–4.

104. Viorst, 'The Storm and the Citadel,' p.100.

105. Ibid.

106. Ghanim Al-Najjar, 'Kuwait: Struggle over Parliament,' *Arab Reform Bulletin*, 4(5), 2006, published by the Carnegie Endowment for International Peace.

107. Ibid.

108. Burke, 'Reaching a Threshold,' p.3.

109. Claire Beaugrand, 'Deconstructing Minorities/Majorities in Parliamentary Gulf States (Kuwait and Bahrain),' *British Journal of Middle Eastern Studies*, 43(2), 2016, p.245.

110. Abdulhadi Khalaf, 'Bahrain's Parliament: The Quest for a Role,' *Arab Reform Bulletin*, 2(5), 2004, published by the Carnegie Endowment for International Peace.

111. Courtney Freer, 'Challenges to Sunni Islamism in Bahrain Since 2011,' *Carnegie Middle East Center*, 6 March 2019.

112. Pascal Ménoret, *Graveyard of Clerics: Everyday Activism in Saudi Arabia* (Stanford: Stanford University Press, 2020), pp.5–6.

113. Miriam Joyce, 'The Bahraini Three on St. Helena, 1956–1961,' *Middle East Journal*, 54(4), 2000, p.614.

114. Sultan Sooud Al Qassemi, 'Jassim Buhejji, a Life for Bahrain,' *Open Democracy*, 28 February 2012.

115. Toby Craig Jones, 'Rebellion on the Saudi Periphery: Modernity, Marginalization, and the Shi'a Uprising of 1979,' *International Journal of Middle East Studies*, 38(2), 2006, pp.226–7.

116. Jafar Al-Shayeb, 'Saudi Arabia: Municipal Councils and Political Reform,' *Arab Reform Bulletin*, 3(9), 2005, published by the Carnegie Endowment for International Peace.

117. Ibid.

118. Ménoret, *Graveyard of Clerics*, p.95.

119. Madawi Al-Rasheed, 'The Saudi Lie,' *London Review of Books* 41(6), 21 March 2019.

120. 'Saudi Women Aim to Create Their Own Municipal Council,' *Al Arabiya*, 1 April 2011.

121. Hatoon Al-Fassi, 'Is Female Suffrage in the Gulf Important?', *LSE Middle East Centre blog*, 16 December 2017.

122. Transcript of Hatoon Al-Fassi interview with Rachel Martin on Weekend Edition Sunday, in 'Saudi Women React to Election Results,' *NPR*, 20 December 2015.

123. Amy Austin Holmes, 'The Base that Replaced the British Empire: De-Democratization and the American Navy in Bahrain,' *Journal of Arabian Studies*, 4(1), 2014, pp.32–3.

124. Khalaf, 'Labor Movements in Bahrain.'

125. Abdo Baaklini, 'Legislatures in the Gulf Area: The Experience of Kuwait, 1961–1976,' *International Journal of Middle East Studies*, 14(3), 1982, pp.373–4.

126. Mehran Kamrava, 'Preserving Non-Democracies: Leaders and State Institutions in the Middle East,' *Middle Eastern Studies*, 46(2), 2010, p.258.

127. Neil Partrick, 'Kuwait's Foreign Policy (1961–1977): Non-Alignment, Ideology and the Pursuit of Security,' *PhD dissertation*, London School of Economics and Political Science, 2006, pp.140–1.

128. Michael Herb, 'Kuwait: The Obstacle of Parliamentary Politics,' in Joshua Teitelbaum (ed.), *Political Liberalization in the Persian Gulf* (London: Hurst & Co., 2009), pp.140–1.

129. Abdul-Reda Assiri, *Kuwait's Foreign Policy: City-State in World Politics* (Boulder: Westview Press, 1990), pp.71–3; Mary Ann Tétreault, 'Independence, Sovereignty, and Vested Glory: Oil and Politics in the Second Gulf War,' *Orient*, 34(1), 1993, p.91; Pete Moore, *Doing Business in the Middle East: Politics and Economic Crisis in Jordan and Kuwait* (Cambridge: Cambridge University Press, 2004), p.133; Pete Moore and Bassel Salloukh, 'Struggles under Authoritarianism: Regimes, States, and Professional Associations in the Arab World,' *International Journal of Middle East Studies*, 39(1), 2007, pp.63–4.

130. Alhajeri, 'Citizenship and Political Participation,' p.168.

245

131. Quoted in Marc Owen Jones, *Political Repression in Bahrain* (Cambridge: Cambridge University Press, 2020), p.127.

132. Ibid.

133. Luciano Zaccara, 'Comparing Elections in Gulf Cooperation Council Countries after the Arab Spring: The United Arab Emirates, Oman, and Kuwait,' *Journal of Arabian Studies*, 3(1), 2013, pp.81–2.

134. Michael Herb, 'Democratization in the Arab World? Emirs and Parliaments in the Gulf,' *Journal of Democracy*, 13(4), 2002, p.43.

135. 'Qatar Election,' *Gulf States Newsletter*, 44(1128), 17 June 2021, p.1.

136. Hassan Abdel Rahim El Sayed, 'Will the Tribe be the Basis for Determining the Electoral Districts for the Upcoming Qatari Shura Council?,' *Doha Institute for Graduate Studies*, 29 March 2021.

137. Ramola Talwar Badam, 'Sheikh Khalifa: UAE's Federal National Council to be 50 Per cent Women,' *The National*, 8 December 2018.

138. 'Saudi Royal Appointments Underscore Conservative Influence,' *Gulf States Newsletter*, 29 October 2020, p.5.

139. Marwa Shalaby and Laila Eliman, 'Women in Legislative Committees in Arab Parliaments,' *Comparative Politics*, 53(1), 2020, p.139; Charlotte Lysa and Andrew Leber, 'Onwards and Upwards with Women in the Gulf,' *Middle East Research and Information Project (MERIP)*, 11 January 2018.

140. Andrzej Kapiszewski, 'Elections and Parliamentary Activity in the GCC States: Broadening Political Participation in the Gulf Monarchies,' in Abdulhadi Khalaf and Giacomo Luciani (eds.), *Constitutional Reform and Political Participation in the Gulf* (Dubai: Gulf Research Centre, 2006), p.99.

141. Kraetzschmar, 'Associational Life under Authoritarianism,' pp.197–9.

142. Quoted in Mariwan Kanie, 'Civil Society, Language and the Authoritarian Context: The Case of Saudi Arabia,' *Orient*, 4, 2012, p.53.

143. Naomi Sakr, 'Women and Media in Saudi Arabia: Rhetoric, Reductionism and Realities,' *British Journal of Middle Eastern Studies*, 35(3), 2008, p.389.

144. Ian Skeet, *Oman: Politics and Development* (London: Macmillan, 1992), pp.121–2.

145. Moore, *Doing Business in the Middle East*, pp.130–2.

146. Hasan Tariq Al Hasan, 'Bahrain Bids its Economic Reform Farewell,' *Open Democracy*, 8 July 2012.

147. Michelle Dunne, 'Interview with Ali al-Rashed, Kuwaiti National Assembly Member and Candidate,' *Arab Reform Bulletin*, 6(4), 2008, published by the Carnegie Endowment for International Peace.

148. Amr Hamzawy, 'Interview with Badr al-Nashi, President of the Islamic Constitutional Movement (ICM),' *Arab Reform Bulletin*, 4(3), 2006, published by the Carnegie Endowment for International Peace.

5.   OPPOSITION

1. See, for example, Giacomo Luciani, 'Allocation vs. Production States: A Theoretical Framework,' in Giacomo Luciani (ed.), *The Arab State* (London: Routledge, 1990), p.76.

2. Gwenn Okruhlik, 'Rentier Wealth, Unruly Law, and the Rise of Opposition: The Political Economy of Oil States,' *Comparative Politics*, 31(3), 1999, pp.295–315; Jessie Moritz, 'Oil and Societal Quiescence: Rethinking Causal Mechanisms in Rentier State Theory,' in Michael Herb and Marc Lynch (eds.), *The Politics of Rentier States in the Gulf*, POMEPS Studies 33, 2019, pp.40–3; Jim Krane, *Energy Kingdoms: Oil and Political Survival in the Persian Gulf* (New York: Columbia University Press, 2019).

3. See, for example, the essays in Lawrence Potter (ed.), *The Persian Gulf in Modern Times: People, Ports, and History* (New York: Palgrave Macmillan, 2014); and Mehran Kamrava (ed.), *Gateways to the World: Port Cities in the Persian Gulf* (London: Hurst & Co., 2016).

4. Fahad Ahmad Bishara, 'The Many Voyages of Fateh Al-Khayr: Unfurling the Gulf in the Age of Oceanic History,' *International Journal of Middle East Studies*, 52(3), 2020, p.402.

5. Ahmad Suba'i, *My Days in Mecca*, translated and edited by Deborah Akers and Abubaker Bagader (Boulder: FirstForumPress, 2009), p.105.

6. Matthew Heaton, 'Decolonizing the Hajj: Nationalist Politics and Pilgrimage Administration in the British Empire in the Mid-Twentieth Century,' *Journal of Imperial and Commonwealth History*, 49(2), 2021, p.292.

7. Abdul Sheriff, *Dhow Cultures of the Indian Ocean: Cosmopolitanism, Commerce and Islam* (London: Hurst & Co., 2010), p.250.

8. Michael Christopher Low, *Imperial Mecca: Ottoman Arabia and the Indian Ocean Hajj* (New York: Columbia University Press, 2020), pp.305–6.

9. Rosie Bsheer, 'A Counter-Revolutionary State: Popular Movements and the Making of Saudi Arabia,' *Past and Present*, 238, 2018, p.237.

10. Kristi Barnwell, 'Overthrowing the Shaykhs: The Trucial States at the Intersection of Anti-Imperialism, Arab Nationalism, and Politics, 1952–1966,' *The Arab Studies Journal*, 24(2), 2016, p.74; see also Omar AlShehabi, *Contested Modernity: Sectarianism, Nationalism, and Colonialism in Bahrain* (London: OneWorld Academic, 2019); Toby Matthiesen, 'Migration, Minorities, and Radical Networks: Labour Movements and Opposition Groups in Saudi Arabia, 1950–1975,' *International Review of Social History*, 59(3), 2014; and Abdel Razzaq Takriti, *Monsoon Revolution: Republicans, Sultans, and Empires in Oman, 1965–1976* (Oxford: Oxford University Press, 2016 edition).

11. See, for example, Gwenn Okruhlik, 'Rentier Wealth,' pp.295–315.

12. Abdulhadi Khalaf, 'Labor Movements in Bahrain,' *Middle East Report 132*, May/June 1985.

13. Mahdi Abdalla Al-Tajir, *Bahrain 1920–1945: Britain, the Shaikh and the Administration* (London: Croom Helm, 1987), pp.173–4.

14. Emile Nakhleh, *Bahrain: Political Development in a Modernizing Society* (Lanham: Lexington Books, 2011 edition), p.77.

15. John Chalcraft, 'Migration Politics in the Arabian Peninsula,' in David Held and Kristian Coates Ulrichsen (eds.), *The Transformation of the Gulf: Politics, Economics and the Global Order* (London: Routledge, 2012), pp.74–5.

16. Robert Vitalis, *America's Kingdom: Mythmaking on the Saudi Oil Frontier* (London: Verso, 2009), pp.93–5.

17. Madawi Al-Rasheed, *A History of Saudi Arabia* (Cambridge: Cambridge University Press, 2010 edition), pp.95–6.

18. Pascal Ménoret, *Graveyard of Clerics: Everyday Activism in Saudi Arabia* (Stanford: Stanford University Press, 2020), p.50.

19. Nathan Citino, *From Arab Nationalism to OPEC: Eisenhower, King Sa'ud, and the Making of U.S.-Saudi Relations* (Bloomington: Indiana University Press, 2002), pp.55–9.

20. Which itself was rebranded as Qatar Energy in 2021.

21. Hassan Mohammad Abdulla Saleh, 'Labor, Nationalism, and Imperialism in Eastern Arabia: Britain, the Shaikhs and the Gulf Oil Workers in Bahrain, Kuwait and Qatar, 1932–1956,' *PhD dissertation*, University of Michigan, 1991, p.109.

22. Sultan Sooud Al Qassemi, 'Jassim Buhejji: A Life for Bahrain,' *Open Democracy*, 28 February 2012.

23. Ibid.

24. Hamad Ebrahim Abdulla, 'Sir Charles Belgrave and the Rise and Fall of Bahrain's National Union Committee, January 1953 to April 1957,' *PhD dissertation*, University of East Anglia, 2016, p.6.

25. Louis Allday, 'Charles Belgrave—The Adviser,' *Qatar Digital Library*, 14 October 2014.

26. Miriam Joyce, 'The Bahraini Three on St. Helena, 1956–1961,' *Middle East Journal*, 54(4), 2000, pp.615–16.

27. Interview with Ivor Thomas Mark Lucas CMG, 25 January 2005, available online at The British Diplomatic Oral History Programme, Churchill College, University of Cambridge, https://www.chu.cam.ac.uk/media/uploads/files/Lucas_EeLXGb4.pdf, p.7.

28. Joyce, 'Bahraini Three,' p.616.

29. Mehran Kamrava, 'Preserving Non-Democracies: Leaders and State Institutions in the Middle East,' *Middle Eastern Studies*, 46(2), 2010, p.254.

30. Rowena Abdul Razak, 'When Guns Are Not Enough: Britain's Response to Nationalism in Bahrain, 1958–63,' *Journal of Arabian Studies*, 7(1), 2017, p.72.

31. Athol Yates and Ash Rossiter, 'Forging a Force: Rulers, Professional Expatriates, and the Creation of Abu Dhabi's Police,' *Middle Eastern Studies*, 56(4), 2020, pp.6–7.

32. Tancred Bradshaw, 'Security Forces and the End of Empire in the Trucial States, 1960–1971,' *Middle Eastern Studies*, 56(6), 2020, p.2; Laleh Khalili, *Sinews of War and Trade: Shipping and Capitalism in the Arabian Peninsula* (London: Verso, 2020), p.204.

33. Riad El-Rayyes, 'Arab Nationalism in the Gulf,' in B.R. Pridham (ed.), *The Arab Gulf and the Arab World* (Abingdon: Routledge, 2016 edition), p.75.

34. Ash Rossiter, *Security in the Gulf: Local Militaries before British Withdrawal* (Cambridge: Cambridge University Press, 2020), p.170.

35. Farah Al-Nakib, 'Modernity and the Arab Gulf States: The Politics of Heritage, Memory, and Forgetting,' in Mehran Kamrava (ed.), *Routledge Handbook of Persian Gulf Politics* (Abingdon: Routledge, 2020), p.68.

36. Fred Halliday, *The Middle East in International Relations: Power, Politics and Ideology* (Cambridge: Cambridge University Press, 2005), p.232.

37. Mandana Limbert, 'Trade, Mobility, and the Sea,' *International Journal of Middle East Studies*, 50(3), 2018, p.587. See also Fahad Ahmad Bishara, *Sea of Debt: Law and Economic Life in the Western Indian Ocean, 1780–1950* (Cambridge: Cambridge University Press, 2017).

38. William Beeman, 'Gulf Society: An Anthropological View of the Khalijis—Their Evolution and Way of Life,' in Lawrence Potter (ed.), *The Persian Gulf in History* (New York: Palgrave Macmillan, 2009), pp.148–9.

39. Haila Al-Meikaimi, 'The Impact of Islamic Groups and Arab Spring on the Youth Political Movement in Kuwait,' *Journal of South Asian and Middle Eastern Studies*, 36(1), 2012, p. 47.

40. Muhammad Morsy Abdullah, *The United Arab Emirates: A Modern History* (London: Routledge, 2016 edition), p.112.

41. John Chalcraft, 'Migration and Popular Protest in the Arabian Peninsula and the Gulf in the 1950s and 1960s,' *International Labor and Working-Class History*, 79, 2011, p.29.

42. Kamal Osman Salih, 'The 1938 Kuwait Legislative Council,' *Middle Eastern Studies*, 28(1), 1992, pp.70–2.

43. Abdulrahman Alebrahim, *Kuwait's Politics before Independence: The Role of the Balancing Powers* (Berlin: Gerlach Press, 2019), p.157 and p.218.

44. Abdulrahman Alebrahim, 'Kuwaiti-Zubayri Intellectual Relations until the Beginning of the Twentieth Century: 'Abd al-'Aziz al-Rushayd as an Example,' in Marc Owen Jones, Ross Porter, and Marc Valeri (eds.), *Gulfization of the Arab World* (Berlin: Gerlach Press, 2018), p.136.

45. Ibid. p.145.

46. Jörg Matthias Determann, *Historiography in Saudi Arabia: Globalization and the State in the Middle East* (London: I.B. Tauris, 2021 edition), pp.65–6.

47. Ulrike Freitag, 'The Falah School in Jeddah: Civic Engagement for Future Generations?,' *Jadaliyya*, 6 May 2015.

48. Abdullah, *United Arab Emirates*, p.112.

49. Matthiesen, 'Migration, Minorities, and Radical Networks,' p.490.

50. Ménoret, *Graveyard of Clerics*, p.50.

51. Nathan Citino, *Envisioning the Arab Future: Modernization in U.S.-Arab Relations, 1945–1967* (Cambridge: Cambridge University Press, 2017), p.122.

52. Matthiesen, 'Migration, Minorities, and Radical Networks,' p.487.

53. Chalcraft, 'Migration and Popular Protest,' p.41.

54. Khalili, *Sinews of War*, p.204; Michael Herb, *The Wages of Oil: Parliaments and Economic Development in Kuwait and the UAE* (Ithaca: Columbia University Press, 2014), p.84.

55. Shafeeq Ghabra, 'Voluntary Associations in Kuwait: The Foundation of a New System?,' *Middle East Journal*, 45(2), 1991, p.211.

56. Gawdat Bahgat, 'Education in the Gulf Monarchies: Retrospect and Prospect,' *International Review of Education*, 45(2), 1999, pp. 129–30.

57. Sharon Stanton Russell, 'Politics and Ideology in Migration Policy Formulation: The Case of Kuwait,' *International Migration Review*, 23(1), 1989, pp. 29–33.

58. Ido Zelkovitz, 'A Paradise Lost? The Rise and Fall of the Palestinian Community in Kuwait,' *Middle Eastern Studies*, 50(1), 2014, p. 87.

59. Ibid. pp.87–8 and p.94.

60. Ali Alkandari, 'The Development of Kuwaiti Islamists' Political Ideology: The Administration of the Kuwaiti Supreme Committee and the Free Kuwait Campaign During the Second Gulf Crisis 1990–91,' *Middle Eastern Studies*, 55(5), 2019, p.787.

61. May Seikaly, 'Women and Social Change in Bahrain,' *International Journal of Middle East Studies*, 26(3), 1994, p.419.

62. Barnwell, 'Overthrowing the Shaykhs,' pp.74–5.

63. Abdel Razzaq Takriti, 'Political Praxis in the Gulf: Ahmad al-Khatib and the Movement of Arab Nationalists, 1948–1969,' in Jens Hanssen and Max Weiss (eds.), *Arabic Thought against the Authoritarian Age: Towards an Intellectual History of the Present* (Cambridge: Cambridge University Press, 2018), p.97.

64. Ibid. pp.97–8.

65. Ibid. p.105.

66. Eran Segal, 'Merchants' Networks in Kuwait: The Story of Yusuf al-Marzuk,' *Middle Eastern Studies*, 45(5), 2009, p.712; Fahad Ahmad Bishara, 'The Many Voyages of Fateh Al-Khayr: Unfurling the Gulf in the Age of Oceanic History,' *International Journal of Middle East Studies*, 52(3), 2020, p.400.

67. Abdulrahman Alebrahim, 'The Neglected Sheikhdom at the Frontier of Empires and Cultures: An Introduction to al-Zubayr,' *Middle Eastern Studies*, 56(4), 2020, p.521.

68. Fatma Al-Sayegh, 'Merchants' Role in a Changing Society: The Case of Dubai, 1900–90,' *Middle Eastern Studies*, 34(1), 1998, p. 92; C.A. Bayly, 'Indian and Arabic Thought in the Liberal Age,' in Jens Hanssen and Max Weiss (eds.), *Arabic Thought beyond the Liberal Age: Towards an Intellectual History of the Nahda* (Cambridge: Cambridge University Press, 2016), p.328.

69. AlShehabi, *Contested Modernity*, pp.110–11 and p.115.

70. Nelida Fuccaro, *Histories of City and State in the Persian Gulf: Manama Since 1800* (Cambridge: Cambridge University Press, 2009), p.177.

71. Ibid. p.179.

72. Miriam Joyce, *Kuwait 1945–1996: An Anglo-American Perspective* (London: Frank Cass, 1998), p.32.

73. Talal Al-Rashoud, 'Schools for the Arab Homeland: Kuwait's Educational Mission in Sharjah,' in Sultan Sooud Al Qassemi and Todd Reisz (eds.), *Building Sharjah* (Basel: Birkhauser, 2021), p.4 and pp.11–12.

74. Ibid. p.13.

75. Joyce, *Kuwait 1945–1996*, pp. 92–4; Fred Halliday, *Arabia without Sultans* (London: Saqi Books, 2002 edition), p.445.

76. Gerd Nonneman, 'Saudi-European Relations 1902–2001: A Pragmatic Quest for Relative Autonomy,' *International Affairs*, 77(3), 2001, p.656. Saudi Arabia also cut diplomatic relations with France and the United Kingdom in 1956—they were restored in 1962 and 1963, respectively.

77. David Rundell, *Vision or Mirage: Saudi Arabia at the Crossroads* (London: I.B. Tauris, 2020), p.185.

78. Determann, *Historiography in Saudi Arabia*, pp.53–4.

79. Chalcraft, 'Migration and Popular Protest,' p.37.

80. Neil Partrick, 'Kuwait's Foreign Policy (1961–1977): Non-Alignment, Ideology and the Pursuit of Security,' *PhD dissertation*, London School of Economics and Political Science, 2006, pp.131–4.

81. In 1971, PFLOAG renamed itself the Popular Front for the Liberation of Oman and the Arabian Gulf, and in 1974 the movement split into two separate Omani and Bahraini branches. See Claire Beaugrand, 'In and Out Moves of the Bahraini Opposition: How Years of Political Exile Led to an Opening of an International Front During the 2011 Crisis in Bahrain,' in Abdulhadi Khalaf, Omar AlShehabi, and Adam Hanieh (eds.), *Transit States: Labour, Migration and Citizenship in the Gulf* (London: Pluto Press, 2015), p.217.

82. J.E. Peterson, 'Oman's Diverse Society: Southern Oman,' *Middle East Journal*, 58(2), 2004, pp.258–9.

83. William Brewer, 'Yesterday and Tomorrow in the Persian Gulf,' *Middle East Journal*, 23(2), 1969, p.155.

84. Clive Jones, 'Military Intelligence, Tribes, and Britain's War in Dhofar, 1970–1976,' *Middle East Journal*, 65(4), 2011, pp.558–60.

85. Joseph Kéchichian, 'Trends in Saudi National Security,' *Middle East Journal*, 53(2), 1999, p.239; Jeremy Jones and Nicholas Ridout, 'Democratic Development in Oman,' *Middle East Journal*, 59(3), 2005, p.387.

86. Fred Lawson, *Bahrain: The Modernization of Autocracy* (Boulder: Westview Press, 1989), p.85.

87. Ahmed Nagi, 'Eastern Yemen's Tribal Model for Containing Conflict,' Carnegie Middle East Center research paper, 31 March 2020, available online at https://carnegie-mec.org/2020/03/31/eastern-yemen-s-tribal-model-for-containing-conflict-pub-81403

88. Takriti, *Monsoon Revolution*, p.1.

89. Fred Halliday, 'The Gulf in International Affairs: Independence and after,' in B.R. Pridham (ed.), *The Arab Gulf and the Arab World* (London: Routledge, 2016 edition), p.100.

90. Dale Eickelman, 'From Theocracy to Monarchy: Authority and Legitimacy in Inner Oman, 1935–1957,' *International Journal of Middle East Studies*, 17(1), 1985, p.5.

91. Takriti, *Monsoon Revolution*, p.54.

92. Halliday, *Arabia without Sultans*, p.362.

93. Eickelman, 'Theocracy to Monarchy,' p.20.

94. Ibid. p.20.

95. Jeremy Jones and Nicholas Ridout, *A History of Modern Oman* (Cambridge: Cambridge University Press, 2015), p.137.

96. Ibid. p.169.

97. Halliday, *Arabia without Sultans*, p.366.

98. Interview with Sir Donald Hawley, 7 August 2007, available online at The British Diplomatic Oral History Programme, Churchill College, University of Cambridge: https://www.chu.cam.ac.uk/media/uploads/files/Hawley.pdf, p.37.

99. Interview with Sir Terence Joseph Clark KBE CMG, 8 November 2002, available online at The British Diplomatic Oral History Programme, Churchill College, University of Cambridge: https://www.chu.cam.ac.uk/media/uploads/files/Clark.pdf, p.38.

100. Simon Smith, 'The Making of a Neo-Colony? Anglo-Kuwaiti Relations in the Era of Decolonization,' *Middle Eastern Studies*, 37(1), 2001, p.169.

101. Partrick, 'Kuwait's Foreign Policy,' pp.163–5.

102. 'Politics and Defence,' *Gulf States Newsletter*, 8(226), 5 December 1983, p.6; Rory Miller, *Desert Kingdoms to Global Powers: The Rise of the Arab Gulf* (New Haven: Yale University Press, 2016), p.200.

103. Joseph Nevo, 'Religion and National Identity in Saudi Arabia,' *Middle Eastern Studies*, 34(3), 1998, pp.38–9.

104. Joseph Kéchichian, 'The Role of the Ulama in the Politics of an Islamic State: The Case of Saudi Arabia,' *International Journal of Middle East Studies*, 18(1), 1986, p.57.

105. Fred Halliday, 'In a Time of Hopes and Fears,' *British Journal of Middle Eastern Studies*, 36(2), 2009, p.174.

106. Jamal Khashoggi, 'Neo-Islamists: A New Direction in Saudi Arabia's Islamic Opposition?,' *Arab Reform Bulletin*, 2(3) 2004, pp.6–7.

107. David Commins, 'Introduction to the English Edition,' in Nasir al-Huzaimi, *The Mecca Uprising: An Insider's Account of Salafism and Insurrection in Saudi Arabia* (London: I.B. Tauris, 2021), p.46.

108. Joseph Kostiner, 'On Instruments and their Designers: *The Ikhwan* of Najd and the Emergence of the Saudi State,' *Middle Eastern Studies*, 21(3), 1985, p.319; Thomas Hegghammer and Stephane Lacroix, 'Rejectionist Islamism in Saudi Arabia: The Story of Juhayman Al-'utaybi Revisited,' *International Journal of Middle East Studies*, 39(1), 2007, p.105.

109. Gregory Gause, 'Regional Influences in Experiments in Political Liberalization in the Arab World,' in Rex Brynen, Bahgat Korany, and Paul Noble (eds.), *Political Liberalization and Democratization in the Arab World: Volume 1. Theoretical Perspectives* (Boulder: Lynne Rienner Publishers, 1995), p.289; Ghabra, 'Voluntary Associations in Kuwait,' p.206.

110. Haila Al-Mekaimi, 'The Impact of Islamic Groups and Arab Spring on the Youth Political Movement in Kuwait,' *Journal of South Asian and Middle Eastern Studies*, 36(1), 2012, p.47.

111. Steve Monroe, 'Salafis in Parliament: Democratic Attitudes and Party Politics in the Gulf,' *Middle East Journal*, 66(3), 2012, p.421; Mary Ann Tétreault, *Stories of Democracy: Politics and Society in Contemporary Kuwait* (New York: Columbia University Press, 2000), p.66.

112. Terrance Carroll, 'Islam and Political Community in the Arab World,' *International Journal of Middle East Studies*, 18(2), 1986, p.189.

113. Barbara Zollner, 'Prison Talk: The Muslim Brotherhood's Internal Struggle During Gamal Abdel Nasser's Persecution, 1954 to 1971,' *International Journal of Middle East Studies*, 39(3), 2007, p.412 and p.419.

114. For a comprehensive assessment of Yusuf Al-Qaradawi, see Bettina Graf and Jakob Skovgaard-Petersen (eds.), *Global Mufti: The Phenomenon of Yusuf Al-Qaradawi* (Oxford: Oxford University Press, 2009).

115. Courtney Freer, *Rentier Islamism: The Influence of the Muslim Brotherhood in Gulf Monarchies* (Oxford: Oxford University Press, 2018), pp.56–7.

116. Commins, 'Introduction to the English Edition,' pp.40–1.

117. David Roberts, 'Qatar and the Muslim Brotherhood: Pragmatism or Preference?,' *Middle East Policy*, 21(3), 2014, pp.85–7.

118. Courtney Freer, 'The Muslim Brotherhood in the Emirates: Anatomy of a Crackdown,' *Middle East Eye*, 17 December 2015.

119. Michael Farquhar, 'Saudi Petrodollars, Spiritual Capital, and the Islamic University of Medina: A Wahhabi Missionary Project in Transnational Perspective,' *International Journal of Middle East Studies*, 47(4), 2015, pp.701–2.

120. David Commins, *TheWahhabi Mission and Saudi Arabia* (London: I.B. Tauris, 2009), p.164.

121. Ibid. p.703.

122. Determann, *Historiography in Saudi Arabia*, p.57.

123. Laurence Louër, *Transnational Shia Politics: Religious and Political Networks in the Gulf* (London: Hurst & Co., 2008), pp.124-5.

124. Pascal Ménoret, *The Saudi Enigma: A History* (London: Zed Books, 2005), p.106.

125. Sarah Yizraeli, *Politics and Society in Saudi Arabia: The Crucial Years of Development, 1960–1982* (London: Hurst & Co., 2012), pp.74–5; Kamal Osman Salih, 'Kuwait Primary (Tribal) Elections 1975–2008: An Evaluative Study,' *British Journal of Middle Eastern Studies*, 38(2), 2011, p.147.

126. Hegghammer and Lacroix, 'Rejectionist Islamism,' pp.111–12.

127. Stephanie Cronin, 'Tribes, Coups and Princes: Building a Modern Army in Saudi Arabia,' *Middle Eastern Studies*, 49(1), 2013, p.23.

128. Mahan Abedin, 'Saudi Shi'a Wait and See as New Light Falls on Islam's Old Divide,' in Joshua Craze and Mark Huband (eds.), *The Kingdom: Saudi Arabia and the Challenge of the 21st Century* (London: Hurst & Co., 2009), p.66.

129. Toby Craig Jones, 'Rebellion on the Saudi Periphery: Modernity, Marginalization, and the Shi'a Uprising of 1979,' *International Journal of Middle East Studies*, 38(2), 2006, pp.218–19.

130. Dilip Hiro, *ColdWar in the IslamicWorld: Saudi Arabia, Iran and the Struggle for Supremacy* (London: Hurst & Co., 2018), p.66.

131. James Bill, *The Eagle and the Lion: The Tragedy of American-Iranian Relations* (New Haven: Yale University Press, 1988), pp.268–9; Louër, *Transnational Shia Politics*, p.177.

132. Gregory Gause, *The International Relations of the Persian Gulf* (Cambridge: Cambridge University Press, 2009), p.48.

133. Hasan Tariq Alhasan, 'The Role of Iran in the Failed Coup of 1981: the IFLB in Bahrain,' *Middle East Journal*, 65(4), 2011, pp.604–6.

134. Rosemarie Said Zahlan, *The Making of the Modern Gulf States* (Reading: Ithaca Press, 1998 edition), pp.52–3.

135. Khaldoun Al-Naqeeb, 'The Shia of Kuwait and Minority Politics,' 1996, available online at: The Khaldoun Alnaqeeb Archive, https://www.khaldounalnaqeeb.com/en/index.jsp

136. Madawi Al-Rasheed, 'God, the King and the Nation: Political Rhetoric in Saudi Arabia in the 1990s,' *Middle East Journal*, 50(3), 1996, p.371.

137. Mahan Abedin, 'Saudi Dissent More than Just Jihadis,' in Joshua Craze and Mark Huband (eds.), *The Kingdom: Saudi Arabia and the Challenge of the 21st Century* (London: Hurst & Co., 2009), p.35.

138. Stephane Lacroix, 'Understanding Stability and Dissent in the Kingdom: The Double-Edged Role of the Jama'at in Saudi Politics,' in Bernard Haykel, Thomas Hegghammer, and Stephane Lacroix (eds.), *Saudi Arabia*

in Transition: Insights on Social, Political, Economic and Religious Change (Cambridge: Cambridge University Press, 2015), p.170.

139. Ménoret, *Graveyard of Clerics*, p.72.

140. Madawi Al-Rasheed, *Muted Modernists: The Struggle Over Divine Politics in Saudi Arabia* (London: Hurst & Co., 2015), p.9.

141. Raed Abdulaziz Alhargan, 'Saudi Arabia: Civil Rights and Local Actors,' *Middle East Policy*, 19(1), 2012, p.132.

142. Roel Meijer, 'Citizenship in Saudi Arabia,' *Middle East Journal*, 70(4), 2016, p.671.

143. Madawi Al-Rasheed, 'Abdullah al-Hamid: Saudi Human Rights Advocate and "National Hero",' *Middle East Eye*, 24 April 2020.

144. Fatma Al-Sayegh, 'Post-9/11 Changes in the Gulf: The Case of the UAE,' *Middle East Policy*, 11(2), 2004, p.113.

145. Louay Bahry, 'Elections in Qatar: A Window of Democracy Opens in the Gulf,' *Middle East Policy*, 6(4), 1999, p.121.

146. Ghabra, 'Voluntary Associations in Kuwait,' p.207.

147. Zoltan Pall, 'Kuwaiti Salafism and Its Growing Influence in the Levant,' *Carnegie Endowment for International Peace*, 7 May 2014.

148. Courtney Freer, 'Exclusion-Moderation in the Gulf Context: Tracing the Development of Pragmatic Islamism in Kuwait,' *Middle Eastern Studies*, 54(1), 2018, p.8; Katherine Meyer, Helen Rizzo, and Yousef Ali, 'Changed Political Attitudes in the Middle East: The Case of Kuwait,' *International Sociology*, 22, 2007, p.292.

149. Mary Ann Tétreault, 'Kuwait's Unhappy Anniversary,' *Middle East Policy*, 7(3), 2000, p.72.

150. J.E. Peterson, 'Oman: Three and a Half Decades of Change and Development,' *Middle East Policy*, 11(2), 2004, p.134.

151. Ibid.; see also Jeremy Jones and Nicholas Ridout, 'Democratic Development in Oman,' *Middle East Journal*, 59(3), 2005, p.380; Abdullah Juma Alhaj, 'The Politics of Participation in the Gulf Cooperation Council States: The Omani Consultative Council,' *Middle East Journal*, 50(4), 1996, pp.566–7.

152. Jones and Ridout, *A History of Modern Oman*, pp.219–20.

153. Alhaj, 'Politics of Participation,' p.383.

154. Toby Jones, 'Seeking a "Social Contract" for Saudi Arabia,' *Middle East Report 228*, 2003.

155. Mary Ann Tétreault and Haya al-Mughni, 'Gender, Citizenship and Nationalism in Kuwait,' *British Journal of Middle Eastern Studies*, 22(1), 1995, pp.71–2.

156. Robert Vitalis, *Oilcraft: The Myths of Scarcity and Security that Haunt U.S. Energy Policy* (Stanford: Stanford University Press, 2020), p.98.

157. Jamal Khashoggi, 'By Blaming 1979 for Saudi Arabia's Problems, the Crown Prince is Peddling Revisionist History,' *Washington Post*, 3 April 2018.

158. Gwenn Okruhlik, 'Saudi Arabian-Iranian Relations: External Rapprochement and Internal Consolidation,' *Middle East Policy*, 10(2), 2003, p.116.

159. Pete Moore and Bassel Salloukh, 'Struggles under Authoritarianism: Regimes, States, and Professional Associations in the Arab World,' *International Journal of Middle East Studies*, 39(1), 2007, p.79.

160. Ibid. p.64.

161. Madawi Al-Rasheed, 'The Shia of Saudi Arabia: A Minority in Search of Cultural Authenticity,' *British Journal of Middle Eastern Studies*, 25(1), 1998, pp.129–30.

162. Monroe, 'Salafis in Parliament,' p.419.

163. Kristian Coates Ulrichsen, 'Bahrain: Evolution or Revolution?,' *Open Democracy*, 1 March 2011.

6.   RESPONSES

1. Christian Reus-Smit, 'Constructivism and the Structure of Ethical Reasoning,' in Richard Price (ed.), *Moral Limit and Possibility in World Politics* (Cambridge: Cambridge University Press, 2008), p.53.

2. Barry Buzan, Ole Wæver, and Jaap de Wilde, *Security: A New Framework for Analysis* (Boulder: Lynne Rienner Publishers, 1998), p.23.

3. Morten Kelstrup, 'Globalization and Societal Insecurity in the Securitization of Terrorism and Competing Strategies for Global Governance,' in Stefano Guzzini and Dietrich Jung (eds.), *Contemporary Security Analysis and Copenhagen Peace Research* (London: Routledge, 2004), p.112.

4. Patrick Conge and Gwenn Okruhlik, 'The Power of Narrative: Saudi Arabia, the United States and the Search for Security,' *British Journal of Middle East Studies*, 36(3), 2009, pp.365–6.

5. Rory Miller, *Desert Kingdoms to Global Powers: The Rise of the Arab Gulf* (New Haven: Yale University Press, 2016), p.62.

6. Odd Arne Westad, *The Global Cold War: Third World Intervention and the Making of Our Times* (Cambridge: Cambridge University Press, 2005), p.3.

7. Mary Ann Tétreault, 'La Longue Durée and Energy Security in the Gulf,' *British Journal of Middle Eastern Studies*, 36(3), 2009, p.378; Frederick Anscombe, *The Ottoman Gulf: The Creation of Kuwait, Saudi Arabia, and Qatar, 1870–1914* (New York: Columbia University Press, 1997), p.172.

8. Toby Craig Jones, '"Energy Security": Genealogy of a Term,' *Middle East Report 271*, 2014.

9. Madawi Al-Rasheed and Loulouwa Al-Rasheed, 'The Politics of Encapsulation: Saudi Policy Towards Tribal and Religious Opposition,' *Middle Eastern Studies*, 32(1), 1996, p.111.

10. Toby Matthiesen, 'Migration, Minorities, and Radical Networks: Labour Movements and Opposition Groups in Saudi Arabia, 1950–1975,' *International Review of Social History*, 59(3), 2014, pp.473–4; Rosie Bsheer, 'A Counter-Revolutionary State: Popular Movements and the Making of Saudi Arabia,' *Past and Present*, 238, 2018, pp.235–6.

11. Matthiesen, 'Migration, Minorities, and Radical Networks,' p.484.

12. Nathan Citino, *From Arab Nationalism to OPEC: Eisenhower, King Sa'ud, and the Making of U.S.-Saudi Relations* (Bloomington: Indiana University Press, 2002), pp.119–20.

13. David Long, *The United States and Saudi Arabia: Ambivalent Allies* (Boulder: Westview Press, 1985), p.112.

14. Gregory Brew, '"Our Most Dependable Allies": Iraq, Saudi Arabia, and the Eisenhower Doctrine, 1956–1958,' *Mediterranean Quarterly*, 26(4), 2015, p.92.

15. Victor McFarland, *Oil Powers: A History of the U.S.-Saudi Alliance* (New York: Columbia University Press, 2020), p.47.

16. Jacob Abadi, 'Saudi Arabia's Rapprochement with Israel: The National Security Imperatives,' *Middle Eastern Studies*, 55(3), 2019, pp.437–8.

17. 'Note for the Record,' by J.F. Mayne, private secretary to the Secretary of State for Defence, 27 April 1975, London: The National Archives, file FCO 93/782, Attitude of Saudi Arabia to Arab-Israeli Dispute.

18. Ibid. p.217.

19. Peter Baker and Susan Glasser, *The Man Who Ran Washington: The Life and Times of James A. Baker III* (New York: Doubleday, 2020), p.179.

20. Laurence Louër, *Transnational Shia Politics: Religious and Political Networks in the Gulf* (London: Hurst & Co., 2008), p.177.

21. Gregory Gause, *The International Relations of the Persian Gulf* (Cambridge: Cambridge University Press, 2009), p.48.

22. Al-Rasheed, 'Politics of Encapsulation,' p.112.

23. Quoted in Miller, *Desert Kingdoms to Global Powers*, p.51.

24. Gwenn Okruhlik, 'Saudi Arabian-Iranian Relations: External Rapprochement and Internal Consolidation,' *Middle East Policy*, 10(2), 2003, p.116.

25. 'Too Close for Comfort,' *Gulf States Newsletter*, 8(178), 11–24 January 1982, p.2; 'The Conduct of the Trial,' *Gulf States Newsletter*, 8(186), 3–16 May 1982, p.4; Steven Wright, 'Iran's Relations with Bahrain,' in Gawdat Bahgat, Anoushiravan Ehteshami, and Neil Quilliam (eds.), *Security and Bilateral Issues between Iran and Its Arab Neighbours* (Cham: Springer, 2017), p.68.

26. Toby Matthiesen, 'Hizbullah al-Hijaz: A History of the Most Radical Saudi Shi'a Opposition Group,' *Middle East Journal*, 64(2), 2010, pp.184–5.

27. Yoel Guzansky, 'Defence Cooperation in the Arabian Gulf: The Peninsula Shield Force Put to the Test,' *Middle Eastern Studies*, 50(4), 2014, pp.644–5.

28. Roham Alvandi, 'Muhammad Reza Pahlavi and the Bahrain Question, 1968–1970,' *British Journal of Middle Eastern Studies*, 37(2), 2010, p.165.

29. Gerd Nonneman, 'The Gulf States and the Iran-Iraq War: Pattern Shifts and Continuities,' in Lawrence Potter and Gary Sick (eds.), *Iran, Iraq, and the Legacies of War* (New York: Palgrave Macmillan, 2004), p.177.

30. Miller, *Desert Kingdoms to Global Powers*, p.210.

31. Youssef Ibrahim, 'Saudi Arabia to Build Causeway to Bahrain,' *New York Times*, 3 December 1979.

32. 'The Iranian Threat is Bad Enough without American Help,' *Saudi Arabia Newsletter*, 9, 8–21 October 1979, p.4.

33. Munira Fakhro, 'The Uprising in Bahrain: An Assessment,' in Gary Sick and Lawrence Potter (eds.), *The Persian Gulf at the Millennium: Essays in Politics, Economy, Security, and Religion* (London: Palgrave Macmillan, 1997), p.184; Miller, *Desert Kingdoms to Global Powers*, p.211.

34. Quoted in Kristian Coates Ulrichsen, 'Gulf States: Studious Silence Falls on Arab Spring,' *Open Democracy*, 25 April 2011. The Bahrain Independent Commission of Inquiry set up by King Hamad in July 2011 to examine the 2011 unrest, found in its report, published in November 2011, that there was no evidence to support the assertions that Iran had played a role in the protest movement.

35. Miller, *Desert Kingdoms to Global Powers*, p.105.

36. Quoted in Conge and Okruhlik, 'Power of Narrative,' p.362.

37. Toby Craig Jones, 'Embracing Crisis in the Gulf,' *Middle East Report 264*, 2012.

38. Karen DeYoung, 'Clinton Defends U.S. Stance on Syria, Bahrain,' *Washington Post*, 7 November 2011.

39. Ibrahim Hatlani, 'Bahrain between its Backers and the Brotherhood,' *Carnegie Endowment for International Peace*, 20 May 2014.

40. Justin Gengler, *Group Conflict and Political Mobilization in Bahrain and the Arab Gulf: Rethinking the Rentier State* (Bloomington: Indiana University Press, 2015), pp.156–7.

41. Scheherezade Faramarzi, 'Kuwait's Muslim Brotherhood,' *Jadaliyya*, 18 April 2012.

42. Sami Atallah, 'The Gulf Region: Beyond Oil and Wars: The Role of History and Geopolitics in Explaining Autocracy,' in Ibrahim Elbadawi and Samir Makdisi (eds.), *Democracy in the Arab World: Explaining the Deficit* (Abingdon: Routledge, 2011), pp.189–91.

43. Ellen Lust-Okar, 'Divided They Rule: The Management and Manipulation of Political Opposition,' *Comparative Politics*, 36(2), 2004, pp.160–1.

44. Atallah, 'Gulf Region,' pp.189–91.

45. Alan Munro, *An Arabian Affair: Politics and Diplomacy Behind the Gulf War* (London: Brassey's, 1996), p.46 and p.205.

46. Katherine Meyer, Helen Rizzo, and Yousef Ali, 'Changed Political Attitudes in the Middle East: The Case of Kuwait,' *International Sociology*, 22, 2007, p.292.

47. Mary Ann Tétreault, 'Kuwait's Unhappy Anniversary,' *Middle East Policy*, 7(3), 2000, pp.68–70.

48. Stephen Sackur, 'In Kuwait,' *London Review of Books*, 14(4), 27 February 1992.

49. Meshal Al-Sabah, *Gender and Politics in Kuwait: Women and Political Participation in the Gulf* (London: I.B. Tauris, 2013), p.109.

50. Sharon Stanton Russell and Muhammad Ali Al-Ramadhan, 'Kuwait's Migration Policy Since the Gulf Crisis,' *International Journal of Middle East Studies*, 26(4), 1994, p.580.

51. 'Kuwaitis Blame Ruling Family Feuds for Instability,' *AFP*, 14 May 2008.

52. 'Kuwaitis to Vote in Parliamentary Election Tomorrow,' *AFP*, 16 May 2008.

53. Ali Zaid Al Zu'abi, 'Prospects for Political Reform in Kuwait: An Analysis of Recent Events,' *Arab Reform Brief* 8, Arab Reform Initiative, 2006, p.4.

54. Kristian Coates Ulrichsen, 'Politics and Opposition in Kuwait: Continuity and Change,' *Journal of Arabian Studies*, 4(2), 2014, pp.222–3.

55. Rivka Azoulay, *Kuwait and Al-Sabah: Tribal Politics and Power in an Oil State* (London: I.B. Tauris, 2020), pp.172–3 and pp.179–80.

56. Anastasia Nosova, 'The Merchant Elite and Parliamentary Politics in Kuwait: The Dynamics of Business Political Participation in a Rentier State,' *PhD dissertation*, London School of Economics and Political Science, 2016, p.160; Shafeeq Ghabra, 'Voluntary Associations in Kuwait: The Foundation of a New System?,' *Middle East Journal*, 45(2), 1991, p.204.

57. Daniel Brumberg, 'Liberalization versus Democracy: Understanding Arab Political Reform,' *Democracy and Rule of Law Project Paper No.37*, *Carnegie Endowment for International Peace*, 2003, p.6; Steven Cook, 'Getting to Arab Democracy: The Promise of Pacts,' *Journal of Democracy*, 17(1), 2006, p.64.

58. Abdulhadi Khalaf, 'Labor Movements in Bahrain,' *Middle East Report 132*, May/June 1985, available online at: https://merip.org/1985/05/labor-movements-in-bahrain/

59. Especially the imposition of an upper, appointed chamber that went against the initial promise that the unicameral elected assembly of 1975 would be revived.

60. Abd al-Nabi Al Ekry, 'Bahrain: Al-Wefaq and the Challenges of Participation,' *Arab Reform Bulletin*, 5(4), 2007, published by the Carnegie Endowment for International Peace.

61. Edward Burke, 'Bahrain: Reaching a Threshold,' *FRIDE Working Paper No.61*, 2008, p.14.

62. 'Bahrain Shia MPs Walk Out over Population Row,' *Reuters*, 14 May 2008.

63. Simon Mabon, 'The End of the Battle for Bahrain and the Securitization of Bahraini Shi'a,' *Middle East Journal*, 73(1), 2019, pp.40–1.

64. Jane Kinninmont, 'Assessing Al-Wefaq's Parliamentary Experiment,' *Arab Reform Bulletin*, 5(8), 2007, published by the Carnegie Endowment for International Peace.

65. Omar AlShehabi, 'Bahrain's Fate: On Ibrahim Sharif and the Misleadingly Dubbed "Arab Spring",' *Jacobin*, January 2014.

66. Laurence Louër, 'Bahrain's National Dialogue and the Ever-Deepening Sectarian Divide,' *Carnegie Endowment for International Peace*, 29 June 2011.

67. Ellen Lust, 'Opposition Cooperation and Uprisings in the Arab World,' *British Journal of Middle Eastern Studies*, 38(3), 2011, p.433.

68. Toby Craig Jones and Ala'a Shehabi, 'Bahrain's Revolutionaries,' *Foreign Policy*, 2 January 2012.

69. Anon., 'Popular Protest in North Africa and the Middle East (VIII): Bahrain's Rocky Road to Reform,' *International Crisis Group Middle East / North Africa Report No.111*, 28 July 2011, p.2.

70. Ibid. p.12.

71. Ibid. p.13.

72. Hamad Albloshi and Michael Herb, 'Karamet Watan: An Unsuccessful Nonviolent Movement,' *Middle East Journal*, 72(3), 2018, p.415.

73. Ibid. p.416.

74. 'Kuwaiti Youth Groups Merge into One Party,' *AFP*, 29 February 2012; Mona Kareem, 'Kuwait Youth Movement Reignites Opposition,' *Al-Monitor*, 26 September 2013.

75. Mary Ann Tétreault, 'Kuwait's Annus Mirabilis,' *Middle East Report (Online)*, 7 September 2006.

76. Elizabeth Dickinson, 'Youth Movement Helps to Set Kuwait's Political Agenda,' *The National*, 22 July 2012.

77. Kristin Smith Diwan, 'Parliamentary Boycotts in Kuwait and Bahrain Cost Opposition,' *Arab Gulf States Institute in Washington*, 6 July 2016.

78. 'Bahrain: New Anti-Terrorism Amendments Pave the Way to Further Abuses,' *Bahrain Institute for Rights and Democracy*, 22 December 2014.

79. 'Low Voter Turnout and Plans for Further Protests Signal More Trouble ahead for Kuwait,' *Gulf States Newsletter*, 36(937), 6 December 2012, p.1.

80. Hamad Al-Jasser, 'Kuwait Seeks to Deter Tribes from Supporting Opposition,' *Al-Monitor*, 23 May 2013.

81. Kristin Smith Diwan, 'Kuwait Takes a Breather,' *Foreign Policy*, 9 August 2013.

82. 'Election Law Amendment Represents Fresh Blow to Kuwaiti Opposition Groups,' *Gulf States Newsletter*, 40(1020), 28 July 2016, p.1.

83. Fred Lawson, 'Keys to the Kingdom: Current Scholarship on Saudi Arabia,' *International Journal of Middle East Studies*, 43(4), 2011, p.743.

84. Roel Meijer, 'Citizenship in Saudi Arabia,' *Middle East Journal*, 70(4), 2016, pp.669–70.

85. Madawi Al-Rasheed, 'The Shia of Saudi Arabia: A Minority in Search of Cultural Authenticity,' *British Journal of Middle Eastern Studies*, 25(1), 1998, p.136.

86. David Rundell, *Vision or Mirage: Saudi Arabia at the Crossroads* (London: I.B. Tauris, 2020), p.240.

87. Toby Matthiesen, 'The Shi'a of Saudi Arabia at a Crossroads,' *Middle East Report (Online)*, 6 May 2009.

88. Toby Craig Jones, 'Rebellion on the Saudi Periphery: Modernity, Marginalization, and the Shi'a Uprising of 1979,' *International Journal of Middle East Studies*, 38(2), 2006, p.217.

89. Lawson, 'Keys to the Kingdom,' p.742.

90. Al-Rasheed, 'Shia of Saudi Arabia,' p.137 (footnote 45).

91. Pascal Ménoret, *Graveyard of Clerics: Everyday Activism in Saudi Arabia* (Stanford: Stanford University Press, 2020), p.74.

92. 'UAE: Terrorism Law Threatens Lives, Liberty,' *Human Rights Watch*, 3 December 2014.

93. Stephanie Kirchgaessner, 'Saudi Woman Given 34-Year Prison Sentence for Using Twitter,' *The Guardian*, 16 August 2022.

94. Aziz El Yaakoubi and Rosalba O'Brien, 'Qatar Jails Four Election Protestors, Including Three for Life,' *Reuters*, 13 May 2022.

95. Clive Jones and John Stone, 'Britain and the Arabian Gulf: New Perspectives on Strategic Influence,' *International Relations*, 13(4), 1997, p.19.

96. Madawi Al-Rasheed, 'Saudi Religious Transnationalism in London,' in Madawi Al-Rasheed (ed.), *Transnational Connections and the Arab Gulf* (Abingdon: Routledge, 2005), p.161; Christa Salamandra, 'Cultural Construction, the Gulf and Arab London,' in Paul Dresch and James Piscatori (eds.), *Monarchies and Nations: Globalisation and Identity in the Arab States of the Gulf* (London: I.B. Tauris, 2005), p.74.

97. Al-Rasheed, 'Saudi Religious Transnationalism,' p.161.

98. Mamoun Fandy, 'Information Technology, Trust, and Social Change in the Arab World,' *Middle East Journal*, 54(3), 2000, p.384.

99. Jon Anderson, 'Producers and Middle East Internet Technology: Getting beyond "Impacts",' *Middle East Journal*, 54(3), 2000, p.423. King Fahd issued a decree in March 1997 that called for the drafting of guidelines for internet use in Saudi Arabia; these were completed in January 1999. See Douglas Jehl, 'Riyadh Journal: The Internet's 'Open Sesame' is Answered Warily,' *New York Times*, 18 March 1999.

100. Sean Foley, *Changing Saudi Arabia: Art, Culture and Society in the Kingdom* (Boulder: Lynne Rienner Publishers, 2021 edition), p.84 and p.117.

101. Naomi Sakr, 'Reflections on the Manama Spring: Research Questions Arising from the Promise of Political Liberalization in Bahrain,' *British Journal of Middle Eastern Studies*, 28(2), 2001, p.231.

102. Ahmed Al Omran, 'Saudi Arabia Revives Efforts to Draw Dissidents Home,' *Financial Times*, 14 July 2019.

103. Hussain Al-Qatari, 'Kuwait Sentences 3 Royal Family Members for Insulting Judges,' *Arab News*, 31 May 2016; Ahmed Azem, 'Qatar's Ties with the Muslim Brotherhood Affect Entire Region,' *The National*, 17 May 2012.

104. Mohanad Hage Ali, 'Exiles on the Bosphorus,' *Carnegie Endowment for International Peace*, 10 March 2020.

105. Madawi Al-Rasheed, *The Son King: Reform and Repression in Saudi Arabia* (London: Hurst & Co., 2020), pp. 318–20.

106. Ibid.

107. Ahmed Al Omran, 'Saudi Arabia Revives Efforts to Draw Dissidents Home,' *Financial Times*, 14 July 2019.

7. DISTRIBUTION

1. Sulayman Khalaf, 'Camel Racing in the Gulf. Notes on the Evolution of a Traditional Cultural Sport,' *Anthropos*, 94(1), 1999, p. 85.

2. James Onley and Sulayman Khalaf, 'Shaikhly Authority in the Pre-Oil Gulf: An Historical-Anthropological Study,' *History and Anthropology*, 17(3), 2006, pp. 197–8.

3. Michael Herb, 'The Origins of Kuwait's National Assembly,' *LSE Kuwait Programme Paper Series 39*, 2016, p. 11; Marc Valeri, 'Nation-Building and Communities in Oman Since 1970: The Swahili-Speaking Omani in Search of Identity,' *African Affairs*, 104(424), 2007, pp. 482–3; Sandhya Rao Mehta and James Onley, 'The Hindu Community in Muscat: Creating Homes in the Diaspora,' *Journal of Arabian Studies*, 5(2), 2015, p. 166; Ulrike Freitag, 'A Twentieth Century Merchant Network Centered on Jeddah: The Correspondence of Muhammad b. Ahmad Bin Himd,' *Northeast African Studies*, 17(1), 2017, pp. 103–5.

4. Jill Crystal, 'Civil Society in the Arabian Gulf,' in August Richard Norton (ed.), *Civil Society in the Middle East: Volume Two* (Leiden: Brill, 1996), p. 262.

5. Victoria Penziner Hightower, 'Pearling and Political Power in the Trucial States, 1850–1930: Debts, Taxes, and Politics,' *Journal of Arabian Studies*, 3(2), 2013, pp. 222–4.

6. Mary Ann Tétreault, 'A State of Two Minds: State Cultures, Women, and Politics in Kuwait,' *International Journal of Middle East Studies*, 33(2), 2001, p. 203.

7. Abdullah Alhajeri, 'The Bedouin: Kuwaitis Without an Identity,' *Middle Eastern Studies*, 51(1), 2015, p. 26.

8. Salwa Alghanim, *The Reign of Mubarak Al-Sabah: Shaikh of Kuwait 1896–1915* (London: I.B. Tauris, 1998), pp. 139–40; Farah Al-Nakib, *Kuwait*

Transformed: A History of Oil and Urban Life (Stanford: Stanford University Press, 2016), pp.30–1.

9. J.E. Peterson, *Saudi Arabia under Ibn Saud: Economic and Financial Foundations of the State* (London: I.B. Tauris, 2018), p.10; Dawn Chatty, 'Rituals of Royalty and the Elaboration of Ceremony in Oman: View from the Edge,' *International Journal of Middle East Studies*, 41(1), 2009, p.42.

10. Nelida Fuccaro, *Histories of City and State in the Persian Gulf: Manama Since 1800* (Cambridge: Cambridge University Press, 2009), p.76 and p.88.

11. Farah Al-Nakib, 'Inside a Gulf Port: The Dynamics of Urban Life in Pre-Oil Kuwait,' in Lawrence Potter (ed.), *The Persian Gulf in Modern Times: People, Ports, and History* (New York: Palgrave Macmillan, 2014), p.203.

12. Fatma Al-Sayegh, 'Merchants' Role in a Changing Society: The Case of Dubai, 1900–90,' *Middle Eastern Studies*, 34(1), 1998, p.91; Waleed Al-Munais, 'Social and Ethnic Differentiation in Kuwait: A Social Geography of an Indigenous Society,' *PhD dissertation*, School of Oriental and African Studies, 1981, pp.95–6; May Al-Arrayed Shirawi, 'Education in Bahrain—1919–1986: An Analytical Study of Problems and Progress,' *PhD dissertation*, Durham University, 1987, pp.61–2.

13. Shirawi, 'Education in Bahrain,' p.63.

14. Fahad Ahmad Bishara, Bernard Haykel, Steffen Hertog, Clive Holes, and James Onley, 'The Economic Transformation of the Gulf,' in J.E. Peterson (ed.), *The Emergence of the Gulf States: Studies in Modern History* (London: Bloomsbury, 2018), pp.196–8.

15. Fahad Ahmad Bishara, 'Mapping the Indian Ocean World of Gulf Merchants, c.1870–1960,' in Abdul Sheriff and Engseng Ho (eds.), *The Indian Ocean: Oceanic Connections and the Creation of New Societies* (London: Hurst & Co., 2014), pp.78–9.

16. Eran Segal, 'Merchants' Networks in Kuwait: The Story of Yusuf al-Marzuk,' *Middle Eastern Studies*, 45(5), 2009, pp.709–10.

17. Easa Saleh Al-Gurg, *The Wells of Memory: An Autobiography* (London: John Murray, 1998), p.41.

18. James Onley, 'Transnational Merchants in the Nineteenth Century: The Case of the Safar Family,' in Madawi Al-Rasheed (ed.), *Transnational Connections and the Arab Gulf* (Abingdon: Routledge, 2005), pp.68–9.

19. Ulrike Freitag, *A History of Jeddah: The Gate to Mecca in the Nineteenth and Twentieth Centuries* (Cambridge: Cambridge University Press, 2020), pp.230–1.

20. Michael Field, *The Merchants: The Big Business Families of Saudi Arabia and the Gulf States* (Woodstock: The Overlook Press, 1985), p.24.

21. Kristian Coates Ulrichsen, *The Gulf States in International Political Economy* (Basingstoke: Palgrave Macmillan, 2015), pp.22–3.

22. Guillemette Crouzet, 'The British Empire in India, the Gulf Pearl and the Making of the Middle East,' *Middle Eastern Studies*, 55(6), 2019, p.869.

23. Niklas Haller, 'A Labyrinth in the Sand: British Boundary-Making and the Emergence of the Emirati Territorial State,' *PhD dissertation*, University of Exeter, 2019, 2019, pp.121–2.

24. Guillemette Crouzet, *Inventing the Middle East: Britain and the Persian Gulf in the Age of Global Imperialism* (Montreal: McGill-Queen's University Press, 2022), p.120.

25. Haller, 'Labyrinth in the Sand,' pp.121–2.

26. Atef Suleiman, *The Petroleum Experience of Abu Dhabi* (Abu Dhabi: Emirates Center for Strategic Studies and Research, 2007), pp.68–9.

27. John Bulloch, *The Gulf: A Portrait of Kuwait, Qatar, Bahrain and the UAE* (London: Century Publishing, 1984), p.119.

28. Allen Fromherz, *Qatar: A Modern History* (Washington, D.C.: Georgetown University Press, 2012), p.119; Jill Crystal, *Oil and Politics in the Gulf: Rulers and Merchants in Kuwait and Qatar* (Cambridge: Cambridge University Press, 1990), pp.5–6.

29. Jill Crystal, 'Coalitions in Oil Monarchies: Kuwait and Qatar,' *Comparative Politics*, 21(4), 1989, p.430.

30. Mahdi Abdalla Al Tajir, *Bahrain 1920–1945: Britain, the Shaikh and the Administration* (London: Croom Helm, 1987), pp.252–4.

31. Haller, 'Labyrinth in the Sand,' p. 122; Crystal, *Oil and Politics,* p. 119; Edward Henderson, *This Strange Eventful History: Memoirs of Earlier Days in the UAE and Oman* (London: Quartet Books, 1988), p.17.

32. Abdulrahman Alebrahim, *Kuwait's Politics before Independence: The Role of the Balancing Powers* (Berlin: Gerlach Press, 2019), p.234.

33. David Rundell, *Vision or Mirage: Saudi Arabia at the Crossroads* (London: I.B. Tauris, 2020), p.112.

34. Sulayman Khalaf, 'Gulf Societies and the Image of Unlimited Good,' *Dialectical Anthropology*, 17(1), 1992, pp.56-7.

35. Joseph Kostiner, 'On Instruments and their Designers: The *Ikhwan* of Najd and the Emergence of the Saudi State,' *Middle Eastern Studies*, 21(3), 1985, p.303.

36. Freitag, *History of Jeddah*, pp.180–81.

37. Bishara, 'Mapping the Indian Ocean World,' p.88. Bishara adds that many of the properties in Bombay and Bahrain remain in the family's ownership today.

38. Jim Krane, *Energy Kingdoms: Oil and Political Survival in the Persian Gulf* (New York: Columbia University Press, 2019), pp.32–4.

39. Gerald Butt, 'Oil and Gas in the UAE,' in Ibrahim al Abed and Peter Hellyer (eds.), *United Arab Emirates: A New Perspective* (London: Trident Press, 2001), p.187; James Worrall, *Statebuilding and Counterinsurgency in Oman: Political, Military and Diplomatic Relations at the End of Empire* (London: I.B. Tauris, 2014), p.56.

40. Coates Ulrichsen, *The Gulf States*, pp.26–7.

41. William Mulligan of Aramco's Government Relations Department, quoted in Sarah Yizraeli, *Politics and Society in Saudi Arabia: The Crucial Years of Development, 1960–1982* (London: Hurst & Co., 2012), pp.278–9.

42. Giacomo Luciani, *The Arab State* (London: Routledge, 1990), p.69.

43. Khaldoon Al-Naqeeb quoted in Tareq Ismael, Jacqueline Ismael, and Glenn Perry, *Government and Politics of the Contemporary Middle East: Continuity and Change* (London: Routledge, 2016), p.502.

44. Frauke Heard-Bey, *From Trucial States to United Arab Emirates* (Dubai: Motivate Publishing, 2004), pp.296–7.

45. Dale Eickelman, 'From Theocracy to Monarchy: Authority and Legitimacy in Inner Oman, 1935–1957,' *International Journal of Middle East Studies*, 17(1), 1985, p.12.

46. David Edens and William Snavely, 'Planning for Economic Development in Saudi Arabia,' *Middle East Journal*, 24(1), 1970, p.28.

47. Rundell, *Vision or Mirage*, p.161.

48. Rosemarie Said Zahlan, *The Making of the Modern Gulf States* (Reading: Ithaca Press, 1998 edition), p.39.

49. Ali Khalifa Al-Kuwari, *Oil Revenues in the Gulf Emirates: Patterns of Allocation and Impact on Economic Development* (London: Routledge, 2018 edition), p.119.

50. Ragaei El Mallakh, 'The Challenge of Affluence: Abu Dhabi,' *Middle East Journal*, 24(2), 1970, p.140.

51. Simon Bromley, *Rethinking Middle East Politics: State Formation and Development* (Cambridge: Polity Press, 1994), p.120.

52. Al-Kuwari, *Oil Revenues in the Gulf Emirates*, p.94 and p.158.

53. Ibid. p.149.

54. Omar AlShehabi, 'Show Us the Money: Oil Revenues, Undisclosed Allocations and Accountability in Budgets of the GCC States,' *LSE Kuwait Programme Paper Series 44*, 2017, p.6.

55. Ibid. pp.23-7.

56. Hazem Beblawi, 'The Rentier State in the Arab World,' in Giacomo Luciani (ed.), *The Arab State* (London: Routledge, 1990), pp. 87–9.

57. Giacomo Luciani, 'Allocative vs. Production States: A Theoretical Framework,' in Giacomo Luciani (ed.), *The Arab State* (London: Routledge, 1990), pp.71–2.

58. Ibid. p.76.

59. Anh Nga Longva, 'Nationalism in Pre-Modern Guise: The Discourse on Hadhar and Badu in Kuwait,' *International Journal of Middle East Studies*, 38(2), 2006, pp.171–2.

60. Uzi Rabi, 'Oil Politics and Tribal Rulers in Eastern Arabia: The Reign of Shakhbut (1928–1966),' *British Journal of Middle Eastern Studies*, 33(1), 2006, p.38.

61. See, for example, Michael Herb, *The Wages of Oil: Parliaments and Economic Development in Kuwait and the UAE* (Ithaca: Cornell University Press, 2014).

62. Kiren Aziz Chaudhry, *The Price of Wealth: Economies and Institutions in the Middle East* (Ithaca: Cornell University Press, 1997), p.144.

63. Ibid. p.74; Yizraeli, *Politics and Society in Saudi Arabia*, pp.278–80.

64. Gregory Gause, 'The Persistence of Monarchy in the Arabian Peninsula: A Comparative Analysis,' in Joseph Kostiner (ed.), *Middle East Monarchies: The Challenge of Modernity* (Boulder: Lynne Rienner Publishers, 2000), p.186.

65. Rupert Hay, 'The Persian Gulf States and Their Boundary Problems,' *The Geographical Journal*, 120(4), 1954, p.438.

66. Alhajeri, 'The Bedouin,' p.21.

67. Ramon Knauerhase, 'Saudi Arabia's Economy at the Beginning of the 1970s,' *Middle East Journal*, 28(2), 1974, p.127.

68. Nasra Shah, 'Recent Amnesty Programs for Irregular Migrants in Kuwait and Saudi Arabia: Some Successes and Failures,' *Gulf Labor Markets and Migration (GLMM) Explanatory Note 09/2014*, 2014, pp.3–4; 2022 population figures are compiled from the CIA's World Factbook country pages for the six GCC states.

69. See, for example, Matthew Simmons, *Twilight in the Desert: The Coming Saudi Oil Shock and the World Economy* (New York: Wiley, 2006).

70. Robin Mills, *The Myth of the Oil Crisis: Overcoming the Challenges of Depletion, Geopolitics, and Global Warming* (Westport: Praeger, 2008), p.54. In Oman, by contrast, Mandana Limbert observed in 2010 that 'the Omani state has been projecting the twenty-year end of oil for nearly four decades.' See Mandana Limbert, *In the Time of Oil: Piety, Memory, and Social Life in an Omani Town* (Stanford: Stanford University Press, 2010), p.167.

71. Paul Dresch, 'Societies, Identities and Global Issues,' in Paul Dresch and James Piscatori (eds.), *Monarchies and Nations: Globalisation and Identity in the Arab States of the Gulf* (London: I.B. Tauris, 2005), p.16.

72. Steffen Hertog, *Princes, Brokers, and Bureaucrats: Oil and the State in Saudi Arabia* (Ithaca: Cornell University Press, 2010), pp.28–9.

73. Michael Herb, 'A Nation of Bureaucrats: Political Participation and Economic Diversification in Kuwait and the United Arab Emirates,' *International Journal of Middle East Studies*, 41(3), 2009, pp.375–6.

74. Justin Gengler, *Group Conflict and Political Mobilization in Bahrain and the Arab Gulf: Rethinking the Rentier State* (Bloomington: Indiana University Press, 2015), pp.10–11.

75. Anoushiravan Ehteshami and Steven Wright, 'Political Change in the Arab Oil Monarchies: From Liberalization to Enfranchisement,' *International Affairs*, 83(5), 2007, p.914.

76. Gwenn Okruhlik, 'Rentier Wealth, Unruly Law, and the Rise of Opposition: The Political Economy of Oil States,' *Comparative Politics*, 31(3), 1999, p.297.

77. Andrew Leber, 'Resisting Rentierism: Labor Market Reforms in Saudi Arabia' and Jessie Moritz, 'Oil and Societal Quiescence: Rethinking Causal Mechanisms in Rentier State Theory,' both in Michael Herb and Marc Lynch (eds.), *The Politics of Rentier States in the Gulf*, POMEPS Studies 33, 2019, p.34 and p.40.

78. Mehran Kamrava, *Inside the Arab State* (London: Hurst & Co., 2018), p.154.

79. Anastasia Nosova, 'The Merchant Elite and Parliamentary Politics in Kuwait: The Dynamics of Business Political Participation in a Rentier State,' *PhD dissertation*, London School of Economics and Political Science, 2016, p.159.

80. Helene von Bismarck, *British Policy in the Persian Gulf, 1961–1968: Conceptions of Informal Empire* (Basingstoke: Palgrave Macmillan, 2013), p.160.

81. Ibid. p.161.

82. Archibald Lamb, 'Annual Review of Events in Abu Dhabi in 1965,' in Robert Jarman, *Political Diaries of the Arab World: The Persian Gulf. Volume 24: 1963–1965* (Chippenham: Archive Editions, 1998), p.520.

83. John Townsend, *Oman: The Making of the Modern State* (London: Croom Helm, 1977), p.69.

84. Dawn Chatty, 'Rituals of Royalty and the Elaboration of Ceremony in Oman: View from the Edge,' *International Journal of Middle East Studies*, 41(1), 2009, p.43.

85. J.E. Peterson, 'Oman: Three and a Half Decades of Change and Development,' *Middle East Policy*, 11(2), 2004, p.128; Linda Pappas Funsch, *Oman Reborn: Balancing Tradition and Modernization* (Basingstoke: Palgrave Macmillan, 2015), p.60.

86. Abdel Razzaq Takriti, *Monsoon Revolution: Republicans, Sultans, and Empires in Oman, 1965–1976* (Oxford: Oxford University Press, 2016 edition), pp.191–3.

87. 'Appendix: Press Release, 26 July 1970,' in Ian Skeet, *Oman: Politics and Development* (London: Macmillan, 1992), p.164.

88. Crystal, *Oil and Politics*, pp.78–9; Tim Niblock and Monica Malik, *The Political Economy of Saudi Arabia* (Abingdon: Routledge, 2007), pp.110–11; Mary Ann Tétreault, *Stories of Democracy: Politics and Society in Contemporary Kuwait* (New York: Columbia University Press, 2000), p.42; Justin Gengler, 'Understanding Gulf Citizen Preferences Towards Rentier Subsidies,' in Michael Herb and Marc Lynch (eds.), *The Politics of Rentier States in the Gulf*, POMEPS Studies 33, January 2019, pp.51–2.

89. Christopher Davidson, *Abu Dhabi: Oil and Beyond* (London: Hurst & Co., 2009), p.132; Mehran Kamrava, 'Royal Factionalism and Political Liberalization in Qatar,' *Middle East Journal*, 63(3), 2009, p.406.

90. Jim Krane, *Dubai: The Story of the World's Fastest City* (London: Atlantic Books, 2009), pp.267–9.

91. Herb, *Wages of Oil*, p.43.

92. Miriam Lowi, 'Justice, Charity, and the Common Good: In Search of Islam in Gulf Petro-Monarchies,' *Middle East Journal*, 71(4), 2017, p.569.

93. Tétreault, *Stories of Democracy*, p.42; Al-Kuwari, *Oil Revenues in the Gulf Emirates*, p.100.

94. Nadav Samin, *Of Sand or Soil: Genealogy and Tribal Belonging in Saudi Arabia* (Princeton: Princeton University Press, 2015), pp.184–5.

95. Abdulhadi Khalaf, 'The Politics of Migration,' in Abdulhadi Khalaf, Omar AlShehabi, and Adam Hanieh (eds.), *Transit States: Labour, Migration and Citizenship in the Gulf* (London: Pluto Press, 2015), p.48.

96. Longva, 'Nationalism in Pre-Modern Guise,' p.183.

97. Alhajeri, 'The Bedouin,' pp.20–4.

98. Alex Boodrookas, 'Reconceptualizing Noncitizen Labor Rights in the Persian Gulf,' *Brandeis University, Crown Center for Middle East Studies, Middle East Brief No.143*, 2021, p.3.

99. Mehran Kamrava, Gerd Nonneman, Anastasia Nosova, and Marc Valeri, 'Ruling Families and Business Elites in the Gulf Monarchies: Ever Closer?,' *Chatham House Research Paper*, 2016, p.4.

100. J.E. Peterson, 'Rulers, Merchants and Shaikhs in Gulf Politics: The Function of Family Networks,' in Alanoud Alsharekh (ed.), *The Gulf Family: Kinship Policies and Modernity* (London: Saqi Books, 2007), p.30.

101. Giacomo Luciani, 'From Private Sector to National Bourgeoisie: Saudi Arabian Business,' in Paul Aarts and Gerd Nonneman (eds.), *Saudi Arabia in the Balance: Political Economy, Society, Foreign Affairs* (London: Hurst & Co., 2005), p.151.

102. Crystal, *Oil and Politics*, pp.1–2.

103. Peter Lienhardt, *Disorientations: A Society in Flux: Kuwait in the 1950s* (Reading: Ithaca Press, 1993), p.53.

104. Mohamed Al Rumaihi, *Bahrain: Social and Political Change Since the First World War* (London: Bowker, 1976), pp.150–1.

105. The British Bank of the Middle East (BBME) was initially known as the Imperial Bank of Persia and was the state bank of Iran until 1928; it is today a part of the HSBC group. See Adam Hanieh, *Capitalism and Class in the Gulf Arab States* (New York: Palgrave Macmillan, 2011), p.78.

106. Ibid. p.80.

107. Ibid. See also J.O. Ronall, 'Economic Review: Banking Developments in Kuwayt,' *Middle East Journal*, 24(1), 1970, p.92; Mehran Kamrava, 'State-Business Relations and Clientelism in Qatar,' *Journal of Arabian Studies*, 7(1), 2017, p.4.

108. Khalid Almezaini, 'Private Sector Actors in the UAE and their Role in the Process of Economic and Political Reform,' in Steffen Hertog, Giacomo Luciani, and Marc Valeri (eds.), *Business Politics in the Middle East* (London: Hurst & Co., 2013), p.58.

109. Ibrahim Almuhanna, *Oil Leaders: An Insider's Account of Four Decades of Saudi Arabia and OPEC's Global Energy Policy* (New York: Columbia University Press, 2022), p.21.

110. Hertog, *Princes, Brokers, and Bureaucrats*, p.124.

111. Matthew Gray, *Qatar: Politics and the Challenges of Development* (Boulder: Lynne Rienner Publishers, 2013), p.44.

112. 'In Brief: Kuwait,' *Gulf States Newsletter*, 11(283), 24 March 1986, p.9.

113. 'In Brief: Saudi Arabia,' *Gulf States Newsletter*, 13(329), 25 January 1988, p.12.

114. Jim Krane, 'Subsidy Reform and Tax Increases in the Rentier Middle East,' in Michael Herb and Marc Lynch (eds.), *The Politics of Rentier States in the Gulf*, POMEPS Studies 33, 2019, pp.20–1.

115. Rory Miller, *Desert Kingdoms to Global Powers: The Rise of the Arab Gulf* (New Haven: Yale University Press, 2016), p.220 and p.223; Yukari Hino, 'Saudi Arabia Field Report: Another Potential Oil Crisis in the Middle East,' *Brookings Institution,* 2015.

116. Elizabeth Dickinson, 'Kuwait PM Cautions that Welfare State "Unsustainable",' *The National*, 27 October 2013.

117. Daniel Fineren, 'Oman Oil Minister Slams Gulf Culture of Energy Subsidies,' *Reuters*, 10 November 2013.

118. Peter Waldman, 'The $2 Trillion Project to Get Saudi Arabia's Economy Off Oil,' *Bloomberg*, 21 April 2016.

119. Thomas Lippman, 'New Saudi Budget: The Good, the Bad, and the Potentially Ugly,' *LobeLog*, 29 December 2015.

120. Luai Allarakia and Hamad Albloshi, 'The Politics of Permanent Deadlock in Kuwait,' *Arab Gulf States Institute in Washington*, 2021.

121. Richard Balmforth, 'Bahrain MPs Blast Fuel Price Hike in Heated Session,' *Reuters*, 12 January 2016; Aziz El Yaakoubi, 'Bahrain Ditches Subsidy Reform Plan as Political Tensions Simmer,' *Reuters*, 7 May 2019.

122. Sarah Townsend, 'Focus: The Impact of the Bahrain Food Subsidies Row, What it Means for the Wider Region,' *Arabian Business*, 18 September 2015; 'Kuwait Prepares for Another Political Battle after Parliament's Early Dissolution,' *Gulf States Newsletter*, 40(1024), 20 October 2016, p.3.

123. Ibrahim Al Hatlani, 'Costs of Saudi Economic Failures Show Up in Electric Bills,' *Al-Monitor*, 31 August 2016.

124. 'Saudi Arabia Restores Perks to State Employees to Fend Off Unrest,' *The Guardian*, 24 April 2017.

125. 'No Plans for Income Tax, VAT Increase is Temporary: Saudi Crown Prince Mohammed bin Salman,' *Arab News*, 28 April 2021; Davide Barbuscia, 'Bahrain Parliament Approves Value-Added Tax Increase to 10%,' *Reuters*, 8 December 2021.

126. Vinod Noir, 'Oman: No VAT Increase, No Income Tax in 2023,' *Oman Daily Observer*, 20 December 2022.

127. Krane, *Energy Kingdoms*, pp.124–6.

128. Ibid.; Steffen Hertog, 'The "Rentier Mentality" 30 Years On: Evidence from Survey Data,' *British Journal of Middle Eastern Studies*, 47(1), 2020, p.8.

129. Ruba Husani, 'For Gulf Producers, Decarbonization Does Not Mean Zero Oil Production,' *Middle East Institute*, 2022.

130. Saeed Azhar, 'Saudi Aramco Raises IPO to Record $29.4 Billion by Over-Allotment of Shares,' *Reuters*, 12 January 2020; Alexis Montambault Trudelle, 'The Public Investment Fund and Salman's State: The Political Drivers of Sovereign Wealth Management in Saudi Arabia,' *Review of International Political Economy*, 30(2), 2022, pp.11–12.

131. Deena Kamel and Massoud Derhally, 'Saudi Arabia Transfers 4% of Aramco Shares to Sovereign Wealth Fund,' *The National*, 13 February 2022.

132. Oliver McPherson-Smith, 'Diversification, Khashoggi, and Saudi Arabia's Public Investment Fund,' *Global Policy*, 12(2), 2021, p.194.

133. Andrew England and Simeon Kerr, 'The Abu Dhabi Royal at the Nexus of UAE Business and National Security,' *Financial Times*, 24 January 2021; 'Sheikh Tahnoon's Business Empire Expands Again with $10bn Venture Capital Fund,' *Gulf States Newsletter*, 46(1140), 3 February 2022, pp.13–14.

134. Karen Young, 'Sovereign Risk: Gulf Sovereign Wealth Funds as Engines of Growth and Political Resource,' *British Journal of Middle Eastern Studies*, 47(1), 2020, p.96.

135. Matthew Gray, 'A Theory of "Late Rentierism" in the Arab States of the Gulf,' *Georgetown University School of Foreign Service in Qatar, Center for International and Regional Studies Occasional Paper No.7*, 2011, p.1.

136. Mohammed bin Salman and Tahnoon bin Zayed are successors to previous generations of 'business royals' in Gulf States, such as Bahrain's long-serving Prime Minister, Sheikh Khalifa bin Salman Al Khalifa; Qatar's Prime Minister, Sheikh Hamad bin Jassim Al Thani; and Sultan Qaboos's cousin and eventual successor in Oman, Haitham bin Tariq Al Said. See Marc Valeri, 'Oligarchy vs. Oligarchy: Business and Politics of Reform in Bahrain and Oman,' in Steffen Hertog, Giacomo Luciani, and Marc Valeri (eds.), *Business Politics in the Middle East* (London: Hurst & Co., 2012), p.32.

137. Karen Young, *The Economic Statecraft of the Gulf Arab States* (London: I.B. Tauris, 2023), p.129.

138. Nora Derbal, *Charity in Saudi Arabia: Civil Society under Authoritarianism* (Cambridge: Cambridge University Press, 2022), pp.152–3.

139. Jon Gambrell, 'Protests Spread across Once-Quiet Oman as Economy Flounders,' *Associated Press*, 25 May 2021.

140. 'Gulf Arab States Should Cut State Spending Growth: IMF,' *Reuters*, 29 October 2012.

141. Steffen Hertog, 'The Costs of Counter-Revolution in the Gulf,' *Foreign Policy*, 31 May 2011.

8. MILITARIES

1. Wilfred Thesiger, *Arabian Sands* (London: Penguin Books, 1991 edition), pp.271–2.
2. James Onley and Sulayman Khalaf, 'Shaikhly Authority in the Pre-Oil Gulf: An Historical-Anthropological Study,' *History and Anthropology*, 17(3), 2006, p.195.
3. Ibid. p.191.
4. Stephanie Cronin, 'Tribes, Coups and Princes: Building a Modern Army in Saudi Arabia,' *Middle Eastern Studies*, 49(1), 2013, pp.5–6.
5. David Rundell, *Vision or Mirage: Saudi Arabia at the Crossroads* (London: I.B. Tauris, 2020), pp.30–1.
6. Ibid. p.33.
7. Tancred Bradshaw, *The End of Empire in the Gulf: From Trucial States to United Arab Emirates* (London: I.B. Tauris, 2021), p.3.
8. Ash Rossiter, *Security in the Gulf: Local Militaries before British Withdrawal* (Cambridge: Cambridge University Press, 2020), pp.7–8.
9. Donald Hawley, *The Trucial States* (London: George Allen & Unwin, 1970), pp.129–30. More than a century and a half later, the Ruler of Sharjah challenged and dissected the British accusations of Arab piracy, in Sultan bin Mohammed Al Qasimi, *The Myth of Arab Piracy in the Gulf* (London: Croom Helm, 1986).
10. Husain Albaharna, *The Legal Status of the Arabian Gulf States: A Study of Their Treaty Relations and Their International Problems* (Manchester: Manchester University Press, 1968), pp.26–7.
11. Robert Blyth, 'Britain Versus India in the Persian Gulf: The Struggle for Political Control, c.1928–1948,' *Journal of Imperial and Commonwealth History*, 28(1), 2000, pp.104–5.
12. James Onley, 'Britain and the Gulf Shaikhdoms, 1820–1971: The Politics of Protection,' Georgetown School of Foreign Service in Qatar: *Center for International and Regional Studies Occasional Paper*, 2009, pp.6–8.
13. Glencairn Balfour-Paul, *The End of Empire in the Middle East: Britain's Relinquishment of Power in Her Last Three Arab Dependencies* (Cambridge: Cambridge University Press, 1991), p.104.
14. Ibid. p.102.
15. Ash Rossiter, 'Survival of the Kuwaiti Statelet: Najd's Expansion and the Question of British Protection,' *Middle Eastern Studies*, 56(3), 2020, p.384.
16. Fatma Al-Sayegh, 'American Missionaries in the UAE Region in the Twentieth Century,' *Middle Eastern Studies*, 32(1), 1996, p.128.

17. John Slight, 'Global War and Its Impact on the Gulf States of Kuwait and Bahrain, 1914–1918,' *War & Society*, 37(1), 2018, pp.30–1.
18. James Worrall, 'The Missing Link? Police and State-building in South Arabia,' in Clive Jones (ed.), *Britain and State Formation in Arabia 1962–1971: From Aden to Abu Dhabi* (Abingdon: Routledge, 2018), pp.19–20.
19. Mansour Nasasra, 'The Frontiers of Empire: Colonial Policing in Southern Palestine, Sinai, Transjordan and Saudi Arabia,' *Journal of Imperial and Commonwealth History*, 49(5), 2021, pp.900–1.
20. Athol Yates and Ash Rossiter, 'Forging a Force: Rulers, Professional Expatriates, and the Creation of Abu Dhabi's Police,' *Middle Eastern Studies*, 56(4), 2020, pp.4–6.
21. Jill Crystal, 'Public Order and Authority: Policing Kuwait,' in Paul Dresch and James Piscatori (eds.), *Monarchies and Nations: Globalisation and Identity in the Arab States of the Gulf* (London: I.B. Tauris, 2005), p.160.
22. Transcript of interview with Sir Anthony Parsons, 22 March 1996, The British Diplomatic Oral History Programme, Churchill College, University of Cambridge, available online at: https://bdohp.chu.cam.ac.uk/transcripts/
23. Ibid. p.10; J.E. Peterson, 'Oman's Diverse Society: Southern Oman,' *Middle East Journal*, 58(2), 2004, p.268.
24. Frauke Heard-Bey, *From Trucial States to United Arab Emirates* (Dubai: Motivate Publishing, 2004 edition), pp.312–13.
25. Tancred Bradshaw, 'Security Forces and the End of Empire in the Trucial States, 1960–1971,' *Middle Eastern Studies*, 56(6), 2020, p.1.
26. Jeffrey Macris, *The Politics and Security of the Gulf: Anglo-American Hegemony and the Shaping of a Region* (Abingdon: Routledge, 2010), pp.115–16.
27. Richard Scott, 'Independence for Kuwait: British Protection Withdrawn,' *The Guardian*, 20 June 1961. Heath made the announcement to the House of Commons in his capacity as Lord Privy Seal.
28. Simon Smith, 'The Making of a Neo-Colony? Anglo-Kuwaiti Relations in the Era of Decolonization,' *Middle Eastern Studies*, 37(1), 2001, p.160.
29. Ibrahim Al-Marashi, 'Iraq's Gulf Policy and Regime Security from the Monarchy to the Post-Ba'athist Era,' *British Journal of Middle Eastern Studies*, 36(3), 2009, p.455.
30. Ibid. p.458.
31. Smith, 'Making of a Neo-Colony,' p.160.
32. Taylor Fain, 'John F. Kennedy and Harold Macmillan: Managing the "Special Relationship" in the Persian Gulf Region, 1961–63,' *Middle Eastern Studies*, 38(4), 2002, pp.102–4.
33. Paul Foot, 'Bye Bye Baghdad,' *London Review of Books*, 13(3), 7 February 1991.
34. Smith, 'Making of a Neo-Colony,' p.161; David Roberts, 'British National Interest in the Gulf: Rediscovering a Role?,' *International Affairs*, 90(3), 2014, p.671.

35. Rodney Wilson, 'Money, Oil and Empire in the Middle East: Sterling and Postwar Imperialism, 1944–1971,' *Middle Eastern Studies*, 46(3), 2010, p.459.

36. Shohei Sato, 'Britain's Decision to Withdraw from the Persian Gulf, 1964–68: A Pattern and a Puzzle,' *Journal of Imperial and Commonwealth History*, 37(1), 2009, pp.101–2.

37. Wm. Roger Louis, 'The British Withdrawal from the Gulf, 1967–71,' *Journal of Imperial and Commonwealth History*, 31(1), 2003, p.93.

38. Simon Smith, *Britain's Revival and Fall in the Gulf: Kuwait, Bahrain, Qatar, and the Trucial States, 1950–1971* (Abingdon: Routledge, 2013 edition), pp.75–6.

39. M.W. Daly, *The Last of the Great Proconsuls: The Biography of Sir William Luce* (San Diego: Nathan Berg, 2014), p.290.

40. Shohei Sato, *Britain and the Formation of the Gulf States: Embers of Empire* (Manchester: Manchester University Press, 2016), pp.108–9.

41. Joseph Kéchichian, *Faysal: Saudi Arabia's King for All Seasons* (Gainesville: University Press of Florida, 1998), p.195.

42. Richard Mobley, 'The Tunbs and Abu Musa Islands: Britain's Perspective,' *Middle East Journal*, 57(4), 2003, p.643.

43. Simon Smith, *Britain and the Gulf after Empire: Kuwait, Bahrain, Qatar, and the United Arab Emirates, 1971–1981* (Abingdon: Routledge, 2019), p.32.

44. Niklas Haller, 'A Labyrinth in the Sand: British Boundary-Making and the Emergence of the Emirati Territorial State,' *PhD dissertation*, University of Exeter, 2019, p.335.

45. Bradshaw, 'End of Empire,' p.172.

46. Clive Jones and John Stone, 'Britain and the Arabian Gulf: New Perspectives on Strategic Influence,' *International Relations*, 13(4), 1997, pp.9–11.

47. Marc Owen Jones, 'The History of British Involvement in Bahrain's Internal Security,' *Open Democracy*, 8 August 2013.

48. Geraint Hughes, 'A Proxy War in Arabia: The Dhofar Insurgency and Cross-Border Raids into South Yemen,' *Middle East Journal*, 69(1), 2015, p.100.

49. J.E. Peterson, 'Oman: Three and a Half Decades of Change and Development,' *Middle East Policy*, 11(2), 2004, p.132; Sepehr Zabih, 'Iran's Policy toward the Persian Gulf,' *International Journal of Middle East Studies*, 7(3), 1976, p.358.

50. Smith, *Britain's Revival and Fall*, p.24.

51. Ibid.

52. Faisal bin Salman Al-Saud, *Iran, Saudi Arabia and the Gulf: Power Politics in Transition* (London: I.B. Tauris, 2011 edition), p.23.

53. Rory Miller, *Desert Kingdoms to Global Powers: The Rise of the Arab Gulf* (New Haven: Yale University Press, 2016), p.8.

54. See, for example, Souad Al-Sabah, *Abdullah Mubarak Al-Sabah: The Transformation of Kuwait* (London: I.B. Tauris, 2015); Roham Alvandi,

'Muhammad Reza Pahlavi and the Bahrain Question, 1968–1970,' *British Journal of Middle Eastern Studies*, 37(2), 2010, pp.159–77; Noura Saber Al-Mazrouei, *The UAE and Saudi Arabia: Border Disputes and International Relations in the Gulf* (London: I.B. Tauris, 2016).

55. Yoel Guzansky, 'Lines Drawn in the Sand: Territorial Disputes and GCC Unity,' *Middle East Journal*, 70(4), 2016, p.551.

56. Transcript of interview with Brigadier Nicholas Cocking, 5 November 2004, The British Diplomatic Oral History Programme, Churchill College, University of Cambridge, available online at: https://bdohp.chu. cam.ac.uk/wp-content/uploads/sites/8/2022/07/Cocking.pdf

57. Rossiter, 'Security in the Gulf,' p.192.

58. Bradshaw, 'End of Empire,' p.129.

59. Christopher Davidson, *Abu Dhabi: Oil and Beyond* (London: Hurst & Co., 2009), p.63.

60. Jeremy Jones and Nicholas Ridout, *A History of Modern Oman* (Cambridge: Cambridge University Press, 2015), p.185.

61. Hassan Ali Al-Ebraheem, *Kuwait and the Gulf: Small States and the International System* (London: Routledge, 2016 edition), p.69.

62. Abdul-Reda Assiri, *Kuwait's Foreign Policy: City-State in World Politics* (Boulder: Westview Press, 1990), p.76.

63. Abdulkhaleq Abdulla, 'The Gulf Cooperation Council: Nature, Origin and Process,' in Michael Hudson (ed.), *Middle East Dilemma: The Politics and Economics of Arab Integration* (New York: Columbia University Press, 1999), p.154.

64. Anthony Cordesman, quoted in Ibrahim Suleiman Al-Duraiby, *Saudi Arabia, GCC and the EU: Limitations and Possibilities for an Unequal Triangular Relationship* (Dubai: Gulf Research Centre, 2009), p.89.

65. Justin Dargin, 'The Dolphin Project: The Development of a Gulf Gas Initiative,' *Oxford Institute for Energy Studies*, 2008, pp.18–21.

66. 'Abdullah Woos the UAE after Central Bank Split Highlights Lack of Trust in the GCC,' *Gulf States Newsletter*, 33(854), 29 May 2009, p.14.

67. Abdulla Baabood, 'Dynamics and Determinants of the GCC States' Foreign Policy, with Special Reference to the EU,' in Gerd Nonneman (ed.), *Analyzing Middle Eastern Foreign Policies* (London: Routledge, 2005), p.148.

68. Li-Chen Sim, 'Powering the Middle East and North Africa with Nuclear Energy: Stakeholders and Technopolitics,' in Robin Mills and Li-Chen Sim (eds.), *Low Carbon Energy in the Middle East and North Africa* (Cham: Springer, 2021), p.268.

69. Miller, *Desert Kingdoms to Global Powers*, p.68.

70. 'Abd al-Hadi Khalaf, 'The Elusive Quest for Gulf Security,' *Middle East Report 148*, September/October 1987, available online at: https://merip. org/1987/09/the-elusive-quest-for-gulf-security/

71. Joseph Kéchichian, 'The Gulf Security Pact: Another GCC Dilemma,' *Al Jazeera*, 24 February 2014.

72. Assiri, *Kuwait's Foreign Policy*, pp.101–2.

73. Miller, *Desert Kingdoms to Global Powers*, p.82.

74. Amy Austin Holmes, 'The Base that Replaced the British Empire: De-Democratization and the American Navy in Bahrain,' *Journal of Arabian Studies*, 4(1), 2014, pp.25–6; Robert Vitalis, *Oilcraft: The Myths of Scarcity and Security That Haunt U.S. Energy Policy* (Stanford: Stanford University Press, 2020), p.93.

75. Gregory Gause, *The International Relations of the Persian Gulf* (Cambridge: Cambridge University Press, 2009), p.127.

76. Jones and Ridout, *History of Modern Oman*, pp.191–2.

77. Fred Halliday, 'The Gulf in International Affairs: Independence and after,' in B.R. Pridham (ed.), *The Arab Gulf and the Arab World* (London: Routledge, 2016 edition), p.108; Victor McFarland, *Oil Powers: A History of the U.S.-Saudi Alliance* (New York: Columbia University Press, 2020), p.229.

78. Gary Sick, 'The United States and the Persian Gulf in the Twentieth Century,' in Lawrence Potter (ed.), *The Persian Gulf in History* (New York: Palgrave Macmillan, 2009), p.298.

79. Assiri, *Kuwait's Foreign Policy*, pp.113–14.

80. Ibid.

81. Dilip Hiro, *Cold War in the Islamic World: Saudi Arabia, Iran and the Struggle for Supremacy* (London: Hurst & Co., 2018), p.129 and p.134.

82. Anthony Cordesman, *Kuwait: Recovery and Security after the Gulf War* (Boulder: Westview Press, 1997), pp.127–9. See also Michael Gordon, 'At Least 36,000 U.S. Troops Going to Gulf in Response to Continued Iraqi Buildup,' *New York Times*, 10 October 1994.

83. Cordesman, *Kuwait*, pp.127–9.

84. John Fox, Nada Mourtada-Sabbah, and Mohammed al-Mutawa, 'The Arab Gulf Region: Traditionalism Globalized or Globalization Traditionalized?,' in John Fox, Nada Mourtada-Sabbah, and Mohammed al-Mutawa (eds.), *Globalization and the Gulf* (Abingdon: Routledge, 2006), p.24.

85. Abdullah Al-Shayeji, 'Dangerous Perceptions: Gulf Views of the U.S. Role in the Region,' *Middle East Policy*, 5(3), 1997, p.5.

86. See, for example, Adeed Dawisha and I. William Zartman (eds.), *Beyond Coercion: Durability of the Arab State* (Abingdon: Routledge, 1988), and Mehran Kamrava, 'Military Professionalization and Civil-Military Relations in the Middle East,' *Political Science Quarterly*, 115(1), p.68.

87. The connection between war- and state-making was made originally by Charles Tilly, 'War Making and State Making as Organized Crime,' in Peter Evans, Dietrich Rueschemeyer, and Theda Skocpol (eds.), *Bringing the State Back In* (Cambridge: Cambridge University Press, 1985).

88. John Duke Anthony, 'The Union of Arab Amirates,' *Middle East Journal*, 26(3), 1972, pp.277–8.

89. Hamad bin Isa Al Khalifa, *First Light: Modern Bahrain and its Heritage* (London: Kegan Paul International Limited, 1994), p.149.

90. Rosie Bsheer, 'A Counter-Revolutionary State: Popular Movements and the Making of Saudi Arabia,' *Past and Present*, 238, 2018, p.248; Fred Halliday, *Arabia without Sultans* (London: Saqi Books, 2002 edition), pp.68–9.

91. Yezid Sayigh, 'Agencies of Coercion: Armies and Internal Security Forces,' *International Journal of Middle East Studies*, 43(3), 2011, p.403.

92. Laurence Louër, 'Sectarianism and Coup-Proofing Strategies in Bahrain,' *Journal of Strategic Studies*, 36(2), 2013, p.253.

93. 'Hamad-Khalifah Row,' *Gulf States Newsletter*, 22(555), 24 February 1997, p.5.

94. Steffen Hertog, 'Rentier Militaries in the Gulf States: The Price of Coup-Proofing,' *International Journal of Middle East Studies*, 43(3), 2011, p.402.

95. Mark Thompson, 'Assessing the Impact of Saudi Arabia's National Dialogue: The Controversial Case of the Cultural Discourse,' *Journal of Arabian Studies*, 1(2), 2011, p.175.

96. Thomas Hegghammer and Stephane Lacroix, 'Rejectionist Islamism in Saudi Arabia: The Story of Juhayman Al-'utaybi Revisited,' *International Journal of Middle East Studies*, 39(1), 2007, p.109.

97. Jamal Khashoggi, 'By Blaming 1979 for Saudi Arabia's Problems, the Crown Prince is Peddling Revisionist History,' *Washington Post*, 3 April 2018.

98. Cronin, 'Tribes, Coups and Princes,' pp.22–3.

99. Joseph Kéchichian, 'Trends in Saudi National Security,' *Middle East Journal*, 53(2), 1999, p.250.

100. Ibid. p.244.

101. Gawdat Bahgat, 'Nuclear Proliferation: The Case of Saudi Arabia,' *Middle East Journal*, 60(3), 2006, p.424.

102. Jean-François Seznec, 'Democratization in the Arab World? Stirrings in Saudi Arabia,' *Journal of Democracy*, 13(4), 2002, p.35.

103. Claire Beaugrand, *Stateless in the Gulf: Migration, Nationality and Society in Kuwait* (London: I.B. Tauris, 2018), p.106.

104. Ibid. p.124.

105. Ibid. pp.125–6.

106. Zoltan Barany, *Armies of Arabia: Military Politics and Effectiveness in the Gulf* (Oxford: Oxford University Press, 2021), p.124.

107. Ibid. pp.127–8.

108. Zoltan Barany, 'Comparing the Arab Revolts: The Role of the Military,' *Journal of Democracy*, 32(4), 2011, p.31.

109. Mark Mazzetti and Emily Hager, 'Secret Desert Force Set up by Blackwater's Founder,' *New York Times*, 14 May 2011.

110. Ibid.

111. Michael Peel and Andres Schipani, 'Bogota Alarmed by Exodus of Columbian Soldiers to UAE,' *Financial Times*, 3 June 2013.

112. Anthony Parsons, 'Lessons from the Gulf,' *London Review of Books*, 13(6), 21 March 1991.

113. Alan Munro, *An Arabian Affair: Politics and Diplomacy Behind the Gulf War* (London: Brassey's, 1996), p.39.

114. Ibid. p.40; Ghazi Algosaibi, *The Gulf Crisis: An Attempt to Understand* (London: Routledge, 2019 edition), p.27.

115. Thomas Hegghammer, 'Islamist Violence and Regime Stability in Saudi Arabia,' *International Affairs*, 84(4), 2008, p.709.

116. Ibid. p.710.

117. Toby Matthiesen, 'A "Saudi Spring?": The Shi'a Protest Movement in the Eastern Province, 2011–2012,' *Middle East Journal*, 66(4), 2012, pp.637–9.

118. Simon Mabon, 'The End of the Battle for Bahrain and the Securitization of Bahraini Shi'a,' *Middle East Journal*, 73(1), 2019, p.42 and p.46.

119. Yoel Guzansky, 'Defence Cooperation in the Arabian Gulf: The Peninsula Shield Force Put to the Test,' *Middle Eastern Studies*, 50(4), 2014, p.650.

120. 'A Talk with Peninsula Shield Force Commander Mutlaq bin Salem al-Azima,' *Asharq al-Awsat*, 28 March 2011.

121. 'Islamists Plot against Gulf, Says Dubai Police Chief,' *AFP*, 25 March 2012.

122. Kristian Coates Ulrichsen, *Qatar and the Arab Spring* (London: Hurst & Co., 2014), p.155; Mabon, 'End of the Battle for Bahrain,' pp.42–3.

123. Charles Tripp, *The Power and the People: Paths of Resistance in the Middle East* (Cambridge: Cambridge University Press, 2013), pp.113–14.

124. Thomas Fibiger, 'Potential Heritage: The Making and Unmaking of the Pearl Monument in Bahrain,' *Journal of Arabian Studies*, 7(2), 2010, p.195.

125. Amal Khalaf, 'The Many Afterlives of Lulu: The Story of Bahrain's Pearl Roundabout,' in Ala'a Shehabi and Marc Owen Jones (eds.), *Bahrain's Uprising* (London: Zed Books, 2015), pp.135–6.

126. Sami Aboudi, 'Hundreds Flee Saudi Town as Security Forces Clash with Gunmen,' *Reuters*, 1 August 2017.

127. Deborah Wheeler, 'New Media, Globalization and Kuwaiti National Identity,' *Middle East Journal*, 54(3), 2000, p.435.

128. Annelle Sheline, '"Fake News" Tool for Authoritarian Regimes to Silence Citizens,' *The Global Post*, 23 October 2018.

129. James Shires, *The Politics of Cybersecurity in the Middle East* (London: Hurst & Co., 2021), pp.120–3.

130. Marc Owen Jones, *Digital Authoritarianism in the Middle East: Deception, Disinformation and Social Media* (London: Hurst & Co., 2022), pp.141–3.

131. Christopher Davidson, *From Sheikhs to Sultanism: Statecraft and Authority in Saudi Arabia and the UAE* (London: Hurst & Co., 2021), pp.85–90.

132. Albeit not through their collapse. See Christopher Davidson, *After the Sheikhs: The Coming Collapse of the Gulf Monarchies* (London: Hurst & Co., 2012), p.ix.

133. Barany, *Armies of Arabia*, p.90.

134. Joseph Nye, *The Future of Power* (New York: Public Affairs, 2011), p.xiii. For Nye's earlier conception of 'soft' power, see Joseph Nye, *Soft Power: The Means to Success in World Politics* (New York: Public Affairs, 2004).

135. Mehran Kamrava, 'Qatari Foreign Policy and the Exercise of Subtle Power,' *International Studies Journal*, 14(2), 2017, p.93.

136. David Held and Anthony McGrew, 'Introduction,' in David Held and Anthony McGrew (eds.), *Governing Globalization: Power, Autonomy and Global Governance* (Cambridge: Polity Press, 2002), p.5.

137. Kristian Coates Ulrichsen, 'Rebalancing Global Governance: Gulf States' Perspectives on the Governance of Globalization,' *Global Policy*, 2(1), 2011, p.65.

138. Kristian Coates Ulrichsen, *Qatar and the Gulf Crisis* (London: Hurst & Co., 2020).

139. See especially Andreas Krieg (ed.), *Divided Gulf: The Anatomy of a Crisis* (Singapore: Palgrave Macmillan, 2019).

140. Kristian Coates Ulrichsen, 'Qatar's Successful World Cup Signals a New Era in the Gulf and Beyond,' *Arab Center Washington*, 5 January 2023.

141. For culture, see especially miriam cooke, *Tribal Modern: Branding New Nations in the Arab Gulf* (Berkeley: University of California Press, 2014), and Lesley Gray, 'Contemporary Art and Global Identity in the Arabian Peninsula and Azerbaijan,' *Journal of Arabian Studies*, 7(1), 2017.

142. Simon Chadwick, 'Sport-Washing, Soft Power and Scrubbing the Stains,' Asia and the Pacific Policy Society, *Policy Forum*, 24 August 2018.

143. Nicholas McGeehan, 'Qatar 2022: The Backlash,' *Medium*, 16 December 2022; Matt Slater, 'Soccer, Golf, F1, Cycling and More. Saudi Arabia is Buying Sport—This is Why,' *The Athletic*, 10 July 2023.

144. Kristian Coates Ulrichsen, 'What Biden's Visit to Saudi Arabia Can and Cannot Fix,' *Gulf International Forum*, 12 July 2022.

145. C.K. Tan, 'Chinese President Xi Jinping Seals Unprecedented Third Term,' *Nikkei Asia*, 10 March 2023.

146. Martin Hvidt, 'The Dubai Model: An Outline of Key Development-Process Elements in Dubai,' *International Journal of Middle East Studies*, 41(3), 2009.

BIBLIOGRAPHY

Monographs

Abdullah, Muhammad Morsy, *The United Arab Emirates: A Modern History* (London: Routledge, 2016 edition).

Alangari, Haifa, *The Struggle for Power in Arabia: Ibn Saud, Hussein and Great Britain, 1914–1924* (Reading: Ithaca Press, 1998).

Albaharna, Husain, *The Legal Status of the Arabian Gulf States: A Study of Their Treaty Relations and Their International Problems* (Manchester: Manchester University Press, 1968).

Al-Duraiby, Ibrahim Suleiman, *Saudi Arabia, GCC and the EU: Limitations and Possibilities for an Unequal Triangular Relationship* (Dubai: Gulf Research Centre, 2009).

Al-Ebraheem, Hassan Ali, *Kuwait and the Gulf: Small States and the International System* (London: Routledge, 2016 edition).

Alebrahim, Abdulrahman, *Kuwait's Politics before Independence: The Role of the Balancing Powers* (Berlin: Gerlach Press, 2019).

Al-Enazy, Askar, *The Creation of Saudi Arabia: Ibn Saud and British Imperial Policy, 1914–1927* (Abingdon: Routledge, 2010).

Alghanim, Salwa, *The Reign of Mubarak Al-Sabah: Shaikh of Kuwait 1896–1915* (London: I.B. Tauris, 1998).

Algosaibi, Ghazi, *The Gulf Crisis: An Attempt to Understand* (London: Routledge, 2019 edition).

Al-Gurg, Easa Saleh, *The Wells of Memory: An Autobiography* (London: John Murray, 1998).

Al-Huzaimi, Nasir, *The Mecca Uprising: An Insider's Account of Salafism and Insurrection in Saudi Arabia* (London: I.B. Tauris, 2021).

Al Khalifa, Hamad bin Isa, *First Light: Modern Bahrain and Its Heritage* (London: Kegan Paul International Limited, 1994).

Al-Kuwari, Ali Khalifa, *Oil Revenues in the Gulf Emirates: Patterns of Allocation and Impact on Economic Development* (London: Routledge, 2018 edition).

Allen, Calvin and W. Lynn Rigsbee, *Oman under Qaboos: From Coup to Constitution 1970–1996* (London: Frank Cass, 2000).

Al-Mazrouei, Noura Saber, *The UAE and Saudi Arabia: Border Disputes and International Relations in the Gulf* (London: I.B. Tauris, 2016).

Almuhanna, Ibrahim, *Oil Leaders: An Insider's Account of Four Decades of Saudi Arabia and OPEC's Global Energy Policy* (New York: Columbia University Press, 2022).

Al-Nakib, Farah, *Kuwait Transformed: A History of Oil and Urban Life* (Stanford: Stanford University Press, 2016).

Al Qasimi, Sultan bin Mohammed, *The Myth of Arab Piracy in the Gulf* (London: Croom Helm, 1986).

Al-Rasheed, Madawi, *A History of Saudi Arabia* (Cambridge: Cambridge University Press, 2010 edition).

————, *Muted Modernists: The Struggle Over Divine Politics in Saudi Arabia* (London: Hurst & Co., 2015).

————, *The Son King: Reform and Repression in Saudi Arabia* (London: Hurst & Co., 2020).

Al Rumaihi, Mohamed, *Bahrain: Social and Political Change Since the First World War* (London: Bowker, 1976).

Al-Sabah, Meshal, *Gender and Politics in Kuwait: Women and Political Participation in the Gulf* (London: I.B. Tauris, 2013).

Al-Sabah, Souad, *Abdullah Mubarak Al-Sabah: The Transformation of Kuwait* (London: I.B. Tauris, 2015).

Al-Saud, Faisal bin Salman, *Iran, Saudi Arabia and the Gulf: Power Politics in Transition* (London: I.B. Tauris, 2011 edition).

Al-Sharekh, Alanoud and Courtney Freer, *Tribalism and Political Power in the Gulf: State-Building and National Identity in Kuwait, Qatar and the UAE* (London, I.B. Tauris, 2022).

AlShehabi, Omar, *Contested Modernity: Sectarianism, Nationalism, and Colonialism in Bahrain* (London: Oneworld Academic, 2019).

Al Tajir, Mahdi Abdalla, *Bahrain 1920–1945: Britain, the Shaikh and the Administration* (London: Croom Helm, 1987).

Althani, Mohammed A.J., *Jassim the Leader: Founder of Qatar* (London: Profile Books, 2012).

Ansari, Shahid Jamal, *Political Modernization in the Gulf* (Delhi: Northern Book Center, 1998).

Anscombe, Frederick, *The Ottoman Gulf: The Creation of Kuwait, Saudi Arabia, and Qatar, 1870–1914* (New York: Columbia University Press, 1997).

Assiri, Abdul-Reda, *Kuwait's Foreign Policy: City-State in World Politics* (Boulder: Westview Press, 1990).

Azoulay, Rivka, *Kuwait and Al-Sabah: Tribal Politics and Power in an Oil State* (London: I.B. Tauris, 2020).

BIBLIOGRAPHY

Baker, Peter and Susan Glasser, *The Man Who Ran Washington: The Life and Times of James A. Baker III* (New York: Doubleday, 2020).

Balfour-Paul, Glencairn, *The End of Empire in the Middle East: Britain's Relinquishment of Power in Her Last Three Arab Dependencies* (Cambridge: Cambridge University Press, 1991).

Barany, Zoltan, *Armies of Arabia: Military Politics and Effectiveness in the Gulf* (Oxford: Oxford University Press, 2021).

Bayly, C.A., *The Birth of the Modern World 1780–1914* (Oxford: Blackwell Publishing, 2004).

Beasant, John, *Oman: The True-Life Drama and Intrigue of an Arab State* (Edinburgh: Mainstream Publishing, 2002).

Beaugrand, Claire, *Stateless in the Gulf: Migration, Nationality and Society in Kuwait* (London: I.B. Tauris, 2018).

Bill, James, *The Eagle and the Lion: The Tragedy of American-Iranian Relations* (New Haven: Yale University Press, 1988).

Bishara, Fahad Ahmad, *Sea of Debt: Law and Economic Life in the Western Indian Ocean, 1780–1950* (Cambridge: Cambridge University Press, 2017).

Bradshaw, Tancred, *The End of Empire in the Gulf: From Trucial States to United Arab Emirates* (London: I.B. Tauris, 2021).

Bromley, Simon, *Rethinking Middle East Politics: State Formation and Development* (Cambridge: Polity Press, 1994).

Bsheer, Rosie, *Archive Wars: The Politics of History in Saudi Arabia* (Stanford: Stanford University Press, 2020).

Bullard, Reader and E.C. Hodgkin (ed.), *Two Kings in Arabia: Letters from Jeddah 1923–25 and 1936–39: Reader Bullard* (Reading: Ithaca Press, 1993).

Bulloch, John, *The Gulf: A Portrait of Kuwait, Qatar, Bahrain and the UAE* (London: Century Publishing, 1984).

Buzan, Barry, Ole Wæver, and Jaap de Wilde, *Security: A New Framework for Analysis* (Boulder: Lynne Rienner Publishers, 1998).

Chatty, Dawn, *Mobile Pastoralists: Development Planning and Social Change in Oman* (New York: Columbia University Press, 1996).

Chaudhry, Kiren Aziz, *The Price of Wealth: Economies and Institutions in the Middle East* (Ithaca: Cornell University Press, 1997).

Chehabi, H.E. and Juan Linz, *Sultanistic Regimes* (Baltimore: Johns Hopkins University Press, 1998).

Citino, Nathan, *From Arab Nationalism to OPEC: Eisenhower, King Sa'ud, and the Making of U.S.-Saudi Relations* (Bloomington: Indiana University Press, 2002).

———, *Envisioning the Arab Future: Modernization in U.S.-Arab Relations, 1945–1967* (Cambridge: Cambridge University Press, 2017).

Coates Ulrichsen, Kristian, *Insecure Gulf: The End of Certainty and the Transition to the Post-Oil Era* (London: Hurst & Co., 2011).

———, *Qatar and the Arab Spring* (London: Hurst & Co., 2014).

————, *The Gulf States in International Political Economy* (Basingstoke: Palgrave Macmillan, 2015).

————, *The United Arab Emirates: Power, Politics, and Policymaking* (Abingdon: Routledge, 2016).

————, *Qatar and the Gulf Crisis* (London: Hurst & Co., 2020).

Colley, Linda, *The Gun, the Ship, and the Pen: Warfare, Constitutions, and the Making of the Modern World* (London: Profile Books, 2021).

Commins, David, *The Wahhabi Mission and Saudi Arabia* (London: I.B. Tauris, 2009).

————, *The Gulf States: A Modern History* (London: I.B. Tauris, 2012).

cooke, miriam, *Tribal Modern: Branding New Nations in the Arab Gulf* (Berkeley: University of California Press, 2014).

Cordesman, Anthony, *Kuwait: Recovery and Security after the Gulf War* (Boulder: Westview Press, 1997).

Crouzet, Guillemette, *Inventing the Middle East: Britain and the Persian Gulf in the Age of Global Imperialism* (Montreal: McGill-Queen's University Press, 2022).

Crystal, Jill, *Oil and Politics in the Gulf: Rulers and Merchants in Kuwait and Qatar* (Cambridge: Cambridge University Press, 1990).

Daly, M.W., *The Last of the Great Proconsuls: The Biography of Sir William Luce* (San Diego: Nathan Berg, 2014).

Davidson, Christopher, *The United Arab Emirates: A Study in Survival* (Boulder: Lynne Rienner Publishers, 2005).

————, *Dubai: The Vulnerability of Success* (London: Hurst & Co., 2008).

————, *Abu Dhabi: Oil and Beyond* (London: Hurst & Co., 2009).

————, *After the Sheikhs: The Coming Collapse of the Gulf Monarchies* (London: Hurst & Co., 2012).

————, *From Sheikhs to Sultanism: Statecraft and Authority in Saudi Arabia and the UAE* (London: Hurst & Co., 2021).

Dawisha, Adeed and I. William Zartman (eds.), *Beyond Coercion: Durability of the Arab State* (Abingdon: Routledge, 1988).

Derbal, Nora, *Charity in Saudi Arabia: Civil Society under Authoritarianism* (Cambridge: Cambridge University Press, 2022).

Determann, Jörg Matthias, *Historiography in Saudi Arabia: Globalization and the State in the Middle East* (London: I.B. Tauris, 2021 edition).

Ehteshami, Anoushiravan, *Globalization and Geopolitics in the Middle East: Old Games, New Rules* (London: Routledge, 2007).

Field, Michael, *The Merchants: The Big Business Families of Saudi Arabia and the Gulf States* (Woodstock: The Overlook Press, 1985).

Foley, Sean, *Changing Saudi Arabia: Art, Culture and Society in the Kingdom* (Boulder: Lynne Rienner Publishers, 2021 edition).

Freer, Courtney, *Rentier Islamism: The Influence of the Muslim Brotherhood in Gulf Monarchies* (Oxford: Oxford University Press, 2018).

BIBLIOGRAPHY

Freitag, Ulrike, *A History of Jeddah: The Gate to Mecca in the Nineteenth and Twentieth Centuries* (Cambridge: Cambridge University Press, 2020).

Fromherz, Allen, *Qatar: A Modern History* (Washington, D.C.: Georgetown University Press, 2012).

Fuccaro, Nelida, *Histories of City and State in the Persian Gulf: Manama Since 1800* (Cambridge: Cambridge University Press, 2009).

Gause, Gregory, *The International Relations of the Persian Gulf* (Cambridge: Cambridge University Press, 2009).

Gengler, Justin, *Group Conflict and Political Mobilization in Bahrain and the Arab Gulf: Rethinking the Rentier State* (Bloomington: Indiana University Press, 2015).

Ghubash, Hussein, *Oman: The Islamic Democratic Tradition* (Abingdon: Routledge, 2006).

Graf, Bettina and Jakob Skovgaard-Petersen (eds.), *Global Mufti: The Phenomenon of Yusuf Al-Qaradawi* (Oxford: Oxford University Press, 2009).

Gray, Matthew, *Qatar: Politics and the Challenges of Development* (Boulder: Lynne Rienner Publishers, 2013).

Halliday, Fred, *Arabia without Sultans* (London: Saqi Books, 2002 edition).

———, *The Middle East in International Relations: Power, Politics and Ideology* (Cambridge: Cambridge University Press, 2005).

Hammond, Andrew, *The Islamic Utopia: The Illusion of Reform in Saudi Arabia* (London: Pluto Press, 2012).

Hanieh, Adam, *Capitalism and Class in the Gulf Arab States* (New York: Palgrave Macmillan, 2011).

Hawley, Donald, *The Trucial States* (London: George Allen & Unwin, 1970).

Hay, Rupert, *The Persian Gulf States* (Washington, D.C.: Middle East Institute, 1959).

Heard-Bey, Frauke, *From Trucial States to United Arab Emirates* (Dubai: Motivate Publishing, 2004 edition).

Held, David, *Models of Democracy* (Cambridge: Polity Press, 2006 edition).

Hellyer, H.A., *A Revolution Undone: Egypt's Road Beyond Revolt* (London: Hurst & Co., 2016).

Henderson, Edward, *This Strange Eventful History: Memoirs of Earlier Days in the UAE and Oman* (London: Quartet Books, 1988).

Herb, Michael, *All in the Family: Absolutism: Revolution, and Democracy in Middle Eastern Monarchies* (New York: SUNY Press, 1999).

———, *The Wages of Oil: Parliaments and Economic Development in Kuwait and the UAE* (Ithaca: Cornell University Press, 2014).

Herb, Michael and Marc Lynch (eds.), *The Politics of Rentier States in the Gulf*, POMEPS Studies 33, 2019.

Hertog, Steffen, *Princes, Brokers, and Bureaucrats: Oil and the State in Saudi Arabia* (Ithaca: Cornell University Press, 2010).

Hiro, Dilip, *Cold War in the Islamic World: Saudi Arabia, Iran and the Struggle for Supremacy* (London: Hurst & Co., 2018).

Huntingdon, Samuel, *Political Order in Changing Societies* (Yale: Yale University Press, 1968).

Ismael, Tareq, Jacqueline Ismael, and Glenn Perry, *Government and Politics of the Contemporary Middle East: Continuity and Change* (London: Routledge, 2016).

Jones, Jeremy and Nicholas Ridout, *A History of Modern Oman* (Cambridge: Cambridge University Press, 2015).

Joyce, Miriam, *Kuwait 1945–1996: An Anglo-American Perspective* (London: Frank Cass, 1998).

Kamrava, Mehran (ed.), *Gateways to the World: Port Cities in the Persian Gulf* (London: Hurst & Co., 2016).

————, *Inside the Arab State* (London: Hurst & Co., 2018).

Kéchichian, Joseph, *Faysal: Saudi Arabia's King for All Seasons* (Gainesville: University Press of Florida, 1998).

————, *Legal and Political Reforms in Sa'udi Arabia* (Abingdon: Routledge, 2013).

Kelly, S.B., *Desert Dispute: The Diplomacy of Boundary-Making in South-Eastern Arabia, Volume 1* (Berlin: Gerlach Press, 2018).

Khalili, Laleh, *Sinews of War and Trade: Shipping and Capitalism in the Arabian Peninsula* (London: Verso, 2020).

Khuri, Fuad, *Tribe and State in Bahrain: The Transformation of Social and Political Authority in an Arab State* (Chicago: University of Chicago Press, 1980).

Kostiner, Joseph, *The Making of Saudi Arabia 1916–1936: From Chieftaincy to Monarchical State* (Oxford: Oxford University Press, 1993).

Krane, Jim, *Dubai: The Story of the World's Fastest City* (London: Atlantic Books, 2009).

————, *Energy Kingdoms: Oil and Political Survival in the Persian Gulf* (New York: Columbia University Press, 2019).

Krieg, Andreas (ed.), *Divided Gulf: The Anatomy of a Crisis* (Singapore: Palgrave Macmillan, 2019).

Lawson, Fred, *Bahrain: The Modernization of Autocracy* (Boulder: Westview Press, 1989).

Lienhardt, Peter, *Disorientations: A Society in Flux: Kuwait in the 1950s* (Reading: Ithaca Press, 1993).

Limbert, Mandana, *In the Time of Oil: Piety, Memory, and Social Life in an Omani Town* (Stanford: Stanford University Press, 2010).

Long, David, *The United States and Saudi Arabia: Ambivalent Allies* (Boulder: Westview Press, 1985).

Louër, Laurence, *Transnational Shia Politics: Religious and Political Networks in the Gulf* (London: Hurst & Co., 2008).

Low, Michael Christopher, *Imperial Mecca: Ottoman Arabia and the Indian Ocean Hajj* (New York: Columbia University Press, 2020).

Luciani, Giacomo, *The Arab State* (London: Routledge, 1990).

Macris, Jeffrey, *The Politics and Security of the Gulf: Anglo-American Hegemony and the Shaping of a Region* (Abingdon: Routledge, 2010).

Manea, Elham, *Regional Politics in the Gulf: Saudi Arabia, Oman, Yemen* (London: Saqi Books, 2005).

Mann, Michael, *The Sources of Social Power. Volume 1: A History of Power from the Beginning to A.D. 1760* (Cambridge: Cambridge University Press, 1986).

McFarland, Victor, *Oil Powers: A History of the U.S.-Saudi Alliance* (New York: Columbia University Press, 2020).

Ménoret, Pascal, *The Saudi Enigma: A History* (London: Zed Books, 2005).

———, *Graveyard of Clerics: Everyday Activism in Saudi Arabia* (Stanford: Stanford University Press, 2020).

Miller, Rory, *Desert Kingdoms to Global Powers: The Rise of the Arab Gulf* (New Haven: Yale University Press, 2016).

Mills, Robin, *The Myth of the Oil Crisis: Overcoming the Challenges of Depletion, Geopolitics, and Global Warming* (Westport: Praeger, 2008).

Moore, Pete, *Doing Business in the Middle East: Politics and Economic Crisis in Jordan and Kuwait* (Cambridge: Cambridge University Press, 2004).

Munro, Alan, *An Arabian Affair: Politics and Diplomacy Behind the Gulf War* (London: Brassey's, 1996).

Nakhleh, Emile, *Bahrain: Political Development in a Modernizing Society* (Lanham: Lexington Books, 2011 edition).

Niblock, Tim and Monica Malik, *The Political Economy of Saudi Arabia* (Abingdon: Routledge, 2007).

Nye, Joseph, *Soft Power: The Means to Success in World Politics* (New York: Public Affairs, 2004).

———, *The Future of Power* (New York: Public Affairs, 2011).

Owen Jones, Marc, *Political Repression in Bahrain* (Cambridge: Cambridge University Press, 2020).

———, *Digital Authoritarianism in the Middle East: Deception, Disinformation and Social Media* (London: Hurst & Co., 2022).

Pappas Funsch, Linda, *Oman Reborn: Balancing Tradition and Modernization* (Basingstoke: Palgrave Macmillan, 2015).

Peterson, J.E., *Saudi Arabia under Ibn Saud: Economic and Financial Foundations of the State* (London: I.B. Tauris, 2018).

Potter, Lawrence (ed.), *The Persian Gulf in Modern Times: People, Ports, and History* (New York: Palgrave Macmillan, 2014).

Quentin Morton, Michael, *Buraimi: The Struggle for Power, Influence and Oil in Arabia* (London: I.B. Tauris, 2013).

Rabi, Uzi (ed.), *Tribes and States in a Changing Middle East* (London: Hurst & Co., 2016).

Rich, Paul, *Creating the Arabian Gulf: The British Raj and the Invasions of the Gulf* (Lanham: Lexington Books, 2009).

Risse, Marielle, *Community and Autonomy in Southern Oman* (London: Palgrave Macmillan, 2019).

Rossiter, Ash, *Security in the Gulf: Local Militaries before British Withdrawal* (Cambridge: Cambridge University Press, 2020).

Rugh, Andrea, *The Political Culture of Leadership in the United Arab Emirates* (New York: Palgrave Macmillan, 2007).

Runciman, David, *Politics* (London: Profile Books, 2014).

Runciman, W.G., *A Treatise on Social Theory. Vol. II: Substantive Social Theory* (Cambridge: Cambridge University Press, 1989).

Rundell, David, *Vision or Mirage: Saudi Arabia at the Crossroads* (London: I.B. Tauris, 2020).

Said Zahlan, Rosemarie, *The Origins of the United Arab Emirates: A Political and Social History of the Trucial States* (London: Macmillan, 1978).

———, *The Making of the Modern Gulf States* (Reading: Ithaca Press, 1998 edition).

———, *The Creation of Qatar* (Abingdon: Routledge, 2016 edition).

Samin, Nadav, *Of Sand or Soil: Genealogy and Tribal Belonging in Saudi Arabia* (Princeton: Princeton University Press, 2015).

Sato, Shohei, *Britain and the Formation of the Gulf States: Embers of Empire* (Manchester: Manchester University Press, 2016).

Scott Huyette, Summer, *Political Adaptation in Sa'udi Arabia: A Study of the Council of Ministers* (Abingdon: Routledge, 2019 edition).

Sheriff, Abdul, *Dhow Cultures of the Indian Ocean: Cosmopolitanism, Commerce and Islam* (London: Hurst & Co., 2010).

Shires, James, *The Politics of Cybersecurity in the Middle East* (London: Hurst & Co., 2021).

Simmons, Matthew, *Twilight in the Desert: The Coming Saudi Oil Shock and the World Economy* (New York: Wiley, 2006).

Skeet, Ian, *Oman: Politics and Development* (London: Macmillan, 1992).

Smith, Simon, *Britain's Revival and Fall in the Gulf: Kuwait, Bahrain, Qatar, and the Trucial States, 1950–1971* (Abingdon: Routledge, 2013 edition).

———, *Britain and the Gulf after Empire: Kuwait, Bahrain, Qatar, and the United Arab Emirates, 1971–1981* (Abingdon: Routledge, 2019).

Strobl, Staci, *Sectarian Order in Bahrain: The Social and Colonial Origins of Criminal Justice* (Lanham: Lexington Books, 2018).

Suba'i, Ahmad, *My Days in Mecca*, translated and edited by Deborah Akers and Abubaker Bagader (Boulder: FirstForumPress, 2009).

Suleiman, Atef, *The Petroleum Experience of Abu Dhabi* (Abu Dhabi: Emirates Center for Strategic Studies and Research, 2007).

Takriti, Abdel Razzaq, *Monsoon Revolution: Republicans, Sultans, and Empires in Oman, 1965–1976* (Oxford: Oxford University Press, 2016 edition).

Taryam, Abdullah Omran, *The Establishment of the United Arab Emirates 1950–1985* (London: Croom Helm, 1987).

Tétreault, Mary Ann, *Stories of Democracy: Politics and Society in Contemporary Kuwait* (New York: Columbia University Press, 2000).

Thesiger, Wilfred, *Arabian Sands* (London: Penguin Books, 1991 edition).

Townsend, John, *Oman: The Making of the Modern State* (London: Croom Helm, 1977).

Tripp, Charles, *The Power and the People: Paths of Resistance in the Middle East* (Cambridge: Cambridge University Press, 2013).

Valeri, Marc, *Oman: Politics and Society in the Qaboos State* (London: Hurst & Co., 2009).

Vitalis, Robert, *America's Kingdom: Mythmaking on the Saudi Oil Frontier* (London: Verso, 2009).

————, *Oilcraft: The Myths of Scarcity and Security That Haunt U.S. Energy Policy* (Stanford: Stanford University Press, 2020).

Von Bismarck, Helene, *British Policy in the Persian Gulf, 1961–1968: Conceptions of Informal Empire* (Basingstoke: Palgrave Macmillan, 2013).

Westad, Odd Arne, *The Global Cold War: Third World Intervention and the Making of Our Times* (Cambridge: Cambridge University Press, 2005).

Wiener, Scott, *Kinship, State Formation and Governance in the Arab Gulf States* (Edinburgh: Edinburgh University Press, 2022).

Wilkinson, John, *The Imamate Tradition of Oman* (Cambridge: Cambridge University Press, 1987).

Worrall, James, *Statebuilding and Counterinsurgency in Oman: Political, Military and Diplomatic Relations at the End of Empire* (London: I.B. Tauris, 2014).

Yizraeli, Sarah, *The Remaking of Saudi Arabia: The Struggle between King Sa'ud and Crown Prince Faysal, 1953–1962* (Tel Aviv: The Moshe Dayan Center for Middle Eastern and African Studies, 1997).

————, *Politics and Society in Saudi Arabia: The Crucial Years of Development, 1960–1982* (London: Hurst & Co., 2012).

Young, Karen, *The Economic Statecraft of the Gulf Arab States* (London: I.B. Tauris, 2023).

Book chapters

Abdulla, Abdulkhaleq, 'The Gulf Cooperation Council: Nature, Origin and Process,' in Michael Hudson (ed.), *Middle East Dilemma: The Politics and Economics of Arab Integration* (New York: Columbia University Press, 1999).

Abedin, Mahan, 'Saudi Shi'a Wait and See as New Light Falls on Islam's Old Divide,' in Joshua Craze and Mark Huband (eds.), *The Kingdom: Saudi Arabia and the Challenge of the 21st Century* (London: Hurst & Co., 2009).

————, 'Saudi Dissent More than Just Jihadis,' in Joshua Craze and Mark Huband (eds.), *The Kingdom: Saudi Arabia and the Challenge of the 21st Century* (London: Hurst & Co., 2009).

Abu 'Aliyya, 'Abd al-Fattah Hasan, 'Early Roots of Projects to Settle the Bedouins in the Arabian Peninsula,' in Fahd al-Semmari (ed.), *A History of the Arabian Peninsula* (London: I.B. Tauris, 2010).

Al Busaidi, Badr, 'Oman's Approach to Development,' in Anoushiravan Ehteshami and Steven Wright (eds.), *Reform in the Middle East Oil Monarchies* (Reading: Ithaca Press, 2008).

Al-Dakhil, Khalid, 'Abdullah Streamlines Saudi Succession Plans but Limits the Power to Choose,' in Joshua Craze and Mark Huband (eds.), *The Kingdom: Saudi Arabia and the Challenge of the 21st Century* (London: Hurst & Co., 2009).

Alebrahim, Abdulrahman, 'Kuwaiti-Zubayri Intellectual Relations until the Beginning of the Twentieth Century: 'Abd al-'Aziz al-Rushayd as an Example,' in Marc Owen Jones, Ross Porter, and Marc Valeri (eds.), *Gulfization of the Arab World* (Berlin: Gerlach Press, 2018).

Alhamad, Laila, 'Formal and Informal Venues of Engagement,' in Ellen Lust-Okar and Saloua Zerhouni (eds.), *Political Participation in the Middle East* (Boulder: Lynne Rienner Publishers, 2008).

Al-Khwaiter, 'Abd Al-Aziz ibn 'Abd-Allah, 'King Abdul Aziz: His Style of Administration,' in Fahd al-Semmari (ed.), *A History of the Arabian Peninsula* (London: I.B. Tauris, 2010).

Al Lawati, Nawra and Gail Buttorf, 'Working Women in the Oil Monarchies,' in Mehran Kamrava (ed.), *Routledge Handbook of Persian Gulf Politics* (Abingdon: Routledge, 2020).

Almezaini, Khalid, 'Private Sector Actors in the UAE and their Role in the Process of Economic and Political Reform,' in Steffen Hertog, Giacomo Luciani, and Marc Valeri (eds.), *Business Politics in the Middle East* (London: Hurst & Co., 2013).

Al-Nakib, Farah, 'Inside a Gulf Port: The Dynamics of Urban Life in Pre-Oil Kuwait,' in Lawrence Potter (ed.), *The Persian Gulf in Modern Times: People, Ports, and History* (New York: Palgrave Macmillan, 2014).

———, 'Modernity and the Arab Gulf States: The Politics of Heritage, Memory, and Forgetting,' in Mehran Kamrava (ed.), *Routledge Handbook of Persian Gulf Politics* (Abingdon: Routledge, 2020).

Al-Rasheed, Madawi, 'Circles of Power: Royals and Society in Saudi Arabia,' in Paul Aarts and Gerd Nonneman (eds.), *Saudi Arabia in the Balance: Political Economy, Society, Foreign Affairs* (London: Hurst & Co., 2005).

———, 'Saudi Religious Transnationalism in London,' in Madawi Al-Rasheed (ed.), *Transnational Connections and the Arab Gulf* (Abingdon: Routledge, 2005).

———, 'Royal Rule in a Time of Change,' in Joshua Craze and Mark Huband (eds.), *The Kingdom: Saudi Arabia and the Challenge of the 21st Century* (London: Hurst & Co., 2009).

———, 'Mystique of Monarchy: The Magic of Royal Succession in Saudi Arabia,' in Madawi Al-Rasheed (ed.), *Salman's Legacy: The Dilemmas of a New Era in Saudi Arabia* (London: Hurst & Co., 2017).

Al-Rashoud, Talal, 'Schools for the Arab Homeland: Kuwait's Educational Mission in Sharjah,' in Sultan Sooud Al Qassemi and Todd Reisz (eds.), *Building Sharjah* (Basel: Birkhauser, 2021).

Al-Sadhan, Abdulrahman, 'The Modernization of the Saudi Bureaucracy,' in Willard Bening (ed.), *King Faisal and the Modernization of Saudi Arabia* (London: Croom Helm, 1980).

Antoniades, Alexis, 'The Gulf Monetary Union,' in Mehran Kamrava (ed.), *The Political Economy of the Persian Gulf* (London: Hurst & Co., 2012).

Atallah, Sami, 'The Gulf Region: Beyond Oil and Wars: The Role of History and Geopolitics in Explaining Autocracy,' in Ibrahim Elbadawi and Samir Makdisi (eds.), *Democracy in the Arab World: Explaining the Deficit* (Abingdon: Routledge, 2011).

Baaboud, Abdulla, 'Dynamics and Determinants of the GCC States' Foreign Policy, with Special Reference to the EU,' in Gerd Nonneman (ed.), *Analyzing Middle Eastern Foreign Policies* (London: Routledge, 2005).

Bannerman, J.P., 'The Impact of the Early Oil Concessions in the Gulf States,' in R.I. Lawless (ed.), *The Gulf in the Early Twentieth Century: Foreign Institutions and Local Responses* (Durham: Centre for Middle East and Islamic Studies, 1986).

Bayly, C.A., 'Indian and Arabic Thought in the Liberal Age,' in Jens Hanssen and Max Weiss (eds.), *Arabic Thought Beyond the Liberal Age: Towards an Intellectual History of the Nahda* (Cambridge: Cambridge University Press, 2016).

Beaugrand, Claire, 'In and Out Moves of the Bahraini Opposition: How Years of Political Exile Led to an Opening of an International Front During the 2011 Crisis in Bahrain,' in Abdulhadi Khalaf, Omar AlShehabi, and Adam Hanieh (eds.), *Transit States: Labour, Migration and Citizenship in the Gulf* (London: Pluto Press, 2015).

Beblawi, Hazem, 'The Rentier State in the Arab World,' in Giacomo Luciani (ed.), *The Arab State* (London: Routledge, 1990).

Beeman, William, 'Gulf Society: An Anthropological View of the Khalijis – Their Evolution and Way of Life,' in Lawrence Potter (ed.), *The Persian Gulf in History* (New York: Palgrave Macmillan, 2009).

Bishara, Fahad Ahmad, 'Mapping the Indian Ocean World of Gulf Merchants, c.1870–1960,' in Abdul Sheriff and Engseng Ho (eds.), *The Indian Ocean: Oceanic Connections and the Creation of New Societies* (London: Hurst & Co., 2014).

Bishara, Fahad Ahmad, Bernard Haykel, Steffen Hertog, Clive Holes, and James Onley, 'The Economic Transformation of the Gulf,' in J.E. Peterson (ed.), *The Emergence of the Gulf States: Studies in Modern History* (London: Bloomsbury, 2018).

Butt, Gerald, 'Oil and Gas in the UAE,' in Ibrahim al Abed and Peter Hellyer (eds.), *United Arab Emirates: A New Perspective* (London: Trident Press, 2001).

Chalcraft, John, 'Migration Politics in the Arabian Peninsula,' in David Held and Kristian Coates Ulrichsen (eds.), *The Transformation of the Gulf: Politics, Economics and the Global Order* (London: Routledge, 2012).

Chay, Clemens, 'Parliamentary Politics in Kuwait,' in Mehran Kamrava (ed.), *Routledge Handbook of Persian Gulf Politics* (Abingdon: Routledge, 2020).

———, 'Dissecting the Spatial Relevance of the Diwaniyya in Kuwait,' in Suzi Mirgani (ed.), *Informal Politics in the Middle East* (London: Hurst & Co., 2021).

Commins, David, 'Introduction to the English Edition,' in Nasir al-Huzaimi, *The Mecca Uprising: An Insider's Account of Salafism and Insurrection in Saudi Arabia* (London: I.B. Tauris, 2021).

Crystal, Jill, 'Civil Society in the Arabian Gulf,' in August Richard Norton (ed.), *Civil Society in the Middle East: Volume Two* (Leiden: Brill, 1996).

———, 'Public Order and Authority: Policing Kuwait,' in Paul Dresch and James Piscatori (eds.), *Monarchies and Nations: Globalisation and Identity in the Arab States of the Gulf* (London: I.B. Tauris, 2005).

Davidson, Christopher, 'The Impact of Economic Reform on Dubai,' in Anoushiravan Ehteshami and Steven Wright (eds.), *Reform in the Middle East Oil Monarchies* (Reading: Ithaca Press, 2008).

Dresch, Paul, 'Societies, Identities and Global Issues,' in Paul Dresch and James Piscatori (eds.), *Monarchies and Nations: Globalisation and Identity in the Arab States of the Gulf* (London: I.B. Tauris, 2005).

El-Rayyes, Riad, 'Arab Nationalism in the Gulf,' in B.R. Pridham (ed.), *The Arab Gulf and the Arab World* (Abingdon: Routledge, 2016 edition).

Fakhro, Munira, 'The Uprising in Bahrain: An Assessment,' in Gary Sick and Lawrence Potter (eds.), *The Persian Gulf at the Millennium: Essays in Politics, Economy, Security, and Religion* (London: Palgrave Macmillan, 1997).

Fox, John, Nada Mourtada-Sabbah, and Mohammed al-Mutawa, 'The Arab Gulf Region: Traditionalism Globalized or Globalization Traditionalized?,' in John Fox, Nada Mourtada-Sabbah, and Mohammed al-Mutawa (eds.), *Globalization and the Gulf* (Abingdon: Routledge, 2006).

Gause, Gregory, 'Regional Influences in Experiments in Political Liberalization in the Arab World,' in Rex Brynen, Bahgat Korany, and Paul Noble (eds.), *Political Liberalization and Democratization in the Arab World: Volume 1. Theoretical Perspectives* (Boulder: Lynne Rienner Publishers, 1995).

———, 'The Persistence of Monarchy in the Arabian Peninsula: A Comparative Analysis,' in Joseph Kostiner (ed.), *Middle East Monarchies: The Challenge of Modernity* (Boulder: Lynne Rienner Publishers, 2000).

Halliday, Fred, 'The Gulf in International Affairs: Independence and After,' in B.R. Pridham (ed.), *The Arab Gulf and the Arab World* (London: Routledge, 2016 edition).

Held, David and Anthony McGrew, 'Introduction,' in David Held and Anthony McGrew (eds.), *Governing Globalization: Power, Autonomy and Global Governance* (Cambridge: Polity Press, 2002).

Herb, Michael, 'Kuwait: The Obstacle of Parliamentary Politics,' in Joshua Teitelbaum (ed.), *Political Liberalization in the Persian Gulf* (London: Hurst & Co., 2009).

Joffe, George, 'Boundary Delimitation: The Role of History,' in George Joffe and Richard Schofield (eds.), *Geographic Realities in the Middle East and North Africa: State, Oil and Agriculture* (Abingdon: Routledge, 2021).

Kamrava, Mehran, 'Politics in the Persian Gulf: An Overview,' in Mehran Kamrava (ed.), *Routledge Handbook of Persian Gulf Politics* (Abingdon: Routledge, 2020).

Kapiszewski, Andrzej, 'Elections and Parliamentary Activity in the GCC States: Broadening Political Participation in the Gulf Monarchies,' in Abdulhadi Khalaf and Giacomo Luciani (eds.), *Constitutional Reform and Political Participation in the Gulf* (Dubai: Gulf Research Centre, 2006).

Kelstrup, Morten, 'Globalization and Societal Insecurity in the Securitization of Terrorism and Competing Strategies for Global Governance,' in Stefano Guzzini and Dietrich Jung (eds.), *Contemporary Security Analysis and Copenhagen Peace Research* (London: Routledge, 2004).

Khalaf, Abdulhadi, 'Rules of Succession and Political Participation in the GCC States,' in Abdulhadi Khalaf and Giacomo Luciani (eds.), *Constitutional Reform and Political Participation in the Gulf* (Dubai: Gulf Research Center, 2006).

————, 'The Politics of Migration,' in Abdulhadi Khalaf, Omar AlShehabi, and Adam Hanieh (eds.), *Transit States: Labour, Migration and Citizenship in the Gulf* (London: Pluto Press, 2015).

Khalaf, Amal, 'The Many Afterlives of Lulu: The Story of Bahrain's Pearl Roundabout,' in Ala'a Shehabi and Marc Owen Jones (eds.), *Bahrain's Uprising* (London: Zed Books, 2015).

Krane, Jim, 'Subsidy Reform and Tax Increases in the Rentier Middle East,' in Michael Herb and Marc Lynch (eds.), *The Politics of Rentier States in the Gulf*, POMEPS Studies 33, 2019.

Lacroix, Stephane, 'Understanding Stability and Dissent in the Kingdom: The Double-Edged Role of the Jama'at in Saudi Politics,' in Bernard Haykel, Thomas Hegghammer, and Stephane Lacroix (eds.), *Saudi Arabia in Transition: Insights on Social, Political, Economic and Religious Change* (Cambridge: Cambridge University Press, 2015).

Lamb, Archibald, 'Annual Review of Events in Abu Dhabi in 1965,' in Robert Jarman, *Political Diaries of the Arab World: The Persian Gulf. Volume 24: 1963–1965* (Chippenham: Archive Editions, 1998).

Leber, Andrew, 'Resisting Rentierism: Labor Market Reforms in Saudi Arabia,' in Michael Herb and Marc Lynch (eds.), *The Politics of Rentier States in the Gulf*, POMEPS Studies 33, 2019.

Luciani, Giacomo, 'Allocation vs. Production States: A Theoretical Framework,' in Giacomo Luciani (ed.), *The Arab State* (London: Routledge, 1990).

————, 'From Private Sector to National Bourgeoisie: Saudi Arabian Business,' in Paul Aarts and Gerd Nonneman (eds.), *Saudi Arabia in the Balance: Political Economy, Society, Foreign Affairs* (London: Hurst & Co., 2005).

————, 'Democracy vs. Shura in the Age of the Internet,' in Abdulhadi Khalaf and Giacomo Luciani (eds.), *Constitutional Reform and Political Participation in the Gulf* (Dubai: Gulf Research Centre, 2006).

Lust-Okar, Ellen, 'Taking Political Participation Seriously,' in Ellen Lust-Okar and Saloua Zerhouni (eds.), *Political Participation in the Middle East* (Boulder: Lynne Rienner Publishers, 2008).

Mirgani, Suzi, 'An Overview of Informal Politics in the Middle East,' in Suzi Mirgani (ed.), *Informal Politics in the Middle East* (London: Hurst & Co., 2021).

Moritz, Jessie, 'Oil and Societal Quiescence: Rethinking Causal Mechanisms in Rentier State Theory,' in Michael Herb and Marc Lynch (eds.), *The Politics of Rentier States in the Gulf*, POMEPS Studies 33, 2019.

———, 'Rentier Political Economies in the Gulf Oil Monarchies,' in Mehran Kamrava (ed.), *Routledge Handbook of Persian Gulf Politics* (Abingdon: Routledge, 2020).

Niblock, Tim, 'Social Structure and the Development of the Saudi Arabian Political System,' in Tim Niblock (ed.), *State, Society and Economy in Saudi Arabia* (London: Croom Helm, 1982).

Niethammer, Katja, 'Opposition Groups in Bahrain,' in Ellen Lust-Okar and Saloua Zerhouni (eds.), *Political Participation in the Middle East* (Boulder: Lynne Rienner Publishers, 2008).

Nonneman, Gerd, 'The Gulf States and the Iran-Iraq War: Pattern Shifts and Continuities,' in Lawrence Potter and Gary Sick (eds.), *Iran, Iraq, and the Legacies of War* (New York: Palgrave Macmillan, 2004).

———, 'Political Reform in the Gulf Monarchies: From Liberalization to Democratization? A Comparative Perspective,' in Anoushiravan Ehteshami and Steven Wright (eds.), *Reform in the Middle East Oil Monarchies* (Reading: Ithaca Press, 2008).

Onley, James, 'Transnational Merchants in the Nineteenth Century: The Case of the Safar Family,' in Madawi Al-Rasheed (ed.), *Transnational Connections and the Arab Gulf* (Abingdon: Routledge, 2005).

Peterson, J.E., 'Rulers, Merchants and Shaikhs in Gulf Politics: The Function of Family Networks,' in Alanoud Alsharekh (ed.), *The Gulf Family: Kinship Policies and Modernity* (London: Saqi Books, 2007).

———, 'Bahrain: Reform – Promise and Reality,' in Joshua Teitelbaum (ed.), *Political Liberalization in the Persian Gulf* (London: Hurst & Co., 2009).

———, 'Sovereignty and Boundaries in the Gulf States: Settling the Peripheries,' in Mehran Kamrava (ed.), *International Politics of the Persian Gulf* (New York: Syracuse University Press, 2011).

Power, Greg, 'The Difficult Development of Parliamentary Politics in the Gulf: Parliaments and the Process of Managed Reform in Kuwait, Bahrain and Oman,' in David Held and Kristian Coates Ulrichsen (eds.), *The Transformation of the Gulf: Politics, Economics and the Global Order* (Abingdon: Routledge, 2012).

Quilliam, Neil, 'Political Reform in Bahrain: The Turning Tide,' in Anoushiravan Ehteshami and Steven Wright (eds.), *Reform in the Middle East Oil Monarchies* (Reading: Ithaca Press, 2008).

Rabi, Uzi, 'Oman: "Say Yes to Oman, No to the Tribe!",' in Joshua Teitelbaum (ed.), *Political Liberalization in the Persian Gulf* (London: Hurst & Co., 2009).

Reus-Smit, Christian, 'Constructivism and the Structure of Ethical Reasoning,' in Richard Price (ed.), *Moral Limit and Possibility in World Politics* (Cambridge: Cambridge University Press, 2008).

Salamandra, Christa, 'Cultural Construction, the Gulf and Arab London,' in Paul Dresch and James Piscatori (eds.), *Monarchies and Nations: Globalisation and Identity in the Arab States of the Gulf* (London: I.B. Tauris, 2005).

Shehabi, Ala'a and Marc Owen Jones, 'Bahrain's Uprising: The Struggle for Democracy in the Gulf,' in Ala'a Shehabi and Marc Owen Jones (eds.), *Bahrain's Uprising* (London: Zed Books, 2015).

Sick, Gary, 'The United States and the Persian Gulf in the Twentieth Century,' in Lawrence Potter (ed.), *The Persian Gulf in History* (New York: Palgrave Macmillan, 2009).

Sim, Li-Chen, 'Powering the Middle East and North Africa with Nuclear Energy: Stakeholders and Technopolitics,' in Robin Mills and Li-Chen Sim (eds.), *Low Carbon Energy in the Middle East and North Africa* (Cham: Springer, 2021).

Sowayan, Saad, 'Top-down Fight against Corruption Leaves Saudis Wondering Who Will Watch the Watchdogs,' in Joshua Craze and Mark Huband (eds.), *The Kingdom: Saudi Arabia and the Challenge of the 21st Century* (London: Hurst & Co., 2009).

Takriti, Abdel Razzaq, 'Political Praxis in the Gulf: Ahmad al-Khatib and the Movement of Arab Nationalists, 1948–1969,' in Jens Hanssen and Max Weiss (eds.), *Arabic Thought against the Authoritarian Age: Towards an Intellectual History of the Present* (Cambridge: Cambridge University Press, 2018).

Tétreault, Mary Ann, 'Kuwait: Slouching towards Democracy?,' in Joshua Teitelbaum (ed.), *Political Liberalization in the Persian Gulf* (London: Hurst & Co., 2009).

Thatcher, Mark, 'Governing Markets in the Gulf States,' in David Held and Kristian Ulrichsen (eds.), *The Transformation of the Gulf: Politics, Economics and the Global Order* (Abingdon: Routledge, 2012).

Tilly, Charles, 'War Making and State Making as Organized Crime,' in Peter Evans, Dietrich Rueschemeyer, and Theda Skocpol (eds.), *Bringing the State Back In* (Cambridge: Cambridge University Press, 1985).

Valeri, Marc, 'Oligarchy vs. Oligarchy: Business and Politics of Reform in Bahrain and Oman,' in Steffen Hertog, Giacomo Luciani, and Marc Valeri (eds.), *Business Politics in the Middle East* (London: Hurst & Co., 2012).

———, 'Towards the End of the Oligarchic Pact? Business and Politics in Abu Dhabi, Bahrain, and Oman,' in Kristian Coates Ulrichsen (ed.), *The Changing Security Dynamics of the Persian Gulf* (London: Hurst & Co., 2017).

Weber, Max, 'Politics as a Vocation,' in H.H. Gerth and C. Wright Mills (translated and edited), *From Max Weber: Essays in Sociology* (New York:

Oxford University Press, 1946), available online at: http://fs2.american.edu/dfagel/www/Class%20Readings/Weber/PoliticsAsAVocation.pdf

Worrall, James, 'The Missing Link? Police and State-building in South Arabia,' in Clive Jones (ed.), *Britain and State Formation in Arabia 1962–1971: From Aden to Abu Dhabi* (Abingdon: Routledge, 2018).

Wright, Steven, 'Iran's Relations with Bahrain,' in Gawdat Bahgat, Anoushiravan Ehteshami, and Neil Quilliam (eds.), *Security and Bilateral Issues between Iran and its Arab Neighbours* (Cham: Springer, 2017).

Journal articles

Aarts, Paul, 'Oil, Money and Participation: Kuwait's Sonderweg as a Rentier State,' *Orient*, 32, 1991.

Abadi, Jacob, 'Saudi Arabia's Rapprochement with Israel: The National Security Imperatives,' *Middle Eastern Studies*, 55(3), 2019.

Abdul Razak, Rowena, 'When Guns Are Not Enough: Britain's Response to Nationalism in Bahrain, 1958–63,' *Journal of Arabian Studies*, 7(1), 2017.

Abou-Alsamh, Rasheed, 'Saudi Municipal Elections Raise Hopes,' *Arab Reform Bulletin*, 3(2), 2005.

Al-Atawneh, Muhammad, 'Is Saudi Arabia a Theocracy? Religion and Governance in Contemporary Saudi Arabia,' *Middle Eastern Studies*, 45(5), 2009.

Al-Azri, Khalid, 'Change and Conflict in Contemporary Omani Society: The Case of Kafa'a in Marriage,' *British Journal of Middle Eastern Studies*, 37(2), 2010.

Albloshi, Hamad and Michael Herb, 'Karamet Watan: An Unsuccessful Nonviolent Movement,' *Middle East Journal*, 72(3), 2018.

Al-Dakhil, Khalid, '2003: Saudi Arabia's Year of Reform,' *Arab Reform Bulletin*, 2(3), 2004.

Al-Ebraheem, Hassan, 'The Gulf Crisis: A Kuwaiti Perspective: An Interview with Hassan Al-Ebraheem,' *Journal of Palestine Studies*, 20(2), 1991.

Alebrahim, Abdulrahman, 'The Neglected Sheikhdom at the Frontier of Empires and Cultures: An Introduction to al-Zubayr,' *Middle Eastern Studies*, 56(4), 2020.

Al Ekry, Abd al-Nabi, 'Bahrain: Al-Wefaq and the Challenges of Participation,' *Arab Reform Bulletin*, 5(4), 2007.

Alhaj, Abdullah Juma, 'The Politics of Participation in the Gulf Cooperation Council States: The Omani Consultative Council,' *Middle East Journal*, 50(4), 1996.

———, 'The Political Elite and the Introduction of Political Participation in Oman,' *Middle East Policy*, 7(3), 2000.

Alhajeri, Abdullah, 'The Bedouin: Kuwaitis Without an Identity,' *Middle Eastern Studies*, 51(1), 2015.

Al-Hamad, Turki, 'Will the Gulf Monarchies Work Together?,' *Middle East Quarterly*, 1997.

Alhargan, Raed Abdulaziz, 'Saudi Arabia: Civil Rights and Local Actors,' *Middle East Policy*, 19(1), 2012.

Alhasan, Hasan Tariq, 'The Role of Iran in the Failed Coup of 1981: The IFLB in Bahrain,' *Middle East Journal*, 65(4), 2011.

Alkandari, Ali, 'The Development of Kuwaiti Islamists' Political Ideology: The Administration of the Kuwaiti Supreme Committee and the Free Kuwait Campaign During the Second Gulf Crisis 1990–91,' *Middle Eastern Studies*, 55(5), 2019.

Al Kitbi, Ebtisam, 'Women's Political Status in the GCC States,' *Arab Reform Bulletin*, 2(7), 2004.

Al-Marashi, Ibrahim, 'Iraq's Gulf Policy and Regime Security from the Monarchy to the Post-Ba'athist Era,' *British Journal of Middle Eastern Studies*, 36(3), 2009.

Al-Meikaimi, Haila, 'The Impact of Islamic Groups and Arab Spring on the Youth Political Movement in Kuwait,' *Journal of South Asian and Middle Eastern Studies*, 36(1), 2012.

Al-Mughni, Haya, 'The Politics of Women's Suffrage in Kuwait,' *Arab Reform Bulletin*, 2(7), 2004.

Al-Najjar, Ghanim, 'Kuwait: Struggle over Parliament,' *Arab Reform Bulletin*, 4(5), 2006.

Al Qassemi, Fahim bin Sultan, 'A Century in Thirty Years: Sheikh Zayed and the United Arab Emirates,' *Middle East Policy*, 6(4), 1999.

Al-Rasheed, Madawi, 'Durable and Non-Durable Dynasties: The Rashidis and Sa'udis in Central Arabia,' *British Journal of Middle Eastern Studies,* 19(2), 1992.

———, 'God, the King and the Nation: Political Rhetoric in Saudi Arabia in the 1990s,' *Middle East Journal*, 50(3), 1996.

———, 'The Shia of Saudi Arabia: A Minority in Search of Cultural Authenticity,' *British Journal of Middle Eastern Studies*, 25(1), 1998.

———, 'Saudi Arabia Post 9/11: History, Religion and Security,' *Middle Eastern Studies*, 43(1), 2007.

Al-Rasheed, Madawi and Loulouwa Al-Rasheed, 'The Politics of Encapsulation: Saudi Policy Towards Tribal and Religious Opposition,' *Middle Eastern Studies*, 32(1), 1996.

Al-Rumaihi, Mohammad, 'Kuwait: Oasis of Liberalism?' *Middle East Quarterly*, 1994.

Al-Sayegh, Fatma, 'American Missionaries in the UAE Region in the Twentieth Century,' *Middle Eastern Studies*, 32(1), 1996.

———, 'Merchants' Role in a Changing Society: The Case of Dubai, 1900–90,' *Middle Eastern Studies*, 34(1), 1998.

———, 'Post-9/11 Changes in the Gulf: The Case of the UAE,' *Middle East Policy*, 11(2), 2004.

Al-Shayeb, Jafar, 'Saudi Arabia: Municipal Councils and Political Reform,' *Arab Reform Bulletin*, 3(9), 2005.

Al-Shayeji, Abdullah, 'Dangerous Perceptions: Gulf Views of the U.S. Role in the Region,' *Middle East Policy*, 5(3), 1997.

Alvandi, Roham, 'Muhammad Reza Pahlavi and the Bahrain Question, 1968–1970,' *British Journal of Middle Eastern Studies*, 37(2), 2010.

Amir, Mordechai, 'The Consolidation of the Ruling Class and the New Elites in Saudi Arabia,' *Middle Eastern Studies*, 23(2), 1987.

Anderson, Jon, 'Producers and Middle East Internet Technology: Getting beyond "Impacts",' *Middle East Journal*, 54(3), 2000.

Anderson, Lisa, 'Absolutism and the Resilience of Monarchy in the Middle East,' *Political Science Quarterly*, 106(1), 1991.

Anthony, John Duke, 'The Union of Arab Amirates,' *Middle East Journal*, 26(3), 1972.

Baaklini, Abdo, 'Legislatures in the Gulf Area: The Experience of Kuwait, 1961–1976,' *International Journal of Middle East Studies*, 14(3), 1982.

Babar, Zahra, 'The "Enemy Within": Citizenship-Stripping in the Post-Arab Spring GCC,' *Middle East Journal*, 71(4), 2017.

Bahgat, Gawdat, 'Education in the Gulf Monarchies: Retrospect and Prospect,' *International Review of Education*, 45(2), 1999.

———, 'Nuclear Proliferation: The Case of Saudi Arabia,' *Middle East Journal*, 60(3), 2006.

Bahry, Louay, 'The Opposition in Bahrain: A Bellwether for the Gulf?,' *Middle East Policy*, 5(2), 1997.

———, 'Elections in Qatar: A Window of Democracy Opens in the Gulf,' *Middle East Policy*, 6(4), 1999.

Barany, Zoltan, 'Comparing the Arab Revolts: The Role of the Military,' *Journal of Democracy*, 32(4), 2011.

Barnwell, Kristi, 'Overthrowing the Shaykhs: The Trucial States at the Intersection of Anti-Imperialism, Arab Nationalism, and Politics, 1952–1966,' *The Arab Studies Journal*, 24(2), 2016.

Beaugrand, Claire, 'Deconstructing Minorities/Majorities in Parliamentary Gulf States (Kuwait and Bahrain),' *British Journal of Middle Eastern Studies*, 43(2), 2016.

Bill, James, 'The Plasticity of Informal Politics: The Case of Iran,' *Middle East Journal*, 27(2), 1973.

Bishara, Fahad Ahmad, 'The Many Voyages of Fateh Al-Khayr: Unfurling the Gulf in the Age of Oceanic History,' *International Journal of Middle East Studies*, 52(3), 2020.

Blyth, Robert, 'Britain Versus India in the Persian Gulf: The Struggle for Political Control, c.1928–1948,' *Journal of Imperial and Commonwealth History*, 28(1), 2000.

Bradshaw, Tancred, 'Security Forces and the End of Empire in the Trucial States, 1960–1971,' *Middle Eastern Studies*, 56(6), 2020.

Brew, Gregory, "'Our Most Dependable Allies": Iraq, Saudi Arabia, and the Eisenhower Doctrine, 1956–1958,' *Mediterranean Quarterly*, 26(4), 2015.

Brewer, William, 'Yesterday and Tomorrow in the Persian Gulf,' *Middle East Journal*, 23(2), 1969.

Brumberg, Daniel, 'Democratization in the Arab World? The Trap of Liberalized Autocracy,' *Journal of Democracy* 13(4), 2002.

Bsheer, Rosie, 'A Counter-Revolutionary State: Popular Movements and the Making of Saudi Arabia,' *Past and Present*, 238, 2018.

Carroll, Terrance, 'Islam and Political Community in the Arab World,' *International Journal of Middle East Studies*, 18(2), 1986.

Chalcraft, John, 'Migration and Popular Protest in the Arabian Peninsula and the Gulf in the 1950s and 1960s,' *International Labor and Working-Class History*, 79, 2011.

Chatty, Dawn, 'Rituals of Royalty and the Elaboration of Ceremony in Oman: View from the Edge,' *International Journal of Middle East Studies*, 41(1), 2009.

Coates Ulrichsen, Kristian, 'Rebalancing Global Governance: Gulf States' Perspectives on the Governance of Globalization,' *Global Policy*, 2(1), 2011.

———, 'Politics and Opposition in Kuwait: Continuity and Change,' *Journal of Arabian Studies*, 4(2), 2014.

———, 'Kuwait as a Mediator in Regional Affairs: The Gulf Crises of 2014 and 2017,' *The International Spectator*, 56(4), 2021.

Conge, Patrick and Gwenn Okruhlik, 'The Power of Narrative: Saudi Arabia, the United States and the Search for Security,' *British Journal of Middle East Studies*, 36(3), 2009.

Cook, Steven, 'Getting to Arab Democracy: The Promise of Pacts,' *Journal of Democracy*, 17(1), 2006.

Cox, Robert, 'Social Forces, States and World Orders: Beyond International Relations Theory,' *Millennium: Journal of International Studies*, 10(2), 1981.

Cronin, Stephanie, 'Tribes, Coups and Princes: Building a Modern Army in Saudi Arabia,' *Middle Eastern Studies*, 49(1), 2013.

Crouzet, Guillemette, 'The British Empire in India, the Gulf Pearl and the Making of the Middle East,' *Middle Eastern Studies*, 55(6), 2019.

Crystal, Jill, 'Coalitions in Oil Monarchies: Kuwait and Qatar,' *Comparative Politics*, 21(4), 1989.

Dekmejian, R. Hrair, 'Saudi Arabia's Consultative Council,' *Middle East Journal*, 52(2), 1998.

Dunne, Michelle, 'Interview with Ali al-Rashed, Kuwaiti National Assembly Member and Candidate,' *Arab Reform Bulletin*, 6(4), 2008.

Edens, David and William Snavely, 'Planning for Economic Development in Saudi Arabia,' *Middle East Journal*, 24(1), 1970.

Ehteshami, Anoushiravan and Steven Wright, 'Political Change in the Arab Oil Monarchies: From Liberalization to Enfranchisement,' *International Affairs*, 83(5), 2007.

Eickelman, Dale, 'From Theocracy to Monarchy: Authority and Legitimacy in Inner Oman, 1935–1957,' *International Journal of Middle East Studies*, 17(1), 1985.

El Mallakh, Ragaei, 'The Challenge of Affluence: Abu Dhabi,' *Middle East Journal*, 24(2), 1970.

Fain, Taylor, 'John F. Kennedy and Harold Macmillan: Managing the "Special Relationship" in the Persian Gulf Region, 1961–63,' *Middle Eastern Studies*, 38(4), 2002.

Fakhro, Elham, 'Land Reclamation in the Arabian Gulf: Security, Environment, and Legal Issues,' *Journal of Arabian Studies*, 3(1), 2013.

Fandy, Mamoun, 'Information Technology, Trust, and Social Change in the Arab World,' *Middle East Journal*, 54(3), 2000.

Farah, Tawfic and Faisal Al-Salem, 'Political Efficacy, Political Trust, and the Action Orientations of University Students in Kuwait,' *International Journal of Middle East Studies*, 8(3), 1977.

Farquhar, Michael, 'Saudi Petrodollars, Spiritual Capital, and the Islamic University of Medina: A Wahhabi Missionary Project in Transnational Perspective,' *International Journal of Middle East Studies*, 47(4), 2015.

Fibiger, Thomas, 'Potential Heritage: The Making and Unmaking of the Pearl Monument in Bahrain,' *Journal of Arabian Studies*, 7(2), 2010.

Fjaertoft, Torgeir, 'The Saudi Arabian Revolution: How Can it Succeed?,' *Middle East Policy*, 25(3), 2018.

Freer, Courtney, 'Exclusion-Moderation in the Gulf Context: Tracing the Development of Pragmatic Islamism in Kuwait,' *Middle Eastern Studies*, 54(1), 2018.

Freitag, Ulrike, 'Helpless Representatives of the Great Powers? Western Consuls in Jeddah, 1830s to 1914,' *Journal of Imperial and Commonwealth History*, 40(3), 2012.

————, 'A Twentieth Century Merchant Network Centered on Jeddah: The Correspondence of Muhammad b. Ahmad Bin Himd,' *Northeast African Studies*, 17(1), 2017.

Gause, Gregory, 'Saudi Arabia Over a Barrel,' *Foreign Affairs*, 79(3), 2000.

Gengler, Justin, 'Royal Factionalism, the Khawalid, and the Securitization of "the Shi'a Problem" in Bahrain,' *Journal of Arabian Studies*, 3(1), 2013.

Ghabra, Shafeeq, 'Voluntary Associations in Kuwait: The Foundation of a New System?,' *Middle East Journal*, 45(2), 1991.

Gray, Lesley, 'Contemporary Art and Global Identity in the Arabian Peninsula and Azerbaijan,' *Journal of Arabian Studies*, 7(1), 2017.

Guzansky, Yoel, 'Defence Cooperation in the Arabian Gulf: The Peninsula Shield Force Put to the Test,' *Middle Eastern Studies*, 50(4), 2014.

————, 'Lines Drawn in the Sand: Territorial Disputes and GCC Unity,' *Middle East Journal*, 70(4), 2016.

Halliday, Fred, 'In a Time of Hopes and Fears,' *British Journal of Middle Eastern Studies*, 36(2), 2009.

Hamzawy, Amr, 'Interview with Badr al-Nashi, President of the Islamic Constitutional Movement (ICM),' *Arab Reform Bulletin*, 4(3), 2006.

Hay, Rupert, 'The Persian Gulf States and Their Boundary Problems,' *The Geographical Journal*, 120(4), 1954.

———, 'The Impact of the Oil Industry on the Persian Gulf Shaykhdoms,' *Middle East Journal*, 9(4), 1955.

Heard-Bey, Frauke, 'Conflict Resolution and Regional Cooperation: The Role of the Gulf Cooperation Council 1970–2002,' *Middle Eastern Studies*, 42(2), 2006.

Heaton, Matthew, 'Decolonizing the Hajj: Nationalist Politics and Pilgrimage Administration in the British Empire in the Mid-Twentieth Century,' *Journal of Imperial and Commonwealth History*, 49(2), 2021.

Hegghammer, Thomas, 'Islamist Violence and Regime Stability in Saudi Arabia,' *International Affairs*, 84(4), 2008.

Hegghammer, Thomas and Stephane Lacroix, 'Rejectionist Islamism in Saudi Arabia: The Story of Juhayman Al-'Utaybi Revisited,' *International Journal of Middle East Studies*, 39(1), 2007.

Herb, Michael, 'Democratization in the Arab World? Emirs and Parliaments in the Gulf,' *Journal of Democracy*, 13(4), 2002.

———, 'Princes and Parliaments in the Arab World,' *Middle East Journal* 58(3), 2004.

———, 'A Nation of Bureaucrats: Political Participation and Economic Diversification in Kuwait and the United Arab Emirates,' *International Journal of Middle East Studies*, 41(3), 2009.

Hertog, Steffen, 'Petromin: The Slow Death of Statist Oil Development in Saudi Arabia,' *Business History*, 50(5), 2008.

———, 'Rentier Militaries in the Gulf States: The Price of Coup-Proofing,' *International Journal of Middle East Studies*, 43(3), 2011.

———, 'The "Rentier Mentality" 30 Years On: Evidence from Survey Data,' *British Journal of Middle Eastern Studies*, 47(1), 2020.

Holmes, Amy Austin, 'The Base that Replaced the British Empire: De-Democratization and the American Navy in Bahrain,' *Journal of Arabian Studies*, 4(1), 2014.

Hughes, Geraint, 'A Proxy War in Arabia: The Dhofar Insurgency and Cross-Border Raids into South Yemen,' *Middle East Journal*, 69(1), 2015.

Hvidt, Martin, 'The Dubai Model: An Outline of Key Development-Process Elements in Dubai,' *International Journal of Middle East Studies*, 41(3), 2009.

Jones, Clive, 'Military Intelligence, Tribes, and Britain's War in Dhofar, 1970–1976,' *Middle East Journal*, 65(4), 2011.

Jones, Clive and John Stone, 'Britain and the Arabian Gulf: New Perspectives on Strategic Influence,' *International Relations*, 13(4), 1997.

Jones, Jeremy and Nicholas Ridout, 'Democratic Development in Oman,' *Middle East Journal*, 59(3), 2005.

Jones,Toby Craig, 'Rebellion on the Saudi Periphery: Modernity, Marginalization, and the Shi'a Uprising of 1979,' *International Journal of Middle East Studies*, 38(2), 2006.

Joyce, Miriam, 'The Bahraini Three on St. Helena, 1956–1961,' *Middle East Journal*, 54(4), 2000.

Kamrava, Mehran, 'Military Professionalization and Civil-Military Relations in the Middle East,' *Political Science Quarterly*, 115(1), 2000.

———, 'Royal Factionalism and Political Liberalization in Qatar,' *Middle East Journal*, 63(3), 2009.

———, 'Preserving Non-Democracies: Leaders and State Institutions in the Middle East,' *Middle Eastern Studies*, 46(2), 2010.

———, 'Qatari Foreign Policy and the Exercise of Subtle Power,' *International Studies Journal*, 14(2), 2017.

———, 'State-Business Relations and Clientelism in Qatar,' *Journal of Arabian Studies*, 7(1), 2017.

Kanie, Mariwan, 'Civil Society, Language and the Authoritarian Context: The Case of Saudi Arabia,' *Orient*, 4, 2012.

Kéchichian, Joseph, 'The Role of the Ulama in the Politics of an Islamic State: The Case of Saudi Arabia,' *International Journal of Middle East Studies*, 18(1), 1986.

———, 'Trends in Saudi National Security,' *Middle East Journal*, 53(2), 1999.

Keshavarzian, Arang, 'Geopolitics and the Genealogy of Free Trade Zones in the Persian Gulf,' *Geopolitics*, 15(2), 2010.

Khalaf, Abdulhadi, 'What the Gulf Ruling Families Do When They Rule,' *Orient*, 44, 2003.

———, 'Bahrain's Parliament: The Quest for a Role,' *Arab Reform Bulletin*, 2(5), 2004.

Khalaf, Sulayman, 'Gulf Societies and the Image of Unlimited Good,' *Dialectical Anthropology*, 17(1), 1992.

———, 'Camel Racing in the Gulf. Notes on the Evolution of a Traditional Cultural Sport,' *Anthropos*, 94(1), 1999.

Khalaf, Sulayman and Hassan Hammoud, 'The Emergence of the Oil Welfare State: The Case of Kuwait,' *Dialectical Anthropology*, 12(3), 1987.

Khashoggi, Jamal, 'Neo-Islamists: A New Direction in Saudi Arabia's Islamic Opposition?,' *Arab Reform Bulletin*, 2(3) 2004.

Kinninmont, Jane, 'Assessing Al-Wefaq's Parliamentary Experiment,' *Arab Reform Bulletin*, 5(8), 2007.

Knauerhase, Ramon, 'Saudi Arabia's Economy at the Beginning of the 1970s,' *Middle East Journal*, 28(2), 1974.

Kostiner, Joseph, 'On Instruments and their Designers: The *Ikhwan* of Najd and the Emergence of the Saudi State,' *Middle Eastern Studies*, 21(3), 1985.

Kraetzschmar, Hendrik, 'Associational Life under Authoritarianism: The Saudi Chamber of Commerce and Industry Elections,' *Journal of Arabian Studies*, 5(2), 2015.

Lawson, Fred, 'Keys to the Kingdom: Current Scholarship on Saudi Arabia,' *International Journal of Middle East Studies*, 43(4), 2011.

Limbert, Mandana, 'Trade, Mobility, and the Sea,' *International Journal of Middle East Studies*, 50(3), 2018.

Longva, Anh Nga, 'Nationalism in Pre-Modern Guise: The Discourse on Hadhar and Badu in Kuwait,' *International Journal of Middle East Studies*, 38(2), 2006.

Lori, Noora, 'Time and Its Miscounting: Methodological Challenges in the Study of Citizenship Boundaries,' *International Journal of Middle East Studies*, 52(4), 2020.

Louër, Laurence, 'Sectarianism and Coup-Proofing Strategies in Bahrain,' *Journal of Strategic Studies*, 36(2), 2013.

Louis, Wm. Roger, 'The British Withdrawal from the Gulf, 1967–71,' *Journal of Imperial and Commonwealth History*, 31(1), 2003.

Lowi, Miriam, 'Justice, Charity, and the Common Good: In Search of Islam in Gulf Petro-Monarchies,' *Middle East Journal*, 71(4), 2017.

Lucas, Russell, 'Monarchical Authoritarianism: Survival and Political Liberalization in a Middle Eastern Regime Type,' *International Journal of Middle East Studies*, 36(1), 2004.

———, 'Rules and Tools of Succession in the Gulf Monarchies,' *Journal of Arabian Studies*, 2(1), 2012.

Lust, Ellen, 'Opposition Cooperation and Uprisings in the Arab World,' *British Journal of Middle Eastern Studies*, 38(3), 2011.

Lust-Okar, Ellen, 'Divided They Rule: The Management and Manipulation of Political Opposition,' *Comparative Politics*, 36(2), 2004.

Mabon, Simon, 'The End of the Battle for Bahrain and the Securitization of Bahraini Shi'a,' *Middle East Journal*, 73(1), 2019.

Matthiesen, Toby, 'Hizbullah al-Hijaz: A History of the Most Radical Saudi Shi'a Opposition Group,' *Middle East Journal*, 64(2), 2010.

———, 'A "Saudi Spring?": The Shi'a Protest Movement in the Eastern Province, 2011–2012,' *Middle East Journal*, 66(4), 2012.

———, 'Migration, Minorities, and Radical Networks: Labour Movements and Opposition Groups in Saudi Arabia, 1950–1975,' *International Review of Social History*, 59(3), 2014.

———, 'Centre-Periphery Relations and the Emergence of a Public Sphere in Saudi Arabia: The Municipal Elections in the Eastern Province, 1954–1960,' *British Journal of Middle Eastern Studies*, 42(3), 2015.

McPherson-Smith, Oliver, 'Diversification, Khashoggi, and Saudi Arabia's Public Investment Fund,' *Global Policy*, 12(2), 2021.

Mehta, Sandhya Rao and James Onley, 'The Hindu Community in Muscat: Creating Homes in the Diaspora,' *Journal of Arabian Studies*, 5(2), 2015.

Meijer, Roel, 'Citizenship in Saudi Arabia,' *Middle East Journal*, 70(4), 2016.

Meyer, Katherine, Helen Rizzo, and Yousef Ali, 'Changed Political Attitudes in the Middle East: The Case of Kuwait,' *International Sociology*, 22, 2007.

Miller, Judith, 'Creating Modern Oman,' *Foreign Affairs*, 76(3), 1997.

Mobley, Richard, 'The Tunbs and Abu Musa Islands: Britain's Perspective,' *Middle East Journal*, 57(4), 2003.

Monroe, Steve, 'Salafis in Parliament: Democratic Attitudes and Party Politics in the Gulf,' *Middle East Journal*, 66(3), 2012.

Montambault Trudelle, Alexis, 'The Public Investment Fund and Salman's State: The Political Drivers of Sovereign Wealth Management in Saudi Arabia,' *Review of International Political Economy*, 30(2), 2022.

Moore, Pete and Bassel Salloukh, 'Struggles under Authoritarianism: Regimes, States, and Professional Associations in the Arab World,' *International Journal of Middle East Studies*, 39(1), 2007.

Nasasra, Mansour, 'The Frontiers of Empire: Colonial Policing in Southern Palestine, Sinai, Transjordan and Saudi Arabia,' *Journal of Imperial and Commonwealth History*, 49(5), 2021.

Nevo, Joseph, 'Religion and National Identity in Saudi Arabia,' *Middle Eastern Studies*, 34(3), 1998.

Niblock, Tim, 'Democratization: A Theoretical and Practical Debate,' *British Journal of Middle Eastern Studies*, 25(2), 1998.

Nonneman, Gerd, 'Saudi-European Relations 1902–2001: A Pragmatic Quest for Relative Autonomy,' *International Affairs*, 77(3), 2001.

Nosova, Anastasia, 'The Voice and Loyalty of Business in Kuwait: Merchant Politics in Times of Contestation,' *British Journal of Middle Eastern Studies*, 45(2), 2018.

Okruhlik, Gwenn, 'Rentier Wealth, Unruly Law, and the Rise of Opposition: The Political Economy of Oil States,' *Comparative Politics*, 31(3), 1999.

———, 'Saudi Arabian-Iranian Relations: External Rapprochement and Internal Consolidation,' *Middle East Policy*, 10(2), 2003.

Onley, James and Sulayman Khalaf, 'Shaikhly Authority in the Pre-Oil Gulf: An Historical-Anthropological Study,' *History and Anthropology*, 17(3), 2006.

Penziner Hightower, Victoria, 'Pearling and Political Power in the Trucial States, 1850–1930: Debts, Taxes, and Politics,' *Journal of Arabian Studies*, 3(2), 2013.

Peterson, J.E., 'Oman's Diverse Society: Southern Oman,' *Middle East Journal*, 58(2), 2004.

———, 'Oman: Three and a Half Decades of Change and Development,' *Middle East Policy*, 11(2), 2004.

———, 'Tribe and State in the Arabian Peninsula,' *Middle East Journal*, 74(4), 2021.

Rabi, Uzi, 'Oman's Foreign Policy: The Art of Keeping All Channels of Communication Open,' *Orient* 46(4), 2005.

———, 'Oil Politics and Tribal Rulers in Eastern Arabia: The Reign of Shakhbut (1928–1966),' *British Journal of Middle Eastern Studies*, 33(1), 2006.

Raphaeli, Nimrod, 'Demands for Reforms in Saudi Arabia,' *Middle Eastern Studies*, 41(4), 2005.

Rathmell, Andrew and Kirsten Schulze, 'Political Reform in the Gulf: The Case of Qatar,' *Middle Eastern Studies*, 36(4), 2000.

Roberts, David, 'British National Interest in the Gulf: Rediscovering a Role?,' *International Affairs*, 90(3), 2014.

———, 'Qatar and the Muslim Brotherhood: Pragmatism or Preference?,' *Middle East Policy*, 21(3), 2014.

Ronall, J.O., 'Economic Review: Banking Developments in Kuwayt,' *Middle East Journal*, 24(1), 1970.

Rossiter, Ash, 'Survival of the Kuwaiti Statelet: Najd's Expansion and the Question of British Protection,' *Middle Eastern Studies*, 56(3), 2020.

Rugh, William, 'Emergence of a New Middle Class in Saudi Arabia,' *Middle East Journal*, 27(1), 1973.

———, 'The United Arab Emirates: What Are the Sources of Its Stability?,' *Middle East Policy*, 5(3), 1997.

Sakr, Naomi, 'Reflections on the Manama Spring: Research Questions Arising from the Promise of Political Liberalization in Bahrain,' *British Journal of Middle Eastern Studies*, 28(2), 2001.

———, 'Women and Media in Saudi Arabia: Rhetoric, Reductionism and Realities,' *British Journal of Middle Eastern Studies*, 35(3), 2008.

Salameh, Mohammad and Mohammad al-Sharah, 'Kuwait's Democratic Experiment: Roots, Reality, Characteristics, Challenges, and Prospects for the Future,' *Journal of Middle Eastern and Islamic Studies* (in Asia), 5(3), 2011.

Salih, Kamal Osman, 'The 1938 Kuwait Legislative Council,' *Middle Eastern Studies*, 28(1), 1992.

———, 'Kuwait Primary (Tribal) Elections 1975–2008: An Evaluative Study,' *British Journal of Middle Eastern Studies*, 38(2), 2011.

Sato, Shohei, 'Britain's Decision to Withdraw from the Persian Gulf, 1964–68: A Pattern and a Puzzle,' *Journal of Imperial and Commonwealth History*, 37(1), 2009.

Sayigh, Yezid, 'Agencies of Coercion: Armies and Internal Security Forces,' *International Journal of Middle East Studies*, 43(3), 2011.

Schofield, Richard, 'International Boundaries and Borderlands in the Middle East: Balancing Context, Exceptionalism and Representation,' *Geopolitics*, 23(3), 2018.

Segal, Eran, 'Merchants' Networks in Kuwait: The Story of Yusuf al-Marzuk,' *Middle Eastern Studies*, 45(5), 2009.

———, 'Political Participation in Kuwait: Diwaniyya, Majlis and Parliament,' *Journal of Arabian Studies*, 2(2), 2012.

Seikaly, May, 'Women and Social Change in Bahrain,' *International Journal of Middle East Studies*, 26(3), 1994.

Seznec, Jean-François, 'Democratization in the Arab World? Stirrings in Saudi Arabia,' *Journal of Democracy*, 13(4), 2002.

Shalaby, Marwa and Laila Eliman, 'Women in Legislative Committees in Arab Parliaments,' *Comparative Politics*, 53(1), 2020.

Slight, John, 'Global War and Its Impact on the Gulf States of Kuwait and Bahrain, 1914–1918,' *War & Society*, 37(1), 2018.

Smith, Simon, 'The Making of a Neo-Colony? Anglo-Kuwaiti Relations in the Era of Decolonization,' *Middle Eastern Studies*, 37(1), 2001.

Stanton Russell, Sharon, 'Politics and Ideology in Migration Policy Formulation: The Case of Kuwait,' *International Migration Review*, 23(1), 1989.

Stanton Russell, Sharon and Muhammad Ali Al-Ramadhan, 'Kuwait's Migration Policy Since the Gulf Crisis,' *International Journal of Middle East Studies*, 26(4), 1994.

Stephenson, Lindsey, 'Women and the Malleability of the Kuwaiti Diwaniyya,' *Journal of Arabian Studies*, 1(2), 2011.

Talha Çiçek, M., 'Negotiating Power and Authority in the Desert: The Arab Bedouin and the Limits of the Ottoman State in Hijaz, 1840–1908,' *Middle Eastern Studies*, 52(2), 2016.

Telhami, Shibley, 'Arab Public Opinion and the Gulf War,' *Political Science Quarterly*, 108(3), 1993.

Tétreault, Mary Ann, 'Civil Society in Kuwait: Protected Spaces and Women's Rights,' *Middle East Journal*, 47(2), 1993.

———, 'Independence, Sovereignty, and Vested Glory: Oil and Politics in the Second Gulf War,' *Orient*, 34(1), 1993.

———, 'Kuwait's Unhappy Anniversary,' *Middle East Policy*, 7(3), 2000.

———, 'A State of Two Minds: State Cultures, Women, and Politics in Kuwait,' *International Journal of Middle East Studies*, 33(2), 2001.

———, 'La Longue Durée and Energy Security in the Gulf,' *British Journal of Middle Eastern Studies*, 36(3), 2009.

Tétreault, Mary Ann and Haya al-Mughni, 'Gender, Citizenship and Nationalism in Kuwait,' *British Journal of Middle Eastern Studies*, 22(1), 1995.

Thompson, Mark, 'Assessing the Impact of Saudi Arabia's National Dialogue: The Controversial Case of the Cultural Discourse,' *Journal of Arabian Studies*, 1(2), 2011.

———, 'Societal Transformation, Public Opinion and Saudi Youth: Views from an Academic Elite,' *Middle Eastern Studies*, 53(5), 2017.

Valeri, Marc, 'Nation-Building and Communities in Oman Since 1970: The Swahili-Speaking Omani in Search of Identity,' *African Affairs*, 104(424), 2007.

Viorst, Milton, 'The Storm and the Citadel,' *Foreign Affairs*, 75(1), 1996.

Wehrey, Frederick, 'Saudi Arabia: Shi'a Pessimistic about Reform, but Seek Reconciliation,' *Arab Reform Bulletin*, 5(5), 2007.

Wheeler, Deborah, 'New Media, Globalization and Kuwaiti National Identity,' *Middle East Journal*, 54(3), 2000.

Wilson, Rodney, 'Money, Oil and Empire in the Middle East: Sterling and Postwar Imperialism, 1944–1971,' *Middle Eastern Studies*, 46(3), 2010.

Yates, Athol and Ash Rossiter, 'Forging a Force: Rulers, Professional Expatriates, and the Creation of Abu Dhabi's Police,' *Middle Eastern Studies*, 56(4), 2020.

Young, Karen, 'Sovereign Risk: Gulf Sovereign Wealth Funds as Engines of Growth and Political Resource,' *British Journal of Middle Eastern Studies*, 47(1), 2020.

Zabih, Sepehr, 'Iran's Policy toward the Persian Gulf,' *International Journal of Middle East Studies*, 7(3), 1976.

Zaccara, Luciano, 'Comparing Elections in Gulf Cooperation Council Countries after the Arab Spring: The United Arab Emirates, Oman, and Kuwait,' *Journal of Arabian Studies*, 3(1), 2013.

Zelkovitz, Ido, 'A Paradise Lost? The Rise and Fall of the Palestinian Community in Kuwait,' *Middle Eastern Studies*, 50(1), 2014.

Zollner, Barbara, 'Prison Talk: The Muslim Brotherhood's Internal Struggle During Gamal Abdel Nasser's Persecution, 1954 to 1971,' *International Journal of Middle East Studies*, 39(3), 2007.

Working papers and policy briefs

Al-Dabbagh, May and Lana Nusseibeh, 'Women in Parliament and Politics in the UAE: A Study of the First Federal National Council Elections,' *Dubai School of Government / Ministry of Federal National Council Affairs paper*, February 2009.

Allarakia, Luai and Hamad Albloshi, 'The Politics of Permanent Deadlock in Kuwait,' *Arab Gulf States Institute in Washington*, 2021.

AlShehabi, Omar, 'Show Us the Money: Oil Revenues, Undisclosed Allocations and Accountability in Budgets of the GCC States,' *LSE Kuwait Programme Paper Series 44*, 2017.

Al-Sulayman, Faris, 'Rethinking State Capitalism in the Gulf States: Insights from the China-Focused Literature,' *King Faisal Center for Research and Islamic Studies,* Special Report, 2021.

Alwuhaib, Mohammad, 'Kuwait: The Crisis and Its Future,' *Arab Reform Brief*, 63, 2012, published by the Arab Reform Initiative.

Al Zu'abi, Ali Zaid, 'Prospects for Political Reform in Kuwait: An Analysis of Recent Events,' *Arab Reform Brief*, 8, 2006, published by the Arab Reform Initiative.

Anon., 'Popular Protests in North Africa and the Middle East (VIII): Bahrain's Rocky Road to Reform,' *International Crisis Group Middle East / North Africa Report No.11,* 28 July 2011.

Boodrookas, Alex, 'Reconceptualizing Noncitizen Labor Rights in the Persian Gulf,' *Brandeis University, Crown Center for Middle East Studies, Middle East Brief No.143*, 2021.

Brumberg, David, 'Liberalization Versus Democracy: Understanding Arab Political Reform,' *Democracy and Rule of Law Project Paper No.37, Carnegie Endowment for International Peace*, 2003.

Burke, Edward, 'Bahrain: Reaching a Threshold,' *FRIDE Working Paper No.61*, 2008.

Dargin, Justin, 'The Dolphin Project: The Development of a Gulf Gas Initiative,' *Oxford Institute for Energy Studies*, 2008.

Gray, Matthew, 'A Theory of "Late Rentierism" in the Arab States of the Gulf,' *Georgetown University School of Foreign Service in Qatar, Center for International and Regional Studies Occasional Paper No.7*, 2011.

Herb, Michael, 'The Origins of Kuwait's National Assembly,' *LSE Kuwait Programme Paper Series 39*, 2016.

Hino, Yukari, 'Saudi Arabia Field Report: Another Potential Oil Crisis in the Middle East,' *Brookings Institution*, 2015.

Husani, Ruba, 'For Gulf Producers, Decarbonization Does Not Mean Zero Oil Production,' *Middle East Institute*, 2022.

Kamrava, Mehran, Gerd Nonneman, Anastasia Nosova, and Marc Valeri, 'Ruling Families and Business Elites in the Gulf Monarchies: Ever Closer?,' *Chatham House Research Paper*, 2016.

Onley, James, 'Britain and the Gulf Shaikhdoms, 1820–1971: The Politics of Protection,' Georgetown School of Foreign Service in Qatar: *Center for International and Regional Studies Occasional Paper*, 2009.

Peterson, J.E., 'The Emergence of Post-Traditional Oman,' *Working Paper No.5, Durham Middle East Papers Sir William Luce Publication Series*, 2005.

Salisbury, Peter, 'Risk Perception and Appetite in UAE Foreign and National Security Policy,' *Chatham House Research Paper*, 2020.

Shah, Nasra, 'Recent Amnesty Programs for Irregular Migrants in Kuwait and Saudi Arabia: Some Successes and Failures,' *Gulf Labor Markets and Migration (GLMM) Explanatory Note 09/2014*, 2014.

Smith Diwan, Kristin, 'Parliamentary Boycotts in Kuwait and Bahrain Cost Opposition,' *Arab Gulf States Institute in Washington*, 6 July 2016.

PhD dissertations

Abdulla, Hamad Ebrahim, 'Sir Charles Belgrave and the Rise and Fall of Bahrain's National Union Committee, January 1953 to April 1957,' *PhD dissertation*, University of East Anglia, 2016.

Alhajeri, Abdullah, 'Citizenship and Political Participation in the State of Kuwait: The Case of the National Assembly (1963–1996), *PhD dissertation*, University of Durham, 2004.

Al-Munais, Waleed, 'Social and Ethnic Differentiation in Kuwait: A Social Geography of an Indigenous Society,' *PhD dissertation*, School of Oriental and African Studies, 1981.

Haller, Niklas, 'A Labyrinth in the Sand: British Boundary-Making and the Emergence of the Emirati Territorial State,' *PhD dissertation*, University of Exeter, 2019.

Nosova, Anastasia, 'The Merchant Elite and Parliamentary Politics in Kuwait: The Dynamics of Business Political Participation in a Rentier State,' *PhD dissertation*, London School of Economics and Political Science, 2016.

Partrick, Neil, 'Kuwait's Foreign Policy (1961–1977): Non-Alignment, Ideology and the Pursuit of Security,' *PhD dissertation*, London School of Economics and Political Science, 2006.

Saleh, Hassan Mohammad Abdulla, 'Labor, Nationalism, and Imperialism in Eastern Arabia: Britain, the Shaikhs and the Gulf Oil Workers in Bahrain, Kuwait and Qatar, 1932–1956,' *PhD dissertation*, University of Michigan, 1991.

Shirawi, May Al-Arrayed, 'Education in Bahrain – 1919–1986: An Analytical Study of Problems and Progress,' *PhD dissertation*, Durham University, 1987.

Thafer, Dania, 'Obstacles to Innovation in Rentier Economies: States, Elites, and the Squandering of the Demographic Dividend,' *PhD dissertation*, American University, 2020.

Media and online resources

ABC News
AFP
Al Arabiya
Al Jazeera
Al-Monitor
AMEinfo
Arab Center Washington
Arab Gulf States Institute in Washington
Arab News
Arabian Business
Aramco World
Asharq al-Awsat
Asia and the Pacific Policy Society
Associated Press
Bahrain Institute for Rights and Democracy
Bloomberg
Carnegie Endowment for International Peace
Carnegie Middle East Center
Churchill College, University of Cambridge, The British Diplomatic Oral History Programme
CNBC
Doha Institute for Graduate Studies
Doha News
Financial Times

Forbes
Foreign Affairs
Foreign Policy
GlobalPost
Gulf Daily News
Gulf International Forum
Gulf News
Gulf States Newsletter
Heinrich Boll Stiftung
Human Rights Watch
Irish Times
Jacobin
Jadaliyya
Khaleej Times
LobeLog
London Review of Books
LSE Middle East Centre
Medium
Middle East Eye
Middle East Report
Middle East Research and Information Project (MERIP)
NBC News
New York Times
Nikkei Asia
NPR
Oman Daily Observer
Open Democracy
Oxford Analytica
Public Library of U.S. Diplomacy
Qatar Digital Library
Reuters
Saudi Arabia Newsletter
The Athletic
The Economist
The Guardian
The Khaldoun Alnaqeeb Archive
The National
The National Archives
The New Yorker
The Peninsula
Washington Post

INDEX

Note: Page numbers followed by "*t*" refer to tables.